DATE DUE

ESSENTIALS OF
OPERATIONS MANAGEMENT

ESSENTIALS OF

OPERATIONS MANAGEMENT

SCOTT T. YOUNG
DePaul University

$SAGE

Los Angeles • London • New Delhi • Singapore • Washington DC

For information:

SAGE Publications, Inc.
2455 Teller Road
Thousand Oaks, California 91320
E-mail: order@sagepub.com

SAGE Publications India Pvt. Ltd.
B 1/I 1 Mohan Cooperative
   Industrial Area
Mathura Road, New Delhi 110 044
India

SAGE Publications Ltd.
1 Oliver's Yard
55 City Road
London EC1Y 1SP
United Kingdom

SAGE Publications Asia-Pacific Pte. Ltd.
33 Pekin Street #02-01
Far East Square
Singapore 048763

Printed in the United States of America

Library of Congress Cataloging-in-Publication Data

Young, Scott T.
Essentials of operations management / Scott T. Young.
        p. cm.
Includes bibliographical references and index.
ISBN 978-1-4129-2570-9 (pbk.)
    1. Production management. 2. Management. I. Title.

TS155.Y68 2009
658.5—dc22   2008031847

This book is printed on acid-free paper.

09   10   11   12   13   10   9   8   7   6   5   4   3   2   1

Acquisitions Editor:	Lisa Cuevas Shaw
Associate Editor:	Deya Saoud
Editorial Assistant:	MaryAnn Vail
Production Editor:	Astrid Virding
Copy Editor:	QuADS Prepress (P) Ltd.
Typesetter:	C&M Digitals (P) Ltd.
Proofreader:	Scott Oney
Indexer:	Kathy Paparchontis
Cover Designer:	Gail Buschman
Marketing Manager:	Jennifer Reed Banando

Brief Contents

Detailed Contents

Preface

E ssentials of Operations Management is intended to teach the students of operations management what they really need to know. Prior to becoming a college professor, I was a materials manager, so I came to the field with a working knowledge of hospital operations.

For 20 years, I have taught from what appear to be encyclopedias with ancillary products that served to raise the price to the student. *Essentials* is designed as an alternative to that approach.

Essentials also delivers a very real shift in content. The content of this book is quite different from that of the 25 other available books. The 80-20 rule is practiced—with 80% of the material addressing services and 20% manufacturing, reflecting where our students will work and, again, what they need to know. (The content is often 80-20 in the other direction.)

New material is offered on important topics such as sustainable development and the balanced scorecard, both rarely addressed in operations texts. An entire chapter is devoted to human resource issues in operations management. Having spent 20 years lecturing on operations methods and techniques and constantly reminding students that the only truly good operations manager is one who can manage people, I wrote a chapter to address that issue.

The Case of the Supply Chain Killer, a murder mystery novella, is included in the *Instructor's Manual* and can be downloaded for students. It is a just-for-fun episode of an operations manager who gets caught up in mystery. In the novella, operations issues arise throughout. The novella is representative in tone of what this book is all about, a conversational journey through the mechanics of operations and how they affect our work lives.

This book represents a change of pace in material, tone, and size. It will not work well for those who really desire to teach management science within an operations management course. No, this is a Management book, with a capital *M*.

Scott T. Young

Acknowledgments

This book has one author's name listed, but it is really the culmination of a career of interactions with colleagues. The tone of this book ultimately reflects involvement with mentors, colleagues, and students. This book is dedicated to the following:

My wife: Dr. Luciana Young

Our family: Maui, Oahu, and "GiGi"

My mentors: At Georgia State University

Dissertation Chairman: Gene Groff

My professors: Tom Clark, Richard Deane, and Walter Riggs

My fellow grad students at Georgia State University: Caron St. John (Clemson), John Angelidis (St. John's), Wing Fok (Loyola, New Orleans), Kern Kwong (Cal State, Louisiana), Faramarz Parsa (West Georgia), Nabil Ibrahim (Augusta State), Ming Jun (New Mexico), Mehdi Kaighobodi (Florida Atlantic), Lilian Fok (University of New Orleans), Jim Pullin (retired, University of Central Florida), Ronnie Richardson (Southern Tech), Ben Harrison, and Jean Hanebury

My POM colleagues at the University of Utah: T. S. Lee (now at Chinese University of Hong Kong), Gary Thompson (Cornell), Susan Chesteen, Don Wardell, Leslie Morgan, and Alysse Morton (Westminster)

My doctoral students at the University of Utah: Xiande Zhao (Chinese University of Hong Kong), Kristie Seawright (BYU), Winter Nie (IMD), Rohit Verma (Cornell), John Goodale (Oregon), Mellie Pullman (Portland State), Kristi Yuthas (Portland State), and Scott Metlen (Idaho)

My POM colleagues at DePaul University: Lori Cook, Dan Heiser, Gilles Reinhardt, Kathy Dhanda, Bin Jiang, Rajesh Tyagi, Gayle Landuyt, John Olson (St. Thomas), and Serge Karalli (Cal State, Sacramento)

My staff at DePaul University: Dianne Cichanski, Margaret Elliott, Nell Shields, Erin Espeland, and Wendy Musielak

The deans at DePaul University: Ray Whittington and, previously, Arthur Kraft (Chapman)

The deans at the University of Utah: John Seybolt and Jack Brittain

The students I have enjoyed my experiences with, mostly at DePaul University and the University of Utah, and also at Pan Asia, Taiwan (thanks to Steve Tsai and Joanna Liu); BIBF in Bahrain; City University of Hong Kong; Groupe ESC–Tours, France; Groupe ESC–Lille, France; and Georgia State University

Nell Shields of Grant Thornton: For her work on the *Instructor's Manual*

My editors: Al Bruckner, the Sage editor who encouraged me to write this, and Deya Saoud, who helped me immensely with the editorial reviews

The reviewers: Who greatly influenced the content and shape of the book—

Stephen N. Chapman, *North Carolina State University*

Murray J. Côté, *University of Florida*

Gene Fliedner, *Oakland University*

Benito E. Flores, *Texas A&M University*

Mark G. Haug, *University of Kansas*

Mehdi Kaighobadi, *Florida Atlantic University*

Elias T. Kirche, *Florida Gulf Coast University*

Yung Jae Lee, *Saint Mary's College of California*

Deborah E. Morrow, *Park University*

David L. Olson, *University of Nebraska*

Jun Ru, *University of Texas at Dallas*

I thank you all for your assistance.

CHAPTER 1

Introduction to Operations Management and Productivity

SOURCE: © Matjaz Boncina/istockphoto.com

> **Learning Objectives**
>
> In this chapter, we will
>
> - Introduce the topic of operations management
> - Trace the development of the field
> - Note applications of operations management to airplane manufacturing, hotels, and universities

Introduction to Operations Management

When you start to read this book, you may not exactly know what operations management is, yet you have been affected by it countless times this very day. The book you hold in your hand has the function of operations management to thank for putting it there.

Let us begin by noticing how many "parts" there are in this book. There is a cover, some kind of binding that holds the book together, and paper. The book is created by laying out photographs and text and checking to make sure that there are no mistakes. Invariably, there are errors that escape the several people who review the textbook, including the author.

The process of assembling finished pages into the form of a book is the function of operations management. Then, the book is distributed across the globe to eager readers. The publisher wants to get the book into the hands of students and professors in time for the beginning of the school term, so the scheduling of deliveries to a bookstore is planned, ideally in advance. Again, this is an operations management function.

Operations management is frequently termed *production and operations management*, or POM. This stems from the field's beginnings in a factory; thus the word *production*. However, operations management is a discipline that encompasses all organizations, and since over 70% of the workforce is involved in the service industries, this book will stick with the term *operations* management.

Operations management is essentially the process of making things. To manufacture a product, we must source the materials from suppliers. We must have a location to build the product and, after we receive the materials, arrange a system to assemble or produce the new product. A materials manager is responsible for ensuring that the inventory is adequate for production, and a purchasing agent is responsible for buying the materials. A production scheduler matches the product orders with a sales forecast to get the factory running smoothly. The quality management aspect guarantees that the product is free of defects.

Service organizations, that is, hospitals, hotels, restaurants, and retailing, do the same things that manufacturers do. They forecast, schedule, select the right location and layout, ensure quality, and manage inventory. In a sense, their process is to convert customers into satisfied customers. If they get the quality right, the customers will return. If they don't, the customers alert other potential customers to avoid the establishment.

When you awake in the morning, perhaps your first step is to stagger to the coffee pot and brew a pot. In the haze of the morning fog, with your rumpled hair and morning breath, you may notice that this coffee pot is a manufactured product that was assembled in some far corner of the globe and ordered by a retailer, where you bought it when the last one broke down. You hope that it is a reliable product that was built through an effective production system.

Your next step in the morning may be to get the morning newspaper, so you stagger outside in your slippers, holding tight to your bathrobe so as not to scare your neighbors, and retrieve it from the damp lawn. It did not land there from outer space. The process of delivering that newspaper to your front lawn involves arranging all the news stories, printing the papers, and distributing them to sub-scribers and news vendors. Operations management is hard at work, all through the process. The newspaper may eventually be recycled; and sometime in the future, you may be reading from a paper that somebody else read from last year.

Or you may get the news from television. Viewers pretty much take for granted that there will be a news anchor, reporters, and a weather forecaster. What we don't see is the frantic behind-the-scenes producers, camera people, schedulers, lighting experts, makeup team, and so on, who get the show on the air. Every day these unsung technicians do their operations jobs to exhaustion.

On this particular morning, you may opt to have breakfast at a fast-food restau-rant. You step into a waiting line—which, by the way, is monitored for length by the manager to determine the optimal number of cashiers to staff the place—and place an order. This sets into motion a preestablished production system, often resem-bling an assembly line in manufacturing.

You may take public transportation to get to school or work. In the case of trains and buses, a schedule has been mapped out that the drivers and engineers attempt to hold to. This schedule is designed to optimally deliver passengers in order to make full use of the vehicles. The schedulers probably have more routes operating in the "rush" hours. Planning a schedule that meets the demand is the domain of operations management.

When operations management is handled smoothly, the system is seamless and unnoticeable. A university makes a class schedule that is heavily influenced by the demand for similar classes in the previous year. Once the schedule is set, faculty are matched to the classes. An undergraduate program takes high school graduates and puts them into an educational system with the goal of creating educated college graduates. A graduate program takes college graduates and tries to create educated, advanced-degree graduates. Operations management is essentially a conversion process. In manufacturing firms, it is the successful conversion of raw materials to finished goods. In services, it is the conversion of a customer from an incomplete to a finished state. A hungry customer is converted into a well-fed and happy cus-tomer at a restaurant. A high school graduate is converted into a college graduate.

The testing aspects and the teaching evaluation process are elements of the qual-ity system in a university. The final element of quality probably is how successful the students are in work and life. If you graduate from University X, then you represent that university in all you do. Anytime someone runs for political office, it is mentioned where he or she attended college. If an officeholder turns out to be a crook, it is a black mark against his or her education. Thus, universities desire to send out educated and ethical graduates. Our "inspectors," so to speak, are the employers.

If you have no problem getting the classes you need and you really enjoy them, then perhaps you will graduate, succeed, and donate millions back to the university. If all goes well, the operations function is usually seamless and invisible.

There are more jobs in operations management than in any other function in business. Operations positions include materials manager, purchasing agent, buyer, scheduler, manufacturing manager, general operations manager, and the supervisors for the line employees. It is very often a route to the top of the organization, since people in operations are typically the most in tune with what goes into actually making the product. The operations managers work in coordination with the marketing executive, who must understand how to sell the product and how best to promote and distribute it. Operations managers must share information with the finance and accounting executives, who are primarily concerned with the numbers on the balance sheets and investments. It is the operations manager who is in the trenches of business, working with the product and supporting the service. With the numbers employed in the operations function, it is no surprise that many business students find themselves in operations jobs, whether they majored in accounting, human resources, or finance.

The Development of the Field

Modern operations management can probably be traced to Frederick Taylor's (1911/2005) *The Principles of Scientific Management*, although Alexander Hamilton wrote "On the Production of Manufactured Goods" in 1800. Taylor's principles of specialized labor and time and motion studies became popular in the early part of the 20th century and were mocked in Charlie Chaplin's classic silent film *Modern Times*. Taylor's methods, simply put, were designed to get the most out of workers, but they treated workers as cogs in a machine.

Taylor (1911/2005) began his work with the statement, "The principle object of management should be to secure the maximum prosperity for the employer, coupled with the maximum prosperity for each employee" (p. 9).

Taylor's work revolved around four major principles:

1. Methods from scientific study should replace rule-of-thumb methods.

2. Workers should be selected, trained, and developed using scientific methods.

3. Scientific methods should be written as a rule and standard operating procedure.

4. Once an acceptable level of performance has been established, a pay system that has rewards for performance above the acceptable level should be established.

Frank and Lillian Gilbreth (Gilbreth & Carey, 1948) advanced the field of scientific management by employing motion picture photography to study time and motion. They applied their own time-and-motion principles to family life, leading to a humorous book and a funny film, *Cheaper by the Dozen.* The remake of the film, starring Steve Martin, changed everything—the parents were no longer industrial analysts but a football coach and a writer.

The Hawthorne studies (Gillespie, 1993) were industrial productivity studies conducted at the Hawthorne Works of the Western Electric Company. The study was designed to find the effect of lighting on productivity and fatigue. The researchers discovered that as lighting in the plant increased, so did the output of the workers. When they decreased the lighting, productivity continued to rise. Their conclusion, called the "Hawthorne effect," was that the workers were so pleased that someone was paying attention to them that they worked harder without any regard to the lighting. This sparked an entire field of humanistic studies of work and reduced the importance of scientific management.

Operations management can best be described as a synthesis of industrial engineering, operations research, and service management. Economics played an important role in making operations management a requirement in business schools. The recession of the late 1970s and the rise of Japanese manufacturing led to a series of reflective articles in the *Harvard Business Review.*

The Middle Eastern oil embargo of the mid-1970s caused the price of oil and gasoline to rise rapidly, and consumers sought new automobiles that were more fuel efficient. For the first time, consumers embraced models from Toyota, Nissan, and Honda. The new converts to Japanese automobiles quickly noticed that their vehicles were remarkably superior in quality, too.

The refocus on operations and quality led to a resurgence in POM. Professors of industrial engineering and operations research switched their allegiance to POM, bringing a manufacturing bias to the field. Although services make up around 75% of our economy and 75% of MBA students go to work in service industries, the textbooks were written with a manufacturing slant. Operations managers have the imperative to deliver goods and services effectively and efficiently no matter what type of business. Let's take a look at the basics of operations management in a manufacturing situation and compare them with some service applications.

Operations Management at Boeing

To illustrate the production process at Boeing (O'Neal & Greising, 2005), the airplane manufacturer, we can take a look at the development of the new 7E7 airplane. Boeing designed this plane with composite materials rather than steel. The plane required a completely new manufacturing process. Suppliers in Japan, Italy, and Texas built the fuselage and wing. Each section was then sent to the main plant in Seattle to be assembled.

The fuselage was placed on a spindle and rotated until multiple layers created the fuselage skin. The production of a new plane does not mean that a company can simply step it through the way the previous model was produced. Here, in one company, we have so many operational issues going on:

1. Who will be our suppliers for the new plane?

2. Where will we assemble the final product?

3. How will it affect our current workforce? With over 30,000 layoffs in recent years, Boeing must be careful when it takes new orders that it has the workforce to get the job done on time.

4. Quality in an airplane has to be 100%, so new materials require all sorts of testing to guarantee the safety of the plane.

5. How do we set up an effective chain of suppliers so that we have an efficient production process?

6. How do we lay out the facility to accommodate manufacture of this new airplane?

7. How do we incorporate the new materials involved in production into our existing inventory system?

Airline companies order new planes years in advance of delivery because it takes months to build one plane. This puts operations into focus because of the pressure to deliver on time and with perfect quality.

Operations Management at a Luxury Hotel

Hotel patrons take for granted that all the operations in a hotel are successfully carried out. But things can go wrong: A toilet does not flush. A showerhead leaks. The housekeeping staff forgets your room, or bursts in on you when you are taking a nap and have a "Do not disturb" sign on the door.

Here are functions that are part of operations in a hotel:

1. *The reservation system:* In this system rooms are checked for availability.

2. *Employee labor scheduling:* After comparing hotel occupancy rates and times, staffing is matched to optimize customer service.

3. *Customer service:* Customer problems arise and have to be handled. A customer service incident damages the reputation of the hotel.

4. *Linen and towel distribution:* The amount of linen distributed is a function of occupancy. Timely delivery must be handled by knowing which hotel patrons have checked out and which ones have continuing stays.

5. *Laundry:* The use of water and detergents is an operations function.

6. *Purchasing:* The purchasing agent sources supplies such as toilet paper, shampoo, soap, restaurant supplies, and so on, trying to obtain quality supplies at a low price.

7. *Event coordination:* A special event requires additional resources to ensure that it is run smoothly.

Peripheral functions that coordinate with operations would include the maintenance or engineering department and the janitorial or housekeeping departments.

These functions are operational in nature but are usually supervised by managers with special training in these fields.

Operations Management at Your University

The fact that you are in a particular classroom at a particular time and are being taught by a certain professor is all operations management at work. Typically, the schedule is set by studying the demand in the previous year. Sometimes, changing the time affects the demand. Sometimes, changing the professor can alter demand. If your favorite professor is changed to a different course and is replaced by an unpopular substitute, word-of-mouth can kill a course's demand.

The university's purchasing department is responsible for furnishing the room with all the equipment and supplies that are needed. There is nothing worse for a professor than to arrive in a room that lacks equipment.

Academic departments monitor classes to make sure that the enrollments are adequate, the professors show up, the class is conducted successfully, the evaluations are distributed, and the students have a rewarding experience. Students come to class with a variety of motivations. Some just "wanna have fun." Passing the course is enough. Others want to get exceptional grades to prepare for graduate school. Whatever the motivation of the students, the professor must meet their expectations.

The teaching evaluations are a form of quality control, as the students give administrators their two cents on how the class was conducted. The professor assigns a grade, another form of quality control.

As you commute back home at the end of the day, if you look around, you will see operations at work in every store you pass by and in the mode of transportation you have selected. If you are driving, there is someone out there who has the responsibility to make sure the roads and streets are clear. If snow and ice have fallen, trucks must be scheduled to shovel the roads and drop salt or sand on the roadways to prevent slippage. Operations management, it is certain, is going on all around you.

This book is organized with the core issues and themes of operations setting the stage. It begins with topics about the management of operations jobs and the strategic aspects of the discipline. Then, we move into the planning aspects of operations. The third section is involved with supply chain management topics.

Part I: Management and Strategy

Chapter 2: "Productivity and Process Analysis." This chapter involves the core aim of operations—to improve productivity—and illustrates how to improve business processes with which to achieve that goal.

Chapter 3: "Operations Strategy." Organizations exist in a competitive world, and operations must be integral to an organization's strategy. Arguably, *all* operations are now global. We source and sell internationally. This chapter concentrates on the most global aspects of operations.

Chapter 4: "Managing the Operations Workforce." In the past, operations management textbooks have tended to explain away the importance of managing people to accomplish operational goals. Many problem-solving methods are introduced with a disclaimer, "Then you have to get your people to perform!" To address this issue, this book sets out a primer on human resource management, specifically for operations.

Chapter 5: "The Balanced Scorecard Approach to Operations." This is a measurement approach that is a good way to monitor operations performance. The basics of this method are discussed, and the operations scorecard is reviewed.

Chapter 6: "Total Quality Management." This chapter addresses the basic issues of quality and customer service. It presents the elementary tools used to build a quality system and outlines the steps in Six Sigma quality.

Chapter 7: "Sustainable Operations." A neglected area of operations is how we responsibly handle waste and conserve our resources. The importance of green operations cannot be overlooked, and this textbook shows why.

Part II: Planning

Chapter 8: "Forecasting and Aggregate Planning." How do we determine how many products to make, how many employees to hire, or how many should work certain hours? This chapter shows methods of forecasting for production.

Chapter 9: "Scheduling for Operations." This chapter looks at a number of scheduling situations and provides methods for handling them. Labor scheduling, machine scheduling, and job shop scheduling are reviewed.

Chapter 10: "Facility Location." Where do we place our offices and plants, and how many do we have? These are the fundamental questions addressed in this chapter. In periods of expansion and downsizing, these all-important strategic decisions require systematic study.

Chapter 11: "Facility Layout and Waiting Lines." How do we effectively lay out our plant or service so that we can efficiently produce our goods and services? This chapter looks at different situational approaches to layout and addresses waiting-line management.

Part III: Inventory, Logistics, and Supply Chain Management

Chapter 12: "Supply Chain Management." Supply chain management follows the logistics from the suppliers of raw materials, through production, and into the customer's hands. It is an umbrella term covering all logistics and materials management.

Chapter 13: "Inventory Management and Purchasing." This chapter discusses how to manage independent-demand inventory, typically used in retailing, hospitals, and most services. Sourcing is a critical operations function, and the principles of purchasing are presented here.

Chapter 14: "Resource Planning." This chapter studies manufacturing inventory management, covering enterprise resource planning (ERP), materials resource planning, and just-in-time production methods.

Chapter 15: "Project Management." An operations management task often involves projects. This chapter reviews methods for managing projects.

Projects

1. Spend the day observing operations management at work during your commute, where you study, and where you dine.

2. Find out who sets up the college's class schedule, and ask that person how he or she goes about it.

References

Gilbreth, F. B., & Carey, E. G. (1948). *Cheaper by the dozen.* New York: Thomas Y. Crowell.

Gillespie, R. (1993). *Manufacturing knowledge: A history of the Hawthorne experiments.* Cambridge, UK: Cambridge University Press.

Hamilton, A. (1800). *On the production of manufactured goods.* Retrieved September 20, 2008, from www.press.uchicago.edu/misc/chicago/910687.html

O'Neal, M., & Greising, D. (2005, January 12). Boeing bets big on a plastic plane. *Chicago Tribune,* pp. 1, 20–21.

Taylor, F. W. (2005). *The principles of scientific management.* Fairfield, IA: 1st World. (Original work published 1911)

PART I

Management and Strategy

CHAPTER 2

Productivity and Process Analysis

SOURCE: © Dan Tero/istockphoto.com

Productivity

The dilemma of all operations managers is how to increase productivity without sacrificing quality. This is the essential core of operations management—producing as many as possible with as little input as possible. Managers are constantly faced with job cuts yet are expected to produce the same quality product with fewer people to do it. As a result, we are faced with trying to find new and better ways of working, of getting by with less.

Productivity is calculated as the ratio of output to input. What can we produce given the available labor hours or labor dollars, or the available materials or equipment costs? It is the measurement system that provides managers with the information they need to know about how effectively the work is performed.

Every industry has its important set of measurements that act as a scorecard for managers. In the hospital, the administrator is concerned with the ratio of the average length of patient stay to the number of labor hours. A reduction in length of stay, corresponding to an improvement in patient care statistics (however they are measured), with the labor inputs kept equal, could result in an improvement in the hospital's financial health, so these are important productivity measurements for the administrator to analyze (see Table 2.1).

National Productivity and Compensation

Productivity differs across the globe, due to differences in infrastructure, capabilities, and skills. Corporations look at both factors when they select a plant site. When comparing, say, Taiwan with Ireland, they will examine a number of factors, but productivity and wages figure greatly in the decision of where to locate a facility. Tables 2.2 and 2.3 provide 2005 data for productivity and compensation. The manufacturing output uses that country's 1992 productivity to set an index of 100. A number greater than 100 indicates an improvement over the 1992 index. A number of 150, for example, would mean that output had increased by 50%.

Table 2.2 does not show total productivity. What it does show is improvement, with Korea making the greatest improvement since 1992 and Italy the least.

Table 2.1   Productivity Measurements

Type of Company	Type of Work	Measures
Airline	Reservations	Reservations/hr
	Baggage handling	Bags handled/hr
		Bags lost/bags handled
Hospitals	Patient care	Average length of patient stay
		Revenue/patient
Auto manufacturer	Assembly line	Cars/day
		Cars/labor hr
Call center	Customer service	Calls/labor hr
		Effectiveness/call
Book publisher	Book sales	Sales/printed copies
	Book distribution	Books/shipment
Baseball stadium	Ticket sellers	Tickets/labor hr
	Concessionaires	Revenue/game
Movie theater	Ticket sellers	Tickets/labor hr
	Concessions	Revenue/day
Restaurant	Food sales	Sales/hr
		Sales/labor hr
Retailer	Department store workers	Sales/sq. ft
		Sales/labor hr

Table 2.2   2005 Output per Hour in Manufacturing

Country	Output
United States	193.2
United Kingdom	140.0
Canada	139.1
Australia	143.7
Japan	158.2
Korea	300.4
Taiwan	196.5
Belgium	144.9
Denmark	141.6
France	169.2
Germany	154.8
Italy	110.3
Netherlands	161.7
Norway	132.0
Spain	121.5
Sweden	241.9

SOURCE: www.bls.gov

Table 2.3   Index of Hourly Compensation in U.S. Dollars for Manufacturing
Workers in 16 Countries (United States = 100)

Country	Index
United States	100
Canada	101
Mexico	11
Australia	105
Hong Kong	24
Japan	92
Korea	57
New Zealand	63
Singapore	32
Taiwan	27
Czech Republic	26
France	104
Germany	140
Ireland	96
Switzerland	129
United Kingdom	109

Measurements in Sports

To illustrate how productivity measurements are managed, let us examine a situation in a typical baseball game. Assume that a miracle has happened, and we are in the World Series, and it is the Chicago Cubs versus the New York Yankees. Carlos Zambrano is pitching for the Cubs in the seventh inning, and the batter is the Yankees shortstop, Derek Jeter. Zambrano is a right-handed pitcher, and the game is at night in Chicago. There is one out, a runner is on third base, and the score is Cubs 2, Yankees 0.

The managers of both teams are loaded with statistics for this particular situation. The Cubs manager, Lou Piniella, knows that Zambrano has thrown 95 pitches and that Zambrano is usually effective until he has thrown 110 pitches. He knows Zambrano's record against right-handed batters at night in Wrigley Field, where the game is played.

Similarly, the Yankees manager, Joe Girardi, knows Jeter's batting average against right-handed pitchers at night and with runners on third base with less than two out in the seventh inning. So far in the game, Jeter has batted three times and was grounded out twice and has struck out once. Perhaps in the Yankees dugout is a substitute who has batted three times against Zambrano in the past and has two hits. Would Girardi substitute for Jeter in this situation? It is doubtful for a lot of reasons.

Who would replace Jeter at shortstop? Three times at bat is not statistically enough information to make a decision in such an important situation. Although Jeter is batting 0.000 and the substitute is batting 0.667 against Zambrano, it makes no sense to make the substitution.

Managers in business are faced with similar situations. They are bombarded with productivity information, and they must then make decisions that may be counter to what the numbers say. Maybe the manager of baggage service for an airline gets a report that productivity is way down, that the number of bags handled per hour has dropped this week from the week before. However, the manager knows of other factors: The snowstorm that stopped planes one day explains the whole situation.

Virtually every job has some sort of productivity measurement that can be applied to it. The postman's productivity can be measured in volume of mail delivered per day, number of houses visited per day, or number of miles put on the car per day.

An attorney's productivity would be measured in some way to get billable hours. It could be obtained by seeing the results of the cases and comparing that with how much time and labor goes into each case.

If we were to measure the productivity of a police homicide department, we would look at the percentage of solved murders and then tie it to the number of labor hours per case.

At a supermarket, the cashier's productivity could be determined by the speed with which products are scanned and the percentage of items "rescanned." The productivity of commissioned salespersons is obviously measured by their sales, but is that the whole story?

To build a good productivity system, it is necessary to study the jobs, ask the employees to comment on the measurements, and consider combining a number of measurements into one productivity index.

Productivity Indexes

Sink (1985) derived a multiple measurement system called a **multiple-criteria measurement** (MCM) model. In this model, several measurements are aggregated into one score. In the following example, there are two measurements: output and quality. Each measurement is scaled, so that 10 points is the best possible score, 9 the next best, and so on (Table 2.4).

Table 2.4   Multiple-Criteria Index

Score	Output (Pumpkins)	Quality (%)
10	150	100
9	140	98
8	130	95
7	120	92
6	110	90
5	100	87
4	90	84
3	80	80
2	70	77
1	60	75
Weight	0.60	0.40

If a worker carved 127 pumpkins with 91% quality, the worker would receive a score of 7.7 for the output and 6.5 for the quality. Multiplying the measures by the weights, we get

$$(7.7 \times 0.6) + (6.5 \times 0.4) = 7.22.$$

The worker's score of 7.22 would be compared with the score of other workers doing the same job.

In professional football, quarterbacks are compared by using a similar measurement system. A scoring system is devised for a number of categories, and each quarterback is then indexed against this system. The categories are as follows: completion percentage (Cmp.), yards per attempt (Yds./Att.), percentage of touchdowns per attempt (TD), and percentage of interceptions per attempt (Int.).

According to www.nfl.com, the scores are derived in this way:

1. *Completion percentage:* Subtract 30 from the percentage of passes that are thrown for completions, and then multiply by 0.05.

2. *Yards per attempt:* Subtract 3 from the number of yards per passing attempt, and then multiply by 0.25.

3. *Touchdown percentage:* Multiply the percentage of touchdown passes per passing attempt by 0.2.

4. *Interception percentage:* Multiply the percentage of interceptions per passing attempt by 0.25, and then subtract 2.375 from that number.

The scores for each category are added together. The sum is divided by 6 and multiplied by 100, which converts it into a rating on a scale from 0 to 158.3.

Examples of quarterback scores from 2004:

	Yds.	Att.	Cmp.	TD	Int.	Rating
Manning, IN	4,557	497	336	49	10	121.1
Culpepper, MN	4,717	548	379	39	11	110.9

SOURCE: www.nfl.com

This is an example of an elaborate productivity system. A similar exercise could be applied to almost any worker.

In the case of a sales representative, we could consider actual sales, sales growth, market share in the territory, new customers, and retained customers.

Consider a real-estate agent. Total sales do not tell the whole story. It is also important that a high percentage of the homes listed are sold. Here is an example of a possible multicriterion index for an agent (Table 2.5).

Table 2.5   MCM for Real Estate

Score	Total Sales ($)	Percentage of Listings Sold	Percentage of Lookers Who Buy
10	3,000,000	100	20
9	2,500,000	95	18
8	2,000,000	90	15
7	1,500,000	85	12
6	1,000,000	80	10
5	750,000	75	7
4	500,000	70	5
3	400,000	65	3
2	350,000	60	2
1	300,000	55	1
Weight (%)	50	25	25

An agent whose sales total $1,750,000 in a year, with 60% of listings sold and 75% of customers buying, would score as follows:

	Score		Weight (%)
Sales	7.5	×	50
Percentage of listings	2	×	25
Percentage of buyers	5	×	25
Total score	5.5		

This score may be good or bad depending on how it compares with others of a similar background.

Time Studies

When studying the productivity of a worker, it is expected that the individual is performing his or her tasks in the most efficient manner possible. The field of industrial engineering is a discipline that studies work processes. There are several approaches to examining a job. The job must be broken down into micromotions, the actual movements of the hand or body.

To sign a piece of paper, a person has to do several motions:

1. Reach for the pen

2. Grasp the pen

3. Lift the pen

4. Write

It is to that level of detail that a number of micromotions are combined. Another way to add micromotions is to consult a predetermined table of motions.

Ultimately, a job is the combination of a number of different tasks. A professor's job includes these tasks:

1. Lecturing

2. Writing examinations

3. Grading examinations

4. Research

5. Committees

6. Planning vacations

A hotel front desk clerk's job includes these tasks:

1. Greeting registrants

2. Registering the guests

3. Credit card processing

4. Key distribution

5. Telling customers where the elevators are

6. Telling customers where the restrooms are

After all the tasks of a job are identified, there are several ways to study the worker's capacity to perform these tasks. One method is to do a **work sample**. A work sample involves studying the worker for a certain period of time. This could be done with a videotape. It is best that the worker does not know that he or she is being observed, because the actual act of observation can influence the performance.

For example, if we were to study a teller at a drive-through window of a bank, we might collect samples during the first 5 min of every hour the bank is open. From these observations, we can learn the following:

1. The percentage of time the teller is involved with customers

2. The rate of arrival of customers

3. The rate of service of the teller

4. Behaviors that may need correcting, for instance, flirting with customers and asking them for their phone numbers

A second way to study work is to do a **time study** with a stopwatch. If you want to learn how long it takes for a fast-food cashier to process an order of six items for a customer, we turn on the watch and time the transaction. Many order entry systems can do these calculations as transactions occur. The information system can yield startling information of how different the productivity of two workers may be:

	Worker A	Worker B
Time at register (min)	220	220
No. of customers	68	142
Sales/customer	5.30	7.02

Worker B manages mores sales per customer, while also processing more than twice the number of customers.

Wiki Productivity

Wiki, software that allows users to add and edit inclusions in open Web pages, offers a new direction in workforce collaboration and decision making. Wikipedia is the biggest example of how a wiki works, with users continuously updating the Web encyclopedia. The same principle can be applied to the workforce.

> A new kind of business is emerging—one that opens its doors to the world, co-innovates with everyone (especially customers), shares resources that were previously closely guarded, harnesses the power of mass collaboration, and behaves not as a multinational but as something new: a truly global firm. These companies are driving important changes in their industries and rewriting many rules of competition. (Tapscott & Williams, 2006)

Wikinomics offers a more collaborative workplace, using the Web. In the United States, where the concept of quality circles, work groups that met after work to discuss solutions to business problems, did not catch on, wikis may help in resurrecting the concept.

Process Analysis

Work is the sum total of a number of processes. Whatever the job is, the operations manager must effectively design the movement of work through these processes.

The manager of the accounts payable function must process the payment of invoices in an efficient manner. The manager of the purchasing function must process the ordering of supplies and equipment. If a manager suspects that the process can be improved, an analysis should be undertaken. The first step in **process analysis** is to understand it. There are five steps involved. The five steps form an acronym: **DMAIC** (Define-Measure-Analyze-Improve-Control).

Step 1: *Define.* What process needs to be improved? Who will participate in the project for improving this process? Who are the customers? Who are the workers involved in the process? In this step, we interview customers and process workers to find out the scope of the project.

Step 2: *Measure.* In this step, we chart the process with some sort of flowchart or map. Input and output measurements are determined. Preliminary data are collected.

Step 3: *Analyze.* What causes problems? Reduce the list of causes.

Step 4: *Improve.* Find solutions for the problem, and design an implementation plan.

Step 5: *Control.* Make sure the improved process stays in control.

This chapter will focus on the first two steps, Define and Measure.

Define

A starting point for process improvement campaigns is to identify the processes that have the most impact on customers and the profitability of the firm. Process analysis can have a major financial impact; so it is crucial that time not be spent on nonessential activities. One fast-food restaurant chain did a process analysis to discover why one store in a region was much less profitable than the others. They discovered that the servers were passing out five or six catsup packets to each customer! Their solution was to place catsup and mustard dispensers in the store and cease to give out packets. The result was a savings of thousands of dollars per year!

The Process Project

This book devotes an entire chapter to project management. Once a project team is formed and the key processes have been identified, the team must learn about the existing process. In their book on Six Sigma processes, George, Rowlands, Price, and Maxey (2005) suggested a *Kaizen* approach to process improvement. *Kaizen* is a Japanese term that means, roughly, "continuous improvement." The definition stage alone involved the following:

- Defining the process objectives
- Selecting a project leader
- Preparing training materials
- Collecting information
- Planning logistics for meetings
- Covering for absences from the day-to-day workplace
- Arranging management participation
- Making appointments

Harrington (1991) outlined a number of questions to ask the workers involved in the process:

1. *What is your job description?* Some employees have not been told what exactly their job requires. A specific job description and a thorough orientation go a long way in starting a new employee off in the right direction.

2. *How were you trained?* Some problems with the process stem from improper training. With this question, the manager can find out if there were mistakes in the training of the worker and correct them.

3. *Who is your customer?* Many workers fail to see the link between their work and the worker who is next in line in the process. Fellow employees are "customers" of the work.

4. *What would happen if you were not at work?* This question addresses where the worker fits into the process. "If no one did my job, it wouldn't even be noticed" is not the correct reply. The order taker on the telephone has to have all the credit card information and an errorless order to pass on to the shipping workers who prepare the items for delivery.

5. *What prevents you from doing error-free work?* If mistakes are made, what causes them? An employee might answer that there is a simple solution—get me a taller chair!

6. *What would you do if you were the manager?* Employees are much like Monday-morning quarterbacks, who criticize every move of the football coach in the game the day before. Workers go home to their families and complain about the mistakes made by their idiot managers! They then espouse a number of ideas to their families that may have some merit. "OK, if you were in charge, what would you do?" They may be suspicious and think this is a trick question, but the idea is to get them to open up.

7. *What do you do?* A different question from the job description one—this question asks for a real explanation of job duties. This description may differ from the job description and may reveal that the process worker is doing some wrong things.

8. *How do you know your output is good?* All workers should be given an explanation of what constitutes good work. Sometimes they are working without knowing this all-important definition of a quality standard to attain.

9. *How can we make your job easier?* They may never have been asked if there were some actions management could take to help them do a better job. They certainly would appreciate the question.

These are important questions the operations manager should ask, so that he or she can truly understand how the work is getting done.

The Voice of the Customer

After interviewing the process workers, the customer should be consulted for suggestions. First, the process analyst must find the *right* customers to ask. That means some market research to determine who the customers who buy the product or use the service are.

One Saturday morning at the bagel shop is probably adequate to gather such information, if it is the bagel restaurant you want to study.

Questions to ask the customer:

1. Why do you come here?

2. What improvements would you suggest to the store?

3. What are your favorite aspects of the place?

4. What are your favorite products?

5. Are you dissatisfied with any of the services that are offered?

Many times, customers can see things that companies cannot. After all, most of their customers have their own workplaces that they can compare on business processes.

Measure

A beginning point in the measurement phase of process analysis is to draw a picture. There are a number of different charting methods. A flowchart of the process is a helpful approach to detect inefficient actions. There are several basic charting symbols, including the most basic ones shown in Figure 2.1.

Other types of charting methods include the following:

• *Value stream mapping:* Identifies value-added and non-value-added activities and includes some performance data.

• *SIPOC diagram (suppliers, inputs, process, outputs, customers):* Provides a complete analysis of inputs and outputs that goes from the supplier of the process to the customer of the process.

• *Deployment flowchart:* Arranges processes according to functions (purchasing, accounts payable, etc.).

• *Transportation diagram:* Provides a diagram of work flow (see Figure 2.2).

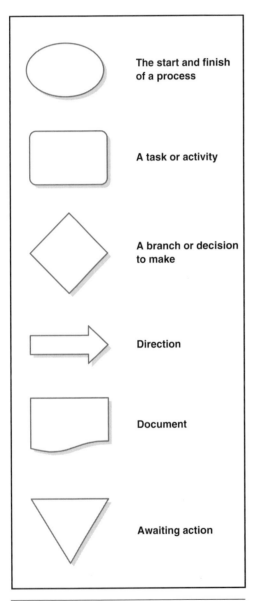

The start and finish of a process

A task or activity

A branch or decision to make

Direction

Document

Awaiting action

Figure 2.1   Flowchart Icons

SOURCE: Leinaker, Sanders, and Hild (1996) and Tenner and DeToro (2000).

The Process of Making Red Wine

All products follow a production process in a sequence of steps. The making of red wine, which is different from the process of making white wine, by necessity starts with the selection of the vineyard and the grape. The location is key to the success of the wine because the soil, the sunlight, and the climate are important factors.

After the grapes are picked, the stems are removed (but not always), and the grapes are crushed. The crushed grapes are placed inside a tank, and yeast is added. Fermentation of the grapes begins, and skins are placed over the liquid. After fermentation is complete, the wine is pressed, put in barrels, and aged. Finally, it is bottled.

This sounds like a simple process; yet every year, the wine tastes different from two next-door neighbors making cabernet sauvignon. That is why there is still an element of art in the wine-making process.

Compare winemaking with the process of making a McDonald's French fry. These fries taste the same everywhere in the world. It is doubtful if we will see a day when we have French fry connoisseurs conducting taste tests and pronouncing the year the French fry was made and what part of Idaho the potato came from.

UPS 12-Step Unloading Process

UPS goes to great lengths to streamline the process of delivering packages. The process of delivering one package from a shelf involves 12 steps:

1. Shift into the lowest gear or park.

2. Turn off the ignition and engage the parking brake.

3. Release the seat belt with the left hand.

4. Open the door.

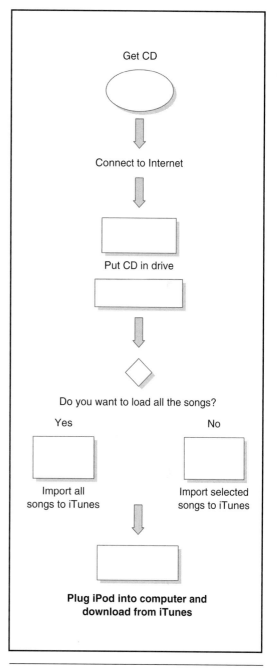

Figure 2.2 Example of Process: Transferring a CD to an iPod

5. Place the key on the ring finger.

6. Select the package.

7. Only select packages from the selection area.

8. Close the door.

9. Pick up the DIAD (delivery information acquisition device).

10. Fasten the DIAD to the belt clip.

11. Look both ways before stepping into the street.

12. Hold on to the handrail and exit the truck.

The UPS industrial engineers have determined that picking a package from a shelf should take 15.5 s and from the floor, 25.1 s. Picking three packages from a shelf should take 29.6 s and five packages from the rear door, 65.5 s.

The very action of Step 5 is instructive. Without the routine of going through these 12 steps over and over again, it becomes very easy to absentmindedly misplace the car keys. How embarrassing it would be for a UPS driver (Hira, 2007) to have to call for a new key! But they are human like the rest of us, who are always losing keys, checkbooks, and eyeglasses. For those with a tendency to lose things, the best approach is to always perform the same steps. Every day, the keys are placed in the same location. If you forget and leave them in a coat pocket, it leads to a panic-stricken search for them the next day!

How to Analyze a Process

Getting From Home to the Airport

There are a number of decision points and processes involved in getting from your home, office, or hotel to your scheduled flight at the airport:

Decision Point 1: What time is the departure? The time of departure can affect what transportation method one takes to the airport. If the flight is before or after the rush hour, traffic is reduced, making the drive or taxi ride a speedy alternative.

Decision Point 2: How many bags will you carry, and how many bags will you check in? If you opt to check bags on the plane, it will add some time for processing the bags. If you have a number of bags, carrying them around becomes a hassle, and a taxi looks like a desirable alternative.

Decision Point 3: How will you get there? Compare some transportation options available for one commuter to Chicago's O'Hare airport:

Transportation Option	Cost ($)	Avg. Time
Electric train	3.50 return ticket	1 hr 40 min (varies by location)
Taxi	36.00	30 min
Drive and park	16/day	48 min
Someone drops you	6	30 min

If the commuter is cost sensitive and has the time, the electric train is a great option. On the other hand, carrying four suitcases and transferring trains would make it a drag—in more ways than one!

Decision Point 4: Will you carry your laptop? If so, this adds hassle at the airport, adds a bag to your luggage, but gives you a portable office on location.

Decision Point 5: Do you check in with the sky cab or go to the automated kiosk? If you only have carry-on luggage, the lines are shorter.

Decision Point 6: Will you eat or buy magazines/books prior to the metal detectors or after? Similarly, do you use a restroom prior to the metal detectors or after? The first question is easy to answer if there is a rule of thumb: If the flight boards in less than an hour, go through the detectors first. On the second issue, only your bladder knows for sure.

Decision Point 7: Do you board as soon as your seating area is announced, or do you hang out until the last minute? That, again, depends on whether you have luggage to stow.

The sometimes mad rush to the airport can be avoided if one has carefully outlined this process and determined the answers to these decision points in advance.

The Process of Getting U2 Tickets

Getting a ticket for popular sporting events and concerts can be a challenge. One method has been to assign a wristband to potential ticket buyers, then randomly assign a numbered wristband to begin the line of ticket sales.

The Irish group U2 tried a method of ticket sales that backfired. They told concertgoers that they could join the U2 fan club for $40 and get advance sales of concerts. What U2 did not realize was that so many people thought it was infinitely better to pay the $40 than it was to stand in line that so the fans who paid the money outnumbered the concert's total capacity by a wide margin. In fact, few of them procured tickets.

It was an unfortunate way to discover that a new process was worse than the old one.

The Process of Getting Elected President of the United States

If you are a U.S. citizen, there is a complicated process in getting elected president. Before the process even begins, the candidate must have minimally good looks, a lot of money, and friends in high places and must not have any secret affairs or be involved in business scandals. The best candidate will probably have been a member of the Boy Scouts or Girl Scouts, played several sports growing up, had a sterling grade point average through school, been loved by all teachers, and either made a fortune in business or inherited a lot of money. The candidate will most likely be married, with 2.2 children and a dog. Unless the candidate lives in California, he or she will probably have spent some time in a political office, such as governor of the home state or U.S. senator. The person should not have extreme views, left wing or right wing, on any issue.

Once all these ingredients are in place, the fun begins. Here are some key steps of the process:

1. Conduct a feasibility study. The candidate should commission a study to ascertain his or her chances of getting elected. Does the candidate have name recognition in all regions of the United States?

2. Build a staff. The candidate needs several key people, a campaign manager, a budget manager, a public relations adviser, an issues adviser, and a speechwriter or two.

3. Take positions on every potential campaign issue imaginable. Voters will want to know what you think of farm aid, foreign aid, and Band-Aid.

4. Invade the states that have the preliminary primaries. Without victories in the early primaries, the chances of gaining momentum through the convention are slim. The public relations team must find every conceivable way to get free ink and airtime.

5. Fund-raising continues at an increasing rate if the early primaries are positive.

6. Establish a national staff. The staffers must find important individuals in every state who are willing to make an early commitment to your campaign and spend the time to organize support and funds in their home states.

7. Gain momentum. If the challengers slowly self-destruct and withdraw from the race, ask each of them to join your team in exchange for some good tickets to future U2 concerts.

8. Work the convention. The convention is where supporters are supposed to follow through with their promised-for votes. A lot of wining and dining and promising go on here.

9. Don't say anything stupid between the convention and the election that will offend any constituency in any state.

10. Have an acceptance speech and a concession speech at hand on election night.

11. If you win, you are the next president. If you lose, write a book about the experience. If you lost weight while campaigning, write a book on weight loss.

In Chapter 15, you will notice many similarities between process analysis and projects. An election campaign is a process in that you must successfully follow a series of steps to win the election. It is also a project with many tasks that can be handled simultaneously.

Streamlining

Harrington (1991) suggested a number of approaches for **streamlining** processes:

1. Eliminate bureaucracy. Organizations seem to love to make things complicated, adding layers of management that become bottlenecks to progress.

2. Eliminate duplication. The process analyst should look for places where work may be duplicated, and eliminate the excess.

3. Assess value added. The most important process improvements should be aimed at those processes in which value is added to the customer. These improvements will have the biggest financial impact.

4. Simplify. The old acronym KISS (Keep it simple, stupid!) applies at all times.

5. Reduce cycle time. Make it a goal to reduce process time while improving efficiency.

6. Proof errors. The operations manager must "idiot-proof" a process. This must be done by imagining how a stupid person will mess it up. For example, the IRS places a message on the return envelope, "Did you remember to sign?" This message helps protect them against the most frequent error in income tax statements. If you build an airplane, you have to assume that some day someone will want to see if the plane's emergency door will open in midflight; so the engineers have to design a door that will not open unless the plane is on the ground.

7. Simplify language. Business language should be aimed at the elementary-grade level of understanding. Some document writers like to display their impressive vocabularies, and mistakes are made because the workers do not understand the words.

This is an actual real-estate document:

> . . . title company, a state corporation, as duly appointed trustee under deed of trust hereinafter referred to, having received from the holder of obligations thereunder a written request to reconvey, reciting that all sums secured by said deed of trust and the note or notes secured thereby having been surrendered to said trustee for cancellation, does hereby reconvey, without warranty, to the person or persons legally entitled thereto the estate now held by it thereunder.

Do you use these words on a daily basis? *Thereunder, hereinafter, reconvey?* Perhaps these were used in the days of Shakespeare but certainly not today. "Would you reconvey me a cup of coffee?" "I want to marry you for the hereinafter!" Documents like these require attorneys to understand them, so perhaps some of you will go to law school and make a living interpreting them.

Pitfalls in Process Analysis

Jacka and Keller (2002), who advocated what they called *process mapping*, a variation of flowcharting, in their book *Business Process Mapping*, identified a number of pitfalls that can occur during process analysis:

1. *Mapping for mapping's sake:* Creating flowcharts is not the objective of process analysis; improving the process is the goal. Some analysts get caught up so much in flowcharting that they can't see the forest for the trees.

2. *Creating complicated flowcharts that are difficult to read.*

3. *Letting the customer define the process:* Customers can get an analyst offtrack before a conclusion is made.

4. *Not verifying the facts:* An error in charting can lead to the wrong results. Charts should be checked and rechecked for accuracy.

Process Analysis and Lean

The process of analyzing processes with flow diagrams and analyzing the way work is accomplished is an important step in **LEAN production**. This term was first used by the authors James Womack and Daniel Jones in their book *The Machine That Changed the World* (1991) and further defined in their book *Lean Thinking* (2003). This concept, which will be discussed later in this book, is essentially nothing more than a renaming of the Japanese production system, just-in-time (JIT).

The principal aim is to eliminate waste, or *muda*, the Japanese word for waste. This is accomplished by identifying the value stream, the "set of actions required to bring a specific product (whether a good or service, or increasingly, a combination of the two) through the three critical management tasks of any business (Womack & Jones, 2003, p. 19).

After the value stream is identified, wasteful steps are eliminated, and a continuous flow is created. Womack and Jones (2003) pointed out that continuous flow is counterintuitive because work tends to be completed in batches. Womack illustrated this with an example of his daughters, who mailed a newsletter in the following steps:

1. Fold the newsletter.

2. Put on the address labels.

3. Seal the newsletter by sticking the upper and lower parts for mailing.

4. Then put on the stamps.

The daughters established four workstations for the process and passed the newsletter down the line. Womack's alternative method was to perform the four steps on each newsletter, so rather than pass the paper down the line, each line did the four steps individually. His argument was that the wasteful step of four people picking up the piece of paper was eliminated.

Summary

- Productivity is defined as the ratio of outputs to inputs.

- Every industry has its important productivity measurements. A hospital may be concerned with its occupancy rate and mortality rate. An airplane deals with its seat utilization and on-time arrivals and departures. A police department is concerned with minimizing the number of crimes committed.

- Sports offer a glimpse of how to manage given a plethora of productivity measurements, since sports statistics are exactly that. The way a baseball manager makes decisions based on data is not much different from the way a manufacturing manager examines the productivity of workers.

- The multiple criteria measurement index is a way to combine a number of factors into one measurement system.

- Time studies serve as a mechanism to study the amount of time in which a work task can be performed. They are helpful in improving productivity by providing information on what a worker can accomplish.

- Wiki productivity holds potential as a new form that can increase worker collaboration.

- A process analysis involves a thorough study of a process, including diagramming and interviewing process workers.

- DMAIC is a method of improving a process that involves the following steps: Define-Measure-Analyze-Improve-Control.

- Streamlining is an approach to process improvement through process analysis.

- Pitfalls of flowcharting include the tendency to rely too much on charting.

- Process improvement is critical in the success of lean production, or JIT, which emphasizes the elimination of waste.

Key Terms

DMAIC	Streamlining
Kaizen	Time study
Lean production	Voice of the customer
Muda	Wikinomics
Multiple-criteria measurement	Work sample
Process analysis	

Review Questions

1. Define production and operations management.

2. Compare operations management in a hospital with operations in a steel mill.

3. How did Frederick Taylor, the Gilbreths, and the Hawthorne study contribute to modern-day operations management?

4. What is a multicriteria performance index, and how does one analyze the score?

5. What are micromotions?

6. How do you define a job?

7. What is the difference between average time and standard time?

8. What are the best questions to ask a worker in a process?

9. List the methods of streamlining a process.

10. How can wiki software increase productivity in an organization?

Projects

1. Consult a company you are familiar with. Who is "the operations manager"? Ask the person to describe his or her activities.

2. Spend the day observing operations management at work, during your commute, where you study, and where you dine.

3. Find out who sets up the college's class schedule, and ask the person how he or she goes about it.

4. Go to a retailer and discuss with the manager how merchandise is purchased and displayed.

5. Devise an MCM system for a worker at a fast-food restaurant who assembles burgers and other sandwiches, operates the cash register, and cleans the area.

6. Ask a librarian what the main activities of work are, and devise an MCM system for the job.

7. In a sport other than football, devise an MCM system of performance.

8. Ask a woman to tie a necktie. Use a stopwatch to see how fast she does it the first time. Try it again. What is the average time? For men, see how long it takes to put on panty hose. Try it a second time. How well does men's performance compare with women doing the same task?

9. Analyze a process by interviewing process workers and then drawing a flowchart of the work. Criticize the process.

10. Approach a process and make streamlining suggestions.

11. Study the following processes: getting a driver's license, buying a house, selling a house, applying for a car loan, washing your clothes at a Laundromat. Draw flowcharts, and see if you can detect flaws in the process.

CASE 1 Process Diagramming—Double-Chocolate Cookies

Use the diagramming icons to draw a picture of this cookie recipe:

1. Sift together the flour, cocoa, baking powder, and salt in a medium bowl. Set aside.

2. Melt the chocolate in a medium heatproof bowl set over a pan of almost simmering water, stirring once or twice until smooth, and then remove from the heat. In a small bowl, beat the eggs and vanilla lightly with a fork; sprinkle the coffee powder over to dissolve, and set aside.

3. Either by hand or with an electric mixer, beat the butter at medium speed until smooth and creamy, about 5 s. Beat in the sugars until combined, about 45 s. Add the chocolate in a steady stream and beat until combined, about 40 s. Scrape the bottom and sides of the bowl with a rubber spatula. With the mixer at low speed, add the dry ingredients and mix until just combined. Do not overbeat. Cover with plastic wrap and let stand at room temperature until the consistency is scoopable and fudge-like, about 30 min.

4. Meanwhile, adjust the oven racks to the upper- and lower-middle positions, and heat the oven to 350°. Line two baking sheets with parchment paper. Scoop the dough onto the prepared baking sheets with a 1½-in. ice-cream scoop, spacing the mounds of dough about 1½ in. apart.

5. Bake until the edges of the cookies have just begun to set but the centers are still very soft, about 10 min, rotating the baking sheets front to back and top to bottom halfway through the baking time. Cool the cookies on the sheets, about 10 min, slide the parchment with the cookies onto wire racks, and cool to room temperature. Cover one cooled baking sheet with a new piece of parchment paper. Scoop the remaining dough onto the parchment-lined sheet, bake, and cool as directed. Remove the cooled cookies from the parchment with a wide metal spatula.

Makes about 42 cookies.
Ingredients:

2 cups (10 oz) unbleached all-purpose flour

½ cup (1½ oz) Dutch-processed cocoa

2 teaspoons baking powder

½ teaspoon salt

16 oz semisweet chocolate, chopped

4 large eggs

2 teaspoons vanilla extract

2 teaspoons instant coffee or espresso powder

2 tablespoons unsalted butter, softened but still cool

1½ cups light brown sugar

½ cup granulated sugar

How is preparing a recipe like a business process? Was this recipe easy to diagram?

SOURCE: Adapted from *The New Best Recipe* (2004, pp. 779–780).

CASE 2 The Eight Days a Week Fitness Center

King Kwong has owned and operated the Eight Days a Week Fitness Center in Hong Kong for several years. The Fitness Center is located near a shopping mall and City University of Hong Kong and draws a number of students, working professionals, and residents of Kowloon. It is across the street from a railway station and is ideally located. The Fitness Center showed a profit by its second year, and its membership grew rapidly. The Center was able to pay off most of its equipment within the first year, but there were signs of discontentment from the members, who complained of there not being enough towels and about problems with the cleanliness of the locker room.

King decided to study the situation and take whatever course of action he could to correct the situation. Here are some of his figures:

Month and Year	No. of Members	No. of Employees	Avg. Labor Hrs/Employee	Profit (in HK $)
Jan. 2006	850	25	4.8	−27,000
Feb. 2006	1,420	40	4.4	−22,000
Mar. 2006	2,107	53	4.7	−13,000
Apr. 2006	2,745	56	5.2	−6,000
May 2006	2,987	65	4.9	−3,000
Jun. 2006	3,005	70	4.6	1,005
Jul. 2006	3,017	68	4.5	3,000
Aug. 2006	3,030	65	4.6	7,000
Sep. 2006	3,045	62	4.7	15,000
Oct. 2006	3,030	65	4.7	22,000
Nov. 2006	3,027	64	4.5	25,000
Dec. 2006	3,009	65	4.6	29,000
Jan. 2007	3,302	74	4.4	40,000
Feb. 2007	3,290	72	4.3	34,800

For the same period, here are his laundry and housekeeping expenses:

Month and Year	Laundry (HK$)	Housekeeping (HK$)
Jan. 2006	6,000	11,420
Feb. 2006	7,100	11,804
Mar. 2006	8,200	13,300
Apr. 2006	9,300	15,600
May 2006	9,700	18,200
Jun. 2006	9,600	17,900
Jul. 2006	9,600	18,100

Month and Year	Laundry (HK $)	Housekeeping (HK $)
Aug. 2006	9,400	17,700
Sep. 2006	9,100	16,500
Oct. 2006	8,700	16,000
Nov. 2006	8,500	15,800
Dec. 2006	8,600	16,000
Jan. 2007	9,100	16,400
Feb. 2007	9,200	16,600

In December 2006, King asked members to complete customer service questionnaires. On a scale of 1 to 5, with 5 = *most satisfied*, the members gave the following ratings:

	Dec. 2006	Jan. 2007	Feb. 2007
Locker room facilities	3.40	3.30	3.20
Equipment	4.50	4.50	4.35
Fitness staff support	4.90	4.87	4.91
Janitorial staff support	2.20	2.10	2.05
Cleanliness of facility	2.75	2.87	2.56
Exercise classes	3.67	3.45	3.27

Given this information that King has collected, do as follows:

1. Derive a number of productivity ratios that are important to the club.

2. Identify problem areas for King to address.

3. Are there relationships between profitability and service at this institution?

CASE 3   Mehdi's Car Wash

Dr. Mehdi decided to take a break from teaching and invest in a South Florida car wash. He was interested in the productivity of the workers at the car wash, so he studied the number of cars washed versus the number of workers employed every hour for a week. The following table gives the information he collected. What are the productivity rates per hour, and how do they differ across the week?

Time Period	Cars Washed	Workers
7:00 a.m.–7:59 a.m.	6	4
8:00 a.m.–8:59 a.m.	14	8
9:00 a.m.–9:59 a.m.	16	8

(Continued)

(Continued)

Time Period	Cars Washed	Workers
10:00 a.m.–10:59 a.m.	20	8
11:00 a.m.–11:59 a.m.	24	8
12:00 p.m.–12:59 p.m.	42	10
1:00 p.m.–1:59 p.m.	30	10
2:00 p.m.–2:59 p.m.	20	8
3:00 p.m.–3:59 p.m.	35	8
4:00 p.m.–4:59 p.m.	32	8
5:00 p.m.–5:59 p.m.	31	8
6:00 p.m.–6:59 p.m.	37	8
7:00 p.m.–7:59 p.m.	12	6

What staffing considerations might Mehdi consider? If each car wash averages $12, the workers are paid $5 per hour (not including tips), and nonlabor expenses (supplies, overhead, etc.) are $800 per day, what is the expected profit for Mehdi?

CASE 4   Rohit's Pizza

Rohit wants to compare the productivity of his pizza delivery drivers. His company covers an 8-mile radius, and drivers take the orders as they come.
In a 1-week period:

Driver	Deliveries	Hours Worked
Abe	62	30
Buffy	47	30
Adrian	58	30
Rocky	39	24
Sam	48	24
Boris	33	24
Bo	40	24
Tommy	38	20
Elliott	36	20
Missy	45	20

Calculate the productivity rates for each driver.

CASE 5   Hospital Supply Marketing

Caron is a new marketing representative for a hospital supply company. She has a starting salary of $48,000, but after 1 year the salary structure changes to $36,000 plus 5% of total sales. As she reviews her sales for her first year, she is somewhat anxious about her earnings in the next year.

From a productivity standpoint, answer the following:

1. How would you devise an MCM system for a marketing representative that included other variables besides sales?

2. What is the projected income for Caron in the coming year?

3. Should Caron get another job?

Quarter	Sales ($)
1	27,000
2	29,000
3	31,000
4	36,000

CASE 6   Office Productivity

Wing designed a new productivity system for his development office in an effort to increase fund-raising for his university. Each development staff member was to receive a 3% commission on all donations actually collected. It did not matter whether the staffer solicited the donation or not. Here is a comparison of the year prior to implementation of the system and the year after it was implemented:

	2005	2006
Alexandra, Education	175,000	188,000
Bruce, Liberal Arts and Sciences	240,000	310,000
Ed, Business	607,000	547,000
Mildred, Computer Science	100,000	156,000
Kathy, Law	588,000	1,200,000

How much did each staffer earn in commissions? Did the system appear to be working?

Web Sites

The American Productivity and Quality Center: www.apqc.org

The Australian Productivity Commission: pc.gov.au

European automotive production: http://Worldmarketanalysis.com

Explanation of NFL statistics: http://Slate.msn.com

Hong Kong Productivity Council: www.hkpc.org

Marriott Hotel productivity information: www.marriott.com/corporateinfo

Pro football: www.nfl.com

United Kingdom Productivity: statistics.gov.uk

U.S. Bureau of Labor Statistics: www.bls.gov

References

George, M. L., Rowlands, D., Price, M., & Maxey, J. (2005). *Lean Six Sigma pocket toolbook.* New York: McGraw-Hill.

Harrington, H. J. (1991). *Business process improvement.* New York: McGraw-Hill.

Hira, N. A. (2007, November 12). The making of a UPS driver. *Fortune,* 118–129.

Jacka, J. M., & Keller, P. J. (2002). *Business process mapping.* New York: John Wiley & Sons.

Leinaker, M., Sanders, R., & Hild, C. (1996). *The power of statistical thinking.* Reading, MA: Addison-Wesley.

The new best recipe. (2004). By the editors of *Cook's Illustrated.* Brookline, MA: America's Test Kitchen.

Sink, D. S. (1985). *Productivity management: Planning, measurement and evaluation, control and improvement.* New York: John Wiley & Sons.

Tapscott, D., & Williams, A. D. (2006). *Wikinomics.* New York: Portfolio.

Tenner, A., & DeToro, I. J. (2000). *Process redesign.* Upper Saddle River, NJ: Prentice Hall.

Womack, J. P., & Jones, D. T. (1991). *The machine that changed the world.* New York: Harper Perennial.

Womack, J. P., & Jones, D. T. (2003). *Lean thinking.* New York: Free Press.

CHAPTER 3

Operations Strategy

SOURCE: © ShaneKato/istockphoto.com

> ## Learning Objectives
>
> In this chapter, we will study
>
> - The mission's importance to strategy
> - The role of operations management in positioning organizational strategy
> - The role of Operations in the Five Forces
> - How Operations fits within the strategy cycle
> - Nine strategic questions to be addressed by organizations
> - Different ways to use Operations for competitive purposes
> - The importance of Operations to the value chain
> - The stages of dynamic manufacturing

The Mission

All organizations, whether they are for-profit corporations or not-for-profit charitable institutions, compete for customers' dollars. This is fairly easy to notice when shopping. If a customer shops for a purse, there are many different manufacturers to choose from: Coach, Guess, Stone Mountain, Versace, and so on. Each of these purse manufacturers competes for the sale on the basis of styling and price. The customer makes a purchase, and the money goes to the retailer, who replaces it with another purse from that manufacturer.

In the for-profit world, it is not a matter of trying to get all the business and drive everyone else into bankruptcy. Companies are too smart. They have savvy managers who watch their competitors and can quickly imitate them if they can't lead the way with a new strategy. Operations management figures prominently in the successful formulation of a corporate strategy. A lean operations system that gets the product quickly into the hands of the consumer and satisfies the retailer is critical in continued success.

The same is true of nonprofits. Perhaps you have a lot of used clothing and furniture to donate to a charity. Charity A has a system of picking up once a week from your town, while Company B requires you to drop it off. Who do you donate to? Charity A has made your task easier for you. After all, you are *giving* them something.

Strategic management is the process of coming up with a competitive strategy and successfully implementing it. A company must have a clearly defined mission and social responsibility prior to mapping out this strategy. The formulation and implementation of strategies are accomplished by the various business functions: operations, finance, accounting, marketing, research and development, human resource management (HRM), and information systems.

Operations management proved to be the most strategic area in business in the late 1970s and early 1980s. Through the use of production techniques, Japanese manufacturers gained a competitive foothold in the world's markets.

Since that time, companies have found a number of ways to realize the competitive advantage of effective operations.

Operations management should have a strategy that coincides with the organization's overall strategy. This chapter gives an overview of where operations management fits in the strategic planning of businesses.

Once a company plots out how it will compete in the marketplace, functional strategies in operations, marketing, and finance are coordinated and implemented to achieve the company's goals. Effective organizational strategy begins with the mission, a statement of what the organization stands for—a basic explanation of why it exists. This is the starting point for operations management, and *all* management. A floundering organization is one in which all work is merely a job, and no one thinks about what purpose it serves. The better firms focus on accomplishing whatever mission they have set out to fulfill. Typically, an organization's mission is spelled out on the company Web site and etched in employees' memories. Employees should all be able to recite the mission from memory.

Here are some examples.

Ben & Jerry's: The popular Vermont ice cream maker sets out three missions (www.benjerry.com/our_company/our_mission/):

Product Mission: To make, distribute & sell the finest quality all natural ice cream & euphoric concoctions with a continued commitment to incorporating wholesome, natural ingredients and promoting business practices that respect the earth and the environment.

Economic Mission: To operate the Company on a sustainable financial basis of profitable growth, increasing value for our stakeholders & expanding opportunities for development and career growth for our employees.

Social Mission: To operate the company in such a way that actively recognizes the central role that business plays in society by initiating innovative ways to promote the quality of life both nationally and internationally.

Ben & Jerry's is rare in establishing a social mission as a part of its agenda, but it is an important influence on the way the company's ice cream is produced. What the triumvirate of missions accomplishes is that it gives employees a sense that their work is contributing toward a greater good. It may also make customers feel that not only are they indulging their ice cream habit, but in some small way, they are helping some social cause as well.

Honda states on their corporate Web site (www.Honda.com),

It is our mission to improve the lives of customers and communities where we all live, work and play. We will continue to develop and build products in local markets around the world to create value for all of our customers. Our established directions for the 21st century provide a balance of fun for the customer and responsibility for society and the environment.

Positioning Strategies

The operations manager must be very much in tune with the mission of the firm and the overall strategy. Michael Porter (1980), in his classic work, *Competitive Strategy*, outlined three basic **generic strategies**:

1. *Cost leadership*, in which the firm strives to be the low-cost producer in the industry

2. *Differentiation*, in which the company attempts to find a unique product or service

3. *Focus*, where the firm seeks out specific niches in the market

Porter insisted that the road to success was to use a strategy that others were not using. When all firms copy each other, they are all "stuck in the middle," and no one has an edge. However, most companies tend to use some combination of the three generic strategies.

Someone driving on an interstate must make a decision as to what motel to stay at for the evening. If you own a motel on the interstate, the weary passenger usually has dozens of choices on where to settle for the night. There are a number of factors in this decision:

1. How far is the ultimate destination?

2. How far have we driven thus far, and how tired are we?

3. Do we insist on a certain brand name?

4. How much can we afford to pay?

5. Do we want a free breakfast, or do we prefer a plush king bed?

6. Do we want nonsmoking?

7. How close is it to the interstate?

8. If we have pets, will they accept them, and if so, what are the terms?

9. Other: swimming pool, proximity to Pizza Hut, and so on

Maybe the driver is limited to pet-friendly hotels, which severely constrains the decision. Some motel chains routinely accept pets, and customers seek them out, sometimes driving an extra 50 miles to reach one.

Knowing that all customers are looking at these decision factors, one motel owner may decide to sell the rooms for $49, when the going rate is $79. She has 80 available rooms. She had originally priced the same as everyone else but averaged only 50% occupancy. With the price reduction, she increased her occupancy to an average of 90% year-round. How do you calculate the difference in revenue? She now brings in $3,528 per night compared with $3,160 per night. Her expenses were

$3,000 per night in the original scenario, and they now are $3,300 per night. This is an improvement of $68 per night, which is $23,920 per year. In a small motel, that is a significant profit increase.

In small, independent motels, the owner is the operations manager. Since she has elected the low-cost option, her decisions as operations manager must agree with this strategy. For instance, the simple replacement of a showerhead is driven by the most economically priced fixtures on the market. Down the street, at the chain hotel that is appealing to the less cost-conscious customer, a showerhead replacement might be to go with an upgrade; the new improved rain showerhead.

A key aspect of operations management is sourcing; and other than the cost of labor, the cost of supplies and materials is the highest cost incurred by companies. Which vendor a company selects is a function of the organization's strategy. The buyer for Mercedes Benz sedans is not sourcing for the same quality parts as the company manufacturing a low-priced sedan at the entry level of the market.

The Five Forces

A popular approach to industry analysis introduced by Michael Porter (1985) was the **Five Forces of Competition**. Porter described a model in which there were five forces that dictated industry competition:

1. *The power of buyers:* How many buyers are there for the products? If there are few buyers, the sellers have little power and a lower profit margin. If there are many buyers, and enough for all sellers to profit, the sellers have more power over price.

In the hotel industry, room capacity is key to this force. In this industry, there are multiple product groupings. The luxury market does not compete with the economy market. Marriott competes with Westin, Hyatt, and Sheraton. Within specific markets, the actual arena of competition is on a city-by-city basis and depends on the number of available rooms at the time. If Chicago is running at 65% occupancy but New York City is at 85%, there will be more competition in Chicago.

In the automobile-manufacturing industry, each manufacturer has multiple models competing in different price ranges. Some manufacturers have several types of SUVs. Again, the capacity is key to this competitive issue. Manufacturers fight for market share, but they must also be constrained by their production capacity. They want to exactly match the customer demand. Honda has the Acura MDX and the Honda Pilot, two similar SUVs, but the Acura adds amenities and luxury components to warrant an increase in the price tag.

In the soft drink industry, there are a number of buyers that Coca-Cola and Pepsi must pay attention to:

1. Supermarket buyers

2. Amusement parks

3. Restaurants

4. Schools, universities, and so on

5. Theaters

Coca-Cola once competed successfully in the restaurant industry by pointing out to buyers that Pepsi owned several fast-food companies: KFC, Pizza Hut, and Burger King. They argued that for any other restaurant to offer Pepsi would result in revenue going directly into competitive facilities. Pepsi eventually sold these businesses.

2. *The power of suppliers:* How many suppliers provide the commodity? This will determine their power. As long as Monsanto owned a patent on aspartame, it controlled the artificial sweetener market. Once patent protection expired, other companies could offer competing sweeteners, forcing Monsanto to reduce its price.

3. *Barriers to entry:* The industry is affected by the ease or difficulty of entering the market. If it is fairly easy to join the competitive fray, then competition is intense. Entry barriers are created by economies of scale. By producing more, a company can lower its average cost of production, thus improving its profit margin. The high cost of an initial capital investment for production is frequently the biggest barrier to entry in most industries. For example, a new entrant in the soft drink industry will not be able to match the average cost of Coca-Cola and Pepsi because of the economies realized through canning, bottling, and distribution. Therefore, no matter how great the new soft drink is, a new entrant will come in at a higher price.

Creating a brand image is an important entry barrier. A product such as Kleenex ™ eventually becomes the industry standard and is tough to beat without product recognition.

4. *Substituting products:* The industry must heed any product that consumers can purchase as a substitute. A luxury hotel must watch developments in the midprice hotel market, for example, or they risk intruding on their market share and profitability. Some midprice hotels offer free amenities such as wi-fi and free breakfasts, which lure customers away from the luxury hotels.

The soft drink industry would have to watch products such as juices, waters, and energy drinks—perhaps all drinks that are nonalcoholic. It is no coincidence that Coca-Cola and Pepsi offer water, juice, and energy and sports drinks. However, years ago, Coca-Cola failed in its efforts to enter the wine industry. Distinctive competence in one market does not always translate into a market requiring different expertise and knowledge.

5. *Jockeying for competition:* The center ring of competition is in the daily moves and countermoves of the industry. If Ford Motor Company offers an extended warranty on an SUV, the move has to be countered in some way by General Motors, Honda, Toyota, and so on.

Operations management is very involved in the "power of suppliers" in their face-to-face negotiations with suppliers. No other function has greater influence on the organization's cost. Supplier strategies would consider whether or not to limit sourcing to one or a few vendors. Supply chain coordination can create an effective selling tool.

Operations is also important in establishing entry barriers over time by creating systems that are efficient for volume production and the mastery of production technology. Operations management is an integral aspect of all company strategies. When planning the future, the involvement of operations is an absolute necessity.

The Strategy Cycle

Operations managers must participate in strategic planning to accomplish the goals and missions set forth by the organization. An assessment needs to be made: "Where are we now? Where do we want to be? How do we get there?" Operations management has to be apprised of the overall strategies so that it can not only support them but also provide ways to differentiate and best the competition. The operations function is much more than the people who get the product out the door and provide the services to the customer.

Goodstein, Nolan, and Pfeiffer (1993) diagrammed a strategic planning model that forms the **strategy cycle.**

Step 1: Planning to plan

Step 2: Performing a values scan

Step 3: Mission formulation

Step 4: Strategic business modeling

Step 5: Performance audit and gap analysis

Step 6: Integrating action plans

Step 7: Contingency plans

Step 8: Strategy implementation

The operations manager works through these steps in concert with the rest of the organization. "Planning to plan" sounds like a needless exercise, but in fact, many organizations have not gone through a strategic planning process. This step would include some preliminary data gathering. What is the current global economic picture? What is the current and future industry and competitive environment, and what are our strengths, weaknesses, opportunities, and threats (SWOT)? If the planner notes that fuel prices are jumping dramatically and are not likely to decline, it will influence the planning process in many transportation, shipping, and courier industries.

Performing a **values scan** is to arrive at an understanding of the organization's culture and values. What do we stand for? Managers should share the same vision of what the company represents. It helps to have an exercise in which the values are actually spelled out.

The "mission formulation" stage follows; once there is a clear understanding of what the company represents, it is time to articulate what the company intends to accomplish. Missions should be understood to the point where every employee can write the mission at a moment's notice: "We intend to be world leader in providing quality chicken nuggets," for example. This is how Marks and Spencer, the British retailer, describes its mission and values:

Vision: the standard against which all others are measured.
Mission: making aspirational quality accessible to all.
Values: quality, value, service, innovation, and trust.

(www.marksandspencer.com)

Sage Publications, the publishers of this book, states that the company "acquires, develops, markets, and distributes knowledge. By disseminating scholarly and professional materials throughout the world, SAGE sets the standard for innovative, interdisciplinary, and international scholarship."

An operations manager who does not know the mission of his or her organization merely performs a job in a vacuum. Managers have to know what the objective of their work is.

The next step, strategic business modeling, involves identifying the proper lines of business and establishing a number of important performance measurements so that the company can gauge its success. Performance measures would include global sales indicators such as return on investment or return on equity, plus tactical indicators such as inventory turnover.

The Nine Questions for Formulating a Strategy

In setting organizational strategies, all the business functions are involved in the process. Operations must be in sync with the rest of the organization. Koch (2000) cited nine key questions that must be answered in formulating a strategy.

1. *What business are you in?* For the business unit, this means to identify the segments in which the unit competes. For example, printers have a number of different segments: color printers, black and white printers, combination printers/copiers/scanners, and so on. A printer manufacturer would ask if they have the same competitors in each individual segment. If they do, the next question is whether the market shares differ by segments. If they differ, they are likely to be different segments.

Segments are defined as "different products or services, different customers receiving the same service, different regions receiving the same product . . . and different versions of the same product."

The identification of the segment is important in determining distinct strategies for each segment. Take, for example, three universities located in the same city and their market shares according to schools (Table 3.1).

University A has a strong position in the undergraduate program and a weaker position in the professional schools, while University B is the law school leader,

Table 3.1   University Market Shares

Market Shares	University A (%)	University B (%)	University C (%)
Undergraduates	42	37	21
MBA students	19	40	41
Law students	23	45	32

and University C is slightly above University B in the business school arena. Thus, it appears that there are three distinct segments. How the universities compete will differ.

2. *Where do you make the money?* The profitability of each arena is an important strategic piece. If a business corners a market that garners few profits, it is a shallow victory. The return on investment or returns on sales are indicators of the success within the segment. University C may be less concerned about its lower standing with the undergraduate share, because the business and law students are paying higher tuitions and yield more profit.

3. *How good are your competitive positions?* The manager needs to know the market share, the trend in market share, the expected future growth rate, and the return on investment.

Table 3.2, adapted from Koch (2000), reveals relative market shares (RMS). The index is the percentage of the average. With three competitors, the average for each segment is 33.3%, so the RMS is based on the percentage of average:

Table 3.2   Relative Market Share at Three Universities

Percentage of RMS	University A	University B	University C
Undergraduates	1.26	1.11	0.63
MBA students	0.57	1.20	1.23
Law students	0.69	1.35	0.96
RMS Position	**Name**		**Rule of Thumb**
4.0+	Dominance		Extremely strong
1.5–3.9	Clear leadership		Very strong
1.0–1.4	Narrow leadership		Strong
0.7–0.99	Strong follower		Fairly strong
0.3–0.69	Follower		Moderate
Less than 0.3	Marginal		Weak

SOURCE: Koch (2000).

In the undergraduate segment, University A has a narrow leadership. In the MBA segment, both University B and University C have a narrow leadership, and in the law segment, University B has a narrow leadership.

Taking University A's case, they should examine the three segments for sales, profitability, and trend.

Category	Segments	Percentage of Tuition Dollars
Narrow leadership	Undergraduate	70
Strong follower	None	—
Follower	MBA	15
	Law	15

Table 3.3 shows market share of the three universities for the past 3 years.

Table 3.3   Market Share for the Past 3 Years

Market Share	University A (%)			University B (%)			University C (%)		
	2005	2006	2007	2005	2006	2007	2005	2006	2007
Undergraduate	43	42	42	35	36	37	22	22	21
MBA	25	22	19	33	39	40	42	42	41
Law	33	27	23	30	36	45	37	37	32

For University A,

Gaining Share	Holding Share	Losing Share
Undergraduate	MBA	Law

For University B,

Gaining Share	Holding Share	Losing Share
MBA	Law	Undergraduate

For University C,

Gaining Share	Holding Share	Losing Share
Undergraduate	MBA	Law

The Boston Consulting Group devised a **growth/share matrix** that identified the strength of segments by juxtaposing RMS against the market growth rate (Table 3.4).

Table 3.4   Boston Consulting Group's Growth/Share Matrix

Growth rate 20%	Stars		Question marks	
10%	Cash cows		Dogs	
0%				
Relative market share	10×	1.0	0.9	0.1

SOURCE: Koch (2000).

In this matrix, companies with an RMS above 1 and a market growth rate over 20% are "stars." "Cash cows" have the same RMS in markets but are growing at less than 10%. "Dogs" are in markets with lower than 10% growth and have less than a 1.0% market share, and "Question marks" are less than 1.0 in market share in markets with greater than 10% growth.

The rule of thumb is to invest heavily in stars and protect the cash cows. For the question marks, try to strengthen their positions. Dogs that are losing money should be considered candidates for sale.

4. *What skills and capabilities underpin your success?* The managers need to have a good understanding of what it is that they do that brings them success in the marketplace. This is usually referred to as the "distinctive competence" of the firm. Hamel and Prahalad (1994) introduced a similar concept, the "core competence of the corporation." Their description of a core competence is as follows:

A competence is a bundle of skills and technologies rather than a single discrete skill or technology. As an example, Motorola's competence in fast cycle-time production (minimizing the time between an order and the fulfillment of that order) rests on a broad range of underlying skills, including design disciplines that maximize commonality across a product line, flexible manufacturing, sophisticated order-entry systems, inventory management, and supplier management. . . . A core competence represents the sum of learning across individual skill sets and individual organizational units. (p. 223)

If this skill is rare or unusual, a way to capitalize on it should be found.

5. *Is this a good industry to be in?* What is the attractiveness of the industry from the current or future financial point of view? Is it hard to enter with little risk of duplicating products? A good understanding of the trends within the industry is important for this assessment.

6. *What do the customers think?* Marketing research should be conducted to discover how the customers compare your company with the competitors. Sales figures do not tell the whole truth. Customer interviews may reveal upcoming problems with the brand.

7. *What about the competitors?* A good business does not copy its competitors, but it respects them and follows their activities and strategies. Nonprofits are mistaken if they believe that they are not in competition with anyone. They are distinctly competing for donor dollars with other nonprofits. Thus, Public Television must pay attention to the activities of the American Heart Association and the Salvation Army.

8. *How do you raise profits quickly?* Sometimes price reductions result in increased sales and profitability. Price reductions, cost improvements, and increased advertising effectiveness are examples of ways to make a jump in profitability.

9. *How do you build long-term value?* Koch (2000) listed four major ways to build long-term value: cost reductions, price increases, price decreases, and changes in the business mix. Each strategy is situational. For example, if customers rate you highly and you have lower prices, a price increase may be warranted.

Performance Audit and Gap Analysis

A performance audit is conducted by a thorough self-examination. In this step, consultants are often employed to give an outside, unbiased perspective. Sometimes this helps in seeing the world from an outsider's perspective. Basically, the company is trying to determine how far away their current state is from the desired state.

Goodstein et al. (1993) listed a number of ways to reduce a performance gap:

1. *Internal expansion:* Adding new businesses through start-ups, acquisitions or mergers, or strategic alliances.

2. *Increasing the time horizon:* If your plan was to lose 10 lb by Christmas and you have lost only 4 lb, well, let's move the target date to Valentine's Day!

3. *Reducing the objective:* Perhaps it was unattainable. After trying to reach a lofty goal and missing it, reconfiguring the goal may be the answer.

4. *Changing the leadership:* How many times have you seen a new sports coach come in and take the same players a previous coach could do nothing with and mold them into a winner? This can happen in organizations too.

5. *Retrenching:* Getting rid of lines of business that are sapping the organization of resources may help. Addition through subtraction is what we call it.

Implementing Action Plans

The implementation stages include integrating the action plans, adapting with contingency plans, and final implementation. For the operations manager, this means contributing with functional strategies that target the company's mission. The following section enumerates a variety of approaches.

Ways to Compete Through Operations

The Harvard Business School professors Robert Hayes, Steven Wheelwright, and Kim Clark (1988) pointed out in the 1980s that manufacturing had been ignored in the prior decade as a competitive arena for business. Many firms had stopped focusing on improving products and services as a way to compete and had resorted to financial manipulations—that is, mergers and acquisitions, junk bonds, and so on—to grow.

A compensation method based on bottom-line performance had resulted in short-term thinking. Managers postponed capital improvements year after year, managing to look good on the balance sheet, getting promoted, and leaving their successors to do the dirty work. They postponed capital improvements, and factories became obsolete.

The oil embargo in the 1970s was a key event in the quality focus. Faced with rapidly rising gasoline prices, U.S. consumers sought automobiles with better fuel consumption, and they found them in the showrooms of Toyota, Nissan, and Honda. Once they purchased these autos, they quickly found that they were superior to U.S. cars. Consumers reported far fewer defects from the Japanese automobiles than were found in comparable U.S. models.

W. Edwards Deming was the most influential figure in the rededication to quality of products and services. A 1978 documentary *If Japan Can, Why Can't We?* helped bring Deming into prominence in the United States, a fame that he already enjoyed in Japan. In that film, Deming was especially critical of U.S. manufacturing for not having focused on quality improvement like the Japanese did. The VP of manufacturing for Ford saw the broadcast of the program and arranged for Deming to be hired as a Ford consultant. Ford, at that time, had a bad reputation for quality; and some customers thought that "FORD" stood for "fix or repair daily." Within a few years after embracing Deming's methods, Ford could use the slogan, "Quality Is Job One."

A major result of the Total Quality Management movement was a shift in strategic thinking. The Japanese had used a number of operations management techniques skillfully, proving that Operations could serve as a competitive weapon.

The following are operational methods that have been proven to give companies an edge when they can differentiate on one or more of these factors.

Quality

In any industry, there are differences in the quality of goods and services. The ability of a company to offer superior goods is an obvious means to gain market share. In some cases, that choice may be an expensive option. For instance, an automobile manufacturer that chooses to use the most expensive materials in its production will have a higher cost of production, but this may be the ticket to a finer automobile.

Westin Hotels introduced a "Heavenly Bed," in all its hotel rooms. This was a more expensive bed, driving up the costs for the hotel. If the hotel chain noticed that customers preferred sleeping in this bed and shifted their allegiance from other hotel chains with less comfortable beds, that product choice would be a successful strategy.

Flexibility

The ability to offer a production system that could shift product lines quickly can become a strategic advantage. Product and service preferences change quickly, and to become stuck on one method and one product or service can prove fatal to a company.

Honda, for example, produces the Honda Odyssey Minivan and the Acura MDX SUV on the same platform. This reduced overall production costs for a major new product introduction.

Burger King once advertised "Have It Your Way," in an effort to prove that each customer could custom-order his or her own choice of hamburger or sandwich—with or without lettuce, pickles, and so on. This was an attempt to differentiate their company from McDonald's, inferring that the hamburger giant did not offer this service, when, in fact, it did.

Nike Shoes enables customers to order customized shoes online. They are not tailor-made but combine features the customers desire in much the same way Dell or Gateway Computers customizes a computer order.

Inventory Systems

One of the major components of the Japanese production system was the just-in-time (JIT) inventory system. Popularized by Toyota, this system required suppliers to deliver necessary parts to manufacturers when needed. It gave the manufacturer the advantage of not having to bear the cost of carrying inventory.

The suppliers, meanwhile, were forced to increase their shipping costs with more frequent deliveries, so it was a supplier choice to gain business through volume. Particularly during the Oil Embargo of the 1970s, the absence of inventory gave the Japanese manufacturers a tremendous cost advantage over their global counterparts, which had huge inventories. As we shall see in Chapter 13, the carrying cost of inventory can be approximately 25% of the cost of the item.

Accurate inventory information systems, usually integrated in software packages designated for enterprise resource planning (ERP), can be a source of advantage. The complexity of the implementation of a materials resource planning II (MRPII) system often results in partially completed systems. The company that masters inventory systems has the advantage of information and timely reporting. The state of competition being what it is, one company may beat another in business simply because it is better with its inventory systems.

Human Resources Management (HRM)

When annual inventories are taken, perhaps the most significant asset of any company is not counted, and that is the combined skills and knowledge of the workforce. Companies invest in their employees to train them in new skills. Some companies scrimp on their training and education budgets, directly affecting their future. If Company A sends its information systems employees to learn new skills, but Company B does not, and a new skill proves critical in the future, Company A has gained.

The climate of an organization says a lot about how the employees feel about their workplace. If people like where they work, it tends to help get things done. Part of the HRM goal is to increase the quality of work life for the workforce. Compare two companies, one with high employee dissatisfaction and the other with extreme satisfaction, and guess which one is outselling the other.

Speed

With reduced product and service design cycles, speed is of the essence. In manufacturing, computer-aided design (CAD) and computer-aided manufacturing (CAM) significantly reduced the length of time it took to design and build new products. New products and services are introduced at a faster rate, and as consumers' tastes change accordingly, companies must be quick in releasing new, quality-tested products. Companies can ill afford to be late in offering new products and services. At the same time, they must never be premature in rolling out the next generation, or they risk losing customer goodwill if there are quality and service problems.

Location

The location of manufacturing and office facilities is a key strategic consideration. The access to customers, costs for distributing products, and shipping costs for receiving materials are important issues. The relative positioning with regard to competitors is another factor worth considering.

A popular location approach for manufacturing is to place plants in remote, rural locations. This often positions the manufacturer as the best place in the area to seek gainful employment. Employees reward the company with loyalty, and this makes it less likely that they will unionize.

A current location decision is whether to manufacture in foreign or domestic locations. The trade-offs are labor costs and shipping costs. Domestic production may increase labor costs while reducing shipping costs. Foreign production may do the opposite. That is why it is a very important and strategic decision.

Vertical Integration

Vertical integration is when a company owns a business related to its products that it could outsource. For example, the Chicago Bulls' United Center can outsource concessions or do it themselves. The trade-offs are managing the labor force and trying to make a profit or turning it over to some other company with expertise in concessions and taking a percentage of the profits. Another example is in automobile sound systems. These are typically outsourced to companies such as Bose. If an auto manufacturer decided that it could do it better and made its own systems, that would be vertical integration.

The degree to which a company is vertically integrated may play a strategic role. The decision to "make or buy" is not straightforward. To make it yourself gives a number of advantages. Likewise, to outsource to a company with more specific expertise may provide even greater advantages.

Technology

There are two sides to the technology factor—first, the technologies customers want, and second, what technologies can be used to produce. The first factor is a marketing and sales consideration. A personal computer must offer the newest and state-of-the-art features, and the manufacturer must know what changes in features are upcoming. B. F. Goodrich and Goodyear, for example, once had an 85% market share in tires, but they were late in responding to the consumer shift to radial tires, resulting in their losing most of the market.

A current production technology used by the grocery store industry is self-service bar code scanning at checkout. If customers embrace this method of checking out, it enables the store to off-load labor. The company must evaluate the trade-off of reduced labor costs against the cost of the technology. At Home Depot and other stores using these scanners, one employee is assigned to take care of problems that occur in processing.

Airline companies are faced with increasing costs, and the selection of airplanes to include in their fleet is one of the strategic choices Delta, Singapore Air, Swiss Air, or Air France must make.

Blackberry™ Versus iPhone™ Versus Treo™

In 2006, Research in Motion's BlackBerry led Palm Treo and competing PDAs (personal digital assistants) with $3.51 million in sales (see Table 3.5).

A lawsuit for patent infringement against Research in Motion had been settled and had strengthened its position against the Palm Treo. Although its market share slightly declined, Research in Motion had gained 10% in sales.

Table 3.5   Sales and Market Shares in PDAs: 2005–2006

Company	2006 Sales ($ Millions)	Market Share (%)	2005 Sales ($ Millions)	Market Share (%)
Research in Motion (BB)	3.51	19.8	3.19	21.3
Palm Treo	1.97	11.1	2.77	18.5
Hewlett Packard	1.72	9.7	2.27	15.1
Mio	1.52	8.5	0.71	4.8
Sharp	1.43	8.0	0.53	3.6
Others	7.60	43.8	5.5	36.7

The most competitive product, the Palm, had its followers because of its user-friendly address book and task functions. However, the Blackberry was winning on the e-mail user interface.

The playing field changed in the summer of 2007, with the introduction of the Apple iPhone. The iPhone offered not only e-mail and phone capabilities but also a superior Web browser and the added benefit of all the music of an iPod™.

Blackberry had a devoted following, and some fanatics of the device became known as "crackberries" and could be counted on to be secretly scanning their blackberries under the table in the midst of business meetings.

Apple offered to bring into the PDA market another devoted following: that of users who did not want to carry *both* an iPod and a PDA. Apple's new phone offered a number of advantages: brand recognition, an already enthusiastic fan base, an attractively thin package, and the use of its own Web browser, Safari.

The iPhone's limitations included its exclusive cellular agreement with AT&T. Since most cell phone users were locked into agreements with other carriers, this meant adding an additional cell phone account, unless the customer already had a contract with AT&T.

In the first 74 days, Apple sold the iPhone for $599, that is, $200 more than a Blackberry. At that point, they reduced the price by $200 and offered rebates to those buying at the higher price. Their thinking was that the pent-up demand for the iPhone would enable them to sell at a higher price than Blackberry and then they would drop the price after the first wave of purchases. The first wave of purchases? One million dollars in sales in 74 days!

Apple then introduced a new iPod, the iTouch™, which had everything the iPhone had, except the phone capability. Now, customers who were not keen on contracting another cell phone could still get the new, improved iPod, without the hassle.

Apple's introduction of its new product was served from an operations standpoint, from its production experience with iPods. It had a preexisting distribution network that enabled it to quickly supply stores with the new product.

These products will change quickly, and the previous year's model will soon become obsolete. This fast-changing technology puts pressure on the production side of companies to design a production system to deliver defect-free products quickly and make adjustments with each generation of the device.

The Value Chain

Another major contribution by Michael Porter was the **value chain**. The value chain approach illustrates how a business creates value for a customer through a chain of activities that transform inputs into outputs. It deconstructs a business into a number of processes. The primary activities that create value are inbound and outbound logistics, operations, marketing and sales, and service.

Essentially, "inbound and outbound logistics" is the same thing as "supply chain management." The thrust of the value chain is that, other than marketing and sales, operational activities are the primary vehicles for creating customer value.

The first rental car agency to introduce bar code scanning, enabling air passengers to quickly exit the rental car agency and get to the airport, gave that company an advantage (temporarily) via operations. This is a great example because of the needs of airline passengers. They typically arrive at the airport in a state of panic, knowing that they have to penetrate the security lines and may miss their plane. In days of old, a car had to be returned by taking the rental agreement back into the office and completing the purchase with a credit card (after waiting in line). Operations managers look to contribute by finding ways of streamlining the process to get the product or service quickly into the customer's hands.

The following are examples of value chain strategies in various departments:

1. Primary activities:

   a. Inbound logistics

      - JIT or system with numerous inventory turns
      - Location—strategically located near sources
      - Efficient receiving/loading/docking
      - Product tracking systems
      - Hotels and restaurants—valet parking
      - Airlines—ticketing kiosks, sky luggage valets

   b. Operations

      - Automation of production processes
      - Efficiency of inventory and accounting systems
      - Reduced product design cycle
      - Six Sigma quality systems
      - Effective plant layout

   c. Outbound logistics

      - Reduced lead times
      - Product tracking systems
      - Location near markets and buyers
      - Efficient distribution system
      - Airlines—efficient and timely baggage delivery

   d. Marketing and sales

      - Effective market identification
      - Brand loyalty
      - Brand image
      - Effective sales force
      - Effective advertising and promotion

   e. Service

      - Speedy handling of problems
      - Exceeding service expectations
      - Effective warranty system
      - Excellent repair network

2. Support activities:

   a. General administration

- Lean hierarchy
- Decision making with mission
- Good reporting and accounting systems
- Motivational leaders

   b. Human resource management

- Effective selection and recruiting team
- Established and excellent training and development system
- Competitive reward and pay system

   c. Technology

- State-of-the-art production technology
- State-of-the-art products
- Investment in effective research and development
- Creative environment

   d. Procurement

- Excellent supplier relations
- Astute sourcing
- Ethical buying practices

The value chain activities listed as "support activities" include general administration, HRM, research and development, and procurement (purchasing or sourcing). These are the activities, systems, and processes that are the oil to the machinery. If they are done well, no one notices these activities, but they contribute immensely. Procurement and human resources control the biggest portions of expenses of any business and can make a great financial impact on the bottom line.

The Value "Profit" Chain

Heskett, Sasser, and Schlesinger (2003), who popularized "the service profit chain," extended their own ideas to arrive at a **value profit chain**. They based their value profit chain on a couple of key principles, that "customer loyalty and commitment are the primary drivers of growth and profitability" and "value is created by satisfied, committed, loyal, and productive employees" (p. 19). Research has shown that there is a positive relationship among happy customers, happy employees, and profit.

Dynamic Manufacturing

An important work in operations strategy was the publication of Hayes et al.'s *Dynamic Manufacturing* (1988). Their study revealed that they could summarize their findings into four key themes (p. 343):

1. Management makes the difference—we take this for granted. However, within any industry, there are firms that have mastered their software, have effective processes in place, and provide a neat and tidy workplace.

2. A holistic perspective is essential—the best organizations realize the interdependencies of decision making throughout the organization. Marketing must make decisions that coordinate with operations, and research and development with operations.

3. Customer value and competitive advantage should be relentlessly pursued. Some companies measure their successes by utilization rates and productivity numbers. Ultimately, all that matters is pleasing the customer. If your company can do that more effectively than anyone else, it will result in increased market share.

4. Continual learning is the objective. The stronger companies treat the skills of their employees as assets that can be improved on. If Company A knows more about operations than Company B, and it sends its employees to seminars where they learn even more, that hidden inventory of knowledge is increased. In lean times, the weaker companies tend to cut their education budgets, ultimately reducing their chances of a stronger future.

Hayes et al. (1988) outlined **four stages of manufacturing competitiveness:**

Stage 1: *Internally neutral*—In this stage, the operations function simply gets the product made and out the door.

Stage 2: *Externally neutral*—In this stage, companies benchmark against their competitors and try to match their products, services, and strategies.

Stage 3: *Internally supportive*—The third stage represents firms that attempt to use operations strategies that differentiate them from their competitors.

Stage 4: *Externally supportive*—Firms at this stage attempt, on a global basis, to differentiate with operations strategies.

Managers had allowed their capital equipment to become obsolete over the years, primarily because they were being judged on their bottom-line performance annually and thus were delaying making capital expenditures to appease the bottom line.

Strategy Maps

There are seemingly hundreds of authors who excel in diagramming how to earn profits with a simple figure. Kaplan and Norton (2004), the creators of the balanced scorecard, devised still another one. Their book *Strategy Maps* emphasized the importance of effective process design to long-term growth. The key processes they identified were operations management processes, customer management processes, innovation processes, and regulatory and social processes.

Kaplan and Norton identified the customer links with operations processes, and these included decreasing costs, delivering quality and on-time products, and offering a product selection.

Global Strategy

When firms compete internationally, the strategic decisions and tactics get more complicated. For many firms, global competition is merely a fact of life. We find the same hotel chains competing in Hong Kong, Paris, New York City, and Chicago. Apple Computers and Dell Computers compete against foreign companies such as Toshiba across the globe. Over time, consumers tend to forget that Honda and Toyota are Japanese automobiles, Land Rover is British, and Mercedes is German. They are multinational companies.

There are many reasons to go global—for instance, to expand markets, to achieve economies of scale, to seek new resources, and to lower costs. From an operations standpoint, the globalization of the firm means increased logistical effort, the maintenance of quality across the world, and the coordination of assembly. It is possible that a firm can assemble its products in multiple plants and multiple countries. For example, a printer could be partially assembled in Malaysia and shipped to China for final assembly.

Pearce and Robinson (2008) listed competitive strategies for multinational firms:

1. *Niche market exporting:* Products are shipped to an importer in another country.

2. *Licensing:* Technology or patents are offered to foreign companies, often in exchange for access to markets.

3. *Joint ventures:* Two or more companies join forces for a product in a specific market.

4. *Foreign branches:* A headquarters presence is established in a foreign location.

5. *Wholly owned subsidiaries:* The foreign-based company is owned outright.

The Boeing 787 airplane reflects the nature of one global manufacturer's involvement with international business.

Manufactured parts:

Tires	Bridgestone	Japan
Landing gear	Messier-Dowty	France
Center wing box	Fuji	Japan
Fairing	Boeing	Canada
Nose	Onex/Wichita	United States
Forward cabin	Kawasaki	Japan
Engines	G.E.	United States
	Rolls Royce	United Kingdom
Leading edge	Onex/Wichita	United States

(Continued)

(Continued)

Wing box	Mitsubishi	Japan
Trailing edge	Boeing	Australia
Mid-cabin	Vought, Alenia	United States, Italy
Doors	Latecoere	France
Tail	Vought, Alenia	United States, Italy
Stabilizers	Vought, Alenia	United States, Italy
Vertical fin	Boeing	United States

Current orders

Chinese Airlines	60
Nippon Airways	50
Japan Airlines	30
Primaris Airlines	20
Continental Airlines	10
First Choice Airways	6
Ethiopian Airlines	5
Blue Panorama Airlines	4
Vietnam Airlines	4
Air New Zealand	2

SOURCE: Greising and O'Neal (2005).

Conclusion

The operations manager must have an understanding about what his or her company is all about and how it will manage to sell its products given a competitive marketplace. Typically, operations managers are well versed in the mathematical approaches to quality, scheduling, forecasting, and so on. The missing critical point is to know *why* these things must be done in the most effective and efficient manner possible.

When companies become complacent and view operations as simply a mechanism with which to "make the stuff and get it out," what frequently happens is that the competition devises operations strategies to capture the market share and the dormant company watches its profitability get eroded.

Organizations have complex infrastructures and functions, and they are designed to consider how to position their goods and services for sale. The operations manager must create an effective process and a delivery method that customers will perceive to be superior to that of the competition. The sphere of competition in operations is the ultimate product or service. When customers visit a car dealership and behold hundreds of models to choose from, they are looking at the actual work accomplished by operations. Once they drive off the lot, they are still not finished with operations because the performance of the vehicle is the ultimate test of the effective achievement of the manufacturing processes. In the repair shop, the quality function continues throughout the life of the automobile. Preventative maintenance schedules optimize the auto's life span if done systematically.

The aspects of the value profit chain are at work throughout. Employees who love their company work hard to help the customers see the value of their automobiles. A measure of success would be to find out what autos the employees actually drive home. If they love what they are selling, it goes far in convincing the buyers. A visit to a competing dealer may find disgruntled employees arguing over some aspect of compensation. Subtly, the customer can sense the difference.

When a guest opens the door to a hotel room and sees a spacious, tidy, and welcoming room and all efforts made to make his or her stay as comfortable as possible, it leads to repeat business. That clean hotel room, with the well-made bed and clean-smelling pillows, is the result of successful operations, and it gives marketing a product to sell. That is the competitive nature of operations. There is another hotel out there trying to do the same thing and looking for a different and new way to do it, whether it is breakfast in bed or a daily massage.

Summary

- Operations management is a key functional strategy that coordinates with the overall company strategy.

- The three generic strategies are cost leadership, differentiation, and focusing on a niche market.

- The five forces that influence industry competition are jockeying for competition, the power of suppliers, the power of buyers, substitute products, and barriers to entry. Operations management is directly involved in all these forces.

- There are nine key strategic questions a company must address when setting a strategy. Operations management is necessarily an important contributor to strategic positioning.

- The value profit chain concept indicates that happy employees and happy customers are important for making a profit.

- The authors of *Dynamic Manufacturing* discovered that there were four keys to excellence in manufacturing: the belief that management makes a difference, the existence of a holistic decision-making perspective, the relentless pursuit of customer value and competitive advantage, and a dedication to continual learning.

- Global strategy includes niche market exporting, licensing, joint ventures, foreign branches, and wholly owned subsidiaries.

Key Terms

Five Forces of Competition	The strategy cycle
Four stages of manufacturing competitiveness	Value chain
Generic strategies	Value profit chain
Growth/share matrix	Values scan
Strategic management	

Review Questions

1. How does a mission statement differ from the values of an organization? Give an example.

2. What is the benefit of studying the competition when making strategic plans?

3. How do operations strategies differ from strategies in marketing and finance?

4. When selling products in multiple countries, how do operational strategies change from one country to another?

5. Compare the value chain with the value profit chain.

Projects

1. Analyze how a specific company uses operations in its competitive strategy.

2. Analyze the operations strategies employed in one of these industries: airlines, hotels, automobile manufacturing, steel manufacturing, amusement parks.

3. Analyze the strategic planning process in a firm. How long-term is it?

4. Ask a middle-level manager of a large corporation how strategic planning has or has not trickled down to that level of the organization.

5. Using the nine key questions to ask in business strategy, analyze a firm.

CASE 1   The Strategy of a Public Television Station

Dan "the man" Reinhardt stared out of his 47th floor office window, as all executives do when they ponder the future in cases. Dan, the general manager for Channel 33, the public television station in a midwestern metropolitan city, pondered the recent numbers for his donations and compared them with the four competitors he had access to:

Time Period	Public TV ($ Million)	Radio ($ Million)	Museums ($ Million)	Arts ($ Million)
Current year	1.3	0.76	1.0	1.2
Prior year	1.6	0.75	2.1	0.9
2 years prior	2.2	0.65	0.9	0.7

In a 2-year period, he had seen the donations to his station drop by $900,000. In the same time period, the local public radio station had increased donations by 110,000; the museums were up by 100,000; and the combined opera, ballet, and symphony ("the arts") had increased by 500,000. Since many of the supporters of the other institutions were also contributors to public television, he had seen a redistribution of their donations.

Both public television and public radio had two major ways to solicit donations: the telethon or radiothon and direct mail. Channel 33 had six donor nights per year, centered on a high-profile program. In the coming year, he knew he had on tap a documentary on the life of Oprah Winfrey as one fund-raiser. But he had seen a decline in recent years in the number of calls and donations.

On weekends, Dan "the man" took MBA courses at the local prestigious university, and the idea of using some form of operational strategy to increase donations struck him as a great idea, but he did not know where to begin. It had triggered one idea, to allow donors to contribute online. This seemed to be helping in the current year, as contributions were 2% above the rate of the prior year. Yet he was late in this game since all his competitors had already thought of doing this.

As he looked out his office window, he could see an airplane headed across the lake, and for a moment, he wished he were on it, flying to some tropical island where he could get alcoholic drinks with little umbrellas in them and have hula dancers serenading his tanned torso. Then he awoke from his reverie, when little Jimmy Bumstead, his assistant, broke in with some news.

"The numbers on our British series, the Alfie Lohan show, are down by anosther 15% at 7 p.m. And we have a contract for 27 more episodes."

"That is great," Dan said sarcastically. "What do you want me to do about it?"

"I just thought you should know," little Jimmy responded, his face hanging with disappointment.

"We have to turn this monkey in the right direction. Call a meeting of the department heads. We need a retreat to think of some operations strategies, since marketing hasn't worked."

"Where do you want this retreat?"

"Somewhere exotic. How about Bozeman, Montana?"

"Is that where Yellowstone National Park is?"

"It's close enough. If you can't find a good meeting place in Bozeman, try Missoula."

"I didn't know you had such a fondness for Montana."

"I've never been there. But I want to think like a buffalo to solve this one."

Little Jimmy left the room. He knew what to expect: Another management fad would be attempted. Operations strategies? What were they, and how could he apply them? Little Jimmy went to his office to stare out the window, like all junior executives in cases do when they cannot figure out what else to do. Was there a White Sox game today?

CASE 2   The Handheld Computer

The Navawho Corporation has patented a new type of handheld computer that will compete with Palm Pilots, Blackberries, and Sidekicks. The device is attached to a USB connection and enables voice e-mails to be sent through the computer. The company was started with venture capital and anticipates giving away 5,000 to influential writers and celebrities as a promotion. Their hoped-for first-year sales are 15,000 at a price of $60. The cost of making each unit is $11.

The biggest issue for Navawho is that they have no true idea of how many they will sell. Their estimates are based on market research at one college campus, where they presented their device and the alternatives to 100 college students and found that there appeared to be instant appreciation for the product and its price.

They think the capacity of their present warehouse location in East Los Angeles adequate to produce 5,000 a year, and they are scouting for a second location in the event that their projections come true. Also, they estimate that they absolutely must sell a minimum of 7,000 at that price to sustain enough cash flow to continue into a second year, based on their calculations.

They believe that if they are a big hit, economies of scale will reduce the unit cost. Demand of 20,000 should reduce the average cost by $1, and demand of 30,000 should reduce the average cost by $2. Thus far, an investment of $4 million has been pumped into this project. Now, poised to release their product, they have been approached by a major manufacturer to sell out at $15 million. What are the implications of selling out at this juncture? What difficulties do they face as a new entrant?

CASE 3 Pizza Wars

Gustav Jiang owned a pizzeria, Gandhi's Pies, in Lincoln Park, near DePaul University in Chicago. There were four competing pizza joints within six blocks of his store. The pizza had only served foot traffic since opening its doors 10 years earlier and had been a profitable enterprise; but the sight of another pizza shop opening its doors concerned Gustav. The fourth shop, 3.14 Pizza, which appealed to math majors, had cut some of Gustav's business, and the impending opening of Wireless Pizza, a combination Internet café and dining establishment, threatened him even more.

Prior to 3.14's opening, Gandhi's used to sell 60 pizzas per night. The past year had seen a drop to 47 pizzas per night. Gustav estimated the nightly business of his present four competitors as follows:

	Ghandhi's	3.14	P. Hut	Hippie's
2006	47	31	80	36
2005	60	—	75	44

For the first time, Gustav was about to introduce pizza delivery. He estimated that half of his customers came from DePaul's dorms and the rest were people who lived in the neighborhood. In the summer, he would deliver on bicycles, and he purchased a covered motorcycle for winter deliveries. What else could Gustav do to create operational advantages to help his business?

Web Sites

Corporate Web Sites With Information on Their Mission and Values

www.benjerry.com

www.Honda.com

www.Marriott.com

http://Levistrauss.com

http://about.nordstrom.com/aboutus/

Information on Strategic Planning and Operations Strategy

www.mapfornonprofits.org

http://Sps.org.uk

http://brunel.ac.uk

References

Goodstein, L., Nolan, T., & Pfeiffer, J. S. (1993). *Applied strategic planning.* New York: McGraw-Hill.

Greising, D., & O'Neal, M. (2005, February 23). The global factory. *Chicago Tribune*, pp. 1, 20–21.

Hamel, G., & Prahalad, C. K. (1994). *Competing for the future.* Boston: Harvard Business School Press.

Hayes, R., Wheelwright, S., & Clark, K. (1988). *Dynamic manufacturing.* New York: Free Press.

Heskett, J. L., Sasser, W. E., & Schlesinger, L. A. (2003). *The value profit chain.* New York: Free Press.

Kaplan, R. S., & Norton, D. P. (2004). *Strategy maps.* Boston: Harvard Business School Press.

Koch, R. (2000). *The Financial Times guide to strategy.* London: Prentice Hall.

Pearce, J. A., & Robinson, R. B. (2008). *Strategic management.* New York: McGraw-Hill.

Porter, M. E. (1980). *Competitive strategy.* London: Free Press.

Porter, M. E. (1985). *Competitive advantage.* London: Free Press.

CHAPTER 4

Managing the Operations Workforce

SOURCE: © Marcin Balcerzak/istockphoto.com

Learning Objectives

In this chapter, we will study the managerial roles of the operations manager:

- How leadership applies to operations managers
- Motivation principles for operations management
- Change management for operations managers
- Human-centered production
- Basic human resource management (HRM) for operations

(Continued)

(Continued)

- Training and development for operations managers
- Compensation issues in operations management
- The Bottom 10% practices of General Electric and Enron
- Performance reviews for operations positions
- Establishing job satisfaction for operations employees
- Management at Toyota and Wal-Mart

Managing People

An important consideration in studying operations management is that all techniques, algorithms, and methods must be accomplished through people. An operations manager who is skilled in statistical and quantitative analysis but incompetent when it comes to people is not going to get anywhere. To be successful, operations managers must master accomplishing their goals through management. With that in mind, this chapter confronts the basics of "people" management for operations. The chapter will provide an overview of the leadership and HR principles that apply to operations management.

Home Depot is an appropriate starting point to illustrate the people side of the company's success. Home Depot analyzed its management processes and streamlined its hiring practices and performance review processes, placing HR managers in every store. Among their management improvements were the centralization of the purchasing function and the decentralization of HRM. The actions made sense because purchasing can realize economic gains through bulk purchasing and HR managers need to staff locally. The management approach used Six Sigma quality techniques.

An example of how analytical tools (covered in subsequent chapters) can be applied to HRM is seen in Home Depot's analysis of employee retention. They discovered that 95% of the employees who voluntarily left the company had less than 5 years of experience with the company. This was important information, because it showed Home Depot who was going to stick with the company and allowed them to reward longevity.

Henry Mintzberg (1973) identified the key **managerial roles** in his book *The Nature of Managerial Work*:

- *Disseminator*—the individual who reveals company information
- *Disturbance handler*—the person who manages conflict with individuals or problems with management or customers
- *Entrepreneur*—the person who thinks of new programs and products
- *Figurehead*—the person who represents the company at social and business functions
- *Leader*—the person in charge
- *Liaison*—the representative of the employees to other groups of stakeholders

- *Monitor*—the person who makes sure the job is going well
- *Negotiator*—the person responsible for departmental resources
- *Resource allocator*—the one who portions out resources
- *Spokesperson*—the person who makes announcements to groups

All these roles are needed to succeed as a senior operations manager. As the disseminator, the general operations manager has to communicate critical information concerning scheduling, future orders, and anything that affects the workers and supervisors. As the disturbance handler, the senior manager must intervene to smooth any conflicts that might affect the smooth production of goods and services. These might include labor strikes, product shortages, or problems due to inclement weather.

The entrepreneurial side of operations is in finding innovative avenues of income or new and unused ways to use resources—for example, renting out unused warehouse space. The most senior managers in Operations handle the figurehead role. They are the ones who must attend ceremonial functions and plant openings.

Operations managers must demonstrate the leadership qualities discussed in this chapter to achieve the organizational mission. The liaison role is performed when Operations works with other functional managers and customers. The operations manager must work hand in glove with the marketing and accounting managers, be familiar with customers and their needs, and represent their departmental interests to customers.

The monitor role is to stay on top of what production is doing and how service is being accomplished. Operations managers must make sure that their departments are performing well and that jobs are where they are supposed to be. The negotiator role serves in dealing with supplier and customer contracts and arrangements within the firm.

Operations managers act as resource allocators in matching capacity to demand in determining plant location and layout. In general, the spokesperson of operations management will be the senior executive in charge of operations.

Operations managers supervise a number of occupations, some of them skilled, others not. Often, their entire workforce is composed of blue-collar workers.

Here are some of the typical jobs supervised by operations managers:

1. Hotels

    - Maintenance workers
    - Housekeeping workers
    - Front desk, reservations, and service workers
    - Restaurant workers
    - Valet parking
    - Conference workers
    - Gift shop employees

2. Hospitals

    - Engineering and janitorial
    - Laundry

- Materials management
- Purchasing staff
- Parking lot employees
- Cafeteria workers
- Admissions

3. Auto manufacturing

- Assembly-line workers
- Maintenance staff
- Quality control staff
- Receiving and logistics
- MRP/scheduling staff
- Purchasing
- Quality analysts

Leadership for Operations Managers

There is a big difference between leadership and management. Management consists of planning, organizing, and directing employees to accomplish tasks. Leadership involves setting the example that motivates others to accomplish the mission. There have been many studies about leadership, but James Kouzes and Barry Posner (1987) conducted one particularly good one that still applies today. In their study of 550 executives, they discovered 10 behaviors inherent in leaders. These 10 behaviors apply to *all* leaders, not just operations managers.

1. *Search for opportunities.* This is a rather strategic aspect of leadership. Where can we find ways to exploit our competitive advantage? If we are delivering sandwiches daily to an office on the seventh floor, shouldn't we pursue business on all the other floors? Operations management's directive is not merely to get the product to the customer; it is to survey the continents for new ways to gain business, using the tools available.

2. *Experiment and take risks.* Some gambles won't pay off to be sure; but great leaders are always pursuing different approaches that have not been tried before. If grocery stores such as Cub Foods had not tried the approach of allowing their customers to bag their own groceries in exchange for wholesale costs, they would not have succeeded.

3. *Envision the future.* Operations managers should also see where they hope to be 5 years down the road and begin to think about it. Do they need to consider foreign plants to close or open? What if sales triple? If this product dies, what becomes of the plants?

4. *Enlist others.* Managers do not succeed without a crew of able supporters and partners. True leaders know that they are only as good as the people who work with them and for them.

5. *Foster collaboration.* In organizations that have power struggles, nothing is gained except, perhaps, a temporary view of the river that hides the mud that they

are about to get mired in. Teamwork and collaboration are the only ways to accomplish objectives, particularly in large organizations.

6. *Strengthen others.* Investing in people so that they can fulfill their own objectives and helping them achieve their personal goals is a quality found in the best leaders.

7. *Set an example.* Leaders have to live and act the way they want their employees to live and act. A football coach who is caught at a topless bar does not exactly give his players a shining example of how to live their lives off the field.

8. *Plan small wins.* Before tackling the complex problems of the organization, accomplishing smaller jobs and succeeding at them helps boost the confidence of the employees and prepares them for the big task.

9. *Recognize individual contribution.* The best leaders always point out the successes of the people who contribute to the organization's success, *and* they don't dwell on their own accomplishments.

10. *Celebrate accomplishments.* Parties and celebrations to let off steam and boost morale are emblematic of the best leaders.

Kouzes and Posner (1987) also surveyed managers about the characteristics found in superior leaders. The top 10 characteristics were as follows:

1. Honest

2. Competent

3. Forward-looking

4. Inspiring

5. Intelligent

6. Fair-minded

7. Broad-minded

8. Straightforward

9. Imaginative

10. Dependable

Looking at the many jobs of operations managers, it is clear why honesty, competence, and being forward-looking would be the top characteristics. Operations managers are the ones with a realistic understanding of their ability to meet delivery dates. That necessitates dealing with customers with complete honesty, to ensure that they meet the customer's expectations.

Competence is a necessity for such a demanding position. Imagine an incompetent airline scheduler who schedules the same plane to be arriving at an airport 5 min before its next departure. Airline passengers trust that the people handling scheduling, maintenance, baggage handling, and piloting are competent at what they do.

Operations managers must be forward-looking so that they can balance schedules and production throughout the year. Aggregate and capacity planning are essential forward-looking tools for the operations manager.

Power and Leadership

One of the keys to leadership is the type of power the leader commands. There are several types of power:

Legitimate power comes from positional authority—where the leader is in the organizational chart. A general in the military can order a colonel to do something, for example, because he is several rungs higher in the chain of command. Or the chief financial officer can direct the accounting manager to prepare a report.

Reward power stems from the ability of the leader to dole out tangible rewards. The person who distributes raises and incentives holds power over the individuals who are working to earn them.

Coercive power is the power to punish people who do not perform. "If you let the opposing player score 10 points against you, I will not let you play the rest of the game!"

Expert power is when an individual has certain knowledge or skills that are critical to the organization, and thus he or she has a degree of power. An example would be the only person to know the combination to the safe.

Referent power is the earned loyalty a leader gains from skilled management.

If you study any organization, all managers hold a certain type of power. Some of it is earned, and some of it is not.

Motivation

One of the important aspects of management is to find ways to motivate employees. The only thing all employees have in common is that they all differ in what motivates them. Some are totally motivated by money. They will work for any incentives available, overtime, weekends, you name it. Others care little for money but are very driven by recognition. They want to receive praise for their efforts. They get more out of a mention of their name in the company newsletter than they would from a pay raise. Others are wired for power, and still others work purely for the pride they take in the output of their work.

Given the varying needs and motivations of the workforce, the operations manager is faced with meeting schedules and meeting demand, at the right quality in the right amounts. Operations managers have to find a way to keep all their employees motivated and driving toward the fulfillment of the company's mission.

An early study of motivation by Herzberg (Herzberg, Mausner, & Snyderman, 1993) led to his theory of **motivation and hygiene** (basic needs). Herzberg believed that workers need to first have hygiene needs met; and these included pay, working conditions, collegiality, and pleasant working conditions. Motivation needs include the work itself, responsibility, and a sense of accomplishment.

Maslow (1998) came up with a **hierarchy of needs**, with five levels of needs to be filled: (1) physiological, (2) safety, (3) belongingness, (4) esteem, and (5) self-actualization. This hierarchy theorized that a starting point for individuals is that their basic needs for food, water, and shelter must be met. Then, they want to feel safe and secure. The belongingness need would be an affiliation with an employer, a hobby group, a political party, a religion, and so on. The esteem need requires that an individual feel good about himself or herself. The final need is self-actualization, when one's potential is fully realized. It is doubtful that operations managers spend much time theorizing on how they can help all their workers achieve self-actualization, but they should be aware of this basic human need as they attempt to manage their people.

Managing Change

Frequently, organizations are faced with major changes in direction, products, or leadership. Operations managers are often the biggest purveyors of change—introducing new quality initiatives, new projects, and new ways to improve processes. It is normal to expect resistance to change, particularly when there is a lot of work to do. Installing a new software system is so difficult; it can make the outdated package that is currently used more attractive as an alternative.

It is in managing change that the art of leadership comes into play in operations management. For example, if a Six Sigma quality campaign is to be introduced for the betterment of the company, the operations manager must demonstrate why this is an improvement and must wholeheartedly lead the conversion process. Where obstacles exist, whether they are people or inanimate objects, the operations manager has to negotiate the project through to completion.

A review of the past 20 years shows just how much change industry has experienced. Things we take for granted today, such as e-mail, the Internet, GPS systems, fax machines, PDAs, and even cell phones, are new technologies. And they have transformed the way business is conducted. Operations managers have seen campaigns in total quality management (TQM), reengineering, Six Sigma, and Lean, to name a few, and these have all required careful implementation and attention to the uncertainty that new technology and systems bring to employees.

Human-Centered Production

The term **managing underground** came about after a study of miners at the Turris Mine in Illinois. The miners revealed a preference for managers who would solve problems inside the mine over those managers who preferred to stay within the safety of their offices and problem-solve. Young and Nie (1996) applied the term *managing underground* to managers who solved problems at the work source rather than staying in their office, noting that the term could apply to banks, hotels, hospitals, and manufacturers as easily as it could to a mine.

The term **human-centered production** embraces a style of management with the following characteristics:

1. Managing underground

2. Viewing the employees as assets

3. Having product knowledge

Managers who practice human-centered production are involved with their employees at the places they work. The managers understand the needs of their workers and the production needs of the product. They are not expected to dismantle the machinery blindfolded, but they should know how it works. It is the human-centered production manager who comes in on Saturdays and holidays and works overtime to ensure successful accomplishment of departmental goals.

Good managers have to overcome all the personal problems that cloud the days of employees. On a typical day, it can be predicted that several of the people on the staff are bothered by one of a catalog of serious problems: health, financial, marital, or family issues. When people come to work, they are not above thinking and daydreaming all day about their issues and problems at home.

An analogy to World War II movies is appropriate. In the typical World War II movie, we have a squad of American soldiers from diverse backgrounds. *Saving Private Ryan* seemed to capture all the stereotypes—the Kentucky hillbilly sharpshooter who can hit a target 200 yards away, the streetwise kid from the Bronx, the farm boy from Nebraska, and the surfer dude from California. Let's say, for the sake of example, that the Nebraska farm boy has received a letter from his girlfriend announcing the good news that she is 6 months pregnant. The problem is the farm boy has not been home in a year. So he's wandering around the foxhole, his helmet is off, and he's asking stupid questions: "Can you get pregnant months later?" The news is particularly disturbing to him. Meanwhile, the sergeant has to get the Nebraskan in gear. "Hey! They are shooting live bullets at us, and you're going to get us all killed. Put your helmet on and concentrate on the enemy."

This is all similar to what is going on at work. People are wandering around, thinking about their personal problems, not wearing their helmets, and you, the manager, have to redirect them to the mission at hand—getting the product to the customer on time.

Managers cannot get personally involved in their employees' personal problems. That is what we have professional counselors and social workers for, but they can direct a troubled employee to the proper help. Work, sometimes, does resemble war. That's why it is so nice to work for one of those "Best companies to work for" companies. The climate of the workplace goes a great way to improving the quality of life of the individual.

Identities are very much tied to feelings of self-esteem gained from work. You are your job, basically. What is the difference between a job and a career? A job has something of a negative ring to it. You don't tell your dog to go do his career, you tell the dog to do his job. Maybe that is why many people equate their jobs to dog poop. People want to be proud of what they do. They want to say with pride, "I am a fireman. I am a steelworker."

F. W. Murnau's classic film *The Last Laugh* captured much about this identity with work. It was the story of a hotel bell captain who was very proud of his position and his uniform. When he was demoted to washroom attendant, he stole his uniform so he could wear it out of the house. He would change into the attendant's uniform just before reporting to work. The last laugh was when a patron died in the restroom and had a last will and testament that instructed that the first person to discover him after his death would inherit all his wealth. The attendant proceeded to buy the hotel and fire the guy who demoted him. Another silent film of that era, Charlie Chaplin's *Modern Times,* also showed the dehumanization of the mechanization of work in a scene in which the plant engineers, trying to dream up ways to increase productivity, invented a machine to feed the worker so he never had to leave his work station.

Management Control

The control aspect of management is the monitoring system that allows a comparison between what was planned and what has been accomplished. Here, performance standards are set, and measurements are taken to see how the organization's departments have done. A number of financial measures of performance are set, budgets are established, and so on.

HRM in Production and Operations Management

This section will cover the basic principles of HRM as they apply to operations management. The HR function is usually a separate entity in large organizations. When job openings occur within operations, the HR function must be consulted so that the proper procedures are followed in hiring a new employee.

The first step in HR for the operations manager is the recruitment and selection of new employees. This varies according to the skills, knowledge, and credentials required for the job. A mechanical engineer, for example, may be recruited in several ways: newspaper advertising, Internet job lists, trade journals and Internet trade sites, or college recruitment trips for newly degreed job candidates. Internal job postings may be helpful also, as sometimes the best source of new talent is the existing job base. The recruiting phase must establish the required skills and education and set expectations for salary.

Perhaps the most important aspect of management is getting good people to work for you and retaining them.

The selection of the right candidate begins with the initial screening of resumes. In many cases, only a small number of applicants have the right requirements for the job. Once the screening has limited the applicant pool, it gets more serious. For some jobs, aptitude and psychological testing is the norm. Some companies want to know that they get persons with the right personality on their team, so they administer personality tests.

The job interview takes things further as the company tries to see if the applicant will fit into the culture of the group. Companies that are careful in who they hire take this seriously and go to great lengths to make sure that they have a good match. It is important to check references, credentials, and background. Companies should not have to find out 6 months after making a hire that the new hire's entire education is bogus.

The hire of a university professor follows a traditional process:

1. The university has a job opening due to either retirement or someone leaving for another job.

2. The request for approval to recruit and hire is processed, and the administrators sign off on whether they have the budget to continue this faculty position.

3. The department advertises in a number of places: *Chronicle of Higher Education,* specialty trade journals, Internet Web sites. Academic disciplines have annual meetings in which job candidates are interviewed, usually in 30-min to 1-hr sessions.

4. Meanwhile, the candidate pool can be made up of either experienced professors or doctoral students who are looking for their first job as a professor. These people scour the ads and the Internet, looking for a job. They respond to the ads with their resumes and try to make appointments for interviews at meetings.

5. Faculty set up a limited number of interviews. They may see as many as 20 applicants in a 3-day period.

6. After the annual meeting interviews, the faculty search committee compares notes and narrows the field down to three to five people to bring to the university for a campus visit.

7. Campus invitations are made to a select few candidates. These individuals make a presentation, which gives the faculty some idea of their presentation skills and how they might translate into classroom teaching. Usually, the candidate does a number of one-on-one visits with other faculty and administration.

8. After all candidates have been seen, the faculty convene and vote on the candidate to whom they wish to offer the job.

9. The department chairman negotiates with the candidate and tries to get him or her to accept the offer. Sometimes, the candidate accepts another job offer, and the second candidate is then approached, until finally a match is made.

This is the process of selection for university faculty. The expense usually varies according to the knowledge and skills required for the position. Hiring hourly workers is much simpler, although there may be a battery of tests that are administered, either tests for certain skills or psychological tests.

Buhler (2002) provided a list of questions that should not be asked in an interview:

- Are you married?
- Do you have children?
- How much do you weigh?
- How old are you?
- What is your national origin?
- What is your religious affiliation?
- When did you graduate from high school or college? (p. 118)

Finding and retaining good employees is always a challenge for the restaurant industry. Starbucks offers reasonably priced health insurance for employees who work more than 20 hr per week. The coffee chain actually spends more on employee health care costs than it does on coffee beans. But the cost and availability of health care is an attractive option for someone who is looking for a flexible work schedule.

Training and Development

Once an employee is hired, he or she becomes a potential asset for the firm, an asset that can be cultivated and, it is hoped, will serve many years of employment. Training can take a variety of shapes and forms. Usually, there is an orientation to the history, culture, and plus points of the company. That would include a tour of the facilities.

After the employee reports for actual work, there may be a total on-the-job training approach, or training may take place in a classroom, depending on the nature of the work. A machine tools operator would have to be trained at the machine. An amusement park guide would probably start out training in a classroom before venturing out in public. Butchers may attend a school where they are taught how to cut meat. Masseuses and barbers start in a school, working for a cheap price on real customers until they graduate from the school and advance to more higher-priced heads.

The initial training is only the beginning for the new employee. Development takes place over time as the company attempts to add continuing education experiences that make the employees more knowledgeable in their functional specialty.

Many large corporations offer tuition reimbursement for formal education, such as an MBA program, for example. The plethora of workshops, seminars, and trade shows that are available to employees to better themselves are indicators of the commitment a company has to its workforce, by the dollars spent on education.

The success and effectiveness of training programs should be measured. It is important to gauge what learning took place, what changes of behavior resulted, and how the training and development ultimately benefit the organization.

Compensation

How much is the right amount of pay? Pay varies according to occupation, geographical region, and supply of and demand for the particular skill. If you are the only carpenter for miles around, the chances are great that you can set a high price for your services. If people are standing in line for hours to get a chance at one job from several hundred applicants, there is little bargaining power for a good salary. Just be thankful you got the job.

Compensation consists of pay and benefits, which typically take up 25% to 35% of the compensation. Two traits are important in compensation: **internal and external equity**.

External equity is how pay compares within the geographical region. For example, in the Normal, Illinois, area, the major employers include Mitsubishi's auto plant and a Caterpillar tractor plant. Since these are the largest employers, with several thousand workers employed, they set the standard for wages in the region. If a new worker can get $15 per hour, it will influence the ability to hire and pay for any job within driving distance of the plant. A dental hygienist making $8 per hour might consider whether getting paid almost double his usual pay for turning a wrench all day is worth sacrificing the excitement of gazing into people's cavities. It may make the wrench more desirable.

When there are no jobs to be had, possibly the best idea for people is to relocate, although that can be psychologically hard. If a region has 20% unemployment, it is difficult to consider even selling a house, since who will have the money to buy it? So relocation can be very trying financially. However, a move to a place that actually is hiring and where the economy is thriving is a better solution than starvation.

When employees are hard to find, companies have to find ways to lure potential employees with incentives. For several years, the nursing profession has experienced such a shortage that recruiters have gone to places such as the Philippines to offer incentives to nurses to move to the United States.

Internal equity is fairness within the organization. Some systems do not offer merit pay. Instead, employees are paid according to a pay grade and years of service. There is no argument about pay, since you know what it will be and it is periodically adjusted for inflation.

Grade	Start	1	2	3
1	20,000	20,600	21,200	21,800
2	22,000	22,600	23,200	23,800
3	24,000	24,700	25,400	26,100

In this system, the starting salary is determined by the grade and is fixed. Someone starting at Grade 2 would see his or her salary adjustments for the first 3 years. Variations of this method include ranges of salary. In a range-based system, the new employee in Grade 1 might start anywhere from $20,000 to $22,000 depending on experience and the previous pay rate.

In other systems, once a starting salary is established, future pay raises are based on merit. An annual pay raise might be established for an entire unit at 5%, but each individual may get a minimum of 2% and a maximum of 10% depending on his or her performance evaluation. Whatever the system, the employees must feel that it is transparent to them how they can succeed within the system.

Retention

Keeping good employees is a challenge. Initially, there is a honeymoon period. The employee is recruited, told why it is advantageous to join the organization, and trained. Then the employee goes through a trial probationary period, in which the company tries to determine if there is a good fit with the company. Employees then receive annual reviews in which their salary is adjusted, unless they change jobs within the company.

The problem is that over time, salaries may grow noncompetitive as other companies increase their payrolls, and companies may lose some of their people to local competition. That is why it is imperative to know what the going wage rates are and stay current. Employees must have a reason to stay with the company. This may be in the form of some vested retirement plan or increasing vacation with years of service.

Basically, people want to feel needed and valued. If they feel ignored, underpaid, and underappreciated, they may be lost causes. It is very difficult to replace an excellent employee.

Welch's Bottom 10%

While he was CEO of General Electric, Jack Welch had a policy to reward the top 20% of the workforce, maintain and keep happy the next 70%, and notify the bottom 10% that their performance was unacceptable and they should consider finding other employment. Welch claimed that 70% of the bottom 10% would resign of their own accord and the rest would be fired. He defended this system because he felt that it told people where they stood.

Welch was a big believer in performance measurements, going so far as to do annual performance evaluations of his housekeeping staff at his house. This system was also very popular at Enron, where it was called "Rank and yank."

The successor to Welch, Jeffrey Immelt, scrapped the system. According to *Business Week*, Welch valued cost cutting, efficiency, and deal making, while Immelt stresses risk taking, sophisticated marketing, and innovation (Brady, 2005). Welch's system decidedly made managers risk-averse. Time will tell whether Immelt's about-face from Welch's managerial style will work.

This performance review system is controversial. It was used by a very successful company but also at one of the worst-managed companies of all time. It is an example of a managerial policy that will very much affect organizational behavior.

Performance Reviews

An onerous task for managers is to perform an annual performance review for all employees. Companies should have a systematic way to approach this, in which the employees first spell out their accomplishments of the previous year and their perception of their performance, which will then be compared with the point of view of their manager.

Measurable performance is helpful in this process. It is a lot easier to handle a performance review in which an employee has performed 116 audits at a 99% accuracy level than it is to review someone who has no measurable output. The performance appraisal should be a meeting in which a number of things happen:

- The employee's performance is compared with the goals of the organization.
- The positive aspects of performance are discussed.
- The areas needing improvement are discussed.
- The employee's goals and aspirations are stated.
- A plan of action for the upcoming year is drawn up.

If there is disciplinary action to be taken, documentation is very important. In our litigious society, more problems erupt over disciplinary actions and firings than any other aspect of business.

Unless they have committed a particularly egregious act, most employees receive a warning in writing or in consultation before their actual termination. Workers who lose their jobs due to downsizing may receive some sort of severance pay, although that is not always the case.

Job Satisfaction

Ultimately, the challenge of managers is to get high-performing people who enjoy working in the organization. Frequent measurement of job satisfaction helps the manager know how this is going. There have been many attempts to define the variables that are most applicable to the measurement of job satisfaction. James and James (1992) broke job satisfaction into four categories: satisfaction with the job, the work group, the organization, and the leader. Satisfaction in each category depended on the following factors:

1. Satisfaction with the job
   - The opportunity to do challenging work
   - Time given to complete work
   - Prestige of the job within the organization
   - Clarity of information received on the job
   - Work quality requirements for the job
   - Amount of authority given to carry out responsibilities
   - Opportunity for independent thought and action

2. Satisfaction with the work group
   - Cooperation and friendliness of coworkers

3. Satisfaction with the organization
   - Prestige of the organization
   - Training received
   - Opportunity for growth and development
   - Opportunity for promotion

4. Satisfaction with the leader
   - Support received from supervisors
   - Respect and fair treatment
   - Opportunity to influence the supervisor

Team Building

Operations require total coordination and a certain degree of camaraderie to be effective. People often apply for a job and may know a couple of people at the company, and suddenly, they are thrust into the middle of a group of people performing a variety of work tasks and they must fit in instantly. People often work next to someone they would not normally associate with outside work, and perhaps they can't even stand the sight of the person. Yet, at work, things must get done, and it is the manager who has to mold people from disparate backgrounds into a unit.

It would be great if everyone got along and respected each other; but in reality, that is not always the case. You just do the best you can. As we wrote earlier in this chapter, a belief in the mission and the values of the organization is the most important ingredient in the formation of a team. Individual aspirations must be sublimated for the sake of the team. That is why some great athletes do not play for winning teams; they are more concerned with their own accomplishments than for the state of the team. One professional basketball player (Karl Malone of the Utah Jazz) once noted that a teammate would be happier if he scored 30 points in a losing effort than if he scored 10 points in a winning effort.

But what are the secrets for forming a winning team? Rosebeth Moss Kantor (2004) wrote in her book *Confidence* that great teams simply believe that they will win and go out and do it. Similarly, there are teams that expect to lose. They have no confidence and wait for that fatal mistake to turn the tide in the opponents' favor.

Sports coaches and managers are often held up as examples for business managers, because they are able to motivate their players to sublimate their tremendous egos for the benefit of their team.

During the heyday of TQM training in the mid-1980s and early 1990s, it became obvious that a team approach was the only way to successfully implement the quality programs. TQM programs were major project implementations in organizations, and it required all functions of a business to work together to achieve results. Scholtes (Scholtes, Streibel, & Joiner, 2003) saw that **team growth** had these stages:

1. *Forming:* When a brand new team is formed, there is naturally fear and apprehension of what the team is supposed to accomplish. There is pride in being selected as a team member. There is a period of identifying who will do what in the project or task. When a new member of an organization joins an existing team, the team identity and culture will always change subtly. Replacing the team comedian with a somber, no-nonsense, yet competent team member is an example of how team chemistry can be altered by personalities. Professional sports teams now administer psychological and personality questionnaires to prospective draft choices for that very reason. They want to know if a person is the right type for the team. "Addition by subtraction" is when a team member is traded, cut, or asked to leave, and the team grows stronger as a result of that member's absence. A baseball fan might wonder how a team can replace a 40-home-run-per-year player with a weak hitter, but the atmosphere in the dugout improves so much that the team gets better.

There is often a feeling of optimism at the onset of a project, before anything is actually accomplished. If the leadership appears to be in place, team members feel confident that the job will get done. On the other hand, the opposite can be true. In the film *The Dirty Dozen*, a number of convicts were gathered to accomplish what was said to be an impossible task. Their reward was reduced prison time. Since the prisoners basically had nothing to lose by trying to succeed in the project, they saw the impossibility as a challenge, and ultimately succeeded.

2. *Storming:* The work begins, and team behaviors emerge. If there is disunity, it usually crops up shortly after the first problems begin. The project's tone is set, and its chances of success and meeting the mission requirements are set. When new team members join an existing team, they have already moved to the fourth stage of team development, and it is a matter of fitting in.

3. *Norming:* At this point in a team's life cycle, expectations have become clearer, and there is a feeling of greater certainty as to what the team is about and where it is headed. If there is conflict within the group, it needs to be neutralized at this point, or else a culture of negativism will set in.

4. *Performing:* By now, the team is a well-functioning unit, and the kinks have all been worked out.

Scholtes articulated 10 ingredients for a successful team (Scholtes et al., 2003):

1. Clarity in team goals

2. An improvement plan

3. Clearly defined roles

4. Clear communication

5. Beneficial team behaviors

6. Well-defined decision procedures

7. Balanced participation

8. Established ground rules

9. Awareness of the group process

10. Use of the scientific approach (Scholtes refers to the TQM statistical approach.)

The Toyota Way

One of the most successful organizations in the past 30 years has been the Toyota Motor Company. Toyota was one of the biggest winners when gasoline rationing became important in the 1970s. Toyota's system, grounded in the Japanese cultural striving for quality and dictated by the need for smaller plants, stressed quality, flow, and just-in-time (JIT) inventory systems. Liker (2004), in his book *The Toyota Way*, spelled out their philosophies.

Liker studied Toyota for 20 years before summarizing their principles into a management discipline. As shown in Table 4.1, he categorized them into 14 principles—not surprisingly, the same number of principles taught by W. Edwards Deming.

Table 4.1   The Toyota Way

Principle 1	Base management decisions on a long-term philosophy at the expense of short-term financial goals
Principle 2	Create continuous process flow to bring problems to the surface
Principle 3	Use "pull" systems to avoid overproduction
Principle 4	Level out the workload (*Heijunka*)
Principle 5	Build a culture of stopping the assembly line to fix problems, in order to get quality right the first time
Principle 6	Standardized tasks are the foundation for continuous improvement and employee empowerment
Principle 7	Use visual control so no problems are hidden
Principle 8	Use only reliable, thoroughly tested technology that serves your people and processes
Principle 9	Grow leaders who thoroughly understand the work, live the philosophy, and teach it to others
Principle 10	Develop exceptional people and teams who follow your company's philosophy
Principle 11	Respect your extended network of partners and suppliers by challenging them and helping them improve
Principle 12	Go and see for yourself to thoroughly understand the situation (*genchi genbutsu*)
Principle 13	Make decisions slowly by consensus, thoroughly considering all options; implement decisions rapidly
Principle 14	Become a learning organization through relentless reflection (*hansei*) and continuous improvement (*Kaizen*)

SOURCE: Liker (2004).

Let's take a closer look at these principles.

Principle 1: Base your decisions on a long-term philosophy. W. Edwards Deming, a major influence on Toyota, stressed that if a company's focus was on improving the quality of its products and services, the bottom-line business results would follow accordingly. In the long run, Deming believed, businesses should be interested in sustaining, making a profit, and keeping people employed. Deming did not stress trying to find total domination of a market and cutthroat competition. In Chapter 3, we discussed the short-term thinking of many U.S. businesses in the 1980s, partially due to performance systems that awarded bonuses based on bottom-line annual performance. Toyota's long-term philosophy was to generate value to the customer and society.

Principle 2: The right process will produce the right results. An important ingredient for improving quality is the total mapping out of all processes. Toyota was a master of the process of changing production from one vehicle to another.

Principle 3: Use "pull" systems to avoid overproduction: A pull system, to be studied in Chapter 12, focuses on actual customer demand rather than producing to inventory. It creates a smoother system, with less need for inventory.

Principle 4: Level out the workload. This approach matches demand to capacity and tries to avoid uneven workstations.

Principle 5: Build a culture of stopping to fix problems, to get quality right the first time. This principle, called *jidoka*, was a major change of philosophical direction from Western approaches to the assembly line. "Quality at the source" is what it means, providing workers with preventative maintenance duties.

Principle 6: Standardized tasks are the foundations for continuous improvement and employee empowerment. One of the tenets of process improvement is to find the best way to do something and train everyone to do it that one, best way.

Principle 7: Use visual control so that no problems are hidden. Toyota likes to post progress reports like scoreboards around the workplace. This gives workers a constant reminder of how things are going.

Principle 8: Use only reliable, thoroughly tested technology that serves your people and processes. Toyota was much more automated than U.S. automakers, although its philosophy was to use automation to support people rather than replace them.

Principle 9: Grow leaders who thoroughly understand the work, live the philosophy, and teach it to others. Toyota is a company that lives and breathes the philosophy of human-centered production. Managers understand what their workers' jobs require.

Principle 10: Develop exceptional people and teams who follow your company's philosophy. There is a real emphasis on a team-centered approach to management at Toyota. Managers begin their careers together and usually are cross trained and step through levels of the organization for a decade before the top executives are sorted from the group. There is very little turnover at Toyota.

Principle 11: Respect your extended network of partners and suppliers by challenging them and helping them improve. The JIT system requires a close working relationship with suppliers and partners; thus they are treated almost like coworkers to help accomplish goals.

Principle 12: Go and see for yourself to thoroughly understand the situation (*genchi genbutsu*). This is another aspect of human-centered production at Toyota. You have to see it for yourself instead of hearing about it second-hand.

Principle 13: Make decisions slowly by consensus, thoroughly considering all options, but implement decisions rapidly. This is team-based decision making at work.

Principle 14: Become a learning organization through relentless reflection (*hansei*) and continuous improvement (*Kaizen*). *Relentless reflection* sounds contradictory, but it means that you always have to think about what you are doing.

Southwest Airlines

One of the very few airlines to be financially successful in the past 20 years is Southwest Airlines. The late Herb Kelleher, the CEO, imprinted his management stamp on the company, which led the industry in profitability and virtually every success measure. In the book *Nuts*, the authors Kevin and Jackie Freiberg (1996) chronicled Kelleher's principles and the success story of Southwest.

It is all common sense, yet somehow good management eludes many firms. Here is a list of success principles found at Southwest Airlines:

1. Think like an entrepreneur.

2. Create a lean organization. It's difficult to hide poor performance.

3. Stop analyzing, start taking action, and act with a sense of urgency.

4. Anticipate the unexpected. Practice the art of asking "What if . . . ?"

5. Stamp out bureaucracy. To ignite the entrepreneurial spirit, abolish unnecessary meetings, minimize paperwork, and simplify communication.

6. Think like an owner—about your job and your life. Owners focus on results regardless of who's watching.

7. Show your people what you think they're worth.

8. Make your organizational and personal mission, vision, and values clear, then hold the reins loosely.

9. Develop a genuine interest in the knowledge of others: Ask to learn, listen to learn, watch to learn.

10. Train yourself to look beyond what you see.

11. Make information interesting, meaningful, and relevant to everyone. Show everyone what's in it for them.

12. Develop a sincere interest in every family member.

13. Do what you value: Practice what you preach, walk the talk.

14. Lighten up: Don't take yourself too seriously. Associate with fun people. Identify six ways you can lighten up, and then work on them for 6 months.

15. Try to make someone smile or laugh every morning and every night.

16. Show love more often.

17. Life is short: Forgive and forget!

18. Defend your people. The customer may not be right all the time!

19. When it comes to serving others, make sure that "good enough" is never good enough!

Do what you ask others to do.

Nuts would probably make a great practical management textbook, since it avoids management theories and clearly articulates what it takes to have a good time leading a company.

Decision Making in Operations

Examples of the types of decisions that operations managers must make would include the following:

- Selecting a supplier
- Adding or deleting a manufacturing plant
- Adding or deleting a headquarters facility
- Deciding whether to add new equipment
- Deciding on a production plan

Operations managers must make both immediate, day-to-day decisions that keep the production flowing and long-term strategic decisions. A decision matrix is a helpful tool in which estimated payoffs can be evaluated in making a decision (see Table 4.2).

The decision maker has two options, one with a 60% probability of a $25 return and a 40% probability of a $5 return. The second option yields a 60% probability of a $16 return and a 40% probability of $11. Summing the states and comparing them, find the expected value for each option. Option 1 yields an expected value of $(25 \times .6) + (5 \times .4) = \$17$. Option 2 has an expected value of $(16 \times .6) + (11 \times .4) = \$14$. Guess which one wins?

Table 4.2   Probability Decision Matrix

		STATES	
		A (0.60)	B (0.40)
OPTIONS	1	$25	$5
	2	$16	$11

Operations managers are in the business of making lightning-quick decisions, and the pace is probably more harried than that of other functional roles in business. "The plane is stalled in a storm in Philadelphia, so our special shipment cannot make it in time for production to proceed. How do we delay the customer?"

"Our demand pattern is very light in the months of June and July. Should we lay off a number of workers or have them build inventory for the fall?"

"Can we rearrange our office spaces to improve efficiency around here?"

The pace can be intense, but the rewards are equally intense: the sight of the first new product to reach the customer's hands in pleasing, working order; a smile from a departing vacationer who has had a wonderful stay at your hotel; or a promise to continue business from the printer who handled your job in record time.

Conclusion

It is impossible to disregard the HR aspects of the operations manager's job. After all, operations management requires skill in directing people to succeed in fulfilling the organization's mission. This chapter serves as a mini textbook in HRM as applied to operations management.

The operations manager must study leadership and management in addition to mastering tools such as forecasting and inventory planning. This chapter serves as an introduction to the principles of management as applied to the operations function.

Summary

- Operations managers must accomplish their objectives through the successful management of people. Knowing how to use a number of quantitative methods won't help a manager who can't direct people.
- Mintzberg (1973) listed the managerial roles as disseminator, disturbance handler, entrepreneur, figurehead, leader, liaison, negotiator, resource allocator, and spokesperson. Operations managers find themselves performing all these roles.
- Kouzes and Posner (1987) identified 10 **leadership traits**. Operations managers must have leadership skills, just as any other functional manager in business.

- Since organizations experience change at a rapid rate, the ability to manage the change is a critical skill for managers.

- Managing underground is a method of management in which the manager goes to the work site to solve problems rather than staying in the office.

- Recruiting new talent is a necessary function of the operations manager. Finding and keeping employees becomes an important part of the manager's job.

- Once new employees are hired, the initial training begins. Training and development are ways to increase the value of the employee.

- Internal and external equity are important factors in compensation decisions.

- Researchers have found that job satisfaction is achieved when workers are satisfied with their jobs, work groups, organizations, and leaders.

- Team growth has several stages: forming, storming, norming, and performing.

Key Terms

Hierarchy of needs	Managing underground
Human-centered production	Mintzberg's managerial roles
Internal and external equity	Motivation and hygiene
Leadership traits	Team growth

Review Questions

1. How is management different in operations compared with marketing?

2. What are the main functions of HRM?

3. What are the main characteristics of leadership?

4. What is human-centered production?

5. How did Jack Welch's performance system work?

6. Describe the four stages of team growth.

7. What are the major ingredients of a successful team?

8. List the 14 principles of Toyota management.

Projects

1. How would you apply motivation to create a winning basketball team?

2. Analyze a manager you know or work for in terms of leadership characteristics. How does he or she stack up?

3. Next time you go to a fine restaurant, notice the movement of the waiters and servers. What visible signs of management can you detect as you eat your meal? In what areas does the place fall short?

4. Consult with a manager. Find out about how they are evaluated.

5. When registering for classes, how difficult is it to complete the process? What management principles are at work in your attempts to do this?

6. Spend some time at your local bookstore reading about keys to leadership in a variety of books. What do these books have in common? Are any of them unique?

CASE 1 The Department Chair's Dilemma

The chair of the management department, Winter Seawright, was disturbed at two reports of mutinous classes taught by Joe Starstruck. Startstruck taught two classes, one in the day and one at night, and independent of each other, both classes sent representatives to the chair demanding Starstruck's replacement due to poor teaching.

The students said that Starstruck gave a few lectures in which he read directly from slides provided by the textbook and then sat back as students presented project reports the rest of the term. One student noticed that Starstruck was writing his grocery list while a presentation was being made. The student noted that the list included milk, Cheerios, Power Bars, coffee, WD40, Cheer, deodorant, 4 gallons of Ben & Jerry's ice cream, and weight watchers' meals. The student observed that, apparently, the diet was not working.

Starstruck had learned that his contract was not to be renewed into the next year. He had been hired while he was a doctoral student, with very high expectations that he would complete his dissertation and publish numerous papers from his work. Instead, Starstruck embraced a lifestyle of skiing, mountain biking, and traveling. His teaching evaluations were OK to date, but that was before he had learned that his contract would not be renewed. Since there was now no chance that he would ever complete his dissertation, his motivation was nil.

Both classes were so adamant that Starstruck be removed that they threatened to go to the president of the university and complain that they wanted their money back, and if that did not work, they would go to the local television station's consumer program, Gil Heisensteiner's Fraud Show, and make the class visible in the media.

Winter had never been faced with a problem this severe in her department. She had problems with faculty trying to manipulate their evaluations in several ways, and numerous arguments within the faculty, but this was the first out-and-out revolt she had ever faced.

Starstruck taught operations management, which was also Winter's specialty. There was no chance of hiring a replacement adjunct with 7 weeks to go in the 14-week semester. It was either do it herself or ask some of the other operations management faculty to take over the classes. The first step, however, was to discuss the situation with Starstruck. Winter called him into her office.

When Starstruck had made himself comfortable, Winter opened the discussion, "So, I hear you like Ben & Jerry's!"

Discussion Questions

1. Should Winter replace Starstruck or ask him to provide a turnaround strategy for the class?

2. Should the students get a refund?

3. Could this have been avoided in some way?

4. What would you do if you were in Winter's shoes?

CASE 2   The Hospital Days Off

Bart Metlen had been the hospital materials manager for 3 months, and he was going crazy. Every day, he was confronted with a stockout of something important that required him either having a courier from the vendor make a special delivery or going to borrow the item from a neighborhood hospital.

He began tracking his records, and he found that 15% of the time that the hospital departments needed supplies, they were out of stock. When trying to discover the major cause of this, he finally concluded that faulty records were to blame. Approximately 10% of the records were incorrect in their computer inventory system.

Further analysis revealed the major causes of the records getting off: Supplies were sometimes withdrawn from the storeroom by nursing personnel at night without signing out for the supplies. Or the unit of measure was incorrect. For example, a case of film consisted of 12 boxes and was distributed to the X-ray department by boxes. If the X-ray department requested one case, it was appropriate to deduct 12 boxes from the inventory, but sometimes only one box was subtracted, causing a deviation of 11.

The materials management department consisted of 25 employees, who worked in purchasing, receiving and distribution, or the central supply area. Starved for solutions, Metlen finally confronted his employees:

> Here is the problem, people. We are out of stock 15% of the time, and this is causing us to spend a lot of extra time and money in getting rush deliveries. So I offer this challenge to you: If we, as a department, can reduce the stockouts to less than 5%, I will give every one of you an additional day off the following month. I don't care how you get to the 5%, so long as you don't fudge the numbers. Whatever you can, do.

It was a magical solution. Suddenly the employees saw reducing stockouts as a way to get a much earned day off to go fishing or shopping, or simply for sleeping in. The department was totally mobilized and made the goal the very first month and every month Metlen was employed at the hospital.

They found a variety of ways to accomplish this, including cycle counting the inventory to reconcile the balances (covered in Chapter 14). This illustrates a case in which increased productivity was reached through an incentive program, and finding the incentives that motivate employees is one of the challenges of good management.

Discussion Questions

1. What other approaches might Metlen have tried to motivate his employees?

2. Going back to Chapter 1, what performance measures would be important here?

CASE 3   Baseball HR—*Moneyball*

In Michael Lewis's book *Moneyball* (2003), the author describes the personnel policies of the general manager of the Oakland A's, Billy Beane. Beane's management has made the A's a competitive team, despite having one of the lowest payrolls in the major leagues.

Beane has a number of beliefs that are contrary to the popular way of baseball thinking. He frowns on the use of the sacrifice bunt and the stolen base. Why? Because he has statistical evidence that makes a convincing argument that they are not the best decisions to make. His favorite statistic is not the batting average for hitters; it is the on-base percentage; and he looks for players who get a lot of bases on balls.

Beane has a number of player personnel practices that are also not common. He refuses to draft players out of high school because the numbers tell him that college players are better bets. He refuses to sign relief pitchers to mega-million-dollar contracts because he thinks that any closer a team has should save 50 games simply by doing the job.

Moneyball is a testament to the use of data and decision making. It shows how a decision maker can make counterintuitive decisions that pay off.

Discussion Questions

1. Are there comparable approaches to the management of data in other professional sports?

2. In baseball, how does operations management figure in an organization? In pro football? Pro basketball? How is professional sports management different from college sports management?

Web Sites

The art and science of leadership: http://Nwlink.com/~Donclark/leader/leader.html

The Center for Creative Leadership: www.ccl.org

Human Resource Management: http://mapnp.osrg

Society for Human Resource Management: http://shrm.org

UK Operations Management professional society: www.iomnet.org.uk

References

Brady, D. (2005, March 28). The Immelt revolution. *Business Week,* 64–73.
Buhler, P. (2002). *Streetwise human resources management.* Avon, MA: Adams Media.
Freiberg, K., & Freiberg, J. (1996). *Nuts.* New York: Broadway Books.
Herzberg, F., Mausner, B., & Snyderman, B. (1993). *The motivation to work.* Edison, NJ: Transaction.
James, L. R., & James, L. A. (1992). Psychological climate and affect. In C. J. Cranny, P. C. Smith, & E. F. Stone (Eds.), *Job satisfaction* (p. 105). New York: Lexington Books.
Kantor, R. M. (2004). *Confidence.* New York: Crown.
Kouzes, J., & Posner, B. Z. (1987). *The leadership challenge.* San Francisco: Jossey-Bass.

Lewis, M. (2003). *Moneyball: The art of winning an unfair game.* New York: W. W. Norton.

Liker, J. K. (2004). *The Toyota way.* New York: McGraw-Hill.

Maslow, A. (1998). *Toward a psychology of being* (3rd ed.). Hoboken, NJ: John Wiley & Sons.

Mintzberg, H. (1973). *The nature of managerial work.* New York: Harper & Row.

Scholtes, P. R., Streibel, B., & Joiner, B. L. (2003). *The team handbook* (3rd ed.). Madison, WI: Joiner/Oriel.

Young, S. T., & Nie, W. (1996). *Managing global operations.* Westport, CT: Quorum Books.

CHAPTER 5

The Balanced Scorecard Approach to Operations

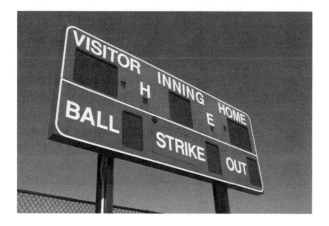

SOURCE: © Michael Krinke/istockphoto.com

Learning Objectives

In this chapter we will

- Study the framework of the "balanced scorecard" (BSC)
- Review the 10 basic questions of the BSC
- Learn how to use the BSC
- Study the importance of the BSC to operations management
- Review applications of the BSC in governmental agencies
- Compare the BSC with a performance dashboard
- Study key performance indicators for academic departments
- Review a case of BSC implementation at a hospital

A s a way to measure nonfinancial performance in an organization, the authors Kaplan and Norton (1996) introduced the "balanced scorecard" (BSC). The **balanced scorecard** approach "balances" customer, internal process, and learning and growth measures against traditional financial measures. Financial indicators never tell the entire story of an organization, since talent, organizational culture, and customer relationships go a long way toward dictating future financial performance.

The increase in adoption of the BSC approach has had an impact on operations management. One of the most important aspects of management is the ultimate question, "How well are we doing?" The BSC helps address the previously intangible aspects to give the manager a bigger picture of performance. This chapter concludes with a discussion of the application of the BSC to two U.S. governmental agencies: the Department of Defense and the Postal Service.

The Framework

The BSC framework has three performance aspects that combine with financial performance:

1. The customer value proposition: What do we offer our customers? Customer satisfaction, customer retention, and customer growth are important by-products of this proposition. That is, they follow directly if the customer values the products and services offered.

2. Internal processes deliver the value to customers. This aspect, discussed in Chapter 1, involved an effective manufacturing/delivery system to customers.

3. Learning and growth relate to the skills, knowledge, and culture of the organization. Also discussed in Chapter 1, this asset is critical to the ultimate success of the organization.

These three performance aspects traditionally have not been tracked to the extent that financial performance measures have been. However, without knowing how a company is doing in these areas, an organization is driving, more or less, without a GPS (Global Positioning System). Yes, the manager knows how to get there, but a GPS sure helps in a strange city!

Questions to Answer

Kaydos (1998) listed 10 basic questions that the BSC should address:

1. *Are we satisfying our customers?* Measures: customer satisfaction, retention, and behavior. Periodic checks of customer satisfaction should gauge the overall satisfaction with the product or service. It is often difficult to get customers to sit down for a survey, and response rates are low, so creative incentives can be used to encourage

an increased response. The larger the response, the more valid the survey. Customer retention, a measurement of whether customers will continue to buy or use the product or service, can be collected at the same time.

2. *Are we satisfying our shareholders?* Measures: financial returns. These measurements are reflected in investing behavior and profitability. If the company's stock is healthy and investors are realizing a nice gain in their investment, shareholders tend to be happy with the decisions of management.

3. *Are we satisfying our stakeholders?* Measures: stakeholder satisfaction and dissatisfaction, retention, and behavior. Since there are numerous stakeholders in a company, employees, customers, board members, the community, and so on, every effort should be made to understand their satisfaction with the help of surveys.

4. *What is happening to our customer base?* Measures: market potential and market growth rate. Marketing research can reveal the market potential and market share within an industry.

5. *Is our company strategy working?* Measures: market share, customer acquisition, customer profitability, product and service profitability, and external factors that affect customers.

6. *Are our individual strategies being properly executed?* Measures: strategic goals and the objectives necessary to achieve them.

7. *Are we serving our customers and stakeholders effectively?* Measures: product and service quality. Here, we use some of the key service quality indicators obtained from a thorough quality system.

8. *Are we operating efficiently?* Measures: process quality and capability, productivity, waste, and product and service costs. These quality measures reflect process indicators rather than customer service quality.

9. *Are stakeholders contributing what they should?* Measures: resource contribution and stakeholder contribution quality.

10. *Are we developing the abilities we need to execute our strategies?* Measures: organizational capabilities, stakeholder capabilities, and infrastructure capabilities. Answering this question requires an analysis of resources and a projection of future demand to make sure the company is prepared for the anticipated trends.

How to Use the BSC

Mobil Oil attributed much of its success in going from last to first in industry profitability to its use of the BSC. An article in the CIO magazine outlined the first steps in the implementation of the BSC:

- *Prepare the organization for change.* Many employees are resistant to change and rather jaded by previous failed efforts to implement programs. Employees have experienced one management fad after another over time, and they get rather tired of them.

- *Devise the right metrics.* Companies need to apply metrics (measurements) that really count toward customer and employee satisfaction, and managers should not measure for the simple love of measuring.

- *Get buy-in at all levels.* If all units are not involved in applying the BSC, there will be only sporadic success.

- *Plan to follow through to completion.* Like any program, checking that milestones are met and implemented is an important action.

First Energy used the following metrics to assess the customer side of the BSC:

- Percentage of projects completed on time and within the budget

- Percentage of projects released to the customer by the agreed-on delivery date

- Client satisfaction as indicated by customer surveys completed at the end of the project

Operations Management and the BSC

Kaplan and Norton (1996) listed four main operations management processes: supplier relationships, producing products and services, delivering products and services, and managing risk.

Examples of measures appropriate to these processes were given by Kaplan and Norton (1996, pp. 70–74):

Supplier relationships
- *Supplier ratings, quality, delivery, and cost:* As Deming points out, suppliers should be rated on more than price, and this provides an aggregate measure for their performance.
- *Cost of purchasing as percentage of purchase price:* This is the overall cost, including labor of the purchasing agents, receiving clerks, and so on.
- *Lead time:* This is the length of time it takes to get supplies from the supplier into the warehouse.
- *On-time delivery percentage:* This measures the actual delivery against the promised delivery date.
- *Percentage of late orders:* This is the percentage of orders that do not meet the promised dates.
- *Percentage of perfect orders received:* This measures the percentage of orders that are 100% complete.
- *Number of suppliers:* This is a number that, it is hoped, can be minimized, since the more suppliers dealt with, the more invoices to pay.
- *Number of outsourcing relationships:* This assumes that outsourcing is a positive step and looks for cost advantages.
- *Cost of purchasing materials:* This is the total cost, including labor cost and the actual cost of the supplies and parts.

Producing products and services

- *Marketing, selling, distribution, and administrative expenses as a percentage of total costs:* An effectiveness measure that it is desirable to minimize
- *Number of processes with substantial improvements:* A subjective measure of process improvements
- *Part-per-million defect rates:* A process quality measurement
- *Cost of inspection and testing:* Another quality measurement
- *Total cost of quality:* Cost of inspection, rework, and so on
- *Cycle time:* The length of time to produce one product
- *Process efficiency:* A proxy for cycle time
- *Percentage of capacity utilization:* Less important than quality but still showing a capability number
- *Equipment reliability:* The performance of machines
- *Flexibility:* The ability to adapt to changing product models
- *Inventory turnover:* The cost of goods sold divided by average inventory
- *Days in receivables:* A performance measurement for the accounts receivable—the lower the better
- *Percentage of stockouts:* An inventory scorecard

Distributing products and services

- *Lead times:* Measure of delivery time to customers
- *On-time delivery percentage:* Meeting promised dates
- *Percentage of items delivered with no defects:* A quality scorecard
- *Number of customer complaints:* A service scorecard
- *Risk management*
- *Bad-debt percentage:* Monitoring customer ability to pay
- *Percentage of uncollectible receivables:* Should be minimized
- *Inventory obsolescence:* Avoiding large inventory quantities of obsolete merchandise
- *Debt-to-equity ratio:* An accounting measure
- *Order backlog:* A good and a bad thing—good in that people want your product and bad in that you can't get it to them yet
- *Technology ranking of products and processes compared with competitors:* A benchmark against competitors

These measures comprise adequate information for a BSC.

Linking the BSC to Strategy

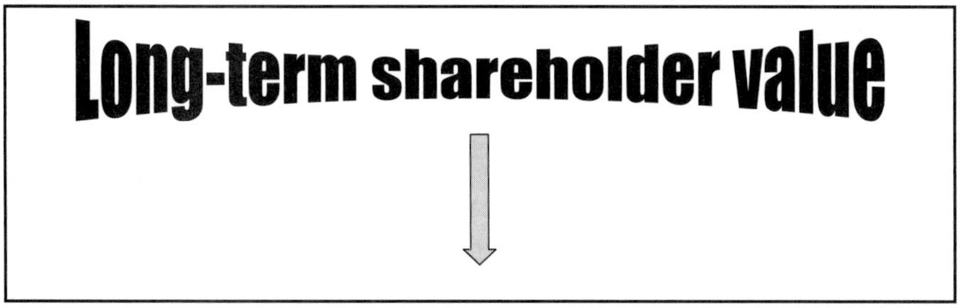

Figure 5.1   A Critical Managerial Target

Kaplan and Norton (2004) sought to show how to apply the BSC to strategy by using "**strategy maps**." These measures show how the financial perspective contributes to long-term value through improved cost structure, increased asset utilization, expanded revenue opportunities, and enhanced customer value. They illustrated this with an eight-stage continuum that led to **strategic outcomes**:

Stage 1. *Mission:* Why we exist

Stage 2. *Values:* What's important today

Stage 3. *Vision:* What we want to be

Stage 4. *Strategy:* Our game plan

Stage 5. *Strategy map:* Translate the strategy

Stage 6. *Balanced scorecard:* Measures and focus

Stage 7. *Targets and initiatives:* What we need to do

Stage 8. *Personal objectives:* What I need to do

Strategic outcomes are satisfied shareholders, delighted customers, efficient and effective processes, and a motivated and prepared workforce.

BSC Implementation

Niven (2003) noted the financial and time considerations a BSC implementation would require. These considerations are really the same as for other major software and programmatic improvements.

- *Employee time:* Employees have to continue with their work while they spend time putting the BSC system into operation.
- *Consulting:* A consultant is often needed to assist in the implementation.
- *Software:* BSC software should be purchased to maintain the scorecard.
- *Educational materials:* Employees will need training and attendance at BSC conferences.
- *Logistical expenses:* Niven (2003) recommends conducting the training offsite, which requires additional expenditures.

The BSC implementation team should include the following:

- *Executive sponsor:* A key executive who assumes ownership of the project and apprises the team of the contribution to the mission and the organization's mission
- *Champion:* The manager who schedules and conducts the meetings and is responsible for training and support

- *Team members:* Employees from different functional areas who help with the delineation of the measurements and are the actual implementers of the BSC

- *Change expert:* A consultant who works with the team and assists with the stress of change on the workforce

Applications of the BSC

Mathys and Thompson (2006) studied the application of the BSC at governmental agencies—the U.S. Post Office and the Department of Defense Financial and Accounting Office (DFAS). The mission and vision of the DFAS are defined in Figure 5.2.

The DFAS Mission and Vision

Mission: Provide responsive, professional finance and accounting services for the people who defend America.

Vision: Best value to our customers
- World-class provider of finance and accounting services
- Trusted, innovative financial partner
- One organization, one identity
- Employer of choice, providing a progressive and professional work environment

---

Figure 5.2   The DFAS Mission and Vision

The following paragraphs are excerpted from Mathys and Thompson's (2006) report.

(DFAS) wrestled over the relationship among the four BSC perspectives. They finally agreed that because DFAS is a service, not-for-profit organization, the key driver was the customer and that the foundation was its people. Improving the skill level of its workforce would allow the talent of the employees to identify the "best" way to improve processes and would solve the problems or needs of the customer. The use of this intellectual talent would improve internal processes, reduce costs and ultimately achieve better customer service. The DFAS pyramidal BSC model [see Figure 5.3] was developed to explain the interrelationships among the perspectives to employees rather than to represent any hierarchy among each of the perspectives.

One of the most difficult behavioral issues or challenges faced by DFAS in implementing the BSC process was the development of metrics. The Leadership Council had great difficulty determining goals and identifying appropriate measures. Finally, they reached a general consensus on 80% of the scorecard goals and measures and decided, rather than spending another 5 months debating the issue, that the BSC should be implemented

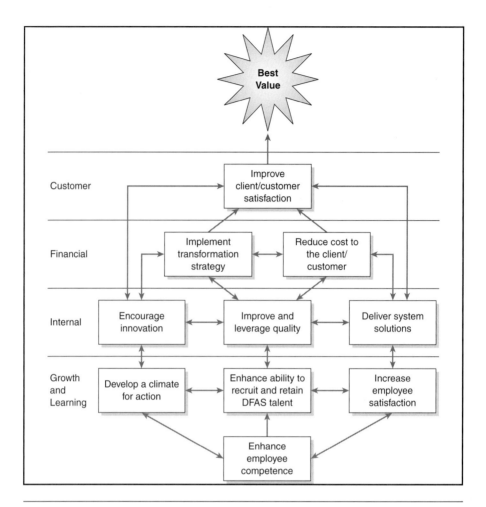

Figure 5.3   Balanced Scorecard Hierarchy

and monitored for potential problems and required changes. At times, what was thought to be the right measurement was found to be deficient—it wasn't measuring the right thing. Leadership realized that this initial score-card was only a first step. It could be improved and adjusted over time. Continuous learning was the key and resulted in BSC revisions each year to include more meaningful metrics and provide a better indication of progress in meeting the overall strategic goals. (pp. 19–27)

While it was fairly easy to develop metrics for business lines that were revenue producing, it was (and continues to be) much more difficult to develop measures and objectives for supporting staff units that were not revenue producing (Figure 5.4).

BSC Benefits

The key benefit of the BSC has been to help managers and supervisors identify and focus on specific goals in order to achieve improved performance and, in doing so, to make them better managers. The BSC goals, in turn, were communicated to

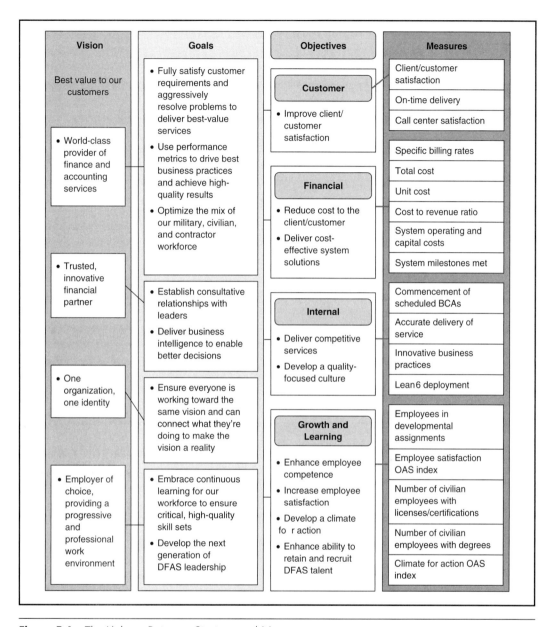

Figure 5.4   *The Linkage Between Strategy and Measures*

all employees, and they helped align managers and employees by making them focus on the same targets. When the BSC targets were achieved, DFAS performance improved, managers reduced costs, employees were proud of their accomplishments, and customers were more satisfied. Publishing the BSC results every month to all employees made the BSC process extremely visible. Everyone was able to see that the BSC was really used and that it really contributed to improvement in the agency. The BSC established a common language or platform, and no matter how much work areas and job functions differed, all managers still focused on the same goals. Even employees in rather unique areas were able to focus on group goals and actually pull together with the rest of the agency as a team to improve overall

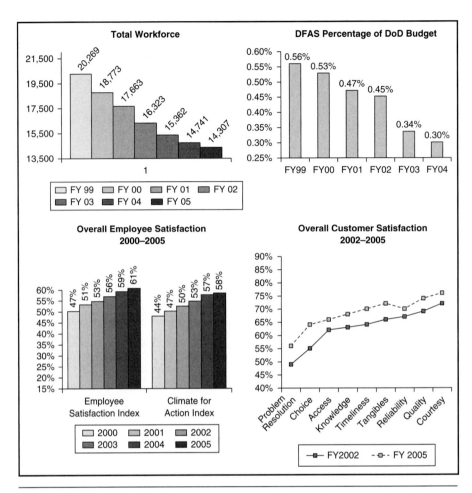

Figure 5.5   DFAS Organizational Results

agency performance. Figure 5.5 shows an example of the positive results achieved from FY 1999 to 2005. Despite a significant decline (roughly 30%) in the total workforce in the past 5 years, there has been consistent improvement in employee and customer satisfaction. At the same time, process costs to DoD (Department of Defense) have been cut almost in half.

One of DFAS's vision statements is "One organization and one identity." Actually, this vision grew from the fact that DFAS came into existence by consolidating many separate organizations, each serving a specific military service or defense agency. One of the Leadership Council's more important tasks was to unite all these various segments toward common goals. Implementing a corporate BSC linked to business line scorecards and individual performance plans was a key step in focusing all levels of the agency on common goals. The BSC was a natural step in the overall process to attain the corporate identity required to achieve its strategic goals and become a world-class provider of finance and accounting services. It provided a tool for senior leadership to focus on the most important issues. As one executive stated, "We take care of a very, very important customer base; people who defend America. So when improvements are made in service deliveries we're doing it for very important people and that's rewarding" (Mathys & Thompson, 2006, p. 27).

The Performance Dashboard

Eckerson (2006) proposed a slightly different approach to measurement, the "**performance dashboard.**" He defined the dashboard as "a multilayered application built on a business intelligence and data integration infrastructure that enables organizations to measure, monitor, and manage business performance more effectively" (p. 10).

Dashboards come in three types: operational, tactical, and strategic. Operational dashboards have the primary purpose of monitoring the organization. Tactical dashboards are used for analysis and strategic dashboards for management. Eckerson (2006) categorizes the BSC as a "strategic" dashboard (see Table 5.1).

Table 5.1   Performance Dashboard Versus Balanced Scorecard

	Dashboard	*Scorecard*
Purpose	Measures performance	Charts progress
Users	Supervisors	Executives, managers
Updates	Right time	Periodic snapshots
Data	Events	Summaries
Display	Visual graphs, raw data	Visual graphs, text

SOURCE: Eckerson (2006).

Eckerson (2006) gave the example of the application of dashboards for Quicken Loans. Loan managers receive a dashboard that shows their team measurements on five important measures. Executives receive a summary screen of six important charts from the loan managers.

Key Performance Indicators for Academic Departments

In setting up a dashboard or scorecard system for academic departments, it is important to start with defining the most important performance metrics. It would seem a difficult task to convert college professors into a scoring system, but it can be done.

Research Productivity

The accrediting bureau of collegiate business schools, AACSB (Association to Advance Collegiate Schools of Business), has two important measures. One measures academic and professional qualifications (AQ and PQ). The other measures the degree of participation the faculty member has with the institution (participating or supporting).

To define AQ, each institution has to come up with a measurable approach to the research productivity of its faculty. This is easiest measured by counting the number of articles in journals, the number of books published, and the number of presentations at conferences. A point system has to quantify these outputs. For example, it might be that to become academically qualified, a faculty member must achieve a total of three points in a 5-year period. One point is awarded for each published article or book. Conference presentations may be awarded a third of a point. So a faculty member with two articles and three presentations would score three points and be determined to be AQ.

The PQ designation would consist of a scoring system for full-time employment, consulting activities and service activities, plus educational credentials. This designation is designed to cover faculty who do not publish yet have much teaching experience. It would also cover faculty who do not have a PhD but have years of either consulting or employment experience. The AQ/PQ score would provide the research productivity information for a dashboard of an academic department.

Teaching Dashboard

Although it is argued that it does not tell the whole story, the "overall" teaching effectiveness of a course is the most important measurement on the dashboard for teaching effectiveness. Other considerations may be the number of different courses taught, the number of students taught, any new courses taught, and the number of teaching conferences attended.

One approach would be to award a score for the overall teaching and then add points for any of the above situations. The faculty member who averages 4.5 on a 5.0 score and teaches two different courses might be awarded a score of 4.6. If he or she teaches three different courses, the score might be 4.7, and so on.

Service Dashboard

The service of college professors is measured by their work inside the university and college, their work for the profession (usually reviewing papers and participating in conferences), and their work for the community. This is a difficult area to quantify and may be best served by a points system.

For example, a committee chairperson may be awarded two points, while a committee member who actively participates receives one point, and so on. Awarding points for service is similar to awarding class participation points in the classroom. It is hard to determine who does the most work, but the judge has to make a subjective call with the information given.

Sedona

A database that does a good job of giving college administrators a dashboard of sorts is Sedona™. Sedona offers a way to input all the information on a professor's activities. The database includes virtually all professorial activities and can convert the information into a scorecard of activity.

Conclusions

Kaplan and Norton's (1996) *Balanced Scorecard* has found acceptance with many organizations, both for-profit and not-for-profit. The scorecard provides a global approach to measurement, combining financial measures with important customer and employee measurements. It functions as both a financial and a productivity system and continues to grow in its application.

Financial measurements used to be the main measurement approach of organizations, but they ignored important customer and employee information that can be captured with the BSC. Operations management's performance is multidimensional, and the BSC is an approach that gives an overview of the important elements of production.

Summary

- The BSC provides a framework for performance leading to customer value and financial performance.

- The following are the 10 basic questions to ask when constructing a BSC:

  Are we satisfying our customers?

  Are we satisfying our shareholders?

  Are we satisfying our stakeholders?

  What is happening to our customer base?

  Is our company strategy working?

  Are our individual strategies being properly executed?

  Are we serving our customers and stakeholders effectively?

  Are we operating efficiently?

  Are stakeholders contributing what they should?

  Are we developing the abilities we need to execute our strategies?

- Mobil Oil found that getting the right metrics, getting buy-in from users, and follow-through are important for successful implementation of the BSC.

- Operations management contributes to the BSC through supplier relationships, producing products and services, delivering products and services, and managing risk.

- There is an eight-stage strategy continuum from the mission that leads to strategic outcomes.

- A key benefit of the BSC is that it can identify and focus on specific measures that lead to improved performance and better management.

Key Terms

Balanced scorecard

Performance dashboard

Strategic outcomes

Strategy map

Review Questions

1. How does the BSC compare with productivity measurement?

2. What would be the major differences of application of a BSC for a governmental agency versus a manufacturing firm?

3. What are the major metric areas in the BSC?

4. How can the use of a BSC improve a firm?

5. Is the BSC applicable to all firms? Is it applicable to your own place of employment?

Projects

1. Find an organization that uses a BSC, and interview employees about the effectiveness of the scorecard and whether its application meant a difference in performance.

2. Create a scorecard for your organization, or one you have access to. After listing possible measurements, review their appropriateness with another employee.

3. Create a BSC for a college athletic department.

CASE 1   Balanced Scorecard for a Hospital

Marge Oliphant, the administrator of the South Tifton Hospital, a 150-bed rural hospital, decided to implement the BSC in her hospital. Her approach was to do a pilot test in the materials management department, a nonpatient care area. The manager, Vernon Clance, was a good choice because he had already submitted reports on inventory levels.

Clance approached his department by breaking down the scorecard into its customary four areas: learning and growth, business processes, customer measures, and financial measures.

With his staff, Clance arrived at these measures:

- Learning and growth

    Staff turnover
    Job satisfaction
    Staff loyalty
    Education (dollars spent)

- Business Processes

  Inventory turnover
  Fill rate
  Accuracy rate
  Responsiveness
  Supplier fill rates
  Productivity (deliveries/labor hour)

- Customer

  Customer (hospital units) satisfaction

- Financial

  Inventory on hand
  Salary expenses
  $/purchase order

Oliphant was impressed with the measurement selection. Clance used job satisfaction and customer satisfaction measurements that he found in a book. Basically, they measured, on a scale from 1 to 5, how happy a person was with the present position, pay, facilities, and so on. The materials management customers were the individual units that received supplies on a daily business. They were surveyed on the responsiveness and accuracy of the supplies they received.

Clance did detect a 93% fill rate (the percentage of orders successfully filled) in the first month, and that became the target of improvement for the next month.

Oliphant then turned to a patient care unit, the intensive-care unit (ICU). This was a 12-bed unit, not as frenetically paced as the emergency room, although the patients were in serious condition. Bob Tallent was the unit manager, a business school graduate in charge of the administrative details of the unit. Bob relished the opportunity to come up with an organized measurement scheme and, with the assistance of the staff, devised these measurements:

- Learning and growth

  Nursing turnover
  Staff turnover
  Training and education dollars
  Job satisfaction
  Staff loyalty

- Clinical and business processes

  Medical errors
  Clerical errors
  In-processing
  Out-processing
  Billing speed
  Responsiveness
  Productivity index

- Customer

  Patient satisfaction
  Family satisfaction
  Physician satisfaction

- Financial

  Revenue per patient
  Cost per patient
  Salary expenses

After 2 months in the ICU and 4 months in materials management, Oliphant extended the trial to Accounts Receivable. The program was intended to go hospital-wide at the end of the year.

Discussion Questions

1. Do these areas give an accurate depiction of what is important in materials management and the ICU?

2. What issues in each area would be important to Accounts Receivable?

3. If the hospital administrator wanted a global scorecard, what would that look like?

CASE 2   Snow Removal in Cook County

Marv Elliott managed the Cook County Snow Removal efforts from November through April each year. In a typical snowstorm, 34 trucks and 3 graders are employed, using approximately 2,500 tons of salt. The drivers are employees of the Cook County Highway Maintenance department.

Marv wanted to set up a performance dashboard for his department. He identified these key issues:

- Reduction of accidents caused by snow and ice
- Speed of delivery of salt and graded roads
- Labor hours to service storms
- Labor hours related to the number of inches of snowfall
- Cost of fuel and miles driven (Cook County covers 577 street and freeway miles)

Assist Marv by designing a performance dashboard for the snow removal department.

Web Sites

The Balanced Scorecard Institute: www.balancedscorecard.org

CIO.com. (n.d.). *How to use the balanced scorecard.* Retrieved November 11, 2007, from www.cio.com/archive/051502/scorecard.html

Norton and Kaplan's BSC site: www.bscol.com

References

Eckerson, W. W. (2006). *Performance dashboards.* Hoboken, NJ: John Wiley & Sons.

Kaplan, R. S., & Norton, D. P. (1996). *The balanced scorecard.* Boston: HBS Press.

Kaplan, R. S., & Norton, D. P. (2004). *Strategy maps.* Boston: HBS Press.

Kaydos, W. (1998). *Operational performance measurement.* Boca Raton, FL: CRC Press.

Mathys, N. J., & Thompson, K. R. (2006). *Using the balanced scorecard at the U.S. Postal Service and the Department of Defense Finance and Accounting Service: Lessons learned.* Washington, DC: IBM Center for the Business of Government.

Niven, P. R. (2003). *Balanced scorecard for government and nonprofit agencies.* Hoboken, NJ: John Wiley & Sons.

CHAPTER 6

Total Quality Management

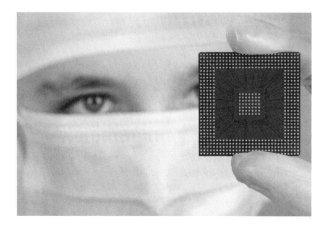

SOURCE: © Oktay Ortakcioglu/istockphoto.com

Learning Objectives

In this chapter, we will

- Trace the history of the total quality management (TQM) movement
- Discuss the many ways in which we define quality
- Review aspects of service quality
- Look at various quality guidebooks
- Study the importance of quality "gaps"
- Discuss the importance of service recovery
- Discover the theories of W. E. Deming and the quality "gurus"

(Continued)

(Continued)

- Learn about the *Lean* concept and its importance to quality
- Study the tools used to measure quality
- Learn the basics of a Six Sigma quality program
- Review the approach to sampling plans
- Review the ISO 9000 quality system
- Study the Malcolm Baldrige and European quality awards
- Study the House of Quality approach to product design

The TQM Movement's History

TQM is a key management philosophy in operations management. The TQM movement gained popularity soon after NBC television sent a film crew to Japan in 1978 to make a documentary titled *If Japan Can, Why Can't We?* The documentary was motivated by the influx of Japanese products in the 1970s, which led other countries to study what the Japanese were doing that was so successful. While making the film, the crew heard repeated references to "Deming." Finally, the filmmakers asked who Deming was. The Japanese were aghast that the Americans did not know him. "He is an American!" they responded. They then explained about the Deming Prize, a Japanese award annually bestowed on a company championing quality in Japan. The film crew tracked Deming to his home and listened to him blast American manufacturing. He credited the Japanese with focusing on quality and said that this focus had led to product improvement and, ultimately, profitability.

The resulting documentary made an impression on executives of the Ford Motor Company. Ford at that time had a poor reputation for quality, and many said that FORD stood for "fix or repair daily." By embracing Deming's methods, Ford was able to turn the corner, and within a few years, the company shed its reputation as the poorest U.S. car manufacturer for quality and rose to the top rank of car manufacturers. This enabled Ford to put on an advertising campaign with the slogan "Quality Is Job One."

Ford was just one of the companies that got caught up in the quality fervor. Company after company started a campaign to improve quality. It may be said that any product bought today is probably better made than a similar product made 30 years ago. This chapter tells the history of that improvement and the methods used to bring it about.

What Is Quality?

People want to make things well. When a pastry chef makes a dessert, he or she is in fact creating a miniature masterpiece that he or she hopes will satisfy the taste buds and make the customer come back for more. When Easton makes steel-shafted arrows, the company aims for the arrows to fly true and straight. When a hotel registers a guest, the management intends that guest to have a totally relaxing stay so that he or she will return.

Quality has been with us since the beginning of time. It is not the norm for someone to awaken in the morning and say, "I can't wait to get to work and see how much I can screw up today!" People are born with an innate desire to produce good things. The challenge of TQM is to tap into that desire and make available quality products and services that customers will covet.

According to Garvin (1984), we define quality in terms of eight different factors:

1. *Performance:* What can the product or service actually do? If we are making stereo systems, there are noise ratios that measure the performance of the speakers. Braking and acceleration distances are measures of automobile performance. Courier services such as UPS and FedEx measure performance by their ability to deliver packages within a certain promised time span.

2. *Aesthetics:* What is the appearance of the product? Is the design so sleek and cool that the customer wants one because of its appearance? A number of products have achieved this. Apple's computers and iPods are examples of products people like not only for their functionality but also because they are small packages simply packed with great features.

Many automobiles have head-turning designs; the Acura RL, the Audi A8, and the Infiniti G5 are classy sedans. The BMW convertibles and Lexus SUVs are very pretty cars. The new lines of Cadillac and Lincoln have restored the popularity of these brands.

Services are also very much affected by the quality of aesthetics; the ambience of a hotel or bank lobby sets a tone of quality. The Peninsula Hotels in Hong Kong and Chicago and the Grand Wailea in Maui are stunning examples of design and architecture.

3. *Reliability:* This is repeatedly performing well. No matter how many times you measure the performance, it is always the same. A starting point for thinking about reliability is to consider the U.S. Postal Service, with the motto that through rain, sleet, or hail, they will get the mail to you. They never promise what time or what day, but they will be there, for sure, delivering the mail.

If you measure an automobile's braking distance while it slows from 100 km/hr to a complete stop, it should always be the same. If you measure the signal-to-noise ratio of some stereo speakers, it should always be the same. Reliability means you can count on something. You have some friends who are reliable and others who may show up if they are invited but may not because they are unreliable.

4. *Conformance:* This is a manufacturing-oriented measure that indicates proximity to product specifications. For instance, a courier may promise next-day delivery 98% of the time. The courier's ability to meet that promise is conformance. If a

contract calls for a minimum of 99% good parts, the ability to meet that specification is called conformance.

5. *Durability:* This is the ability to withstand stress. A number of automobiles "sell" durability. Mercedes Benz and Volvo are examples; these companies advertise their effectiveness in crash testing. Samsonite once had a successful advertising campaign in which its luggage was placed in a cage with a gorilla. Since this was not too different from the way luggage is handled at the airport, it proved to be a good marketing campaign.

6. *Features:* These are added options. Adding features (bells and whistles to standard products, in the customer's eyes) increases the quality of the product. It also increases the chances of defects. Visit Best Buy or Circuit City, and you will encounter dozens of DVD players, DVRs, washing machines, and electronic items. Invariably, added features raise the price—either for the customer or for the manufacturer.

7. *Serviceability:* Products have to be repaired. Services have problems that must be remedied. Any company has to consider how it will take care of service problems well in advance. Customer service often determines how the customer feels about the company based on how a problem has been handled. American Express has a worldwide network of offices to handle problems with travelers' checks and credit cards. They take pride in being able to deliver replacements to customers anywhere in the globe within a couple of days.

A repair network must be established even before a product is released. Apple has installed in its stores a "Genius Bar," in which their best technical minds are put to the task of dealing with problems related to iPod and computer purchases. For the customer, dealing with someone in person is preferable to waiting on hold for hours and never knowing where you are in the queue.

(A product that may be aesthetically pleasing and score high in aesthetic quality may have a poor repair network. But if customers find that they have trouble getting a problem fixed, it is unlikely that they will be repeat customers, however beautiful the product.)

8. *Perceived quality:* This is probably the most important dimension of quality, because it is what the customer believes the quality to be. Conformance and reliability measures are important from a measurement point of view, but what the customer believes is even more important.

Some companies through time have become synonymous with quality, and this has to do mainly with reputation and word-of-mouth.

- *Levi's:* Their jeans are known for their durability and can last for years of normal use. Designer jeans? They come and go as fast as the labels are sewn on them.

- *Nordstrom's:* There are many stories of legendary Nordstrom achievements in customer service, and this has served the company well. The actual differences between their products and those of competitive stores such as, for example,

Nieman-Marcus, Bloomingdale's, and Saks Fifth Avenue in the United States and Marks & Spencer in the United Kingdom may be small, but Nordstrom's has achieved an industry reputation for quality.

- *Honda, Toyota,* and *Nissan* (and *Acura, Lexus,* and *Infiniti*): The Japanese automakers have led in virtually all areas of quality for many years. The Japanese automobile industry adopts new features much more quickly than their Western counterparts. For example, keyless ignition was introduced by Lexus and Acura before BMW and Audi added this feature to their vehicles.

- *Harley Davidson:* The U.S. maker of motorcycles has gathered an almost cult-like following, due to quality, styling, and performance.

- *McDonald's:* A French fry eaten at a McDonald's in Illinois tastes identical to one eaten in Paris or London. That is emblematic of reliability.

- *Leer:* If someone thinks of private, charter planes, they start with Leer. Leer has become synonymous with charter jet quality.

- *Disney:* The Disney brand is only applied to quality entertainment, whether in amusement parks, cruises, or motion pictures.

- *Starwood, Marriott,* and *Hilton:* These companies provide a level of service that you can depend on across the world. They all offer a number of hotels, ranging from luxury to economy brands. Hilton must be the greatest of all, to survive the notoriety of its famous heiress, Paris.

- *Sony, Mitsubishi, Panasonic,* and *Samsung:* Leaders in televisions and electronics products, the three Japanese companies and one Korean company (Samsung) are known for outstanding products and have pretty much monopolized their industry.

- *Costco* and *Sam's Club:* These are leaders in warehouse-type all-purpose stores. Like the French-origin hypermarkets, these stores specialize in reduced prices for groceries and additionally offer discount prices on everything but the kitchen sink, which probably is available too.

- *Coca-Cola* and *Pepsi Cola:* When was the last time you tasted one that was bad right from the store? You may have bought some cans and left them in the car for 2 weeks, and these may have tasted flat; but Coke and Pepsi are examples of food-and-beverage products that are always reliable. (For the most part, quality is always certain in these industries, due to the strict regulations placed on them by the government.)

- *Prada, Hermes,* and *Gucci:* These are dealers in purses, handbags, and other accoutrements popular with the Beverly Hills crowd.

- *Apple:* Its iPod line of products drew attention to the fact that the company, an innovator for many years, continues to offer products that are more innovative than their PC equivalents.

- *Nokia:* They are the leader in cell phones, an industry in which it is hard to keep up with the changes offered by competing PDAs.

- *Barnes & Noble* and *Borders:* Initially criticized for driving independent booksellers out of business, these two companies have revolutionized the book industry by offering superstores with tremendous selections.

- *Starbucks:* Designed according to the concept of the Italian café and neighborhood hangout, they have "lateed" and "frappuccinoed" their way into the mainstream of Western culture.

- *Nike, Adidas, Mizuno, Avia, New Balance, Reebok,* and so on: They are leaders in running and athletic shoes, with innovations such as the air sole.

- *Ben & Jerry's* and *Häagen–Dazs:* These companies bestowed innovative flavors on the ice cream world and 20lb on all their fans.

- *Shimano:* This company is known for its bicycle gearing.

It takes quite some time to gain the status of a "roll-off-the-tongue" name associated with quality. The process begins with a well-designed product with built-in quality and excellent follow-up customer service that gains lifetime allegiance among customers. However, tastes and technologies change. IBM was known for many years as the quality producer of Selectric typewriters, products that will probably some day sit side by side with slide rules at a museum of ancient business technologies.

Service Quality

Berry, Zeithaml, and Parasuraman (1990) conducted the most well-known study on service quality. After studying quality in a number of service industries, they condensed the major dimensions of service quality into the following classes:

- *Tangibles:* The physical appearance of a facility and its personnel

- *Reliability:* Consistency of performance

- *Responsiveness:* The ability to address the customer's needs quickly

- *Assurance:* The levels of skill and knowledge needed to perform the task

- *Empathy:* A feeling for the customer's situation

Tangibles are a form of aesthetics. At the local bank, it is expected that the tellers be neatly dressed and groomed, and their demeanor should be very polite. After all, they are the face of the bank. You would not expect to go to a bank and find the tellers in jeans and T-shirts.

Reliability has been judged in all service industries to be the most important aspect of service quality. Customers want to be able to depend on the company. When a customer sends a DVD back in an envelope to Netflix, he or she expects a quick turnaround. Netflix, meanwhile, must rely on the reliability of the U.S. Postal Service.

When you think of responsiveness, no service company can be more responsive than the police, the fire department, or an ambulance corps responding to a 911 call. Here, the customer is usually in dire straits and in need of immediate help. (Unfortunately, some 911 calls turn out to be bogus, as do more than 90% of fire alarms. This makes it harder for the emergency response organizations to be responsive.)

Assurance is a given when you go to the hospital or deal with a tax accountant. In the hospital, the physician has an MD degree and is an expert in a field. (Physicians do not always agree on the method of treatment, however.) The patient wants to feel secure that the diagnosis is correct and the treatment will be the best available. The customer also expects tax accountants to know what they are doing. A letter from the IRS inviting a discussion about taxes probably lowers the average person's life expectancy.

Similarly, the hospital is where you expect empathy. If you are told you have a life-threatening illness, you expect the person communicating the message to feel your pain. In any case where there is a service problem, the customer needs that kind of sympathy. At the car repair shop, when they tell you it will cost thousands of dollars to repair your engine, you do not want to hear this news from a person who laughs at your plight. You expect condolences. After all, this is costing you an arm and a leg.

Quality Guides

A number of agencies and independent companies have been judging quality and passing on the information to consumers even before the quality revolution of the 1970s. These companies grade hotels and restaurants.

Zagat's: This group does restaurant and hotel guides for major cities and has branched out to movies, golf, and other areas. Frequent diners are asked to rate restaurants in terms of food, ambience, and service, and these ratings yield a total rating.

AAA: The automobile club has been rating hotels and restaurants for many years (their guides are similar to the Mobil guides in the United States and the Michelin guides in Europe). AAA provides many other services, including travel agency, automobile insurance, and towing services.

Michelin: These guides for Europe tell you what sites to see, where to eat, and where to stay. Michelin is an indispensable provider of European information.

Ebert and Roeper: These film critics give a "thumbs up" or a "thumbs down" rating to movies. They are representative of media critics who attempt to give consumers guidance on what to see, what to read, and what music to listen to.

Consumer Reports: The leading publisher of consumer products ratings, this company studies everything from automobiles to laptops.

Quality Gaps

An important concept for managers is that they should strive to match the customer's expectations with what they deliver to the customer. All restaurants are not alike in the ways in which they try to meet the customer's expectations. A restaurant offering an all-you-can-eat buffet for a low price has customers in mind who are probably going to go the entire day without eating and will therefore be looking for a large quantity of food at a low price. They will be casually dressed and often will not bother to remove their baseball caps as they come in. They will pile several hunks of meat—sampling beef, chicken, pork, and fish—on the same plate, add a second plate of vegetables and potatoes, and finish the meal off with three or four desserts. These customers will feel very happy if they have to let their belts out an additional notch as they slide out the door, for they have eaten 6,000 calories for about $8.

Take another type of customer, someone who is going to celebrate a special anniversary at a five-star restaurant, the one that has the highest Zagat rating in the city. A jacket and tie may be required for admittance. The ambience is immediately apparent in the spacing of tables, which are placed so that you cannot eavesdrop on the couple having a conversation close by. The servers are so prompt that they anticipate every request before it is made. The menu consists of exotic entrees that cannot possibly be made at home, many having unpronounceable foreign names, which must taste good since you don't know what they are.

The dishes are also miniature works of art. Carrots appear on the plate arranged in the shape of a log cabin. Sauces are swirled around to make the plate look as if Picasso had designed it. Even a doggie bag comes in the form of an aluminum swan. Music is gentle in the background, the wine is exquisite, and the entire presentation must be extraordinary, as the final bill will be more than you would pay for a Broadway play and almost as much as the cost of a scalped Radiohead ticket.

If a number of surveyors were to wait outside the all-you-can-eat place and a similar number were to await customers coming out of the top-flight restaurant and ask only one question, "How satisfied are you with your dining experience?" they may be very surprised to find that the rating of the all-you-can-eat place matches the score of the top-rated establishment. Are they equal in quality? No way. The all-you-can-eat buffet purchases lower-quality (but still decent) meats and vegetables in large quantities. The restaurants have met the customers' expectations equally well—that is all. Of course, the gourmet restaurant is of higher actual quality, but both achieve customer satisfaction, and that is what quality is all about. It may even be that the all-you-can-eat place makes more money with its mass-production strategy than the gourmet restaurant.

Service Recovery

An important aspect of quality is the ability to overcome a mistake. The moment of truth for a company's reputation comes when it has made a mistake and has to correct it. At that point, the customer is making up his or her mind about how good the company is. How many times have you ordered food at the drive-through window of a fast-food restaurant and returned home to discover that they have either forgotten part of your order or given you the incorrect order? And how many times have you been willing to drive all the way back to have the order corrected? If an incorrect order is returned to a drive-through within 30 min, the customer should receive major compensation. A free meal or free items are warranted in this case.

The best type of **service recovery** is one in which the customer's expectations of recompense are topped. The customer may only expect to receive the two tacos the servers missed; but the restaurant can make amends by offering, in addition, half off on a future order, plus a free dessert. By giving a discount on future business, the firm guarantees the customer's return, which has been put at risk because of the error.

Deming's Points

Deming was much influenced by Walter Shewhart, who wrote *On the Economic Control of Quality* (1931/1980), which advocated using statistical techniques. In fact, the United States used these techniques during the massive war manufacturing effort of World War II, and the statistical methods were still in favor with many military veterans who moved into product manufacturing after the war.

In the 1950s, when Japanese companies sought a way to change the worldwide view that "Made in Japan" meant shoddy products, they brought in the world's then experts, Deming and Joseph Juran. At the same time, the U.S. economy was booming to the point that quality techniques fell into disfavor. Who needs to measure quality when everything we make, we sell? U.S. manufacturers began practicing "planned obsolescence" of their products. Car manufacturers expected consumers to change their automobiles every 3 or 4 years, so they planned major design changes years in advance and only built the product to last for a short time. (It is no wonder that the Japanese seized the opportunity afforded by the oil embargo of the 1970s.)

Deming (1986) believed that a proper business cycle went like this:

1. Make quality the goal. That is the starting point.

2. If you have a quality system, you can reduce costs.

3. If you can reduce costs, you can reduce prices.

4. If you reduce prices, you can make profits.

5. Then, you can stay in business.

Deming's (1986) **14 points**, which formed the basis of his system, are as follows:

1. *Drive out fear!* Many workers have great ideas to improve quality and productivity, but they actually fear that such ideas would enable the company to get by without them and that if they discussed their ideas with management they would lose their jobs. In Deming's view, if a company is to succeed, it has to have an encouraging environment that welcomes ideas and honors them, whether they are good or not. After all, a bad idea turned about slightly may lead to a dramatic improvement in the way things are done.

2. *Make quality the common goal.* The quality organization has a common mission to produce quality, and everyone in the organization should not only understand the mission but also live it. It is said that when a housekeeper at NASA was

asked what her job was, she replied, "Putting a man on the moon." That level of unity of mission will undoubtedly carry over to a firm's success.

3. *Institute training programs.* People have to be trained in the quality methods, which includes training in statistical methods. Often, that means additional training in basic arithmetic and language skills. It is not easy to teach about statistical means and standard deviations when the worker cannot multiply and divide.

4. *Eliminate slogans.* Deming objected to the idea of trying to improve quality by placing encouraging slogans all over the place. He particularly objected to the slogan "Do it right the first time," believing that it implied that workers *would not* do it right unless they were told to do so. He felt that this was demeaning, and workers on the floor in companies that he visited told him so. Quality is not achieved through cheerleading. It is accomplished through hard work and effective systems.

5. *Improve constantly.* There is a tendency to reach a certain level of quality and ease off. Deming wrote that companies should always strive for improvement and not grow complacent and satisfied after reaching a particular goal.

6. *Eliminate obstacles.* Deming believed that it is our innate nature to make good things. Your mother does not cook dinner thinking, "I'm going to make them some slop. I can't wait to see the looks on their faces." Instead, she tries to prepare meals with care, perhaps with an eye toward their nutritive value. The point is that we usually try to make something good. If you are working on your own house, you want to do a good job so things work right. Deming frequently saw a problem in the workplace: Workers wanted to do good work but were not given the proper tools and equipment to do the job. If you are trying to grill hamburgers without a spatula to flip them over with and are using a pocketknife instead, the burgers will fall apart.

7. *Adopt the new philosophy.* A philosophy in which quality is the main goal should emanate from the CEO and spread throughout the organization. It should be the main focus of all actions within the company.

8. *Stop depending on mass inspection.* Prior to Deming, the popular thinking was that the way to increase quality was to hire more inspectors to find defects and then pull the defects from the line. Thus, managers believed that it was more expensive to have higher quality. Deming argued that if the causes of defects were eliminated, it would actually be less expensive to improve quality.

Using systematic sampling plans makes it unnecessary (usually) to inspect every last item. A popular commercial for Hanes underwear once depicted a woman stretching a man's underpants and saying, "It don't say Hanes unless I say it says Hanes." Hanes underwear at that time would come with a little sticker that said "Inspected by Margaret" (or some other woman), apparently with the idea that it would give the wearer great comfort to know that his underwear had been previously inspected. This was nothing more than a marketing gimmick. It was unnecessary for an underwear producer to inspect *every* pair of underwear. If you are sending people on an airplane or into outer space, *then* you may consider 100% inspection. But *underwear?*

9. *End the practice of awarding business on the basis of price alone.* Deming encouraged sourcing that examined quality, price, and service. Those that sourced raw materials based on price alone often got what they paid for. Junk.

10. *Adopt and institute leadership.* Leadership should not be the sole domain of the executive suite. Anyone who has a role with an impact on quality should be given the power to stop the line.

11. *Break down barriers between staff.* (Deming saw the same thing pointed out by Hayes, Wheelwright, and Clark.) A lack of coordination among functional areas in a business is undesirable. If success is to be realized, people have to break down the walls and communicate.

12. *Eliminate numerical quotas for the workforce.* Deming saw it as wrong-headed to set quotas for production, because workers often sacrificed quality in the interests of meeting a quota. Quotas lead to counterproductive behaviors.

13. *Encourage education and self-improvement for everyone.* Continuous improvement as a theme also applies to the workforce. Workers should be encouraged to educate themselves and take advantage of skill-developing seminars and higher education.

14. *Take action to accomplish the transformation.* It is one thing to lay out a wish list. It is another to implement the list. Deming saw taking action as the actual charting of processes (starting with small projects) and following the Shewhart PDCA cycle: Plan-do-check-act.

Other names became important in the TQM movement:

• Walter Shewhart, a manager who worked for Western Electric, wrote the first major work on quality, *On the Economic Control of Quality.* Shewhart's cycle was popularized by Deming and is often credited erroneously to Deming.

• Joseph Juran espoused similar ideas to Deming's and was also instrumental in training Japanese companies. He coedited the massive tome *Juran's Quality Control Handbook* (1951/1988), popularized **Pareto analysis,** and made numerous contributions to the field of quality management (see Juran, 1992; Juran & Godfrey, 1999). His philosophies are organized around a trilogy: quality planning, quality control, and quality improvement. (Quality planning includes discovering the customer's needs, developing processes and process controls, and establishing quality goals. Quality control is the actual monitoring of quality. Quality improvement involves finding causes of problems and solving them.)

• Philip Crosby wrote the best-selling *Quality Is Free* (1980) and was known for introducing two quality campaigns, "Buck-a-Day" and "Zero Defects." His programs involved the cheerleading approaches that Deming found objectionable.

- Arthur Feigenbaum (1951) wrote extensively on *total quality control*. This phrase evolved into *total quality management*, although no one is credited with coming up with that expression.

- Ishikawa, a leading Japanese quality writer, is credited with inventing the "fishbone" diagram.

Lean Operations Management

A natural offshoot of the TQM movement is the "lean" movement. Lean is a systematic approach to eliminating waste *(muda*, in Japanese). It stems from the philosophy of Taiichi Ohno of Toyota, who sought to eliminate waste in inventories and processes, in movement of employees and transportation of goods, in wait time, and in production. Ohno also sought to eliminate products and services that did not fit the customer's wants and needs.

The primary goal of lean is to provide value to the customer. It does this by employing quality management tools, process analysis, and JIT (just-in-time) principles. Womack and Jones (2003) view lean as a five-step process:

1. *Specify value:* Determine what value is in the customer's eyes. What does the customer want out of the product or service? Some business travelers spend half their days in the hotel room on the computer, so naturally they will seek out hotels with free wi-fi. Hotels have had to quickly transform their rooms to accommodate the changes in technology required by their customers.

2. *Identify the value stream:* This step requires an analysis of the value added through the entire supply chain. *Muda* can be found throughout the supply chain, so a concerted effort to enforce lean thinking on all chain members is important.

3. *Flow:* Here we undergo a process analysis, looking for the most efficient way to do things. Womack and Jones (2003) encouraged breaking away from batch production where it did not make sense. They gave the example of two children assigned to process the mailing of a newsletter. The children set up an assembly line for folding, addressing, sealing, stamping, and mailing. The authors noted that this was less efficient than applying the same five steps to one envelope at a time.

4. *Pull:* An aspect of JIT production is that inventory is "pulled" by customer orders. The opposite is a push system, in which there are no actual orders and the manufacturer simply produces to stock. Push usually results in more *muda*.

5. *Perfection:* The final step is when the first four steps have succeeded in reducing *muda* to a minimum and the system operates like a well-oiled machine.

Use of the *lean* philosophy has had impressive results in reducing waste. It will be discussed further in Chapter 12, "Supply Chain Management."

The Quality Tool Kit

One reason why TQM campaigns tend to fade over time is the painstaking record keeping that is required. TQM is a discipline that tends to be discarded when a company rides a wave of success, only to be brought back if times grow lean.

We will introduce the major quality tools using the framework introduced in the process improvement section. Define, measure, analyze, improve, and control (DMAIC) is the order in which the quality tools are employed to map the way to improvement. The DMAIC process is essential in efforts to achieve Six Sigma quality, which is defined later in this chapter.

Define

A beginning point in TQM is to have the numerous processes mapped, so that all the work is being performed in as efficient a manner as possible. The flow charts and diagrams reviewed in Chapter 1 give some indication of how to proceed. Next, we need to discover what defects occur in the system, so that they can be reduced or eliminated. One method for thinking about all the possible causes of a defect uses what is known as the **fishbone diagram** (see Figure 6.1), also called the *cause-and-effect diagram*. With this method, we sort out as many possible causes as we can of problems that may arise.

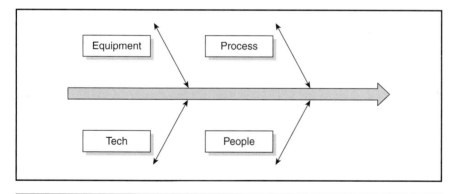

Figure 6.1   Fishbone Diagram

Working through the fishbone diagram, a team can discuss all the causes of a problem and later address them one by one. For example, let us say that the problem is that you are chronically late for work.

In analyzing this problem, start by thinking about what causes you to miss the arrival time of 8 a.m. First, a time study reveals that the average commute time is 35 min but that the commute can take as long as 50 min on a heavy-traffic day. Thus, you must leave no later than 7:10 a.m. to make it on time.

Simply by making the time study, you were able to improve your timeliness record. In the course of 10 days, you left prior to 7:10 a.m. on 7 days and after 7:10 a.m. on only 3 days. During those 3 days, you were late twice. On the 7 days when you left prior to 7:10 a.m., you were late only once, when there was an accident. Your small sample size reveals that the departure time is critically important.

If you are to leave by 7:10 a.m., you must analyze how long it takes to get ready each morning. The morning ritual consists of showering (15 min), having a cup of coffee and a light breakfast (5 min, but simultaneous to applying makeup and dressing), dressing (10 min), and applying makeup and drying hair (30 min). Finally, there are a few assorted minutes taken up with collecting the briefcase and the work for the day, writing notes to yourself, and so on (10 min). On an average day, it takes you 65 min to get out the door. The alarm is set daily for 6:15 a.m. Why is it so difficult to get out the door in 55 min? Because it takes longer than 55 min for you to get ready, that's why!

If you want to get out of the house prior to 7:10 a.m., one of two things has to happen. Either you improve on the time it takes to get ready, or you simply get up 15 min earlier each day. Maybe a haircut could cut 3 min off your hair-drying time. Of course, no one ever got a haircut simply to get to work on time, but this is an example of how a process can be analyzed to improve a problem situation. Selecting the wardrobe the night before could reduce the time it takes to match all the clothes and eliminate the need to try one thing on after another for just the right look.

A fishbone diagram lets you look at every possible cause. Why do we lose baggage? Because people are poorly trained. Why are people poorly trained? Because there is high turnover and little time. Why is there high turnover? Because the pay is too low and the baggage handlers are leaving for jobs at Target. Why is the pay too low? Because the airline is nearly bankrupt and cannot pay anyone any more. Why is the airline nearly bankrupt? Because they are paying pilots $200,000 per year to fly on 4 days a month and executives earn $20 million per year. You get the picture. The fishbone process involves asking "Why?"

The diagram is organized around five "M"s: manpower, methods, materials, machines, and measurements. The approach to each cause is to go through a cycle of five "Why?"s:

We are running out of a certain popular running shoe. Why? It is something to do with people. Why? Employees are not ordering on time. Why? They are not reading the stock reports. Why? They were never trained adequately on the reports. Why? The manager is too busy to train them. Why? The manager is overworked. The process continues until all causes have been exhausted.

Poka Yoke

Often confused with the name of a dance popular at Octoberfests, this is actually a term popularized by the Japanese quality expert Shigeo Shingo, meaning "prevent a mistake." Shingo went to great lengths to create systems that enabled him to conceive of every possible mistake that could be made by humans or machines and then find a way to prevent them all from happening.

The poka yoke process works in three steps: (1) identify the possible mistake; (2) find a way to detect that it is either taking place or about to take place; and (3) have an action plan when it occurs.

The *Lean Six Sigma Pocket Toolbook* (George, Rowlands, Price, & Maxey, 2005) lists seven steps to mistake-proofing:

1. Describe the defect and its effect on customers.

2. Identify the process step where the mistake is discovered and the step where it is created.

3. Detail the standard procedures where the defect is created.

4. Identify errors in deviation from the standard procedure.

5. Investigate and analyze the root cause for each deviation.

6. Brainstorm ideas to eliminate or detect the deviation early.

7. Create, test, validate, and implement mistake proofing devices. (pp. 233–234)

The Scatter Diagram

The scatter diagram (see Figure 6.2) is a graph that juxtaposes two variables against each other when the analyst is looking for some relationship. Perhaps you want to analyze whether there is a relationship between time of day and billing errors.

What does this chart tell you? There are an unusually high number of errors clustered around 2 p.m. Lunchtime explains the low number of errors at noon and 1 p.m. But what happens at 2 p.m.? That is what the quality analyst must find out. The scatter diagram gives a picture, but the analyst must do the interpretation. Perhaps the answer is simple. At 2 p.m., a part-time worker who is error-prone

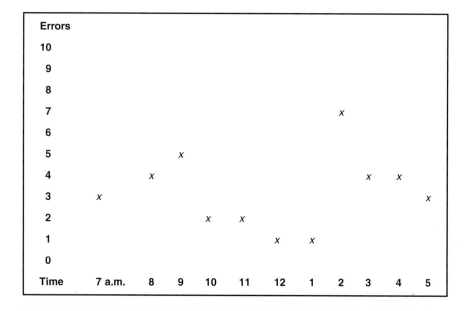

Figure 6.2   Scatter Diagram

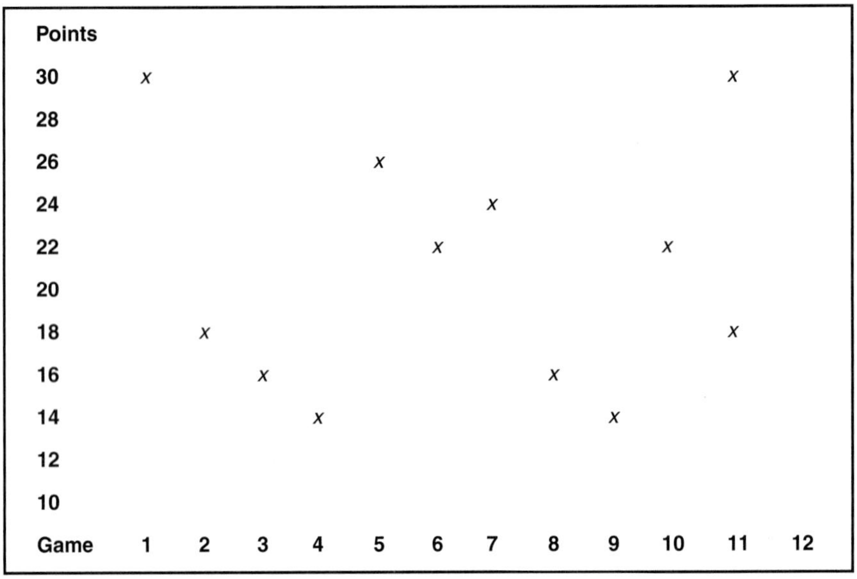

```
Points
30      x                                               x
28
26                              x
24                                  x
22                              x                   x
20
18          x                                       x
16              x                       x
14                  x                       x
12
10
Game    1   2   3   4   5   6   7   8   9   10  11  12
```

Figure 6.3   Run Chart

comes to work and immediately makes mistakes; the number of mistakes is reduced throughout the day simply because the worker's rate of processing diminishes.

Run Charts

A similar approach to examining quality problems is a run chart, which charts continuous progress through time. In this method, the analyst must determine the median of a series of numbers. In a chart of the numbers, a *run* consists of consecutive points in the same grid either above or below the median. By consulting a run chart, the analyst can decide if the patterns are normal or if there are too many runs.

Let us say that a basketball player has scored a median of 20 points per game over the past 12 games (see Figure 6.3).

There are a total of 6 runs here, that is, a series of consecutive points above the median and a series of consecutive points below the median. If there had been an occasion when this player scored exactly on the median, we would have ignored that data point. By consulting a run chart, we can see that when we have 12 points not on the median, any number of runs between 3 and 10 may be considered normal variation (Table 6.1).

What would not have been considered normal would have been one or two runs. In the case of two runs, perhaps the player scored in the first six games above 20 points and in the following six games, below 20 points. Since this is not normal, we would want to find out the cause of this change in performance. It might be simple: The player might have sprained an ankle in the seventh game and could not play as many minutes. Or it might be that he was playing against the best defensive player in the league.

Table 6.1 Run Chart Based on 10 to 25 Observations

No. of Points Not on Median	Lower Limit of Runs	Upper Limit of Runs
10	3	8
11	3	9
12	3	10
13	4	10
14	4	11
15	4	12
16	5	12
17	5	13
18	6	13
19	6	14
20	6	15
21	7	15
22	7	16
23	8	16
24	8	17
25	9	17

SOURCE: George et al. (2005, p. 121).

With 11 runs, the player is up and down during every other game. This would be considered erratic performance, and there would be reason to investigate.

Major causes of problems can be found through a method called *Pareto analysis*. The Pareto principle is that a few causes create most of your problems and if you focus on eliminating the major causes, quality will dramatically improve.

A starting point for this method is to keep a check sheet, analyzing the reasons for each defect or problem. We will use the example of lost baggage. Over a 1-week period, an airline counted 225 bags reported lost, of which 190 were later found. Logging the original reason for the missing 225 bags revealed the following causes:

Incorrect airport code (85 bags)

Wrong passenger took luggage (65 bags)

Baggage handler mistake (50 bags)

Other causes (25 bags)

With three major causes, the airline can focus on all three at once. Investigators can trace which employee is responsible for assigning the wrong airport code and either retrain that employee or send that employee to live in the wrong city. They have less control over the wrong passenger taking luggage, beyond ensuring that each bag has an identification label. (Savvy passengers have some unique identifying mark on their luggage, such as a University of Nowhere sticker or a large florescent tag.)

Every plane has its baggage sorted into destination luggage and connecting luggage, and the connecting luggage is of the highest priority, since it must make the flight. More luggage is lost because of the narrow time span between connecting flights than for any other reason. The bags usually make the next flight, but when the passenger has more than two connecting flights, the odds increase that the bags will follow the passenger in days rather than hours. This is especially true on international flights.

This example shows how a Pareto analysis helps focus on the few main causes; rather than do a complete study of every error, the quality analyst is able to narrow the field to a manageable size.

Measure and Analyze

The measurement phase of DMAIC involves constant monitoring of the process. Record keeping is essential to this step, as it shows quality over time. Reviewing the records, the quality analyst finds the flaws in the process.

Control Charts

At the heart of most quality management systems is the control chart, which shows how the process is performing. By calculating the mean of a variable, samples are plotted on the chart. Control limits are calculated as standard deviations away from the mean. They demonstrate whether or not the process is in control.

There are several control charts in common use. We will review a few major charts: the X-bar chart, the R chart, and the p chart. The X-bar charts the means, the R chart gives the ranges of observations, and the p chart gives the percentage defective.

Revisiting the Mean and Standard Deviation

Before getting into the operation of a control chart, we'll begin with a review of how to calculate the mean and the standard deviation. The mean is simply the average. Add up a series of numbers and divide by n, the number of observations.

The mean of a student's quiz scores:

Quiz scores: 89, 78, 95, 93, 88

Observations: 5

Sum of quiz scores/observations: 443/5 = 88.6

This particular student has a mean grade of 88.6.

The mean of a runner's marathon times:

Marathons: 3:47, 3:40, 3:47, 3:53, 3:34

(In a case involving hours and minutes [3:47 means 3 hr 47 min], we convert to minutes to determine the average.)

Observations: 5

Sum of marathon times/observations: 1121/5 = 224.2 min = 3:44

The average for this marathoner is 3 hr 44 min. (The 0.2 min can be converted into seconds, as 20% of a minute is 12 s.)

The Standard Deviation

The standard deviation measures variation from the mean. It pretty much tells you how consistent the data are. A baseball player who has batting averages of 0.279, 0.285, 0.276, and 0.267 would have a fairly low standard deviation, and we could approximate a fairly good forecast for future performances. Averages of 0.250, 0.317, 0.238, 0.330, and 0.259 would have a very high standard deviation, and we would probably wonder what was wrong when the batter had bad years.

A low standard deviation is more desirable because it shows consistent performance. Of course, we could have consistently bad performance, and in that situation we would try to raise the mean while maintaining consistency.

To calculate a standard deviation, the steps are as follows:

1. Calculate the mean M of X_i observations, $i = 1, \ldots, n$.

2. Calculate the standard deviation:

$$\sqrt{\frac{(X_1 - M)^2 + (X_2 - M)^2 + \ldots + (X_n - M)^2}{n - 1}}$$

Let us go back to the test scores: 89, 78, 95, 93, and 88. The mean is 88.6. The standard deviation is the square root of $\{[(89 - 88.6)^2 + (78 - 88.6)^2 + (95 - 88.6)^2 + (93 - 88.6)^2 + (88 - 88.6)^2]$ divided by 4 (5 observations minus 1)$\}$.

X-Bar Chart

With this and all charts, samples of observations are charted against the statistical mean of all the previous observations. Later in this chapter, we will discuss how to determine the sample size. Let's say we make cereal, and over thousands of samples, we find the mean weight of the boxes to be 32.0 oz. If the sample plan calls for us to measure 10 boxes every hour, we will plot the mean of the 10 boxes on the control chart. The chart has a centerline, which is for the mean, and an upper control limit (UCL) and a lower control limit (LCL). If the sample falls within the control limits, we believe that the process is in control and continue to plot samples unless there appears to be a sample outside the limits.

The implication of falling below the control limits is that we are not producing boxes that weigh enough, so we might get into trouble with the consumers. The implication of being above the control limits is that we are giving away the product.

Calculating the control limits. The equations for this step are as follows:

$$UCL = \bar{X} + A3 \text{ (standard deviation)}$$
$$LCL = \bar{X} - A3 \text{ (standard deviation)}$$

A3 is a function of sample size.

Sample Size	A3	Sample Size	A3
2	2.659	12	0.89
3	1.954	13	0.85
4	1.628	14	0.82
5	1.427	15	0.79
6	1.287	16	0.76
7	1.182	17	0.74
8	1.099	18	0.72
9	1.032	19	0.70
10	0.975	20	0.68
11	0.93		

To begin a control chart, there should be a minimum of 100 continuous observations to set a baseline mean.

Figures 6.4 and 6.5 show X-bar charts. In Figure 6.4, the process is in control because the observations fluctuate between the control limits.

In Figure 6.5, the process is out of control for four sample means, requiring an adjustment. The last six observations stay within the limits but require some monitoring to avoid another out-of-control situation.

The R Chart

The range chart, or R chart, is typically used in conjunction with the X-bar chart, because it makes it possible to arrive at a mean with a series of numbers that are wide apart.

For example, suppose an X bar was at 10, and a sample was taken that included these numbers: 20, 25, 30, 5, 6, 10, 4, 2, 2, 6.

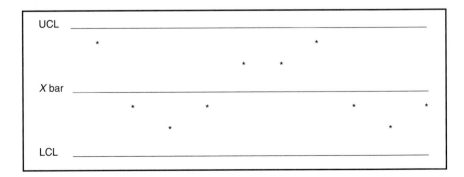

Figure 6.4   Statistical Process Control Chart

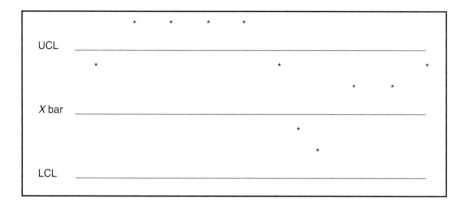

Figure 6.5   Out-of-Control Statistical Process Control Chart

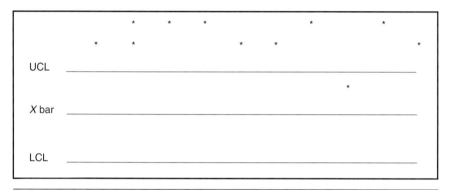

Figure 6.6   *R* Chart Example

The mean of these observations is 10, and so the plot on the *X* bar would make it appear that everything was in control. The range chart would show that the difference between the highest and lowest observations was 28. Clearly, with a mean of 10, this is not good.

In Figure 6.6, all but one observation exceed the upper control limit on this particular *R* chart. No matter what the *X*-bar chart indicates, we have a problem.

The p Chart

The percent-defective chart, or *p* chart, sets the limits on failure rates. The control limit equations are as follows ($\bar{p}$ is centerline):

$$\text{UCL} = \bar{p} + 3\sqrt{\frac{\bar{p}(1 - \bar{p})}{n}}$$

$$\text{LCL} = \bar{p} - 3\sqrt{\frac{\bar{p}(1 - \bar{p})}{n}}$$

Control limits for a $\bar{p}$ of 5 and $n = 10$ are as follows:

$$\text{UCL} = 5 + 3\sqrt{\frac{[5(4)]}{10}}$$

$$\text{LCL} = 5 - 3\sqrt{\frac{[5(4)]}{10}}$$

In Figure 6.7, the observations are all within range.

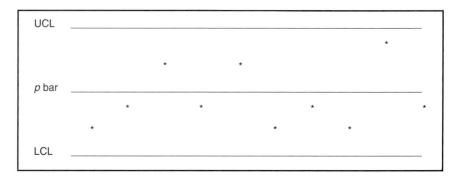

Figure 6.7   Percent-Defective Chart

Other Statistical Approaches

Beyond control charts and graphical means of interpreting data, univariate and multivariate statistics can be employed to discover the *causes* of quality problems. ANOVA (analysis of variance), regression, multiple regression, MANOVA (multivariate analysis of variance), chi-square, and factorial analysis can help determine the reasons why we have problems. Refer to statistics books for these methods.

Improve and Control: Six Sigma

In recent years, a quality program known as Six Sigma, based on achieving strict quality control limits, has become very popular. Allied Signal, General Electric, and Motorola popularized the Six Sigma quest. It is a total immersion in the statistical techniques described here, with varying levels of success awarded to managers undergoing Six Sigma training.

One of the main promoters of Six Sigma was Jack Welch, the CEO of General Electric. Welch believed strongly in the effectiveness of its quality programs and became messianic in spreading the word. For this reason, he is often credited with popularizing the concept.

Six Sigma is equivalent to 3.4 defects per million opportunities. McCarty, Daniels, Bremer, and Gupta (2005) wrote about the difference between 4.6 Sigma, which is at 99.9% quality, and 6 Sigma, which is at 99.9997% quality. Table 6.2 illustrates this difference.

These significant differences indicate why such a high level of quality is pursued.

Table 6.2   A Comparison Between 4.6 Sigma and 6 Sigma

	4.6 Sigma	6 Sigma
Wrong medical prescriptions	4,000/yr	13/yr
Newborns dropped in hospital	3,000/yr	10/yr
Long or short airplane landings	2/day	2/yr
Lost letters	400/hr	1/hr

SOURCE: McCarty et al. (2005).

Company after company has cited major cost savings attributable to their Six Sigma campaigns. McCarty and colleagues (2005) at Motorola listed a four-pronged management system for Six Sigma. Six Sigma

- Is built on the business-process model of organization structure.
- Uses a data-driven management approach based on a unique operational-measurement system.
- Is centered on a model of a high-performing, ethical leadership team.
- Applies a team-based model as its fundamental work unit. (p. 11)

Six Sigma training includes sessions for the senior leadership team, "sponsors" and "champions." This sets the important cultural tone for the embracing of the Six Sigma program. "Green belts" receive 5 to 10 days of training so that they can lead individual projects in the workplace. "Black Belts" receive 4 weeks of training, which gives them the skills to train others and lead Six Sigma improvement teams.

Typically, a Six Sigma quality project is assigned to a team led by a Black Belt. Motorola noted that when their team was assigned 11 months to complete a quality project, participants tended to lose interest in 90 days. Thus, they recommend setting up projects that can be accomplished in cycles of 4 to 6 months.

The DMAIC process is used, employing the techniques used in this chapter. A corporate "dashboard" is a display of progress in the key metrics. The review process is termed the "tollgate" review process at Motorola. Here, the success of the project and the lessons learned are reviewed.

Sampling Plans

An effective plan for sampling products and services is one that minimizes inspection while maximizing quality levels.

In sampling, we have two types of risk of error that might occur: producer's risk, which is the risk that the producer will reject a "good" lot, and consumer's risk, the risk that the consumer will accept a "bad" lot. In statistical terms, when the consumer rejects something that is good, it is a Type 1 error. If the consumer accepts a bad lot, it is considered a Type 2 error.

Assume that a manufacturer of pens samples 100 pens and finds that 8 are bad. The company's hurdle for the lot is 2% defects, and any lot exceeding that is rejected. We would see the producer's risk come into play if the actual percentage of defects in this lot was 1%; because the sample exceeded the number, the pens would have all been discarded.

On the other hand, let's say an office supply company receives 1,000 boxes and they sample 10 boxes; finding them all to be good, the company accepts the entire lot. The consumer risk is that the lot is really bad. Perhaps the defect rate is 10% in the remaining 990 boxes.

Lot tolerance percent defective is a term denoting the level of unsatisfactory quality. The acceptable quality level is defined as the *limit of satisfactory process average. Acceptance sampling* is the term for accepting or rejecting a lot that has already been produced.

ISO 9000

The ISO (International Standards Organization) 9000 is a set of worldwide quality standards that were adopted to facilitate the institution of quality standards in international trade. These standards were introduced in 1987 and quickly became a basic requirement for doing business in Europe. Companies must meet a strict set of standards to achieve ISO certification, without which they are shut out from doing business with many other businesses. There are two kinds of standards:

- Product standards—for technical specifications
- Quality system standards—for process documentation

The quality system requirements concern 20 areas of a business:

1. Management responsibility
2. Quality system
3. Contract review
4. Design control
5. Document and data control
6. Purchasing
7. Control of customer-supplied product
8. Product identification and traceability
9. Process control
10. Inspection and testing
11. Control of inspection, measuring, and test equipment
12. Inspection and test status
13. Control of nonconforming product
14. Corrective and preventive action
15. Handling, storage, packaging, preservation, and delivery
16. Control of quality records
17. Internal quality audits
18. Training
19. Servicing
20. Statistical techniques

ISO certification requires proper documentation of the processes being used in an organization. Its focus is similar to the focus of the Malcolm Baldrige Award process.

The Malcolm Baldrige National Quality Award

The Malcolm Baldrige National Quality Award was established in 1988 by the then president Ronald Reagan to award companies that achieved excellence in quality. It was imitative of the Japanese Deming Prize. To receive the Baldrige Award, companies must meet stringent criteria. The following are the 1998 Criteria for Performance Excellence from the National Institute of Standards and Technology:

1. Leadership	110 points
2. Strategic planning	80
3. Customer and market focus	80
4. Information and analysis	80
5. Human resource focus	100
6. Process management	100
7. Business results	450
Total	1,000 points

The most exciting part of the Baldrige Award is the announcement of the actual measurable results of quality—the statistical measurements provided.

European Foundation for Quality Management Award

The European Foundation for Quality Management award was introduced in 1992, with a heavy emphasis on leadership, processes, and business results. The award is very similar in scoring and intention to the United States's Baldrige Award.

The scoring breakdown for this award is as follows:

Customer satisfaction	200
Business results	150
Processes	140
Leadership	100
People management	90
Resources	90
People satisfaction	90
Policy and strategy	80
Impact on society	60

Other national quality awards of note include the Australian Quality Awards for Business Excellence, Canada's Awards for Excellence, and the Hong Kong Awards for Industry and Awards for Services.

Quality and Design

Product design is usually the domain of engineers and industrial designers. In services, it could be the domain of the marketing department or an interior design division. Operations interfaces with product and service designers by contributing ideas on how to best accomplish the operations of the company with respect to design.

Design for manufacturability (DFM) is a team-based approach to new products. The team consists of marketing, operations, and research and development representatives and a customer representative, who work together to approach a new product or service. IBM used this approach to design one of its first printers. Convinced that existing printers could be improved on, the team designed a product that was easy to build and easy to disassemble and one that customers were very happy with. Operations is always concerned with the "easy-to-build" aspect. Entire new plants are sometimes required so that new products can be built, so it is advantageous to see if there is a way to use existing facilities where possible.

Operations involvement in the design process is critical. A simple example is the 24-hr sale at a department store. Operations knows that this means more labor and this labor has to be scheduled for. Similarly, a phone line has to have increased capacity to accommodate the additional business. The TV show *American Idol* relies on enough capacity for phone lines to manage millions of phone calls in a couple of hours. If only a few phone lines were available, viewers would always get a busy signal and lose interest in calling.

Quality function deployment is similar to DFM in combining the voice of the customer with the expertise of Engineering, Marketing, and Operations to design an optimal product. A matrix called the House of Quality is used to juxtapose customer requirements against product characteristics and design targets that give a picture of the customer's needs versus the state of the product.

Each product characteristic is scored, measured for importance, and compared with the competition's product characteristics. For example, a computer mouse would have the following characteristics: easy to use, doesn't jam, and contoured to the hand. The manufacturer's mouse would be compared, one characteristic at a time, against the competition.

Conclusion

TQM may be called the core business philosophy of many organizations. Without good quality, firms will simply fail. The leading figures in the quality movement, Deming and Juran, established a framework based on measurement and analysis.

The use of graphical and statistical tools to measure quality is a basic requirement for achieving the highest quality. TQM is not simply a matter of cajoling the workforce into delivering quality results. It is the implementation and maintenance of a system that brings success in this arena of business.

Today, Six Sigma campaigns continue in many organizations, showing that the search for improved quality has not been abandoned. Although these programs vary in their degree of success, the effort should always be made to focus on making better products and providing better services.

Summary

- W. Edwards Deming is generally considered to be the founder of the quality movement, having first assisted the Japanese with their quality improvements and then spearheaded a worldwide movement to improve products and services.

- Deming made 14 points that represent his quality philosophy.

- There are many ways to define quality. Garvin offered a number of definitions, using the categories of performance, aesthetics, reliability, conformance, durability, features, and serviceability.

- Research in service quality revealed that the major attributes were tangibles: reliability, responsiveness, assurance, and empathy.

- Consumers use quality guides many times in their daily lives. We use reviews of products and of entertainment and guides to restaurants and hotels to inform our purchasing decisions. Zagat's, Mobil's, AAA's, and Fodor's are examples of such quality guides.

- Quality gaps happen when managers do not understand their customers' expectations.

- Service recovery is important to companies in establishing a quality reputation. It is the way a company responds to a mistake that customers notice.

- Lean operations use quality tools, process analysis, and JIT principles to reduce waste.

- DMAIC (design, measure, analyze, improve, and control) is the process of achieving Six Sigma.

- The tools used to analyze quality include Pareto analysis, scatter diagrams, run charts, control charts, and fishbone diagrams.

- A sampling plan guides the manager in taking a valid random sample of products, to avoid making a complete inspection.

- Most countries offer national quality awards. In the United States, the Malcolm Baldrige Award signifies the highest achievement of quality.

Key Terms

Aesthetics	Conformance
Assurance	Deming's 14 points

Durability	Quality gaps
Empathy	Reliability
Features	Responsiveness
Fishbone diagram	Service recovery
Pareto analysis	Serviceability
Perceived quality	Tangibles
Performance	

Review Questions

1. How is a scatter diagram different from a run chart?

2. What measures of quality are applied to the restaurants in your city?

3. How do you select what movies you will see?

4. What quality applications are found at your college?

5. Discus the application of quality tools with someone who uses them at work.

6. What are Deming's 14 points?

7. How does service quality differ from manufacturing quality?

Projects

1. Investigate a quality system in place at an organization. How many of the quality tools do they employ? Do they use others not listed in this chapter?

2. Find a company that does not have any quality system in place. Make suggestions about tools that may be used in that company for monitoring quality.

3. Here are some statistics about teenage driving (from www.drivehomesafe.com):

- Fourteen percent of deaths due to motor vehicle accidents occur among teenagers.

- Teen deaths due to auto accidents occur on weekends 53% of the time.

- Teen drivers killed in auto accidents had a youth passenger in the car 45% of the time.

- More than one third of teen driving fatalities are attributable to excessive speed.

- The number of teen drivers by the year 2010 will increase from the current 26.1 million to 32 million.

- The 16-year-old population in the United States will increase from 3.5 million in 2005 to 4 million in 2010.

With this information in hand, perform an analysis using the quality tools introduced in this chapter. Then, write a paper on how to improve the alarming statistics on teen driving.

4. Using the data in the Table 6.3 on voting numbers according to age and gender, perform an analysis to determine which demographics need the most attention from those interested in improving voting statistics in the United States.

5. Professor Elliott Ward, the department chairman, is interested in grade inflation. On checking the average grade point average (GPA) of graduating seniors at his university, he has detected an upward trend:

1970	2.37
1975	2.40
1980	2.60
1985	2.71
1990	2.80
1995	2.84
2000	2.87
2005	2.95

Convinced that he has an inflation problem in his own department, he first tracks all class GPAs for one semester. He intends to set up a control chart after finding the mean. His second step will be to provide incentives to students who make poor grades so as to drive the average grades down. Whatever the logic of his plan, these are the data for his semester:

2.30	2.37	2.40	2.45	2.47	2.50	2.52	2.58	2.58	2.61
2.75	2.79	2.88	2.98	3.02	3.06	3.15	3.23	3.27	3.33
3.38	3.41	3.48	3.50	3.54	3.57	3.61	3.64	3.80	3.88

a. Set up the above data with the mean and control limits.
b. How does his department compare with the 2005 mean?

6. Professor Ward decides to look for connections between grades and teaching evaluations. The evaluations below are based on a 5-point scale and correspond to the three rows above (2.30 above corresponds to 4.12 and 2.37 to 3.50, etc.):

4.12	3.50	3.76	4.09	4.32	3.89	3.65	4.40	3.65	2.90
4.09	3.54	4.34	4.50	3.76	2.37	4.43	4.20	3.98	3.65
4.45	4.76	4.65	4.76	3.87	4.87	4.59	4.63	4.88	4.84

a. Set up a scatter diagram using the grades and the evaluations.
b. Is there evidence of a connection between the two variables?

Table 6.3 Reported Voting and Registration by Sex and Age for the United States: November 2004 (in thousands)

	Total Population:	Reported Registered		Not Registered		Reported Voted		Did Not Vote		U.S. Citizen: Reported Registered	Not Registered	Not a Citizen
	No.	No.	%	No.	%	No.	%	No.	%	No.	No.	No.
All races, both sexes	215,694	142,070	65.9	73,624	34.1	125,736	58.3	89,958	41.7	142,070	54,936	18,688
18 to 24 years	27,808	14,334	51.5	13,474	48.5	11,639	41.9	16,169	58.1	14,334	10,564	2,910
25 to 44 years	82,133	49,371	60.1	32,763	39.9	42,845	52.2	39,288	47.8	49,371	21,860	10,902
45 to 64 years	71,014	51,659	72.7	19,355	27.3	47,327	66.6	23,688	33.4	51,659	15,524	3,831
65 to 74 years	18,363	14,125	76.9	4,239	23.1	13,010	70.8	5,354	29.2	14,125	3,635	604
75 years and over	16,375	12,581	76.8	3,794	23.2	10,915	66.7	5,459	33.3	12,581	3,352	442
Male	103,812	66,406	64.0	37,406	36.0	58,455	56.3	45,357	43.7	66,406	27,741	9,665
18 to 24 years	13,960	6,731	48.2	7,229	51.8	5,415	38.8	8,545	61.2	6,731	5,642	1,587
25 to 44 years	40,618	23,403	57.6	17,215	42.4	19,913	49.0	20,705	51.0	23,403	11,435	5,780
45 to 64 years	34,471	24,676	71.6	9,795	28.4	22,520	65.3	11,951	34.7	24,676	7,922	1,873
65 to 74 years	8,438	6,534	77.4	1,904	22.6	6,119	72.5	2,319	27.5	6,534	1,635	269
75 years and over	6,325	5,062	80.0	1,263	20.0	4,489	71.0	1,836	29.0	5,062	1,107	156

	No.	Total Population:								U.S. Citizen:		
		Reported Registered		Not Registered		Reported Voted		Did Not Vote		Reported Registered	Not Registered	Not a Citizen
	No.	No.	%	No.	%	No.	%	No.	%	No.	No.	No.
Female	111,882	75,663	67.6	36,219	32.4	67,281	60.1	44,601	39.9	75,663	27,195	9,024
18 to 24 years	13,848	7,603	54.9	6,245	45.1	6,224	44.9	7,624	55.1	7,603	4,922	1,323
25 to 44 years	41,515	25,967	62.5	15,548	37.5	22,932	55.2	18,583	44.8	25,967	10,425	5,123
45 to 64 years	36,544	26,984	73.8	9,560	26.2	24,807	67.9	11,737	32.1	26,984	7,603	1,957
65 to 74 years	9,926	7,591	76.5	2,335	23.5	6,891	69.4	3,034	30.6	7,591	2,000	335
75 years and over	10,049	7,519	74.8	2,531	25.2	6,426	63.9	3,623	36.1	7,519	2,245	286

SOURCE: U.S. Census Bureau (2004).
NOTE: "Not registered" includes "Did not register to vote," "Do not know," and "Not reported." "Did not vote" includes "Did not vote," "Do not know," and "Not reported."

Problems

1. The following samples were taken of employees' process times as they handled customer transactions in a financial services company.

Sample #	Transaction time (in minutes)
1	5.9
2	6.4
3	6.0
4	7.6
5	6.3
6	5.8
7	6.1
8	5.9
9	6.7
10	5.6
11	6.0
12	5.9
13	6.8
14	6.5
15	6.2
16	6.0
17	5.9
18	5.7
19	6.2

Set up an X-bar chart and an R-chart for this process. Comment on the control process.

2. Alberto monitors the monthly percentage of fraudulent credit-card use at his department store.
(Fraudulent credit-card use includes payments charged to stolen or fraudulent cards and payments
charged to cards used in identity theft.)

Month	%	Volume of transactions
January	1.3	143,000
February	0.9	88,000
March	1.0	85,000
April	1.1	83,000
May	0.8	102,000
June	0.7	109,000
July	0.7	111,000
August	0.8	106,000
September	0.8	114,000

October	0.9	94,000
November	1.1	104,000
December	1.3	190,000

What observations can be made, given this information? What possible means of action could be pursued?

3. In one week, the manager of the hotel Spaghetti Junction counts 25 reservation errors. He reviews the logs of the errors to check the causes of customer complaints:

1. Wanted no-smoking

2. Requested two beds, not one

3. Wanted concierge level

4. Wanted smoking

5. Requested one bed, not two

6. Wrong night assigned

7. Wanted no-smoking

8. Requested one bed

9. Asked for ocean view

10. Wanted no-smoking

11. Wanted four nights, got three

12. Credit card not taken

13. Requested two beds

14. Wanted no-smoking

15. Asked for business suite

16. Wanted smoking

17. Asked for ocean view

18. Got handicapped room

19. Wanted smoking

20. Credit card invalid

21. Requested one bed

22. Told no rooms available, six were

23. Wanted no-smoking

24. Wanted no-smoking

25. Wrong night assigned

Perform a Pareto analysis on the list of 25 errors. How would you group the data and what are your conclusions?

Web Sites

American Automobile Association: www.aaa.com

American Society for Quality: www.asq.org

Australian Quality Awards: www.sai-global.com/improve/awards

Canada's Awards for Excellence: www.nqi.ca

Consumer guides: www.consumerreports.com

Ebert and Roeper: www.tvplex.go.com

Edmunds auto guides: www.edmunds.com

Hong Kong Awards for Industry: www.tid.gov.hk

ISO 9000: www.iso.org

Malcolm Baldrige Award: www.quality.nist.gov

Michelin tires and travel guides: www.michelin.com

Movies, books, and music guides: www.metacritic.com

Zagat's restaurant guides: www.zagats.com

References

Berry, L. L., Zeithaml, V. A., & Parasuraman, A. (1990, Summer). Five imperatives for improving service quality. *Sloan Management Review,* 29–38.

Crosby, P. B. (1980). *Quality is free: The art of making quality certain.* New York: Mentor.

Deming, W. E. (1986). *Out of the crisis.* Cambridge: MIT Press.

Feigenbaum, A. (1951). *Quality control: Principles, practice, and administration.* New York: McGraw Hill.

Garvin, D. A. (1984). What does product quality really mean? *Sloan Management Review, 26*(1), 25–43.

George, M. L., Rowlands, D., Price, M., & Maxey, J. (2005). *The Lean Six Sigma pocket toolbook.* New York: McGraw Hill.

Juran, J. (1992). *Juran on quality by design.* New York: Free Press.

Juran, J. M. (Au.), & Gryna, F. M. (Ed.). (1988). *Juran's quality control handbook* (4th ed.). New York: McGraw-Hill. (Original work published 1951)

Juran, J. M. (Au.), & Godfrey, A. B. (Ed.). (1999). *Juran's quality handbook* (5th ed.). New York: McGraw-Hill.

McCarty, T., Daniels, L., Bremer, M., & Gupta, P. (2005). *The Six Sigma Black Belt handbook.* New York: McGraw Hill.

Shewhart, W. (1980). *On the economic control of quality.* Milwaukee, WI: American Society for Quality Control. (Original work published 1931)

U.S. Census Bureau. (2004). *Voting and registration in the election of November, 2004.* Retrieved August 11, 2008, from www.census.gov/population/www/socdemo/voting/cps2004.html

Womack, J. P., & Jones, D. T. (2003). *Lean thinking.* New York: Free Press.

CHAPTER 7

Sustainable Operations

SOURCE: © sweetym/istockphoto.com

Learning Objectives

In this chapter, we will

- Study the philosophy of sustainable development
- Review the need for a triple bottom line
- Determine the major operations management concerns for air pollution, water pollution, and energy needs
- Study the sustainability efforts in operations management

Why Be Green?

The planet has taken abuse for centuries from the human race, machines, and factories. As society has advanced, so have the problems of pollution. This chapter has the basic premise that Operations must make every effort to operate in a clean environment. Operations managers must take the philosophy that we are managing today as if tomorrow mattered. A hole in the ozone layer created by aerosol sprays used for household products is symptomatic of the problems we face. Operations management is very critical to the sustainability efforts of modern business, as it is the business function that consumes the most resources.

In manufacturing organizations, limiting the pollutants in the air, preserving the purity of the water, and limiting the waste of unused resources is of primary concern. The operations managers in manufacturing have a critical role in the control of resources that are spent. Manufacturing consumes water and energy more than any other part of the organization. Similarly, the operations functions in services such as hotels, hospitals, and restaurants have the most impact on resource allocation. Hospitals must be concerned about their hazardous and toxic waste disposal. Hotels must be concerned about their water usage, particularly in laundry services. The employees of all firms contribute to air pollution simply by driving their cars to work. With the opportunity for tremendous cost savings at stake, operations managers need to study methods of conservation. This chapter will discuss the critical environmental issues for operations management. It is intended as an introduction to the relationship between the environment and businesses, with an emphasis on the operations interface (see Table 7.1). Operations management must partake in sustainable practices not only for the benefit of their employers but also for the sake of the planet.

Table 7.1   Operations and the Environment: Interfaces

Topic	Issue
Quality management	Involves the reduction of waste
Inventory management	Involves minimization of inventory and encourages recycling of materials
Human resource management	Encourages use of public transportation
Facilities location	Construction of green buildings
	Minimization of transportation time
	Use of employee public transportation
Facilities layout	Minimization of waste
	Energy conservation
Forecasting	Minimizes waste
Supply chain management	Reverse supply chain
	Lean operations
	JIT and pollution

Sustainable Development

SOURCE: © José Luis Gutiérrez/istockphoto.com

The term **sustainable development** means that society and businesses must meet their present needs while keeping in mind the needs of future generations. An example of how thinking has changed is found in the "dirty" industries such as chemicals, mining, and oil and gas. In the past, companies within these industries tended to go into a remote region to seek their resources and when the resources were depleted, would simply move on to some new region. Sustainable development requires a rethinking. Now, firms must consider the welfare of the indigenous population in the area where they hope to mine, dig, or open a factory. This means building a health and educational system to accommodate the local citizenry long after the firm closes its doors. Mines get depleted. However, a community remains. In the past, these communities were left to fend for themselves and usually suffered serious poverty and health concerns.

Challenges to sustainability differ from developed economies to emerging and survival economies (see Table 7.2). Survival economies struggle to make ends meet and don't have the means and wherewithal to devote efforts to reduction in pollution.

The Triple Bottom Line

A way of looking at business other than the traditional bottom line is to evaluate success according to the **triple bottom line**: economic prosperity, environmental quality, and social justice. Elkington (2001) set forth ways to measure the bottom lines for environmental quality and social justice.

For environmental issues and indicators, he included the following:

- Legal compliance
- Provisions for fines, insurance, and other legally related costs

Table 7.2 Major Challenges to Sustainability

	Pollution	Depletion	Poverty
Developed economies	Greenhouse gases Use of toxic materials Contaminated sites	Scarcity of materials Insufficient reuse and recycling	Urban and minority unemployment
Emerging economies	Industrial emissions Contaminated water Lack of sewage treatment	Overexploitation of renewable resources Overuse of water for irrigation	Migration to cities Lack of skilled workers Income inequality
Survival economies	Dung and wood burning Lack of sanitation Ecosystem destruction due to development	Deforestation Overgrazing Soil loss	Population growth Low status of women Dislocation

SOURCE: Hart (1997).

- Landscaping
- Abandonment costs
- Emergency and contingency plans
- Life-cycle impacts of products
- Energy, materials, and water usage at production sites
- Potentially polluting emissions, environmental hazards, and risks
- Waste generation
- Consumption of critical natural capital
- Performance against best-practice standards set by leading customers and by green and ethical investment funds.

Operations management is most involved with energy consumption, waste generation, and consumption of natural capital, from this list. Abandonment costs are a facility relocation or downsizing issue for Operations. In many industries, the plant managers must be aware of Environmental Protection Agency (EPA) standards, to reach legal compliance.

Environmental Impact Analysis

When considering possible locations for plants, an important step is the **environmental impact analysis.** The World Bank has categorized these projects into three groups:

Category A projects have significant environmental impact and require intense analysis. Projects that change a local ecosystem or involve resource deployment are classified as Category A.

Category B projects have minor impact and require less scrutiny.

Category C projects do not have adverse environmental impacts.

The assessment includes the impact on local biology; the impact on the atmosphere, water, and earth; the cultural impact in the local community and economy; and the impact on resources, recreation, and conservation.

Operations and Waste

Efforts to have lean operations, with reduced waste or *muda*, are emblematic of environmentally conscious decisions. Garbage should be carefully sorted and recycled. The automobile industry recycles a great percentage of its materials, which turn up in new cars. The same is not true of the personal computer industry.

The reverse supply chain is the mode of transporting damaged or unwanted goods back to a manufacturer. Attention should be given here to having an environmentally sound policy. How are defective products recycled or disposed of? Product design should include cradle-to-grave thinking; that is, what happens to the product when it becomes obsolete?

Operations and the Air

There are many interfaces between operations management and air pollution. In manufacturing, the energy used to cool and heat the plant should be closely monitored. One facility location issue is the energy requirements to run a plant. Service organizations also have to consider their energy usage. A hotel has individual thermostats for room temperature that the guests can control if they wish. However, the spacious lobbies and ballrooms are controlled by hotel management and need to be closely monitored.

Facility planners must consider how the employees will actually get to work. Proximity to public transportation is a definite asset for a company's location. This reduces the cars on the streets. Finally, astute supply chain management reduces the number of trucks and deliveries. Just-in-time (JIT) becomes increasingly expensive when considering the fuel costs necessary to pull it off. Future considerations on the benefits of carrying some inventory to reduce shipments may make some trade-offs necessary in production.

The Air: Global Warming and Climate Changes

Operations managers may feel that they have little impact on the environment, no matter what they do. Society cannot afford to take a casual attitude toward the pollution of the environment, and the operations function does play an important role. Scientists have alerted politicians of the dangers of air pollution. The greenhouse effect is the warming of the earth's atmosphere. There has been some debate on whether or not this is truly occurring. Climate researchers appointed by the

United Nations argued that it was and predicted a 2°C increase in the next century. The two primary causes of global warming are the rise in levels of carbon dioxide in the atmosphere and global deforestation. Carbon dioxide levels have risen from 315 parts per million in 1957 to 368 parts per million in 1999. Eighty-two percent of the carbon dioxide level can be attributed to human factors. The United States alone produces 25% of the carbon dioxide emissions.

There are pros and cons of global warming. If you live in the Great Lakes Region of the United States or Scandinavia, the idea of a warmer winter does not seem so bad. There actually are a number of positive effects.

Positive Effects of Global Warming

The following are the positive effects of global warming:

1. Heating costs are reduced in colder climates, as demand decreases for fossil fuel.

2. Population can shift to colder climates (i.e., Wyoming and Montana).

3. Increased rainfall in some areas gives them more opportunity to increase agricultural output.

4. Crop yields of rice, corn, and wheat may increase.

Harmful Effects of Global Warming

The following are some of the harmful effects of global warming:

1. Summer cooling demand will increase, offsetting the cost gains in reduced heating.

2. Melting of the polar ice caps will increase the sea levels. Coastal properties will be damaged as the coastline shrinks. Cities in danger include the Eastern Corridor of the United States (New York City, Washington, D.C., Boston) and Miami and New Orleans.

3. Rice in lower-coastal-plain areas such as China and Pakistan will be destroyed by floods.

4. The rise in sea levels will increase the damage caused by hurricanes and tropical storms.

5. Droughts in the Great Plains could trigger dust storms like those in the Great Depression.

6. Fish and game in freshwater estuaries would be diminished by salt water.

7. Many plants and animals would become extinct.

8. Health problems would increase with floods and droughts.

9. It would have a major economic impact, causing some winners, some losers. (Chiras, Reganold, & Owen, 2002, pp. 509–510)

Table 7.3   Energy End-Use Sector Sources of U.S. Carbon Dioxide Emissions, 1990–2001

Sector	Million Metric Tons Carbon Equivalent		Percentage of Change	
	1990	2001	1990–2001	2000–2001
Residential	257.5	314.9	22.3	−1.0
Commercial	212.6	279.7	31.5	1.9
Industrial	458.0	452.4	−1.2	−5.4
Transportation	431.4	511.6	18.6	0.8

SOURCE: www.eia.doe.gov

The reduction in industrial use in Table 7.3 may be partially explained by the outsourcing of manufacturing to other countries. Increases in residential and commercial use are partially explained by demographic shifts into the Sunbelt and warmer climates that require more air conditioning. Transportation increases in this period are probably reflective of a relatively stable price of gasoline. However, by 2005, the increasing price of fuel could result in a decline in the carbon dioxide equivalents for transportation. When the price of gasoline becomes exorbitant, people seek more fuel-efficient vehicles or alternative modes of transportation.

The Water: Pollution, Drinking Water, and the Seas and Lakes

The major issues concerning water for operations management are as follows:

How do we conserve it?

How do we avoid polluting it?

How do we protect the purity of our drinking water?

In the United States, 70% of water is used in agriculture. Water is usually treated by industry as an inexhaustible commodity. Firms that have major water needs are the first to seek means to reduce usage. In hotels, asking guests to forgo washing their linen unless requested can result in significant water savings, since it has the effect of cutting water use by one third.

The city of Albuquerque, New Mexico, set a goal of reducing water consumption by 30% in 1994 and met the goal by 2004, dropping from 250 gallons per capita per day to 177 in that time period. Residential customers consumed 50% of the water in the city because the city is high desert and there is limited agriculture. One way the city reduced water consumption was by giving incentives for converting lawn landscaping to xeriscape, which does not require nearly the same amount of water to survive. Businesses were offered $5,000 incentives and residential customers $800. Customers who converted to low-flow toilets received rebates of $125 per toilet. Those who changed from high-water-use washing machines to low-water-use machines were also given rebates (www.cabq.gov).

One of the issues concerning water shortages is simply that water is scarce in some regions and plentiful in others; so how do we borrow from the rich to feed the poor? The California Water Project (CWP) is an example of a water diversion project, using a number of dams, reservoirs, and pumping plants to transport water from the northern parts of the state to the dry south.

Water Pollution

Polluted water poses a serious health risk to humans. It is a critical issue for organizations that they have pure water to operate with and not pollute their outgoing water flows. The most common pollutant of water is soil erosion. Sediment may enter the water by natural means, or it can be pushed into the water by construction or mining. Sediment can carry pesticides into the water and can be harmful to fish.

Nutrient pollution, which comes from fertilizers, sewage, and livestock wastes, can make a lake look and smell like a sewer, taking away its recreational value. Thermal pollution, caused by power, chemical, and steel companies, is deadly to fish populations.

The following extract highlights the importance of clean water:

> If you live in a densely populated area, the last glass of water you drank may already have passed through the bodies of eight other people living upstream from you. Of course, it has been cleansed over and over again after each use. (Chiras et al., 2002, p. 262)

In the United States, the EPA is responsible for safe drinking water. The EPA established many regulations, banned lead pipes, and was vigilant about water standards. Operations managers should take care that their companies do not carelessly pollute the water supply.

In many industries, water is a key ingredient in production. Thus, it is critical not only that the water that goes into manufacturing is clean but that the company is responsible for its waste so that it does not contaminate the local drinking water. In hospitals, water consumption is a big expense, and environmental services are responsible for its safety.

Conservation: Waste and Recycling

Operations management can have a major impact on an organization's efforts at resource conservation, waste reduction, and recycling. A new effort in product design has been called **Design for the Environment** (DFE). In DFE, manufacturers must consider the ultimate disposal of the product after its useful life expires. Where are the Apple II PCs, the Epson printers, and the Compaq portable computers of the early 1980s? Where do we park useless exercise equipment? Garage sales are full of rowing machines, abdominal crunchers, and Bowflex machines. Where do they go when people tire of them? Is there an island somewhere in the South Pacific, the Island of Useless Computers and Exercise Equipment?

Hewlett-Packard's efforts to recycle ink cartridges are emblematic of this effort. A used ink cartridge should not go in your garbage, nor should used motor oil.

Green Buildings

When confronted with building a new facility, a company should consider its environmental impact. Although it is by no means a requirement for production, the state of the art for facilities is a design that has achieved **Leadership in Energy and Environmental Design (LEED) certification**, a designation for environmental standards established by the U.S. Green Building Council (USGBC). The LEED designation has gained increasing popularity as a means of showing good environmental citizenship.

LEED standards are available for new commercial construction, existing buildings, commercial interior projects, core and shell projects, and homes and neighborhood development. A checklist to make a building qualified as LEED certified is provided in Table 7.4.

The USGBC was created for the following purposes:

- To define "green building" by establishing a common standard of measurement
- To promote integrated, whole-building design practices
- To recognize environmental leadership in the building industry
- To stimulate green competition
- To raise consumer awareness of green building benefits
- To transform the building market (www.usgbc.org)

The LEED standards give an indication of what the certifiers consider important. Ten points are awarded for optimizing energy. The company that gets all 10 points here is already more than 25% toward attaining certification. Also scoring high is optimizing the use of alternative materials (5 points) and innovation in operation and upgrades (4 points).

The reduced costs of energy help reduce overall production costs. A LEED-certified building is going to be a more comfortable building. It is obviously easier to build a LEED-certified facility than it is to retrofit an existing building.

ISO 14001

The International Standards Organization, which administers the ISO 9000 quality certification program, is also involved in an environmental certification program, **ISO 14001**. The LEED standards are similar to the types of records a company must keep if they hope to attain the certification. The value of the certification is that it proves a company's commitment to the environment. This is not only a sign of acting in the public interest but also a sign that usually is correlated with the offering of quality products. Companies that take the time and care to certify in both ISO standards are sending the signal that they have well-thought-out standards and processes in getting their products to the marketplace.

Table 7.4   LEED—Existing Building Project Checklist

Sustainable sites	14 possible points
Water efficiency	5 possible points
Energy and atmosphere	23 possible points
Materials and resources	16 possible points
Indoor environmental quality	22 possible points
Innovation in operation, upgrades, and maintenance	5 possible points
Project totals	80 possible points plus 5 for innovations in operations and upgrades
Certified	32–39 points
Silver	40–47 points
Gold	48–63 points
Platinum	64–85 points

Energy

The major sources of energy are oil, coal, and natural gas. These forms are called "nonrenewable" because they cannot be reused. Since oil constitutes the largest component of our energy consumption, there is a worldwide concern about its availability, and moves are on to find alternative sources of energy.

Nuclear energy, derived from uranium, was once considered to be a future energy replacement for oil. However, several accidents, such as Three Mile Island in the United States and Chernobyl in Ukraine, alerted the public to what can happen if there is a nuclear accident.

At Three Mile Island, a failed valve caused radioactive steam to escape from the plant and threaten the community. Fifty thousand people evacuated the area, and it is uncertain, since the event happened in 1979, if there is a lasting effect.

At Chernobyl, Ukraine, in 1986, an explosion killed 31 workers and 237 people suffered acute radiation poisoning. A total of 135,000 people not only were evacuated but also had to be permanently relocated by the government. The damages were estimated at 5 billion U.S. dollars. But the damage to the industry was permanent. The public viewed the risks of an accident to outweigh any benefits the energy form might have.

Renewable energy sources include solar energy, hydropower, and wind power. Electricity can be harnessed from the sun through the use of solar panels that capture the sun's rays and can provide heating for a house or building, plus heat the water.

Hydropower, energy harnessed from rivers, provides 10% of the United States' total electricity. According to Chiras et al. (2002), it offers desirability because it is inexpensive and pollution free. But it is not without disadvantages. Sediment tends to collect and diminish the life of dams, which can last anywhere from 10 to 200 years, depending on the sediment problem. Dams also destroy the scenic beauty of canyons. Lake Powell in Utah and Arizona filled the canyon, which had been on a par with the Grand Canyon for scenic beauty. Today, it is possible to view the beauty only if you have a boat, and then all you can see is the top of the canyon. Imagine the Grand Canyon filled to near its crest!

Wind power is the fastest-growing form of electricity. This energy is free and clean, and renewable. The cost to generate electricity from wind is comparable to that of coal. The negative side of wind power? Some would argue windmills are an eyesore on the landscape. They can also be hazardous to birds.

Company Environmental Efforts

Wal-Mart

Wal-Mart Stores, Inc., made a major investment in environmentally conscious building design with its facility in McKinney, Texas. The store has a number of environmental features:

- The roof of the store collects rainwater for irrigating the grounds.
- The store generates electricity from photovoltaic cells in the skylights.
- It employs energy-efficient light-emitting-diode lighting.
- It uses radiant floor heating produced by burning waste oil from the garage and cooking oil from the kitchen.
- It evenly distributes cool air via fabric ducts, a method saving enough electricity for 70 homes.

Wal-Mart will add a second store with the same configuration in Colorado. The building's designers also designed a green office building for Toyota Motor Company.

Starbucks

Starbucks sells water called "Ethos," with a percentage of the profits going to efforts for clean drinking water across the world.

General Electric

General Electric launched a campaign that it calls Ecoimagination, which includes a $1.5 billion investment into clean technologies, and committed to a reduction in greenhouse gas emissions from its products.

Ford Motor Company

Ford's Web site (www.ford.com) offers extensive information about their environmental efforts. They classify "Environment" within the section "Good Works," and they include information about "clean manufacturing, air and climate, recycling, and nature and wildlife."

Here is what they say about the efforts to make their Canadian plant in Windsor more environmentally friendly:

The Ford Model U Concept is a realistic approach to the future, guided by a powerful, positive vision that follows in the traditions of the Model T by being designed for the masses and addressing social issues, specifically environmental concerns. The Model U represents how using and producing personal transportation can have a positive effect on the planet instead of simply minimizing negative effects.

The Model U is helping encourage development of materials that are safe to produce, use, and recycle over and over again in a cradle-to-cradle cycle. These materials never become waste, but instead are nutrients that either feed healthy soil or the manufacturing processes without moving down the value chain.

Toyota

Toyota, the manufacturer of the popular hybrid, Prius, devotes several pages on its Web site to its environmental efforts in manufacturing. Toyota has sold 150,000 of its energy-saving model, the Prius, as of July 2005. According to Toyota's Web site, besides offering state-of-the-art emission controls in its automobiles, the company recycles 99% of its scrap metal, and it also recycles plastics, paint solvents, oil, and packaging. Its vehicles are 85% recyclable. Toyota is able to recycle foam, copper, and bumpers. Toyota's Kentucky plant recycles more than 100,000 tons per year and 45,000 light bulbs per year. Apparently, they employ people to count light bulbs! The New United Motor Manufacturing, Inc. (NUMMI), a joint venture with General Motors, recycles more than 175,000 gallons of solvent each year (www.toyota.com).

Green Hotels

The Green Hotel Association is an organization dedicated to environmentally sensitive hotels. On its Web site, www.greenhotels.com, it lists a number of energy-saving ideas for hotels and individuals. Some examples include a Toronto hotel that recycles stained tablecloths as napkins. Bicycles in some hotels are rented or loaned as alternative transportation. One Pennsylvania hotel grows its own vegetables on the property.

All industries, whether in manufacturing or services, have to deal with environmental concerns in the coming years. Companies must do so not only for competitive reasons but also for the very survival of the planet. As the future generation of operations managers, today's students must be cognizant of the environmental impact of their decisions.

Summary

1. Operations managers are key individuals in environmental management, with location, layout, and supply chain areas key to this process.

2. Sustainable development means to manage as if tomorrow matters to the company, and to the world.

3. The triple bottom line is a philosophy that recognizes the needs for social and environmental considerations in conjunction with economic decision making.

4. An environmental impact analysis is a preliminary step in locating a new plant.

5. Lean operations are examples of waste reduction and conservation.

6. The reduction in facility air pollution contributes in a small but important way to the reduction of air pollution in the area.

7. Similarly, the prudent consumption of water is an operational issue of importance.

8. LEED provides certification for environmentally sound buildings.

Key Terms

Design for the environment (DFE)

Environmental impact analysis

ISO 14001

Leadership in Energy and Environmental Design (LEED) certification

Sustainable development

Triple bottom line

Review Questions

1. What is meant by the term *sustainable development*?

2. How do the challenges to sustainability differ by national economies?

3. Discuss Hart's "sustainability portfolio."

4. How does poverty influence facility location decisions?

5. How does operations management interface with environmental issues?

6. What is the triple bottom line?

7. Give examples of products "designed for the environment."

8. How does a building earn LEED certification?

9. What are some of the features of Ford's environmental program?

Projects

1. Find a LEED-certified building and visit with the managers of the facility. How has the building increased productivity compared with the output in the previous facility?

2. Discuss a hotel's efforts to meet the standards established by Greenhotels.com.

3. How involved in environmental issues is your local community?

Web Sites

www.ford.com

www.greenhotels.com

www.toyota.com

www.usgbc.org

References

Chiras, D. D., Reganold, J. P., & Owen, O. S. (2002). *Natural resource conservation* (8th ed.). Upper Saddle River, NJ: Prentice Hall.

Elkington, J. (2001). Cannibals with forks: "The triple bottom line" for 21st century business. In R. Starkey & R. Welford (Eds.), *Business and sustainable development* (pp. 20–46). Sterling, VA: Earthscan.

Hart, S. L. (1997). Beyond greening: Strategies for a sustainable world. *Harvard Business Review, January–February,* 66–76.

PART II

Planning

CHAPTER 8

Forecasting and Aggregate Planning

SOURCE: © Skip O'Donnell/istockphoto.com

Learning Objectives

In this chapter, we will

- Study qualitative methods of forecasting
- Review methods of quantitative forecasting, including moving averages, exponential smoothing, and seasonal methods of forecasting
- Study methods of calculating forecasting error
- Review approaches to aggregate operations planning
- Discover how capacity must be considered in planning
- Learn about yield management techniques

Why Should Operations Managers Forecast?

Forecasting is an important tool for the operations manager. Two business functions are most involved in formulating forecasts: marketing and operations. The marketing department makes a demand forecast for the coming periods. Operations then sets a production forecast: How many products will we actually make? The production forecast provides information on staffing, equipment, and supply needs and delivery lead times for customers. Although forecasts are rarely perfect, the *process* of forecasting is an important step in successfully matching staff and supplies with demand.

Marketing forecasts tend to be optimistic in an effort to give high goals for the sales associates to shoot for. A production manager cannot assume that a marketing forecast will be correct. The production manager schedules production by taking the actual customer orders and the forecast into account.

Take the past several years of sales into account for a manufacturer of kitchen sinks:

Year	Sales	% Increase
2004	4,560	11.3
2005	4,700	3.1
2006	4,311	−8.3
2007	4,509	4.6

Confronted with this information, the vice president of marketing would probably tell the sales staff that in 2008 they must sell as many as 5,000 kitchen sinks. It is the sales executive's job to motivate and drive the sales staff to increase sales. However, they can't force customers to buy, and sometimes there are competing products on the market that eat away at the market share. This usually optimistic projection is passed on to the president, and the company budgets to sell that many.

The company does not want to be caught at the end of the year with unsold sinks, as models even in kitchen sinks tend to change with fashion. They want to produce exactly what they will sell. Thus, the production manager must balance the marketing forecast against the actual placed orders to make a plan.

They could gather more information based on the patterns formed:

Year	Sales	% Increase
2000	3,976	6.0
2001	4,302	8.2
2002	4,108	−4.5
2003	4,000	−2.6

Two down years followed a gain in 2001, and then increases in 2004 and 2005 were followed by a 2006 decline and a rebound in 2007 (for years 2004–2007 see table above).

There may be other factors worth examining. After all, new kitchen sinks are installed in new homes, so data on housing starts in the region would be helpful to know. It could be the overall economy, the Dow Jones Industrial Average, who knows?

But experienced operations managers have to look at sales forecasts critically and act conservatively in their estimates. They know the lead time of production, and if sales increase, they can step up production.

Predicting the number of airline customers is handled in a similar way. There are a number of variables that influence airline travel: the cost of fuel, for example. When fuel prices rise, people tend to travel less. When airfares increase as a result of fuel price increases, air travelers decline still more. Air travel is related to average price per airline ticket and the price for certain routes. Airlines sometimes offer special deals to certain locations, and they don't make any money on these deals. What they do is keep people flying, even if the airlines are only making pennies on the flight. Without people in the air, they will go broke.

So, we have a crew of people who must predict how many passengers they will get and plan the number of flights to certain cities based on these projections. If the numbers shrink too much, they will cut flights. If a competitor enters a certain route market, it will cut into their business, so they have to watch the customer's price and the success of the routes.

There are infinite methods of forecasting for the operations manager to choose from, and the rule of thumb is that it does not matter what method you use so long as you are right. A very successful stock market forecaster once used earthquake information to predict the market. His customers did not care how he came out with his predictions, because he was more often right than anyone using traditional methods. Whether you use a dartboard or consult with a psychic, no one will care so long as you are correct.

This chapter outlines traditional forecasting methods and methods of calculating forecasting error. A forecast usually begins with historical data so that the forecaster can be cognizant of any patterns that exist; that is, is the demand seasonal or following a trend?

Qualitative Methods

Some forecasts are prepared without mathematical analysis and are done by talking to either experts or customers. These nonmathematical methods are called **qualitative forecasts.** Marketing research is a qualitative method of forecasting. A company desires an estimate of how a product will fare in the market, so it selects a focus group or a specific demographic and either conducts a product test or constructs a questionnaire to get some idea of the potential success.

New-product introductions are the most difficult to forecast since there is no demand history. The best method in these cases is to mirror the patterns of similar products. If we are introducing a new cookie for which taste testers have given the seal of approval, we should look at the demand patterns of the last new cookie that had a successful reception. Once the new cookie has its own demand pattern, we can use quantitative methods.

Focus groups can be helpful with new products if they are carefully selected to represent the demographic the product is aimed for. Automobile manufacturers spend a lot of money on research on existing cars and future cars. When a customer purchases a car, the manufacturers want to know what demographic the buyer came from. Perhaps a car they intended for males between 19 and 29 years turns out to be purchased in larger numbers by females between 30 and 39 years. Then, they must learn why.

When anticipating the release of a new automobile, the market researchers will bring in thousands of people to look it over and say whether it compares with existing cars and what the chances are that they might buy it.

Motion picture companies test market their films, sometimes even changing the endings or elements of the film after public reaction. There are certain communities that reflect the national demographic they are looking for, so they will select those markets for the test.

There are times when movies may fail in the United States but find a huge audience in foreign markets. "Troy," with Brad Pitt, is an example. It made $133 million in the United States but $364 million in global markets. What does not sell in Peoria, Illinois, may be a hit in Taipei, Taiwan.

Another qualitative method is to involve consultants or experts. Rather than conducting extensive market research, a shortcut might be to ask the industry experts. The **Delphi method** is a process in which a number of experts are asked their opinions in an iterative fashion. If the Delphi method were used in subjective gymnastics scoring, it would work like this:

1. The gymnast performs his or her routine.

2. The judges make their scores.

3. The judges review each other's scores.

4. The routine is examined again via replay.

5. The judges offer their corrected scores.

In the Delphi process, the forecaster reviews the opinions of others and makes changes in his or her own forecast based on these opinions.

Every week in the United States, we have football prognosticators (forecasters) who predict who will win every game. If they were to use the Delphi method, it would probably change some of the predictions. If eight forecasters chose the Green Bay Packers to beat the Cleveland Browns, and two favored the Cleveland Browns, the second round might find one or both of the predictors changing their predictions.

Ultimately, the market forecast without any historic data is just a guess, but an understanding of similar products in similar times may aid the forecaster in coming up with a very close approximation to reality. For example, if a comedy is due to be released the same weekend as two action movies and the test reaction to this comedy is very positive, it can be assured a certain market if it has no other comedy movie to compete with for a few weeks. So the sales team can estimate the audience by looking at prior periods in which two action movies competed with a romantic comedy in the same weekend. The "trailer" or the advertisement for the movie sometimes shows only the good things that happen in a truly awful movie, but they are enough to lure in a wide audience until the word-of-mouth kills the demand. Often, the distributors have already expected a decline in sales for the second weekend.

Quantitative Methods

Moving on to forecasting models that use mathematical approaches to estimate demand, the most important consideration is to understand the pattern of data and have a certain amount of history available. There are many models to choose from. The forecaster tries to pick the right one. A forecasting program with multiple models that switches to the model that is currently doing the best job is a helpful forecasting tool. As soon as another model becomes superior, the focused forecast will switch models.

One statistical approach to making forecasts is **linear regression,** used when the forecaster believes there is a causal variable that can predict the outcome. The equation for linear regression is

$$Y = a + bX,$$

where

Y = the dependent variable to be predicted,

a = the y-axis intercept,

b = the slope of the regression line, and

X = the independent variable used to predict Y.

The slope, b, is found with the equation

$$b = \frac{\Sigma XY - n\bar{X}(\bar{Y})}{\Sigma X^2 - n\bar{X}^2}.$$

Linear regression fits a line to a set of points that minimizes the squares of the distance between the line and each data point.

A simple illustration: Let us say that you believe there is a way to predict your next year's salary according to the number of years worked. Since you are trying to predict salary, Y is the dependent variable, salary, and X is the number of years worked.

Therefore, if

$$Y = 39.57 + 4.83X,$$

we plug in the year number to make a prediction for the year's salary (see Table 8.1):

$$Y = 39.57 + 4.83(12) = 97.53$$
$$Y = 39.57 + 4.83(13) = 102.36$$
$$Y = 39.57 + 4.83(14) = 107.19$$

Table 8.1   A Linear Regression to Predict Future Salary

Year (X)	Salary (Y)	XY	X^2	Y^2
1	48	48	1	2,304
2	51	102	4	2,601
3	54	162	9	2,916
4	54	216	16	2,916
5	58	290	25	3,364
6	68	408	36	4,624
7	75	525	49	5,625
8	82	656	64	6,724
9	84	756	81	7,056
10	87	870	100	7,569
11	93	1,023	121	8,649
Totals				
66	754	5,056	506	59,404

$\bar{X} = 6.0$
$\bar{Y} = 68.55$
$b = 4.83$
$a = \bar{Y} - b(\bar{X}) = 68.55 - 28.98 = 39.57$

Another example here are the enrollment figures for a university:

Year	Enrollment	Year	Enrollment
1990	14,000	2005	22,800
2001	20,300	2006	23,200
2002	21,600	2007	24,800
2003	21,200	2008	26,100
2004	21,400		

From 2001 to 2008, there was enrollment growth; in 1 year, there was a slight decline in enrollment. Eventually, the university will have to consider capacity issues, if it has not already done so.

X	Y	XY	X^2	Y^2
1	20.300	20.300	1	412.09
2	21.600	43.200	4	466.56
3	21.200	63.600	9	449.44
4	21.400	85.600	16	457.96
5	22.800	114.000	25	519.84
6	23.200	139.200	36	538.24
7	24.800	173.600	49	615.04
8	26.100	208.800	64	681.21

Usually, more than one variable is the key to prediction. If you were to predict the population for 2010 in Macon, Georgia, a starting point would be to examine the census for 1980 and 1990. Other important indicators would be unemployment, rate of housing increases, and overall economic health. Trying to combine so many factors in one causal model is not practical. Therefore, multiple regression and other forms of multivariate statistical analysis make more sense.

Time Series Forecasting

Forecasters typically deal with a **time series**—the collection of data points through time. These data points are analyzed for pattern, which can be cyclical, seasonal, or based on some trend. This method of forecasting is dependent on these patterns as the forecaster tries to best match the pattern. Demand might peak every 6 months for some reason. Then there is a rapid decline. This would call for a seasonal forecasting tool.

Perhaps in every 4th year there is a rise in demand for hotels due to a conference that meets in the city on a 4-year cycle. The forecaster would need to use a cyclical method.

Or, maybe, there is a steadily advancing trend coupled with a seasonal pattern. Again, a different model would be applied. One forecasting method does not fit all situations, and the forecaster has to choose the one that works the best for the specific requirement.

Moving Averages

To illustrate a very simple forecasting method, the moving average is a way to predict the next data point. A forecast is made by averaging a number of periods to predict the next period:

January	February	March	April
25	37	41	?

Assume that this is a three-period average. April's forecast would be the average of the first 3 months, 103/3 = 34.3. If the actual demand in April were 47, we would forecast for May by dropping January and averaging the most recent 3 months:

February	March	April	May
37	41	47	? = 125/3 = 41.7

There appears to be an upward trend, and by using a moving average we will continue to lag the demand.

Weighted Moving Average

If the forecaster wanted to assign weights, making the most recent forecast the most important, a three-period forecast with weights would go like this:

January	February	March	April
(0.2)	(0.3)	(0.5)	?
25	37	41	

April = 5 + 11.1 + 20.5 = 36.6.

Again, this method lags the trend, but by weighting the most recent month the highest, we get a closer approximation.

Since this is a moving average, we would move the weights accordingly:

February	March	April	May
(0.2)	(0.3)	(0.5)	?
37	41	47	

May = 7.4 + 12.3 + 23.5 = 43.2.

Noticeably, this method is forecasting that there should be a decline in sales—that is, because the weighting of the early months produces enough weight to drag the forecast down.

Forecasting Error

Forecasters need to know how far off their forecasts are to give them the opportunity to make corrections with the next forecast. The two basic ways to measure forecasting error are **bias,** the average of the errors, and MAD, the **mean absolute deviation,** or the average of the absolute value of the errors. A forecaster would want to examine these measurements to see how far off they have been and hopefully make an adjustment.

Example:

Month	Forecast	Actual	Bias	MAD
Jan.	100	90	+10	10
Feb.	90	105	−15	15
Mar.	100	127	−27	27
Apr.	125	151	−26	26
May	165	158	+7	7
Sum			−51	85

This tells the forecaster that after 5 months bias is $(-51/5) = -10.2$. In other words, they are underforecasting an average of 10.2 each month. In May, they overforecasted, so they may be more conservative and repeat their forecast of 165 for June.

The MAD column shows that in five periods, they are $(85/5) = 17$ off. MAD does not show the direction of the forecasting error, it shows the average absolute amount. The amount of forecasting error; is helpful in making adjustments for future forecasts.

MAD and bias can be combined to form a **tracking signal (TS)**, in which the signal is bias/MAD. In the above example, the TS would be $-10.2/17 = -0.6$. After April, the TS would be $-11/15.3 = -0.719$. The implication is that since the TS is getting closer to 0, it is improving. The TS is a monitoring index to combine the two pieces of error information.

Exponential Smoothing

Moving averages are not very sophisticated methods and are best applied when there is an absence of any trend or seasonality. A step up in sophistication, **exponential smoothing,** is a popular forecasting approach that has several forms. Single-exponential smoothing is a simple method for use when it is suspected that there is no trend or seasonality within the data. The smoothing constant (alpha) is used to consider the forecasting error from one period to the next.

The basic formula is

$$F_t = F_{t-1} + \alpha(A_{t-1} - F_{t-1}),$$

where

F_t = the forecast for the next period,

F_{t-1} = the forecast for the prior period,

α = the smoothing constant (a value between 0.01 and 0.99), and

A_{t-1} = the actual demand in the prior period.

The way this method works is that it makes a forecast based on the forecasting error in the prior period. If we had a prior forecast of 200 and the actual demand was 240, and we decide to use an α of 0.2, we would make a subsequent forecast:

$$F_t = 200 + 0.2(240 - 200) = 208$$

The forecast for the subsequent period would largely depend on the accuracy of the last forecast. In the initial period, when there are no actual data to compare with, the forecasters must start out with their best guess based on all the information they can find.

The α constant is essentially set with a rule of thumb that stable data have a low constant but volatile data have a high constant. This method will always lag any trend, so it is not appropriate in the case of a noticeable trend in the data.

Taking the forecast out one more period and assuming that the actual for the forecasted period was 236, our forecast would change to the following:

$$F_t = 208 + 0.2(236 - 208) = 213.6$$

Ironically, the forecast is higher, although the actual data dropped from 240 to 236. This is really because the forecast of 208 was still below the actual demand, so the forecast would increase.

Double-Exponential Smoothing

If a trend is present, a second smoothing constant is employed. The process of making a trend-adjusted forecast follows a sequence of steps:

1. Make a single exponential forecast, using the previous forecast, actual data, and smoothing constant:

$$F_t = F_{t-1} + \alpha(A_{t-1} - F_{t-1})$$

2. Calculate the trend:

$$T_t = T_{t-1} + \beta(F_t - F_{t-1})$$

3. Add the trend to the forecast:

$$TAF = F_t + T$$

Example:
In the last period, we had a trend-adjusted forecast of 400, the actual demand was 420, and we used 0.2 for both α and β. The trend component in the prior period was found to be 8.

1. $F_t = 400 + 0.2(420 - 400) = 404$

2. $T = 8 + 0.2(404 - 400) = 8.8$

3. $TAF = 404 + 8.8 = 412.8$

TAF here is the trend-adjusted forecast. For the next period, 412.8 becomes F_{t-1}, and 8.8 becomes T_{t-1}.
   We extend out the three periods as follows:

Period	Actual
2	440
3	520
4	560

Steps for Period 2:

1. $F_t = 412.8 + 0.2(440 - 412.8) = 418.24$

2. $T = 8.8 + 0.2(418.2 - 412.8) = 9.88$

3. $TAF = 418.2 + 9.9 = 428.1$

Steps for Period 3:

1. $F_t = 428.1 + 0.2(520 - 428.1) = 446.48$

2. $T = 9.9 + 0.2(446.5 - 428.1) = 13.58$

3. $TAF = 446.5 + 13.6 = 458.1$

Steps for Period 4:

1. $F_t = 458.1 + 0.2(560 - 458.1) = 478.48$

2. $T = 13.6 + 0.2(478.5 - 458.1) = 17.68$

3. $TAF = 478.5 + 17.7 = 496.2$

Note that we are doing some rounding throughout the problem. At this point, we should look at the forecasting error for four periods:

Period	Actual	Forecast	Bias	MAD
1	420	400	20	20
2	440	412.8	27.2	27.2
3	520	428.1	91.9	91.9
4	560	458.1	100.9	100.9

We are getting progressively worse. The most likely solution at this point would be to increase the values of the smoothing constants.

Seasonal Forecasting

Many organizations operate on a seasonal calendar. Amusement parks have predominately summer seasons. Hotels have higher occupancy in certain seasons and have to plan accordingly. Hospitals experience spikes in demand during the summer months, when children are out of school. Universities have their heaviest enrollments in the fall and the lightest enrollments in the summer.

Seasonal patterns require corresponding shifts in planning. A manager needs to be aware of demand patterns for the purposes of staffing and inventory management. Thus, seasonal methods of forecasting are important and helpful tools for the manager.

Seasonality is determined by noting that over time certain periods experience significant changes in demand. An index is calculated for each period to help arrive at a forecast. By knowing the index for a time period, demand can be estimated.

Demand	2005	2006	2007	Total	Average	Index
Jan.	85 units	107	114	306	102	
Feb.	77	91	98	266	88.7	
Mar.	65	72	80	217	72.3	
Apr.	40	31	43	114	38	
May	16	21	14	51	17	
Jun.	8	11	6	25	8.3	
Jul.	4	7	8	19	6.3	
Aug.	8	14	10	32	10.7	
Sep.	28	39	41	108	36	
Oct.	60	65	80	205	68.3	
Nov.	80	87	90	257	85.7	
Dec.	101	120	129	350	116.7	

The index is the percentage of the average. With each new month of data, the indexes will change. When forecasters make an annual forecast, they can take that annual forecast, divide it by the average of the periods, and multiply by the seasonal index to come up with a forecast for that period.

A monthly index is calculated as follows:

Annual forecast = 240,000

January index = 1.20

Monthly average = 240,000/12 = 20,000

January forecast = 20,000 (1.2) = 24,000

Trend Plus Seasonality

In cases where both trend *and* seasonality are present, the forecaster must go back to the prior season to make a forecast. Thus, when using exponential smoothing, it would not be a matter of forecasting from one week or month to the next.

A shortcut approach would be to combine the index with a trend value. Here, we can use 4 years of data to illustrate the sales progression (see Figure 8.1):

Season	Year 1	Year 2	Year 3	Year 4
Winter	120	140	170	210
Spring	160	210	260	300
Summer	180	240	320	400
Fall	80	100	110	120

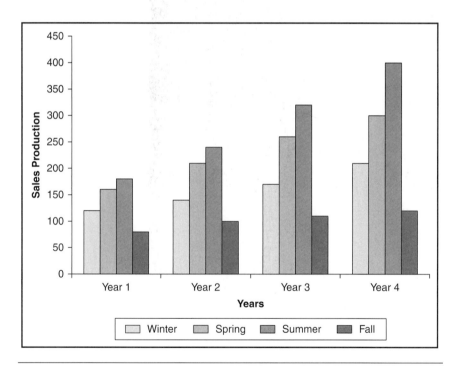

Figure 8.1   Four-Year Sales Progression

With these numbers, we see both seasonality and an upward trend. The seasonal index changes from year to year (see Table 8.2).

Based on this, the forecaster could use either the most recent seasonal index to project the next year or the average index of the 4 years (Winter 0.83, Spring 1.19, Summer 1.44, Fall 0.54).

The growth rate is also of interest to the forecaster. From Year 1 to Year 2, the demand increases 27.7% (from 540 to 690); from Year 2 to Year 3, another 24.6%; and from Year 3 to Year 4, 19.8%. The forecaster could again make a projection in several ways: the most recent growth rate, the trend of the growth rate, or the average growth rate.

Table 8.2 Seasonal Indexes for Four Years

Season	Year 1 Index	Year 2 Index	Year 3 Index	Year 4 Index
Winter	0.89	0.81	0.79	0.82
Spring	1.18	1.22	1.21	1.17
Summer	1.33	1.39	1.49	1.55
Fall	0.59	0.58	0.51	0.47

If our forecaster were to use a 24% increase over the 1,030 units, we would see a projection to 1,277 units. This averages 319 per quarter, so the breakdown by season would apply the index times 319. This arrives at forecasts of Winter 265, Spring 380, Summer 459, and Fall 172. Note that the total is 1,276 instead of 1,277 due to rounding.

Aggregate Planning

The forecast is the tool for breaking a budget into a production plan. How many employees do we need in the next year? What will be our expected inventory and materials needs? Do we have any periods when there are problems with over- and understaffing? An important planning technique for operations is aggregate planning. This involves taking the forecasted demand and making a production plan for a period from 6 months to 1 year. Operations managers must make production plans months ahead so that they can estimate hiring and inventory needs. There are a number of approaches to this process, which we will discuss here.

Method 1: Even Production

One approach is to plan even production throughout the year. This method will accumulate inventories in periods where demand is below production.

Period	Forecast	Production	Ending Inventory
1	1,000	1,000	0
2	900	1,000	100
3	800	1,000	300
4	600	1,000	700
5	900	1,000	800
6	1,200	1,000	600
7	1,500	1,000	100
8	1,000	1,000	100
9	1,100	1,000	0
10	600	1,000	400
11	500	1,000	900
12	500	1,000	1,400

Reviewing the above plan, we see that there would be an average inventory of 5,400/12 = 450 per period. Let us say that the holding cost per unit is $10. That would mean that this production plan would result in inventory costs of $4,500 per month. The advantage of an even production plan is that a stable workforce size could be maintained, minimizing hiring and firing costs.

Labor-related costs are the costs of firing: potential unemployment premiums, downsizing costs, or separation costs. The cost of hiring includes the cost of finding a replacement, whether that is through advertising in the local newspapers, an employment agency, or a headhunter firm. There is also an incurred cost of lost productivity. Workers do not usually walk in the first day and produce the same as an employee who has been working for several years. For a period of time, productivity may be reduced, and this can result in reduced revenues.

Method 2: The "Chase" Strategy

With a "chase" strategy, the **aggregate plan** attempts to produce the demand forecast. With this method, there are minimized inventory costs but increased hiring and firing costs.

Period	Forecast	Plan	Workforce	Hiring	Firing
1	1,000	1,000	100	—	—
2	900	900	90	—	10
3	800	800	80	—	10
4	600	600	60	—	20
5	900	900	90	30	—
6	1,200	1,200	120	30	—
7	1,500	1,500	150	30	—
8	1,000	1,000	100	—	50
9	1,100	1,100	110	10	—
10	600	600	60	—	50
11	500	500	50	—	10
12	500	500	50	—	—

We have to get some realistic estimate of what it takes to hire and fire. Assume we estimate $1,000 to hire and $1,000 to fire. Since the costs are equal, we add the number of hirings and firings (250) and multiply that by 1,000. This would result in annual costs of $250,000. Compare that with the cost of $54,000 in the even production method, and we see that given the trade-offs of carrying inventory or paying to hire and fire workers, it is much more economical to keep the workforce stable. It is imperative, however, that accurate estimates for carrying costs and employment costs are factored into the equation.

Method 3: Paying Overtime

The third basic aggregate planning strategy is to keep the labor force the same size, but increase the work hours by paying overtime. This usually requires paying a 50% premium for hourly workers.

In this case, we will assume that our workers earn $15 per hour and we have to increase their pay with overtime of $7.50 for every added hour. In this example, we assume that we have 10 workers accounting for the period production of 1,000, at the rate of 100 per worker. We will maintain even production, accumulating inventory when demand is less than production. In Periods 10 through 12, we will need to pay overtime. To get an additional 200 in Period 10 will require an increase for each worker from 100 to 120, and that will take an added 32 hr per month (just a round figure) at $32 \times 7.50 = \$240$ for each worker, for a total of $2,400 paid out in overtime:

Period	Forecast	Production	Ending Inventory	Overtime Cost
1	1,000	1.000	0	
2	900	1,000	100	
3	800	1,000	300	
4	600	1,000	700	
5	900	1,000	800	
6	1,200	1,000	600	
7	1,500	1,000	100	
8	1,000	1,000	100	
9	1,100	1,000	0	
10	1,200	1,200	0	2,400
11	1,300	1,300	0	3,200
12	1,100	1,100	0	1,600

Overall, a manager must evaluate the trade-offs of all the aggregate planning strategies. Inventory-holding costs must be factored against the opportunity cost of not having stock to sell. Hiring and laying off workers must be weighed against the problems that can be caused by having an unstable workforce. Overtime pay is an expensive way to go, but sometimes it is necessary to meet a deadline.

Aggregate Planning in Services

Aggregate planning is slightly different in services than it is in manufacturing, because it removes the elements of producing inventory and storing it. Basically, the service aggregate plan is a staffing plan to meet demand.

John Adams House of Shoes has these sales figures for the year 2008:

Month	Sales	Month	Sales
Jan.	120,000	Jul.	180,000
Feb.	80,000	Aug.	200,000
Mar.	130,000	Sep.	210,000
Apr.	150,000	Oct.	170,000
May	170,000	Nov.	140,000
Jun.	190,000	Dec.	220,000

The store is open from 9 to 6 Monday through Saturday and closed on Sunday. From Thanksgiving to Christmas, the working hours are increased—9 to 9.

The store has a manager who earns $80,000 annually and two full-time sales-people earning a basic salary of $40,000 plus a commission on sales, which has averaged to $25,000 annually. The rest of the staff is all part-time. The manager and sales-people work 40-hr weeks, with 3 weeks off for vacation.

An aggregate plan would primarily become a scheduling problem for dealing with the part-timers and tying them to sales. We could do this in a number of ways, but one way would be to look at the demand of each month, attach an index to it, and divide the part-time hours across the month.

Month	Index	Month	Index
Jan.	12	Aug.	20
Feb.	8	Sep.	21
Mar.	13	Oct.	17
Apr.	15	Nov.	14
May	17	Dec.	22
Jun.	19	Total	196
Jul.	18	Average	18.3

Now let us look at how to fit this into a schedule:

Monday	Tuesday	Wednesday	Thursday	Friday	Saturday
M	M	M	M	M	
F1	F1	F1	F1	F1	F1
F2	F2	F2	F2	F2	F2
P1	P1	P1	P1		
P2	P2	P2	P2		

NOTE: M = manager, F = full-time (alternate working Saturdays), and P = part-time.

The part-timers would work a total of 20 hr/week, with 8 hr on Saturday and 3 days of 4 hr each. If there is a constant relationship between sales and labor hours, the seasonal index can give us an indicator of how much we will have to increase the base schedule. In months that have an index of 1.2 or more, it means that our labor demands increase from 160 to 192 hr/week. We could meet this requirement for another 32 labor hours with two additional part-time workers or some combination of new workers and increased hours of the present part-time staff.

Capacity Management

Managers making aggregate plans have to factor in the capacity of the business to ensure that plans are not made that exceed capabilities. Capacity is a limitation of space, workforce, and money. A hospital has a capacity limitation of the number of available beds and the number of employees available to handle 100% capacity of the rooms. Hotels usually have the same considerations. Thus, when doing aggregate planning, one must always consider capacity.

How can you increase capacity? A hotel might be able to add more rooms through a building project, or it could increase the number of employees if the building cannot be expanded.

Manufacturers could increase the production rate in lower-demand periods to build inventory for when the demand outstrips the capacity.

Yield Management

One problem managers frequently must deal with is that all customers want the same thing at the same time. More people go to the movies on Friday and Saturday nights than any other time. More travelers want to go to Florida when school is on vacation than at other times. Faced with demand that fluctuates in peaks and valleys, deals are usually offered to encourage customers to come at off-season times.

This is exactly what airlines do when they price according to customer demand. This method is called **yield management.** Let us look at the differences in prices in 2005 for United Airlines on their Chicago to New York City flights, according to the time of day in the same week:

	Departure ORD		Departure LGA		
Flight No.	Date	Time	Date	Time	Price ($)
1	10/27	11:00 a.m.	10/30	3:00 p.m.	337
2	10/27	11:00 a.m.	10/30	11:00 a.m.	282
3	10/27	6:35 a.m.	10/30	11:00 a.m.	212
4	10/27	6:35 a.m.	10/30	9:20 a.m.	197

What explains the difference in prices? Demand. Flying at 6:35 a.m. requires arriving at the airport at 5:30 a.m. and may mean leaving your house at 5 a.m. That means arriving in New York sleep deprived. On the other hand, it may be necessary to do so. An important business meeting may be scheduled for that day. But the bottom line is that fewer people will desire that departure time. That makes the 11 a.m. departure time more desirable from a body clock point of view, hence the higher price due to the higher demand. Similarly, departing from New York's La Guardia airport is cheaper by an early flight. New Yorkers, no matter what time of day, take extra time to get to the airport. However, departures between 5 p.m. and 7 p.m. can be difficult to make due to the rush-hour traffic.

Motion picture theaters offer discounts to those who come early simply because fewer people do. By evening out the demand pattern and offering discounts, it makes it easier on the facility with regard to parking and concessions. Any time there is a discount offered for a certain time period, it is almost certain that yield management is at work.

The Web site resortdata.com includes a primer on how hotels use yield management: Rates are classed into four groups for three identifiable seasons. High seasons may include special events (a local convention taking up a lot of rooms) during the off-season. The rates vary according to season. For example, a rack rate (when a customer has no discount) could be $80 in the off-season, $120 in a near-peak season, and $170 during peak periods. The objective is to get close to capacity at all times, and yield management is an excellent approach.

Conclusion

In this chapter, we looked at techniques that help the operations manager predict production demands. Several forecasting models are available, but, really, all that matters is accuracy. This chapter looked at qualitative and quantitative models and studied moving averages, exponential smoothing, and linear regression.

Typically, both Operations and Marketing are involved in the process of forecasting. Marketing makes sales forecasts, which are used as information for the production forecasts. Operations must make predictions using whatever information it can access. If a hotel knows that only 92% of actual room reservations register, then it will have to work around that information.

Aggregate planning breaks the forecasts down into seasonal chunks, enabling the budgeting process for staffing and inventory. Also helpful in the planning process are capacity planning and yield management.

Summary

1. Operations managers must make forecasts for production, staffing, and overtime, working with a marketing projection for sales.

2. Qualitative forecasts are made without the use of data, by gathering opinions.

3. Linear regression is a method of forecasting when it is believed that a variable or variables have a causal relationship with the outcome they are trying to forecast.

4. Moving averages are used to forecast a future period based on the most recent periods.

5. Exponential smoothing methods use smoothing constants to make projections, incorporating forecasting error and trend.

6. Forecasting errors are measured according to the amount of error and the direction of the error (overforecasting or underforecasting).

7. Data that show seasonal patterns require an index for each season for proper forecasting.

8. An aggregate plan is a budgetary projection of staffing and inventory requirements for a given time period.

9. Capacity has to be considered in planning so that a company can handle periods when demand exceeds its ability to produce.

10. Yield management is a method for attempting to smooth demand over time by giving incentives to customers during off-peak times.

Key Terms

Aggregate plan	Mean absolute deviation (MAD)
Bias	Qualitative forecasts
Delphi method	Time series
Exponential smoothing	Tracking signal (TS)
Linear regression	Yield management

Problems

1. Here are the Chicago White Sox attendance figures for their 81 home games from 1995 through 2006.

Year	Attendance	Year	Attendance
1995	1,609,773	2001	1,766,172
1996	1,676,416	2002	1,676,416
1997	1,865,222	2003	1,939,594
1998	1,391,146	2004	1,930,537
1999	1,338,851	2005	2,342,834
2000	1,947,799	2006	2,957,414

Predict the White Sox attendance for 2007.

Now examine the division place and the number of wins for the White Sox from 1995 through 2006:

Year	Wins	Games Behind
1995	68	32
1996	85	14
1997	80	6
1998	80	9
1999	75	21
2000	95	+5
2001	83	8
2002	81	13
2003	86	4
2004	83	9
2005	99	—
2006	90	6

    a. Which is more important for predicting the attendance, the previous year or the current year?
    b. What factors would you consider as influencing the sporting event attendance?
    c. What forecasting model would you use to best predict the White Sox attendance?

2. Steven Spielberg is the leading film director of all time when it comes to the box office. Below are a list of the motion pictures he has directed and the box office. Also listed is the opening-weekend box office.

Year	Title	Gross Sales (Millions)	Opening
1974	Sugarland Express	7.5	NA
1975	Jaws	260.0	7.0
1977	Close Encounters of the Third Kind	132.0	5.3
1979	1941	31.7	2.7
1981	Raiders of the Lost Ark	242.3	8.3
1982	E.T.	435.1	11.8
1984	Indiana Jones and the Temple of Doom	179.8	25.3
1985	Color Purple	98.4	1.7
1987	Empire of the Sun	22.2	1.3
1989	Indiana Jones and the Last Crusade	197.1	29.3
1989	Always	43.8	3.7
1991	Hook	119.6	13.5
1993	Jurassic Park	357.0	47.0
1993	Schindler's List	96.0	0.6

(Continued)

(Continued)

Year	Title	Gross Sales (Millions)	Opening
1997	Lost World	229.0	72.1
1997	Amistad	44.2	4.5
1998	Saving Private Ryan	216.5	30.5
2001	A.I. Artificial Intelligence	78.6	29.3
2002	Minority Report	132.0	35.6
2002	Catch Me If You Can	164.6	30.0
2004	The Terminal	77.8	29.0
2005	War of the Worlds	231.7	64.8

Raiders of the Lost Ark was the first movie that Spielberg released in more than 1,000 theaters at once. Previously, it was the practice to limit the number of theaters in the first couple of weeks before going into general release.

   a. Given the above, what would you predict for the next Spielberg movie at the box office?
   b. What factors go into predicting the box office of a motion picture?
   c. Would it make a difference for the movie *War of the Worlds* at the box office if it starred an unknown actor or Tom Cruise?

3. R.E.M. has been a leading band since 1981. After performing for 10 years, their sales skyrocketed with their seventh album, *Out of Time*, which featured the hit single, "Losing My Religion."

Here are the worldwide sales figures of their albums since that time:

Year	Title	Worldwide Sales (Millions)
1991	Out of Time	13
1992	Automatic for the People	18
1994	Monster	10
1996	New Adventures in Hi Fi	5.5
1998	Up	3
2001	Reveal	4
2003	Best of R.E.M.	5
2004	Around the Sun	2

   a. Based on this information, what sales figure would you forecast for the next R.E.M. album?
   b. What forecasting method makes sense in this instance?
   c. What are some of the variables that go into album sales?

4. Joe Wyoming has to make an aggregate plan for the production of knee braces. He is unsure whether to have his workers cover excess demand with overtime. Here are the costs involved:

Overtime cost: $5 an hour.

Required workers: For 175 units per month, 10 workers are needed. One worker is needed for every 10 added units. Alternatively, 10 units equal 100 hr of overtime.

Cost of hiring: $1,000.

Cost of laying off: $2,000.

Inventory carrying cost: $1 per unit.

Cost of each brace: $9.

Month	Demand	Starting Workers
January	175	10
February	195	
March	220	
April	230	
May	250	
June	220	
July	180	
August	170	
September	155	
October	125	
November	115	
December	140	

Approach the above situation and answer the following questions:

a. Make an aggregate production plan, deciding how many to produce per month and whether to carry inventory, vary the number of workers, or work overtime.

b. What is the least costly option?

5. Consider the above situation but with the capacity of the plant set at 200. Make a new aggregate plan.

6. Look at the following demand pattern. What is the best forecasting method for these data? Forecast using several models to see which has the best accuracy.

Period	Demand	Period	Demand
1	1,543	5	1,678
2	1,432	6	1,700
3	1,389	7	1,865
4	1,544	8	1,742

(Continued)

(Continued)

Period	Demand	Period	Demand
9	1,976	17	2,076
10	2,367	18	2,230
11	1,876	19	2,198
12	1,980	20	2,765
13	1,678	21	2,187
14	1,700	22	2,450
15	1,865	23	2,290
16	1,742	24	2,475

CASE 1   Hotel Capacity

In the Mojo Hotel, at 95% occupancy the staff is at top capacity. Two hundred workers staff the hotel, and in the months when the capacity increases to more than 70%, the staff is increased by 1 person for each percentage gain. In other words, an 80% projected capacity would result in 210 workers. This ratio has been perfected through trial and error.

Month	Occupancy (%)	Workers
Jan.	62	200
Feb.	59	200
Mar.	67	200
Apr.	73	203
May	73	203
Jun.	88	218
Jul.	95	225
Aug.	95	225
Sep.	84	214
Oct.	75	205
Nov.	65	200
Dec.	64	200

CASE 2   Manufacturer and Capacity

Month	Capacity	Demand	Production	Inventory
Jan.	1,000	700	900	200
Feb.	1,000	690	900	410
Mar.	1,000	900	900	410

Month	Capacity	Demand	Production	Inventory
Apr.	1,000	1,100	900	210
May	1,000	1,200	1,000	10
Jun.	1,000	900	900	10
Jul.	1,000	900	900	10
Aug.	1,000	800	900	110
Sep.	1,000	800	900	210
Oct.	1,000	900	900	210
Nov.	1,000	1,000	900	110
Dec.	1,000	900	900	110

Here, the manager plans the year and discovers an expected overcapacity demand to appear in April and May. Thus, an even production rate in the first 3 months of the year results in scheduling around the capacity issue.

Web Sites

A cool site on weather forecasting methods: www.research.noaa.gov/k12/index.html

A site on yield management: www.resortdata.com

In-depth site on methods: www.forecastingprinciples.com

Material on aggregate planning: www.enotes.com/management-encyclopedia/aggregate-planning

Scheduling
for Operations

Learning Objectives

The goals of this chapter are to

- Study methods of scheduling for job shop situations
- Learn about establishing a Master Production Schedule (MPS)
- Review topics in labor scheduling
- Review scheduling in different arenas: manufacturing and service. Specific scheduling situations studied include hospital scheduling, train scheduling, sports scheduling, and television production scheduling
- Study Eli Goldratt's Theory of Constraints

Why Do We Need a Schedule?

A primary function of operations management is scheduling. Operations managers must match a labor schedule to the demands of customers. In a fast-food restaurant, the manager has to make sure that there are enough workers to satisfy demand. Customers do not come in at the same arrival rates at the same time of day, so the schedule must vary to match the arrival rates of the customers.

Similarly, a manufacturing plant has to schedule production, so that products can smoothly pass through production and out the door into the customer's hands. It is the matching of production, customers, and the workforce that requires expert scheduling.

The schedule is based partially on the forecasted customer demand. The manager takes the expected number of customers or orders and makes a schedule that will produce to that amount. This is where the art of staffing comes into play.

Students know firsthand how important it is to register for their desired classes early to ensure a spot. The class schedule is set based on a number of factors: enrollments in previous years, projected enrollments, classroom availability, instructor availability, and curriculum requirements. If you take a walk down the hallway and notice classes filled to the brim, it is indicative of good scheduling—to schedule enough classes so the great majority of students can get into all their desired classes. Of course, it does not always work out that way for students.

This chapter will review scheduling in a number of different situations. The job shop schedule and Master Production Schedule are for traditional operations settings. These are the most common topics found in classic operations management texts. However, the basic goals of all schedules are the same—to accomplish work on time. Labor scheduling is a concern for all places of employment. How many people do we need at a certain time of day, and who is scheduled to work? How do we get to work on time? How do we set train schedules to maximize commuter traffic and maintain a schedule? How do we synchronize the scheduling of airplanes and flight crews?

For sports fans, nothing is more important than their team's schedule. The day your favorite sports team's schedule is announced, the dates are put on the calendar, and lives often revolve around that schedule. For the athletic director, setting a schedule that minimizes traveling costs while scheduling a good mix of competition is the goal. In major collegiate sports, the strength of that schedule is a factor in rankings.

The type of scheduling used in companies varies from one industry to another. For this reason, we will review some scheduling applications for different business situations. Commuters in major cities schedule their own workdays around train schedules and become finely tuned to their own departure times from home and work, to make the train on time.

Job Shop Scheduling

Every company has its own approach to scheduling. If a number of customers arrive at Kinko's as the doors open in the morning, how does the manager process them? One method of scheduling to get a number of jobs done in a timely order is called **job shop scheduling**. This method is appropriate for businesses such as printing or copying or a job shop, which is a firm that has different machines to handle different kinds of jobs. Students employ job shop scheduling without being aware of it. If a student has three papers due in a certain time frame, he or she must figure out how to spend his or her time to get the papers finished.

There are a number of scheduling rules that may be assigned to this type of scheduling problem. To illustrate different rules for the same type of situation, consider this scenario:

Lillian Wayne opens the doors to her print shop and is greeted by a line of five customers. They all have jobs that will take several days, so she has to set a schedule to get the best and most efficient results.

Job	Expected No. of Days	Expected Day of Completion
101	6	6
102	5	10
103	4	14
104	8	22
105	7	28

The expected date was Lillian's guess as to when the jobs would be ready, since she was faced with giving each customer an idea of how soon the job could be finished. Unfortunately, the jobs were such that she had to complete them one at a time.

Shortest Processing Time

If Lillian arranged the jobs according to the shortest process time, the jobs would be processed through the plant like this:

Job	Start Day	Finished (Days)	Due (Days)	Lateness (Days)
103	0	4	14	0
102	4	9	10	0
101	9	15	6	9
105	15	22	28	0
104	22	30	22	8

In this example, she was on time for three of the five jobs, with an average lateness of 3.4 days (17 total days for five jobs). Three customers should be pretty satisfied, but two would be displeased.

First Come First Served

If Lillian processed the jobs in the order they were presented to her, the jobs would be processed as given below:

Job	Expected No. of Days	Expected Day of Completion
101	6	6
102	5	10
103	4	14
104	8	22
105	7	28

Job	Start Day	Day Finished	Day Due	Lateness (Days)
101	0	6	6	0
102	6	11	10	1
103	11	15	14	1
104	15	23	22	1
105	23	30	28	2

Here, the results were four of five late jobs, with an average lateness of 1 day per job (five total days late for five jobs). Lillian has more late customers, but it is fairer for the two customers who would be so late if using the shortest process time.

Earliest Due Date

In this example, Lillian scheduled by the earliest due date simply by going first come first serve, but it does not always work out that way. Here is another set of examples.

Job	Process Time (Days)	Due (Days)
A	14	25
B	6	11
C	11	17
D	15	18
E	7	21
F	8	9

Confronted with this set, Lillian should make several tries.

1. *By earliest due date:*

Job	Process Start Day	Process Completion Day	Day Due	Lateness (Days)
F	0	8	9	0
B	8	14	11	3
C	14	25	17	8
D	25	40	18	22
E	40	47	21	26
A	47	61	25	36

This schedule could get Lillian fired.

2. *By the shortest process time:*

Job	Process Start Day	Process Completion Day	Due (Days)	Lateness (Days)
B	0	6	11	0
E	6	13	21	0
F	13	21	9	12
C	21	32	17	15
A	32	46	21	25
D	46	61	18	43

See Figure 9.1.

The first method has 95 total days late. The second method has 95 also, but this time two jobs are on time. The mistake Lillian made up front was not noting that the cumulative flow time of the jobs would take 61 days!

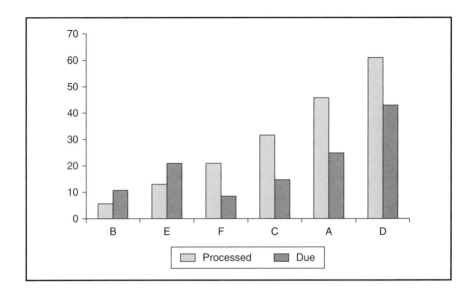

Figure 9.1   Job Shop Scheduling, Processed Versus Due Dates

Another Situation (in Hours)

Assume that you are a print shop manager and you open your doors at 8:00 a.m. and have no previously scheduled jobs. Four people wait in line with jobs of various lengths. Now, it is your turn to schedule them to minimize lateness.

Job	Length	Promised Time
1	2 hr	11:00 a.m.
2	1 hr	9:30 a.m.
3	1 hr 30 min	10:30 a.m.
4	2 hr	11:30 a.m.

The printer takes the jobs, which were handled at the register in the order 1-2-3-4, but she gets them at the same time and looks at the anticipated time. She has a number of choices.

Schedule according to the earliest expected time:

Job	Time	Processing	Expected Time	Lateness
2	1 hr	8:15–9:15 a.m.	9:30 a.m.	0
3	1 hr 30 min	9:15–10:45 a.m.	10:30 a.m.	15 min
1	2 hr	10:45 a.m.–12:45 p.m.	11:00 a.m.	1 hr 45 min
4	2 hr	12:45–2:45 p.m.	11:30 a.m.	3 hr 15 min

This method has three late jobs totaling 5 hr and 15 min.

First come first served:

Job	Time	Processing	Expected Time	Lateness
1	2 hr	8:15–10:15 a.m.	11:00 a.m.	0
2	1 hr	10:15–11:15 a.m.	9:30 a.m.	1 hr 45 min
3	1 hr 30 min	11:15 a.m.–12:45 p.m.	10:30 a.m.	2 hr 15 min
4	2 hr	12:45–2:45 p.m.	11:30 a.m.	3 hr 15 min

Now, the jobs are late a total of 7 hr and 15 min, which is worse.

Scheduling according to the shortest process time gives the same result as the schedule according to the earliest due time. The lesson in this case is that the person making promises has to understand the processing time for a number of jobs before making promises. Unrealistic schedules result in lost customer goodwill.

Johnson's Rule

A method for scheduling jobs that must be processed on two different machines, or processes, and one job at a time, is called **Johnson's Rule**.

The rule works like this:

1. List the times to process each job on both machines and processes.

2. Examine the listed time for all jobs and machines. If the shortest time for any job is listed on the first machine, schedule that job first. If the shortest time for any job is on the second machine, schedule that job last.

3. Once that job is scheduled, reschedule the remaining jobs in the same method.

For example, suppose we have five jobs that have to be scheduled on two machines:

Job	Process Time (Days)	
	Machine A	Machine B
101	6	7
102	4	9
103	8	3
104	5	2
105	10	6

Job 104 has the shortest process time, 2 days, and it is on Machine B. Since these 2 days are on the *second* machine, we place it fifth on the schedule.
   Remaining jobs:

	Process Time (Days)	
Job	Machine A	Machine B
101	6	7
102	4	9
103	8	3
105	10	6

Now, we see that Job 103 has the shortest time, again on Machine B. It will be scheduled fourth.
   Remaining jobs:

	Process Time (Days)	
Job	Machine A	Machine B
101	6	7
102	4	9
105	10	6

Job 102 has the shortest time, so it is scheduled first. The remaining two jobs have the same 6-day processing, 101 on Machine A and 105 on Machine B, so that conveniently plays out that we schedule 101 in the second place and 105 in the third position. Our schedule now looks like this:

Job	Process Time A (Days)	Process Time B (Days)
102	4	9
101	6	7
105	10	6
103	8	3
104	5	2

The actual flow through the plant will run like this. We assume that we start at Day 0, and there is continuous production, so that each successive job starts on the same day the previous one finishes.

Job	Flow Time A (Days)	Flow Time B (Days)
102	0–4	4–13
101	4–10	13–20
105	10–20	20–26
103	20–28	28–31
104	28–33	33–35

Note that Job 101 finished on the first machine on Day 10 but had to wait until Day 13 for Job 102 to complete before commencing processing.

This process of scheduling on two processes, invented by someone named Johnson, is the most effective way to schedule this situation. If you can come up with a better way, write to the author of this book, and we'll see that this new method is named after you.

Take a crack at another scenario, a printing process.

Job	Process A (Days)	Process B (Days)
A	16	11
B	11	14
C	12	7
D	17	18
E	10	9
F	8	19

A note on ties: If there is a tie and it is on the same machine, look to the *other* machine. If the other machine is Process A, schedule the shorter of the two first. If the other machine is Process B, schedule the shorter of the two last.

Our schedule for this situation would be F-B-D-A-E-C.

Job C is scheduled last because it has the shortest time on the second process. Job F goes first because it has the shortest time on the first process. Job E goes next to last because it has the shortest time of the remaining jobs on the second machine. We continue to schedule until all jobs are processed. Our flow times would be as follows:

Job	Time A (Days)	Flow Time (Days)	Time B (Days)	Flow Time (Days)
F	8	0–8	19	8–27
B	11	8–19	14	27–41
D	17	19–36	18	41–59
A	16	36–52	11	59–70
E	10	52–61	9	70–79
C	12	61–73	7	79–86

The process time scheduled for these jobs would be 86 days. Process A is always in use, and so is Process B in this case.

Three Processes

A modification of Johnson's rule would be required to handle any more than two processes. For three processes, we could arrange it so that if the shortest time were on the *second* process, we would schedule that job in the median position. Otherwise, Johnson's rule applies.

Job	Process A (Days)	Process B (Days)	Process C (Days)
A	16	6	11
B	11	12	14
C	12	3	7
D	17	13	18
E	10	14	9
F	8	10	19

Now, our schedule would be changed because Jobs C and A have the shortest processing times, both on the second process. With six jobs, it would mean that we would schedule them into positions three and four. Then, we would schedule Job F first, Job E last, Job B second, and Job D fifth.

Adding a third process brings these jobs to a flow time of 104 days.

Job	A Time (Days)	Flow	B Time (Days)	Flow	C Time (Days)	Flow
F	8	0–8	10	8–18	19	18–37
B	11	8–19	12	19–31	14	37–51
C	12	19–31	3	31–34	7	51–58
A	16	31–47	6	47–53	11	58–69
D	17	47–64	13	64–77	18	77–95
E	10	64–74	14	77–91	9	95–104

Machine Loading

Scheduling that considers capacity requirements is termed *loading*. Jobs that are sequenced to start at the earliest time are scheduled in what is called "forward scheduling." Jobs that are scheduled from the due date to the present date use "backward scheduling." Backward scheduling must assume that a work center can do more than one job at a time, and this may not be realistic.

The Theory of Constraints

Goldratt and Cox's (2004) novel *The Goal* illustrates his theory of production scheduling. The publication gained an audience among operations professionals for its plain sense approach to scheduling around bottlenecks.

The most telling episode in the book is about a Boy Scout hike. The group of Boy Scouts has to spend a lot of time waiting for its slowest hiker, Herbie. Finally, the Scout leader hits on the idea of having Herbie lead the hike because the hikers can, as a group, only get to their destination according to the speed of their slowest hiker. This principle is then applied to machine scheduling. When there is a machine that acts as a constraint (the *Herbie* machine), do what you can to alleviate that constraint.

In the case of the hike, others might carry Herbie's bag for him, or, long term, get him to lose weight. In the production sense, the constraint is what determines the schedule, so resources should address streamlining the constraint.

Goldratt's theory is to find ways to streamline the bottleneck. In a production process involving multiple steps, one or more of the steps are central to the delivery of the product. This constraint is like the turkey in the oven on Thanksgiving. If everyone is waiting for the turkey, you have to be careful about turning the heat up to speed things along, because the end result may ruin the taste. The answer is probably to start the cooking earlier in the process. Goldratt's (1999) **Theory of Constraints** involves five steps (www.goldratt.com):

1. Identify the constraint.
2. Exploit the constraint (i.e., streamline).
3. Synchronize everything else (nonconstraint activities).
4. Elevate performance.
5. Return to Step 1.

The Theory of Constraints consists of three elements. The **Drum** is the rate of production. Goldratt made the analogy of the production rate to that of a drumbeat, a steady pace. The **Buffer** is additional stock that is placed strategically to allow the bottleneck to keep flowing. The **Rope** is the link between the processes that feeds the bottleneck.

The Master Production Schedule

In manufacturing situations, production is scheduled using a **Master Production Schedule** (MPS). This schedule interfaces with the materials requirements planning (MRP) inventory system, discussed later in the book. The schedule is set out a number of periods prior to production and combines two pieces of information, the forecast and actual customer orders. In the short term, the company typically will use the actual orders and produce them. In the longer term, the scheduler will take the greater of the two as a planned schedule. When the schedule gets very close to actual production, it is said to "freeze." This means that the scheduler desires no alterations to the schedule. This might happen a week or two prior to actual production, depending on the industry.

Cox and Blackstone (1998) noted that the purpose of the MPS is to compare the forecast to actual demand and account for existing backlogs and inventory on hand. It is a planning document for scheduling production.

(1) The anticipated build schedule is for those items assigned to the master scheduler. The master scheduler maintains this schedule, and in turn, it becomes a set of planning numbers that drives material requirements planning. It represents what the company plans to produce expressed in specific configurations, quantities, and dates. The MPS is not a sales forecast that represents a statement of demand. The MPS must take into account the forecast, the production plan, and other important considerations, such as backlog, availability of material, availability of capacity, and management policies and goals.

(2) The master schedule is a presentation of demand, forecast, backlog, the MPS, the projected on-hand inventory, and the available-to-promise quantity.

Period	1	2	3	4	5	6	7	8	9	10
Forecast	60	72	57	38	56	60	60	54	47	37
Orders	79	84	54	40	29	21	16	27	11	6
Production	79	84	54	40	29	60	60	54	47	37

In the above scenario, in Periods 1 to 5, we plan to produce the actual orders. We plan to produce the greater of the forecast or actual orders in Periods 6 to 10.

In the following scenario, we are given period forecasts and actual orders. The scheduler will combine this information to make a schedule.

Period	1	2	3	4	5	6	7	8	9	10
Forecast	126	126	157	168	120	120	110	110	100	100
Orders	171	177	145	132	128	115	98	90	87	54

Schedule

Production would go with 171, 177, and 145 in the first three periods and then 168, 128, 120, 110, 110, 100, and 100. The scheduler may decide to freeze the schedule within three periods of production.

The schedule is considered to have a "rolling horizon." As each production period moves forward, the schedule will be frozen short term. For example, after the

171 orders in Period 1 are processed, the 177 orders in Period 2 move into Period 1. The Period 4 orders of 132 will move into Period 3. If any new orders are added, the schedule will freeze production of those orders.

The horizon is considered to have two sections: The first few planning weeks, the closest to the production date, are referred to as the frozen section. This section is rarely changed. The frozen section may be one or two planning periods, usually weeks.

The second section is the open section, in which the planner is comparing the forecast against actual orders. The planner deals with a number of input variables.

- *Beginning inventory:* How much stock is available at the beginning of the period?

- *Gross requirements:* What are the projected outputs for that inventory item?

- *Net requirements:* After subtracting available inventory, the actual needs are calculated.

- *Lot sizes:* If the item must be produced in specific sizes for some reason, for example, if boxes come in lots of 144, that must be factored into production. For example, if the net requirements are 120, but the lot size is 144, then 144 must be produced, leaving an ending inventory of 24.

- *Safety stocks:* Any safety stock must be accounted for so that at the end of a period, there is a minimum amount left.

- *Capacity requirements:* The planner must consider plant capacity when scheduling.

We will review more of the details of the MPS in Chapter 14.

Labor Scheduling

Labor scheduling has to be carefully matched to the schedule for production or customer processing. In office situations, labor scheduling is usually fairly simple. Everyone works regular office hours, typically something like 9 to 5. Salaried managers and staff, who are not paid by the hour, can work overtime without getting additional pay, because they are paid a fixed salary.

The most complicated scheduling problems usually deal with part-time workers employed at fast-food restaurants. Here, the problem is that workers have different hours that they are available to work, often because they attend school. The staffing should be tied to the work flow. There are times when more customers stream in, typically from 12 p.m. to 1 p.m. and from 6 p.m. to 7 p.m.

Let's take a fast-food restaurant scheduling by looking at the customers' arrival rates.

SOURCE: © Marcin Balcerzak/istockphoto.com

Time	Arrivals	Time	Arrivals	Time	Arrivals
6:00–6:15 a.m.	6	6:15–6:30 a.m.	10	6:30–6:45 a.m.	17
6:45–7:00 a.m.	19	7:00–7:15 a.m.	32	7:15–7:30 a.m.	37
7:30–7:45 a.m.	39	7:45–8:00 a.m.	29	8:00–8:15 a.m.	27
8:15–8:30 a.m.	26	8:30–8:45 a.m.	24	8:45–9:00 a.m.	17
9:00–9:15 a.m.	14	9:15–9:30 a.m.	12	9:30–9:45 a.m.	9
9:45–10:00 a.m.	8	10:00–10:15 a.m.	8	10:15–10:30 a.m.	7
10:30–10:45 a.m.	6	10:45–11:00 a.m.	9	11:00–11:15 a.m.	12
11:15–11:30 a.m.	14	11:30–11:45 a.m.	28	11:45 a.m.–12:00 p.m.	31
12:00–12:15 p.m.	47	12:15–12:30 p.m.	53	12:30–12:45 p.m.	57

Time	Arrivals	Time	Arrivals	Time	Arrivals
12:45–1:00 p.m.	43	1:00–1:15 p.m.	35	1:15–1:30 p.m.	21
1:30–1:45 p.m.	17	1:45–2:00 p.m.	12	2:00–2:15 p.m.	11
2:15–2:30 p.m.	9	2:30–2:45 p.m.	8	2:45–3:00 p.m.	7
3:00–3:15 p.m.	17	3:15–3:30 p.m.	19	3:30–3:45 p.m.	22
3:45–4:00 p.m.	24	4:00–4:15 p.m.	21	4:15–4:30 p.m.	19
4:30–4:45 p.m.	13	4:45–5:00 p.m.	20	5:00–5:15 p.m.	17
5:15–5:30 p.m.	22	5:30–5:45 p.m.	29	5:45–6:00 p.m.	37
6:00–6:15 p.m.	43	6:15–6:30 p.m.	51	6:30–6:45 p.m.	50
6:45–7:00 p.m.	41	7:00–7:15 p.m.	32	7:15–7:30 p.m.	27
7:30–7:45 p.m.	20	7:45–8:00 p.m.	14	8:00–8:15 p.m.	10
8:15–8:30 p.m.	8	8:30–8:45 p.m.	6	8:45–9:00 p.m.	5
9:00–9:15 p.m.	8	9:15–9:30 p.m.	8	9:30–9:45 p.m.	9
9:45–10:00 p.m.	12	10:00–10:15 p.m.	15	10:15–10:30 p.m.	12
10:30–10:45 p.m.	10	10:45–11:00 p.m.	12	11:00–11:15 p.m.	8
11:15–11:30 p.m.	6	11:30–11:45 p.m.	4	11:45 p.m.–12:00 a.m.	3

The manager, John Johnson, has a rule that since he has five registers, during the peak hours, he wants 12 employees, with 1 at every register, 1 at the drive-through, and the rest preparing food and cleaning up. At all times, he must have a minimum of 4 employees to keep the place working smoothly. That is basically 1 at the register, 1 at the drive-through, and 1 or 2 preparing food and cleaning. Converting the above schedule to a ratio of customer flow to employees, with 12 the maximum and 4 the minimum, we have a worker need schedule.

Time	Arrivals	Time	Arrivals	Time	Arrivals
6:00–6:15 a.m.	6 (4)	6:15–6:30 a.m.	10 (4)	6:30–6:45 a.m.	17 (5)
6:45–7:00 a.m.	19 (5)	7:00–7:15 a.m.	32 (8)	7:15–7:30 a.m.	37 (9)
7:30–7:45 a.m.	39 (9)	7:45–8:00 a.m.	29 (8)	8:00–8:15 a.m.	27 (8)
8:15–8:30 a.m.	26 (7)	8:30–8:45 a.m.	24 (6)	8:45–9:00 a.m.	17 (5)
9:00–9:15 a.m.	14 (4)	9:15–9:30 a.m.	12 (4)	9:30–9:45 a.m.	9 (4)

Time	Arrivals	Time	Arrivals	Time	Arrivals
9:45–10:00 a.m.	8 (4)	10:00–10:15 a.m.	8 (4)	10:15–10:30 a.m.	7 (4)
10:30–10:45 a.m.	6 (4)	10:45–11:00 a.m.	9 (4)	11:00–11:15 a.m.	12 (4)
11:15–11:30 a.m.	14 (4)	11:30–11:45 a.m.	28 (7)	11:45 a.m.–12:00 p.m.	31(8)
12:00–12:15 p.m.	47 (12)	12:15–12:30 p.m.	53 (12)	12:30–12:45 p.m.	57 (12)
12:45–1:00 p.m.	43 (11)	1:00–1:15 p.m.	35 (9)	1:15–1:30 p.m.	21 (6)
1:30–1:45 p.m.	17 (5)	1:45–2:00 p.m.	12 (4)	2:00–2:15 p.m.	11 (4)
2:15–2:30 p.m.	9 (4)	2:30–2:45 p.m.	8 (4)	2:45–3:00 p.m.	7 (4)
3:00–3:15 p.m.	17 (5)	3:15–3:30 p.m.	19 (5)	3:30–3:45 p.m.	22 (6)
3:45–4:00 p.m.	24 (6)	4:00–4:15 p.m.	21 (6)	4:15–4:30 p.m.	19 (5)
4:30–4:45 p.m.	13 (4)	4:45–5:00 p.m.	20 (5)	5:00–5:15 p.m.	17 (5)
5:15–5:30 p.m.	22 (6)	5:30–5:45 p.m.	29 (8)	5:45–6:00 p.m.	37 (10)
6:00–6:15 p.m.	43 (11)	6:15–6:30 p.m.	51 (12)	6:30–6:45 p.m.	50 (12)
6:45–7:00 p.m.	41 (11)	7:00–7:15 p.m.	32 (8)	7:15–7:30 p.m.	27 (8)
7:30–7:45 p.m.	20 (5)	7:45–8:00 p.m.	14 (4)	8:00–8:15 p.m.	10 (4)
8:15–8:30 p.m.	8 (4)	8:30–8:45 p.m.	6 (4)	8:45–9:00 p.m.	5 (4)
9:00–9:15 p.m.	8 (4)	9:15–9:30 p.m.	8 (4)	9:30–9:45 p.m.	9 (4)
9:45–10:00 p.m.	12 (4)	10:00–10:15 p.m.	15 (4)	10:15–10:30 p.m.	12 (4)
10:30–10:45 p.m.	10 (4)	10:45–11:00 p.m.	12 (4)	11:00–11:15 p.m.	8 (4)
11:15–11:30 p.m.	6 (4)	11:30–11:45 p.m.	4 (4)	11:45 p.m.–12:00 a.m.	3 (4)

NOTE: Workers in parentheses.

This information is for Monday through Friday. The weekend presents totally different arrival rates.

The goal in labor scheduling is to

- maximize customer service,
- minimize labor costs,
- reduce idle work time,

- operate efficiently, and
- maintain high quality.

For the manager to schedule, he has a current workforce that has two full-time employees. There are six employees who work in 2-hr shifts, and the rest work in 4-hr shifts.

Grouping the work needs by hour and using the peak number of employees in any hour as a rule, we have these numbers:

Time	No. of Workers	Time	No. of Workers	Time	No. of Workers
6–7 a.m.	5	7–8 a.m.	9	8–9 a.m.	4
9–10 a.m.	4	10–11 a.m.	4	11 a.m.–12 p.m.	8
12–1 p.m.	12	1–2 p.m.	9	2–3 p.m.	4
3–4 p.m.	6	4–5 p.m.	6	5–6 p.m.	10
6–7 p.m.	12	7–8 p.m.	8	8–9 p.m.	4
9–10 p.m.	4	10–11 p.m.	4	11 a.m.–12 a.m.	4

Studying this information by time blocks and breaking it down to needs, we have the following:

6 a.m.	7 a.m.	8 a.m.	9 a.m.
1 full-time	Add:	(Overstaffed 1)	(Over 1)
4 part-time	4 part-time		
Working 6–8	Working 7–11		

10 a.m.	11 a.m.	12 p.m.	1 p.m.
(Over 1)	Add:	Add:	(Over 3)
7 part-time	1 full-time	11–3	(Second takes break)
4 part-time			
12–2			
7 part-time			
Working 11–3			

2 p.m.	3 p.m.	4 p.m.	5 p.m.
(Over 5)	Add:	No change	
5 part-time 3–7	6 part-time 5–9		

6 p.m.	7 p.m.	8 p.m.	9 p.m.
No change	Add: 1 part-timer 7–11	(Over 6)	No change
Add: 4 part-time 8–12			

This schedule has built in 17 hr of overstaffing. But the reality of staffing of fast-food places is that there is high turnover and high absenteeism. The biggest challenge is simply to put enough part-time, competent bodies in the store that can reliably fill the schedule.

Other Scheduling Applications

SOURCE:© sven herrmann/istockphoto.com

Scheduling applications are used for practically everything that you experience in a typical day. The classes you take, public transportation you use, the production of the material you read—all are prepared with some form of a schedule. The following section gives examples of scheduling methods in various aspects of our lives.

Scheduling Faculty to Classes

Here is the scenario that universities use to schedule classes.

Below are the teaching needs for a management department in a two-semester academic year:

Semester 1		Semester 2	
MGT301	2 days	MGT301	2 days
MGT301	2 nights	MGT301	2 nights
MGT355	1 day	MGT355	1 night
MGT356	1 night	MGT356	1 day

Semester 1		Semester 2	
MGT502	2 days	MGT502	2 days
MGT502	2 nights	MGT502	2 nights
MGT502	2 Saturdays	MGT502	2 Saturdays
MGT510	1 night	MGT510	1 day
MGT515	1 day	MGT515	1 night
MGT525	1 night	MGT525	1 night
MGT798	1 night	MGT798	1 night

Thus, we have a need for 16 sections in the first semester and 16 in the second semester.

The faculty available to teach includes the following:

Name of Faculty	Number of Courses
Nie	4 courses
Goodale	4 courses
Zhao	4 courses
Verma	4 courses
Metlen	4 courses
Seawright	4 courses
Pullman	3 courses

This means that we are five short of a match and these courses will have to be staffed with adjuncts. Adjuncts work during the day, so their availability is limited to night classes.

The match is further complicated by the faculty preferences. Some insist on teaching during the day. Others will only teach at night. Some will never teach on weekends, and others will insist on it. Some faculty do not like to come into the university due to balancing child care duties and other personal responsibilities. However, a good schedule considers the desires of the students first and starts out with a schedule that is designed to maximize student satisfaction.

Railroad Scheduling

Another industry that is totally dependent on effective scheduling is the transportation industry: trains, buses, and airplanes all must schedule to maximize their capacity.

Time zones were originally established due to train accidents. The time zones made sure that the train conductors who passed from one state into another were able to change their watches accordingly if they passed a time zone.

Setting a train schedule is a complicated process. The scheduler has these goals in mind:

1. Maximize passengers per train.

2. Minimize travel time.

3. Maintain a safe schedule.

The Metra/Union Pacific North line is a good example of how train schedules work. There are 27 possible stops from Chicago to Kenosha, Wisconsin. It would be inefficient and slow to stop every train at every stop, so the schedule studies the passenger traffic at every stop to determine how many times to stop at each of the 27 stops. Here is the schedule from 4:30 p.m to 5:45 p.m.

Stop	Time (p.m.)							
Ogilvie Station, Chicago	4:30	4:35	5:07	5:10	5:15	5:21	5:35	5:45
Clybourn	4:38	4:43	—	5:18	5:23	5:29	5:43	—
Ravenswood	—	4:48	—	—	—	5:34	5:49	—
Rogers Park	—	4:53	—	5:26	—	5:38	—	—
Main Street Evanston	—	4:57	—	—	5:33	5:41	—	—
Davis Street	4:48	4:59	—	5:31	5:36	5:44	5:56	—
Central Street	4:51	—	—	5:34	5:38	5:47	—	6:05
Wilmette	—	5:03	5:28	—	5:41	—	—	6:08
Kenilworth	4:55	—	—	5:38	—	5:51	—	6:11
Indian Hill	—	5:07	—	—	5:44	—	—	6:14
Winnetka	4:58	—	—	5:41	—	5:54	6:02	6:17
Hubbard Woods	—	5:11	—	—	5:48	—	6:06	6:20
Glencoe	5:03	—	—	5:46	—	—	6:10	6:24
Braeside	—	5:15	5:36	—	5:52	—	6:14	6:28
Ravinia Park	—	—	—	—	—	—	—	—
Ravinia	5:07	—	—	5:50	5:56	—	6:17	6:31
Highland Park	5:10	5:19	5:42	5:53	5:59	—	6:21	6:35
Highwood	—	5:22	—	—	6:02	—	6:24	—
Fort Sheridan	—	5:25	5:47	5:58	—	—	6:27	6:40
Lake Forest	—	5:29	5:52	—	6:08	—	6:32	6:45
Lake Bluff	—	5:33	5:56	6:04	—	—	6:36	6:50
Great Lakes	—	5:37	—	6:08	6:14	—	—	—
North Chicago	—	5:40	—	6:11	6:17	—	6:41	—
Waukegan	—	5:45	6:06	6:16	6:22	—	6:47	7:00
Zion	—	—	6:15	6:25	—	—	—	—
Winthrop	—	—	6:20	6:30	—	—	—	—
Kenosha, WI	—	—	6:30	6:40	—	—	—	—

Train commuters study the schedule carefully, because the trains typically do not stop at every stop. A commuter who wants to ride from Ogilvie Station to Wilmette during this time frame has a choice of boarding at 4:35 p.m., 5:07 p.m., 5:15 p.m., and 5:45 p.m.

If a commuter who boarded at Main Street, Evanston, and commuted to Waukegan wanted to know which trains were available, he or she would study the schedule to make sure that trains arrived at both stations. Only the trains leaving Main Street at 4:57 p.m. and 5:33 p.m. would work.

The number of train stops at a station is a function of the passenger demand. Note that the Clybourn stop is served six times, while Ravenswood and Rogers Park are served only three times. The train scheduler will log the number of passengers at every stop in determining where the train stops.

The Emergency Room

The emergency room of a hospital presents a different type of scheduling challenge. A certain number of staff will be present during assigned hours and others will be on call for special emergencies. There are a given number of rooms that determine capacity, and they have to coordinate with ambulances to make sure that they can handle everything that comes in. A typical day may have a lot of twisted ankles, fevers, and broken bones. Most hospitals do not have the types of cases you see every week on television.

When catastrophes happen, cities and counties have emergency response systems that allocate the emergency rooms that are available in the area. California can go years without an injury due to earthquake, but it has to have a system of emergency response ready for that eventuality.

To study emergency room scheduling, you must understand that it is a 24-hr operation, but the emergency room is not fully staffed in the wee hours of the morning. Many emergency room physicians spend the entire night on a case, to be sure, and that is accounted for in a call schedule.

The On-Call Schedule

Hospitals are staffed with their own physicians, and private practice physicians have staff privileges enabling them to use the hospital. Ob-gyns usually have staff privileges at several hospitals, giving them the flexibility to deliver babies in the facility their patients desire. Physician schedules include clinic hours in which they examine patients; ward service time in which they must treat all the patients of their specialty who are hospitalized; time spent in surgery; and time on call.

"On call" means that the specialist is available by pager to respond to requests, some of which require a trip to the hospital. The call schedule is made by the unit manager, who determines a fair schedule by equally distributing the work across a time period. The workload usually begins with the input of the physicians, who request that certain days be left free.

A typical scenario: Days on call in 1 month

Wilma			6 days			No Jewish holidays
Lucy			6 days			Prefers Thursdays
Mike			6 days			No Mondays
Kate			6 days			No weekends
Ellen			4 days			
Sue			3 days			

Mon	Tue	Wed	Thu	Fri	Sat	Sun
		1 Wilma	2 Lucy	3 Kate	4 Sue	5 Ellen
6 Wilma	7 Mike	8 Kate	9 Lucy	10 Sue	11 Ellen	12 Wilma
13 Lucy	14 Kate	15 Mike	16 Lucy	17 Wilma	18 Sue	19 Ellen
20 Kate	21 Mike	22 Wilma	23 Lucy	24 Ellen	25 Mike	26 Wilma
27 Kate	28 Mike	29 Wilma	30 Lucy	31 Kate		

Holidays must be equally distributed so that no person gets an unfair distribution of these days in the United States. These holidays include New Year's Day, Memorial Day, Independence Day, Labor Day, Thanksgiving, and Christmas. (Religious holidays should be equally distributed across religions. If someone does not practice a religion, he or she may receive a personal day to balance this out.)

Vacation days also play havoc with a schedule. As a consequence, medical schedules must be plotted out at least 6 months in advance. Once the schedule is set, it is up to the individual physicians to trade whenever something comes up that they would want a night off of call to attend, such as a baseball game, their child's theatrical pageant, an anniversary, and so on.

Scheduling in Sports

Sports scheduling can be complicated by many factors. These factors must be considered.

1. *Availability of a facility:* If the stadium, arena, or field is owned by the team, it is simply a matter of blocking out the facility for the team. After the schedule is made for the team, other events may be scheduled. Most basketball arenas are also used for concerts when the team is not using the facility.

2. *League requirements:* In professional leagues, the schedule is set by the league office. College sports require a certain number of games to be played within the conference, on a rotating home-and-away basis. For example, the University of Georgia will traditionally play Auburn one year in Alabama and the next year in Athens, Georgia. However, every year they will play the University of Florida in Jacksonville, Florida—a "neutral" field. In collegiate conferences, a minimum number of league games must be played every year.

3. *Financial considerations:* In university sports, travel budgets restrict where teams are able to play. Some smaller universities will schedule games in the home stadiums of larger universities simply to generate more revenue than they would otherwise get in a home game. They may lose 63 to 0, but they provide needed funds.

4. *Scheduling the home field advantage:* In university sports, the more games played at home in certain sports, that is, basketball, the better the chance of winning. Experts say that the home court advantage is worth about four to six points per game. However, the team will want to play some games in locations that are attractive to recruits. An annual trip to play Hawaii might be an incentive. Some coaches go so far as to schedule games so that prized recruits can play in front of their families. Similarly, coaches may schedule games so that they can see their own families. This might explain why a team from Kansas might play a game against a team from Philadelphia.

The National Football League Schedule

An interesting approach to scheduling is used by the National Football league in the United States. Each team will play 8 home games and 8 away games. The 16 games are arranged in this way:

1. Each team plays 2 games against its three division opponents, for a total of 6 games.

2. Each team plays the four teams from a division within its conference. The conferences are rotated on 3-year cycles. This process adds 4 games.

3. Each team plays a division from the other conference, on a rotation 4-year cycle. This adds 4 games.

4. There are 2 final games scheduled according to the prior year's standings. First-place teams play the two other division first-place teams. Second-place teams play the two second-place teams.

The Chicago Bears 2007 schedule was set on the final day of 2006, when it won its conference and played in the Super Bowl. It played two games each against its division opponents: Green Bay, Detroit, and Minnesota. It played a game against each team in the NFC division, including Dallas, Philadelphia, New York, and Washington. It played a game against each team in the AFC West from the other conference: San Diego, Kansas City, Oakland, and Denver. Finally, it played games against Seattle and New Orleans based on the prior year's standings. The two games against the prior year's standings provide a measure of parity.

Women's College Basketball

In college basketball, a conference schedule must be met. After that, the schedule is a function of travel budgets and scheduling around examinations. Here, for example, is the DePaul women's basketball schedule for 2007–2008:

Date (mm/dd)	Opponent	Big East	Mode
11/10		@ Southern Illinois	Bus
11/15	Florida International		
11/16	Florida State		
11/25		@ Illinois State	Bus
11/29	Illinois, Chicago		
12/2	Missouri State		
12/8	Loyola, Chicago		
12/12	Chicago State		
12/17		@ Northern Illinois	Bus
12/20		@ Northwestern	Bus
12/28	Texas	@ San Diego tournament	Air
12/30	Appalachian St.	@ San Diego	
1/2	Tennessee		
1/6	Pittsburgh	X	
1/12	@Providence	X	Air
1/15	St. John's	X	
1/19	@Marquette	X	Bus
1/22	@Notre Dame	X	Bus
1/26	Cincinnati	X	
1/29	Syracuse	X	
2/2	Villanova	X	
2/5	@South Florida	X	Air
2/10	Louisville	X	
2/16	@West Virginia	X	Air
2/20	@Georgetown	X	Air
2/24	Notre Dame	X	
2/27	@Rutgers	X	Air
3/1	@Connecticut	X	Bus
3/3	@Seton Hall	X	Bus
3/7	Big East tournament		Air

NOTE: @ = away games, X = Big East conference games.

In this schedule, DePaul has 15 home games and 14 road games. Two of the road games are played at a neutral court in a tournament in San Diego. Of the road games, 5 are played within 150 miles, enabling the team to get to the arena by bus. The 3 games at the end of the schedule, Rutgers, Connecticut, and Seton Hall, are handled in one trip. Six air trips are called for, excluding the Big East tournament, resulting in reduced travel costs.

The Office Schedule

Scheduling clients and patients into offices (doctors, lawyers, accountants, etc.) can be more efficiently handled if the following considerations are made:

1. The average length of time per class of service

2. Outside obligations of the professional (court time, hospital time, etc.)

3. Expecting the unexpected

4. Following up to verify appointments, via telephone calls or contact cards

A problem that most of us experience in a doctor's office is that the physician has an unexpected case that slows the schedule throughout the day. This can be avoided if the office assistant studies the cases for an extended period of time and logs the "unexpected cases." If the schedule accounts for an unexpected, unscheduled 3-hr case, it is no longer unexpected. The difficulty is that it is unpredictable. But the knowledge that such cases occur requires that a buffer be built into the schedule to allow for them. The office would be totally inefficient if it scheduled 100% of the time slots with no consideration for these types of cases.

A certain number of appointments become no-shows, and these also have to be factored in. If 10% of appointments cancel, that is almost 1 hr in a normal work day. There are two actions to be taken: one is to vigilantly reduce that number by contacting the customers to make sure that they show. However, things will happen to make them miss appointments. A second strategy is to overbook. Airlines do this because they do experience a customary no-show rate, and this expectation forces them to oversell planes. Overbooking can have a negative effect when everyone shows up, and airlines alleviate this pain by offering incentives to bump passengers. But few office clients get incentives when they have to wait for 2 hr for their scheduled appointments. That is the trade-off of the office—risking the loss of goodwill at the expense of maximizing revenue.

Television Production Scheduling

Television production is similar to project scheduling, which is discussed in another chapter. However, production schedulers have found traditional business means of scheduling projects to be inferior for handling the complexities of television and the movies. The vast majority of movie production schedulers use software called Movie Magic Scheduling™—a powerful package that visually gives the scheduler a portrait of what and when resources are needed.

The schedule begins with a shooting script. The scheduler must take this script and note all the different locations and sets that are called for in the movie. Television and movies are rarely shot in the same order as the shooting script. Instead, they are shot according to the availability of actors and locations.

The scheduler takes the shooting script and makes a "breakdown sheet." On this sheet, notations are made for each scene as to whether it is interior or exterior, day or night, the location, and the set. Cast members are then placed into the appropriate scenes in which they are set to appear.

The scheduling for television production depends on the type of program. A situation comedy uses fixed sets. Reality shows can vary from one room, à la *Big Brother*, to all over the world, such as *The Amazing Race*. Shows such as *CSI: Miami* have a combination of fixed sets and actual locations in Miami.

To get some idea of the scheduling that would be required, here is an example from a 1995 taping of *Seinfeld*. Each scene is introduced with an exterior shot of where the interior location is supposed to be. These shots are stock footage catalogued over time. This episode has three main plots: in one, a character named Jimmy annoyingly speaks of himself in the third person. "Jimmy had a great game," he says, discussing his basketball game. "Jimmy sells these shoes" (see Table 9.1).

Table 9.1   A "Seinfeld" Episode Scene Breakdown

Scene	Location	Characters	Action
1	A. Comedy club	Jerry	Jerry's monologue
2	B. Locker room	Jerry, Kramer, George, Jimmy	George and Kramer admire Jimmy's basketball shoes, which are specially made for jumping.
3	C. NY Yankee board room	George and Yankee employees	There is a theft problem with the Yankees. George is a suspect because he sweats a lot.
4	D. Dentist's waiting room	Jerry and extras	Jerry is surprised to see a Penthouse magazine in the waiting room.
5	E. Jerry's apartment	Jerry, Elaine, Kramer, and George	Elaine wants to know who the blond guy at the gym is. She needs a date to the Mel Tormé concert.
6	F. Gym	Elaine, Jimmy, blond guy	Jimmy tells Elaine that Jimmy likes her. (He speaks of himself in the third person.) She gets Jimmy's number, thinking it is the blond guy.
7	G. Dentist's office	Kramer, dentist, aide	Kramer gets Novocain.
8	B	Kramer, Jerry, George, and Jimmy	Kramer causes Jimmy to fall in the locker room.
9	B	Add ambulance driver and extra	Jimmy is taken away on a stretcher.
10	H. Street	Kramer, extra	A man thinks Kramer is handicapped due to the Novocain and weird shoes and gives him a ticket to the Mel Tormé benefit.
11	I. Sports store	George, extras	George demos shoes to extras in sports store.
12	E	Kramer, Jerry, and Elaine	They realize Kramer was invited because he looked handicapped.
13	G	Jerry, dentist, aide	Jerry is given gas for anesthesia. He thinks he sees the dentist and aide getting dressed.
14	J. Restaurant	Jerry, Elaine, George	Jerry worries about what happened while he was asleep in the dentist's office. Elaine realizes she has a date with Jimmy and not the blond guy.

Scene	Location	Characters	Action
15	G	Elaine, Jimmy, blond guy, extra	Elaine finds out the blond guy is gay.
16	K. Hotel lobby	Kramer, Elaine, and Jimmy	Jimmy sees Kramer in line and punches him for causing his fall.
17	L. Hotel ballroom	Kramer, Mel Tormé	Kramer now really appears handicapped, and Tormé dedicates a song to him.
18	M. George Steinbrenner's office	George, Steinbrenner stand-in	George is asked about the missing stuff, but he says he would never steal.
19	N. Outside newsstand	Kramer, Jerry	Kramer reads a Penthouse letter about a dentist and his aide taking advantage of an unconscious patient.

Elaine has a crush on a blond guy who works out at the health club, and Jimmy tells her, "Jimmy thinks you are hot." She thinks that Jimmy must be the blond guy. "Jimmy wants your phone number." She obliges, and mistakenly agrees to a date with Jimmy.

The second plot is at Yankee Stadium, where George is suspected of stealing items from the Yankees because whenever they discuss the missing items, he breaks out into a sweat. He sweats for one reason or another that has nothing to do with the thefts.

The third plot involves Kramer. After a trip to the dentist in which he is shot with Novocain, he meets a man on the street waiting for a cab. The man sees that Kramer is wearing these odd shoes (a pair that Jimmy makes) that resemble shoes typical for a person with clubfoot. Hearing Kramer's voice slurred by Novocain, the man feels sorry for him and invites him to the same Mel Tormé dinner that Elaine attends with Jimmy. Meanwhile, Jimmy has a locker-room accident (caused by Kramer) that puts him on crutches. When Jimmy sees Kramer at the benefit, he attacks him, making Kramer seem even more handicapped. Well, it is funnier on television than it sounds on paper!

Character	Scenes
Jerry	1, 2, 4, 5, 8, 9, 12, 13, 14, 19
Kramer	2, 5, 7, 8, 9, 10, 12, 16, 17, 19
Elaine	5, 6, 12, 14, 15, 16
George	2, 3, 5, 8, 9, 11, 14, 18
Jimmy	2, 6, 8, 9, 15, 16
Extras	3, 4, 9, 10, 11, 15, 16
Mel Tormé	17

Location	Scenes	Location	Scenes
A. Comedy club	1	E. Jerry's apartment	5, 12
B. Locker room	2, 8, 9	F. Gym	6
C. Yankee boardroom	3	G. Dentist's office	7, 13
D. Dentist's waiting room	4	H. Street (1)	10

(Continued)

(Continued)

Location	Scenes	Location	Scenes
I. Sports store	11	L. Hotel ballroom	17
J. Restaurant	14	M. Steinbrenner's office	18
K. Hotel lobby	16	N. Outside newsstand	19

Not including the exterior establishing shots, there are 14 different locations in one 20-min Seinfeld episode. The shooting of the script will group according to locations. Most of these are created on the sound stage, where a dentist's waiting room or dentist's office can be easily assembled. The order of shooting usually varies, however. For example, all the scenes in the locker room would be shot consecutively.

Conclusion

A good schedule is required of any organization that intends to operate in a smooth and efficient fashion. The method of scheduling depends on the industry and the situation. In the manufacturing of assembled items, the MPS drives the entire production system.

Students juggle their class schedules with their work schedules. Those who take public transportation are dictated by bus and train schedules. When on vacation, there is a scramble to find flight schedules that match the flyer's needs.

Global business, in fact, is on schedule. Shipments must leave the dock in Hong Kong by a certain time so that they arrive in Los Angeles on time to be unloaded to a train or truck that will deliver them to Kansas City when the customer wants them. If you look at your watch right now, you know where you have to be and when, and all that is best handled by a schedule.

Summary

1. Operations managers establish a schedule for production based on a forecast. It is an important function to the success of balancing production needs against customer needs.

2. There are many types of scheduling, and as in forecasting, the operations manager must find the right tool for the job. The job shop schedule is a type of schedule that prioritizes jobs using rules. Examples of these rules include the shortest processing time, the earliest due date, and the first-come-first-served rule.

3. Eli Goldratt developed the Theory of Constraints, a theory for scheduling machines around bottlenecks; it is a helpful theory with the main idea being to streamline production at the bottleneck task.

4. The MPS is a module used within materials requirements planning (MRP) software, to schedule production using a rolling time horizon.

5. One of the important tasks for Operations is the labor schedule. In this task, the operations manager must match the labor schedule against the customer demand patterns.

Key Terms

Buffer

Drum

Job shop scheduling

Johnson's rule

Master Production Schedule

Rope

Theory of Constraints

Review Questions

1. What are the different approaches to making a job shop schedule? Which do you think works the best?

2. Describe how a Master Production Schedule differs from a production forecast.

3. What are the major factors in establishing a train schedule, a bus schedule, and an airline schedule?

4. How does the National Football League set a schedule for the year?

5. What are the factors for setting a college sports schedule?

6. Why is television production scheduling different from manufacturing scheduling?

7. What are the five steps in the Theory of Constraints?

Problems

1. You are given a series of jobs with expected due dates and processing times. What is the best schedule to minimize average lateness and the number of late jobs?

Job	Processing Time (Days)	Due Date (Days)
1	6	14
2	5	9
3	8	17
4	3	7
5	9	21
6	4	11

2. You are given a series of jobs at your copy shop with expected due times and processing times. What is the best schedule to minimize average lateness and the number of late jobs? You receive all these jobs at 8 a.m.

Job	Processing Time	Due Time
1	5 min	10:00 a.m.
2	5 min	8:30 a.m.
3	5 min	12:00 p.m.
4	1 hr	10:00 a.m.
5	1 min	8:15 a.m.
6	2 hr	4:00 p.m.
7	5 min	8:45 a.m.
8	30 min	12:00 p.m.

Thirty minutes later, you have a series of jobs to add into the mix. Now reschedule.

Job	Processing Time	Due Time
9	5 min	10:00 a.m.
10	5 min	9:00 a.m.
11	1 min	9:00 a.m.
12	15 min	11:00 a.m.
13	1 hr	3:00 p.m.
14	2 hr	5:00 p.m.
15	1 hr	6:00 p.m.

Can you schedule all these jobs, given one machine to work on?

3.   You run a hospital emergency room. You have four rooms available, with a staff of three physicians and four nurses. You categorize incoming patients according to criticality, with 1 being *the most critical cases*, in which you have to drop everything and manage. When all rooms are occupied by critical patients, you must turn away incoming patients to another hospital. Illustrate how you would service the incoming patients for this hospital. Physicians do not have to stay with the patients until completion of treatment. They may interrupt service for a higher-priority patient.

Arrival Time (a.m.)	Patient No.	Criticality	Processing Time (Minutes)
7:02	1421	1	60
7:07	1422	5	15
7:11	1423	2	60
7:17	1424	3	45
7:21	1425	1	120
7:22	1426	4	30
7:31	1427	5	30
7:32	1428	5	15

Arrival Time (a.m.)	Patient No.	Criticality	Processing Time (Minutes)
7:35	1429	5	30
7:41	1430	2	50
7:48	1431	5	30
7:52	1432	5	15
7:55	1433	4	30
7:59	1434	5	30

4. You must process the series of jobs listed below on two machines. Each job must be completed on the first machine before moving to the second, and the machines can only do one job at a time.

Job No.	Time on Machine A (Days)	Time on Machine B (Days)
1010	8	3
1011	7	5
1012	9	6
1013	11	7
1014	5	4
1015	8	8

    a. How many days will it take to complete all jobs?
    b. How much idle time is found on Machine B?
    c. How much waiting time is found on Machine B?

5. Albert Seymour must process the series of jobs listed below on two machines. Each job must complete on the first machine before moving to the second, and the machines can only do one job at a time.

"Task" No.	Time on Machine A (Days)	Time on Machine B (Days)
Fab	1	4
Move	2	5
Embellish	4	6
Polish	3	1
Stock	5	4
Ship	3	7

    a. How many days will it take to complete all jobs?
    b. How much idle time is found on Machine B?
    c. How much waiting time is found on Machine B?

6. What if we add a third machine to the problem?

"Task" No.	Time on Machine A (Days)	Time on Machine B (Days)	Time on Machine C (Days)
Fab	1	4	9
Move	2	5	14
Embellish	4	6	8
Polish	3	1	5
Stock	5	4	6
Ship	3	7	7

   a. How many days will it take to complete all jobs?
   b. How much idle time is found on Machine C?
   c. How much waiting time is found on Machine C?
   d. How would you change the schedule?

Projects

1. Study the schedule of classes at your business school this term. Count the number of courses of production and operations management classes at both the undergraduate and graduate levels and then determine the teaching loads by professor. Ask your professor how many courses he or she teaches and how the schedule is determined.

2. Visit a fast-food restaurant and for several time periods in the day and count the number of workers and the number of customers. Note if any customers leave when the line gets too long.

3. Compare the sports schedules of the past 2 years for the following sports:
   - Football
   - Women's basketball
   - Men's basketball
   - Baseball
   - Women's volleyball

   a. How have the schedules changed from one year to the next?
   b. Discuss the travel involved in the road games.

4. The next time you are on an airplane, and when all services have been concluded, ask the flight attendant about his or her work schedule. How many days per month does he or she typically work? How does he or she count time spent working? How does this compare with the typical office worker's schedule?

5. Interview a shift worker. Discuss how shifts rotate (if they do).

6. Watch a movie, and note every time the location and sets change. Note which actors appear in every scene. Invent a fantasy shooting schedule based on the various locations and sets.

7. Study the major scheduling issues at your workplace.

CASE   Office Scheduling

Dr. Rob Morgan is a psychiatrist with clinics in two locations: Chicago and Chapel Hill, North Carolina. *Originally*, he was based in North Carolina, but several high profile cases in Chicago led him to establish a practice there.

His practice is to schedule 1-hr appointments followed by 15-min breaks. He takes 90 min off for exercise 3 days a week. His basic schedule looks like this:

	Mon	Tue	Wed	Thu	Fri	Sat
Time	Chicago	Chicago	Chicago	NC	NC	NC
8:00–9:00 a.m.	X	X	X	X	X	
9:15–10:15 a.m.	X	X	X	X	X	X
10:30–11:30 a.m.	X	X	X	X	X	X
11:45 a.m.–12:45 p.m.	X	X	X			
1:00–2:00 p.m.	X	X				
2:15–3:15 p.m.	X	X	X	X	X	
3:30–4:30 p.m.	X	X	X	X	X	
4:45–5:45 p.m.	X	X	X	X		

NOTE: X = work hours.

Dr. Morgan takes a flight from Chicago to North Carolina every Wednesday night at 5:45 p.m. He only works until 11:30 a.m. on Saturdays. He takes 6 weeks off per year for vacation and rest.

He employs two receptionists, one at each location. If each of the receptionists were to work 32 hr, how would you suggest that he set the schedule?

Web Sites

www.showbizsoftware.com

www.goldratt.com

References

Cox, J. F., III, & Blackstone, J. H., Jr. (1998). *APICS dictionary* (9th ed.). Falls Church, VA: APICS.
Goldratt, E. (1999). *Theory of constraints.* Great Barrington, MA: North River Press.
Goldratt, E., & Cox, J. (2004). *The goal.* Great Barrington, MA: North River Press.

CHAPTER 10

Facility Location

SOURCE: © Marcelo Wain/istockphoto.com

Learning Objectives

In this chapter, we will study

- Strategic issues in facility location (we will discuss why companies choose specific locations)
- How locations are selected from global, regional, and city sites
- The site selections for IKEA
- The factor-rating method: This method applies a scoring system to location decisions
- bestplaces.net, an Internet source for city research
- The center-of-gravity method, a grid method for selecting locations
- The features of geographic information systems (GIS)
- City-ranking services
- Several locations: Savannah, Chicago, China, India, Taiwan, and Belfast
- The review factors used for closing locations

Where Should We Move?

One of the most strategic decisions in operations management concerns facility location. How many factories do we need, and where do we put them? Where do we have our regional offices? Where do we locate our service stations? Our repair centers? If we need to downsize our locations, where do we begin? The facility location decision basically travels in two directions: We are either expanding or downsizing. Expansion of facilities must be done carefully, because the day may come when we must close locations, and that is infinitely more difficult to do than opening a plant.

Opening a new location is usually a cause for joy, celebration, and parties. Local economies reap the benefits when 3,000 jobs are added, for the multiplier effect of new jobs means additional jobs to service the new workforce. The new workforce has to find places to live, and that adds health to the local real estate markets. They have to find places to shop and get their hair cut, nails done, laundry done, cars serviced, and banking taken care of.

Politicians are always on the alert for potential new employers because that stimulates the economy, and a healthy local economy usually brings with it satisfied voters, keeping the politician in office. Mayors need to strive for a diversified portfolio of businesses. It is dangerous to be reliant on only one employer because if that one suffers, so does the local economy.

On the other side of the coin, when employers have to close locations, there is a real human cost. Closing of a plant with 5,000 workers means that probably 15,000 or more people suffer economically. The real estate market declines, as there is a glut of available homes on the market. All the stores suffer significant declines in sales. Politicians don't get reelected. People go on unemployment or move to places where there are jobs. Michael Moore's film *Roger and Me* detailed the cost to Flint, Michigan, when many jobs were lost as a result of the decline in U.S. auto sales and the move to foreign plants.

In this chapter, we will review the major issues in facility location.

Global Location

Once a decision maker knows what type of facility is needed, that is, manufacturing, headquarters and offices, distribution, and so on, the first big question in global facility location is "In what region of the globe will we locate?" A U.S. company, for example, may desire a manufacturing plant to add to their current three domestic plants. They might consider Asian countries such as China, Taiwan, and Thailand. They may consider Mexico. They might consider India, England, Australia, Brazil, the Czech Republic, Bahrain, or Dubai.

The important considerations a company would need to review include the following:

1. *Labor:* What are the local labor costs?

2. *Skills:* What expertise does the local populace have that we can use?

3. *Shipping:* What would the shipping costs be to major shipping points?

4. *Other costs:* What other cost factors must we be concerned about?

5. *Political stability:* What is the local political climate?

6. *Employers:* What is the record of other employers in the region?

7. *Competition:* Where are our competitors located, and how will this location affect competition?

8. *Economics:* What is the level of unemployment and availability of skilled employees in the area?

9. *Unions:* Is organized labor a factor in the region?

The decision involves numerous trade-offs. One location may offer lower labor costs that are offset by increased shipping costs. Another location may not be up to speed on the ISO standards of quality that the industry may dictate.

From Global to Region

After narrowing the choice down to a specific country, the search narrows to regions, then cities, and then actual sites.

Regional Decisions

The United States has a number of regions offering a completely different set of advantages and disadvantages. Dealing with each region is much like dealing with a number of different countries.

Mercedes Benz located in Alabama after scouting for a place to locate a plant to build SUVs. BMW located in South Carolina. Honda is in Ohio, Nissan in Tennessee, Toyota in California, Mitsubishi in Illinois, and Subaru in Indiana. In the auto industry, it made sense to locate in rather sparsely populated regions, giving the advantage of an area in which workers had few choices of employers. This made the local populace reliant on the company and less likely to form a union. The wages were substantially higher than in other places of employment in each region, so the plant was warmly received. There was also little opportunity for skilled workers—engineers, for example—to find other employment in the region easily. An industrial engineer in Southern Illinois would have to take the day off and drive to Chicago, St. Louis, or Indianapolis to look for similar work. In Detroit, the workers could just take a couple of hours off to interview for a job.

The City and Site

Much of the decision on the actual city (or town) and the place to build centers on the same issues you or I would have to consider if we thought about moving to another place for a job. What is the cost of housing? What are the local amenities? What activities does the local community afford?

Then, there are the obvious business decisions. How do we transport materials from the area? What is the cost of real estate? How high are property taxes? Are there any tax incentives being offered?

IKEA

IKEA, the Scandinavian furniture store, has 35 current locations, after adding 6 in 2007–2008. Their locations are as follows:

Tempe, AZ	Elizabeth, NJ	Burbank, CA
Paramus, NJ	Carson, CA	Long Island, NY
Costa Mesa, CA	Conshohocken, PA	E. Palo Alto, CA
S. Philadelphia, PA	Emeryville, CA	Pittsburgh, PA
San Diego, CA	Frisco, TX	W. Sacramento, CA
Houston, TX	New Haven, CT	Woodbridge, VA
Bolingbroke, IL	Seattle, WA	Schaumberg, IL
Atlanta, GA	Stoughton, MA	Baltimore, MD
College Park, MD	Twin Cities, MN	
2006		
Dublin, CA	Canton, MI	Round Rock, TX
2007–2008		
Orlando, FL	Sunrise, FL	Brooklyn, NY
West Chester, OH	Portland, OR	Draper, UT

IKEA has focused on suburban locations in middle- to high-income neighborhoods. Among the locations not presently served are Denver, Kansas City, and Tampa, each of which fits their profile.

The Factor Rating Method

The simplest approach to a location decision is the **factor rating method**. This method involves the selection of the most important factors contributing to the location decision, weighting them, and summing the totals. For example, let's say we are considering five cities for location: Denver, Chicago, Atlanta, San Francisco, and Baltimore. The decision criteria are cost of living, climate, and recreation. Each city is then compared in the three areas.

We apply weights to the criteria. The weightings will shift the results in favor of those doing well in the most important decision criteria. In this case, we will use 50% for cost of living, 30% for climate, and 20% for recreation.

The scaling can produce quite different results. If we used a 10-point scale on the decision, it might go like this (with 1 being *best*):

	Cost of Living	Climate	Recreation	
	.50	.30	.20	Total points
Denver	5	6	3	4.9
Chicago	7	7	4	6.4
Atlanta	3	3	5	3.4
San Francisco	10	1	2	5.7
Baltimore	3	5	6	4.2

Based on this approach, Atlanta, with the lowest score, would be the preferred choice, since a low score indicates a superior location.

Center-of-Gravity Method

There are a number of different location models that apply to specific situations. The **center-of-gravity method** suits the case in which existing stores must be served by a new distribution center. The objective is to locate the distribution center to serve the stores from the most economical location. The method involves plotting the existing locations on a map and using either distance or average driving time for the number of loads delivered.

Steps:

1. Set up a grid with an arbitrary location of $x = 0$ and $y = 0$.

2. Locate each present store location on a grid, noting its x and y location.

3. Note the number of "loads" shipped to this location. In general, this number represents a dollar volume, quantity volume, or number of shipments.

4. Plug the x, y coordinates and loads into this equation:

Center X = $[(x_1 \times \text{loads}) + (x_2 \times \text{loads}) + (x_3 \times \text{loads}) + \ldots + (x_n \times \text{loads})]/\#\text{loads}$
Center Y = $[(y_1 \times \text{loads}) + (y_2 \times \text{loads}) + (y_3 \times \text{loads}) + \ldots + (y_n \times \text{loads})]/\#\text{loads}$

Suppose we have three existing locations:

	x	y	Loads
Provo	10	0	100
Salt Lake	2	40	500
Ogden	2	70	100

$$x = [(10 \times 100) + (2 \times 500) + (2 \times 100)]/700$$
$$x = 2200/700 = 3.9$$

$$y = [(0) + (40 \times 500) + (70 \times 100)]/700$$
$$y = 27000/700 = 38.6$$

This location of $x = 4$ and $y = 39$ would be approximately 1 mile to the south of Salt Lake City.

The location decision maker would weigh this information but not necessarily locate exactly where the method dictates.

Here is another example, with the turf much larger:

Existing locations:

	x	y	Loads
Reno	0	0	1,000
Sacramento	250	0	2,000
Salt Lake	500	0	2,000
Denver	1,100	100	3,000

Our center-of-gravity-determined location is as follows:

$$x = [(250 \times 2000) + (500 \times 2000) + (1100 \times 3000)]/8000 = 600$$
$$y = (100 \times 3000)/8000 = 37.5$$

This location would be approximately 100 miles to the east of Salt Lake City and 37 miles north—somewhere on the way to Denver, which has the biggest load requirement.

Geographic Information Systems (GIS)

What is GIS?

Today, many firms employ **geographic information systems (GIS)** to analyze location-type decisions. GIS databases include information about addresses, buildings, and streets and demographic and census information.

There are three approaches to GIS:

1. *The database approach:* GIS is a geodatabase, describing the geographic world.

2. *The map approach:* GIS includes map sets of the earth, enabling analysis and editing.

3. *The model approach:* By combining data sources and applying analytic functions, new data sets can be created.

Examples of Applications. The Web site www.gis.com gives several examples of useful applications of GIS technology.

Bank of America analyzed the geographic distribution of the bank's deposits in relation to the deposit potential in New York City. This showed them on a map where they should concentrate on increasing their coverage.

An emergency medical service in Florida plotted emergency calls and response times. This gave them a visual picture of how long it was taking to respond to calls in various zones.

When the Shuttle Columbia exploded on reentry over Texas in 2003, a GIS system was used to model the expected distribution of debris. It did this with incredible accuracy.

What Can You Do With GIS?

Map Where Things Are. Mapping where things are lets you find places that have the features you're looking for and see where to take action.

1. *Finding a feature:* People use maps to see where or what an individual feature is.

2. *Finding patterns:* Looking at the distribution of features on the map instead of just an individual feature, you can see patterns emerge.

Maps of the locations of earthquake hazards are essential for creating and updating building codes used in the United States. Online, interactive earthquake maps, as well as seismicity and fault data, are available at earthquake.usgs.gov.

Map Quantities. People map quantities, such as where the most and least are, to find places that meet their criteria and take action or to see the relationship between places. This gives an additional level of information beyond simply mapping the location of features.

A map created by the Center for the Evaluative Clinical Sciences at Dartmouth Medical School showed the number of children under 18 years per clinically active pediatrician for a particular study area.

For example, a catalog company selling children's clothes would want to find ZIP codes not only around their store but also where there are many young families with relatively high income. Or public health officials might want to map not only physicians but also the number of physicians per 1,000 people in each census tract to see which areas are adequately served and which are not.

Map Densities. While you can see concentrations by simply mapping the locations of features, in areas with many features, it may be difficult to see which areas have a higher concentration than others. A density map lets you measure the number of features using a uniform unit, such as acres or square miles, so that you can clearly see the distribution.

Mapping density is especially useful when mapping areas such as census tracts or counties, which vary greatly in size. On maps showing the number of people per census tract, the larger tracts might have more people than the smaller ones. But some smaller tracts might have more people per square mile—a higher density.

Find What's Inside. Use GIS to monitor what's happening and to take specific action by mapping what's inside a specific area. For example, a district attorney would monitor drug-related arrests to find out if an arrest is within 1,000 ft of a school—if so, stiffer penalties will apply.

Find What's Nearby. Find out what's occurring within a set distance of a feature by mapping what's nearby.

The Pacid Disaster Center has developed and applied a vulnerability-exposure-sensitivity-resilience model to map people and facilities (what's nearby) exposed to flood risk in the Lower Mekong River Basin.

Map Change. Map the change in an area to anticipate future conditions, decide on a course of action, or evaluate the results of an action or policy.

1. By mapping where and how things move over a period of time, you can gain insight into how they behave. For example, a meteorologist might study the paths of hurricanes to predict where and when they might occur in the future.

2. *Map change to anticipate future needs.* For example, a police chief might study how crime patterns change from month to month to help decide where officers should be assigned.

3. *Map conditions before and after an action or event to see the impact.* A retail analyst might map the change in store sales before and after a regional ad campaign to see where the ads were most effective (www.gis.com/whatisgis/dowithgis.html).

Operations management can use GIS for all types of location decisions. For instance, to locate a new gas station, we would want to know the traffic patterns by time of day. Since people are more likely to stop for fuel *after* work, we want to know in what direction they will be traveling from 5 p.m. to 7 p.m. and locate on that side of the street.

If you want to locate a new retail store, you'll need to know the demographics of the area, the location of competitors in the area, and the traffic patterns. It is helpful to know the per capita income and the age breakdown of the local population. You're not going to do well with a day care center in a retirement community!

Fast-Food Locations

Major fast-food chains use GIS systems to find the best places to locate a new restaurant. A number of key factors play into the decision, which would be similar for a gas station or a convenience store.

1. *Traffic patterns:* An actual estimate of traffic flows by time of day plays into this decision. Sales are greater for fast-food restaurants in the evening, so the best location would have greater traffic flow in the evening than in the morning. For example, one side of the street may have heavy traffic in the morning as people drive to work, whereas traffic is heavier on the other side of the street in the evening, when they return. Thus, the fast-food restaurant, and the gas station, would be more likely to get business on the "evening" side of the street.

2. *Ease of entry:* The ease of getting in and out of the restaurant is a key consideration. If there is a cement median blocking a left-hand turn into the restaurant, then that alone will cut into the business.

3. *Competition:* It is not necessarily bad to locate within spitting distance of the competition, as long as the traffic patterns dictate enough demand. However, to find a great location with no competition enables the restaurant to enjoy a nice period of profits until the competition locates next door.

4. *Other nearby businesses:* Locating near a gas station, even next door, is a good thing because customers tend to group their stops. It is also smart to locate on the way to a popular attraction or store.

5. *Demographic trends:* A study of the local incomes, crime rates, and real estate trends is important to make sure the company is not locating in an area that is declining.

A lot of thought must go into the location of a fast-food restaurant, a small business, or even an office, such as an accounting specialist, shoe repair, hair salon, or any other business. The small businessperson often has a great concept for a business but makes a poor location decision that cuts into the business.

www.bestplaces.net

An application of the factor-rating method is found at bestplaces.net. This site takes a number of factors in selecting a city and enables the user to weight each factor in making a decision. This process for an individual is similar to what a firm would go through in selecting a location.

For example, let's say we have two individuals finishing college who want to find a job in certain types of cities. Student #1 prefers warmth above all factors. She or he prefers a job in a city that is near the beach. Student #2 prefers a small city (under 300,000 in population) with a low cost of living and low crime rate. After plugging in their ratings in the site, the factors are summarized and the best cities determined.

Student #1:

1. Orlando	2. Ft. Myers, FL	3. San Francisco, CA
Economy B	Economy B	Economy C
Housing C+	Housing B–	Housing C+
Education C+	Education C	Education A–
Health B–	Health C	Health A
Crime C–	Crime C	Crime C+
Recreation A	Recreation B	Recreation A+
Culture A–	Culture C–	Culture A+

Student #2:

1. Bellingham, WA	2. Ft. Collins, CO	3. Bremerton, WA
Economy B–	Economy B	Economy B–
Housing B–	Housing B–	Housing C+
Education C+	Education B–	Education C
Health C–	Health B–	Health C
Crime B–	Crime B	Crime B–
Recreation B+	Recreation A+	Recreation A+
Culture C	Culture C–	Culture C
Transportation C+	Transportation C–	Transportation C–

Cities Ranked and Rated

Sperling and Sander's (2007) book, *Cities Ranked and Rated*, was published in 2004, ranking more than 400 U.S. cities in nine categories:

1. *Economy and jobs:* This category looks at employment levels and projected growth. It may change drastically from year to year for cities dependent on specific industries.

2. *Cost of living:* This is derived from the U.S. Bureau of Labor Statistics Cost of Living Index. It includes the cost of housing, utilities, food, gasoline, and so on.

3. *Climate:* This ranking seeks out the nicest weather by finding the climates with mild weather.

4. *Education:* This factor is derived by graduation rates and availability of higher education.

5. *Health and health care:* This ranking is a "mix of health hazard and healthcare attributers."

6. *Crime:* Crime is determined by property rates.

7. *Transportation:* This ranking is a function of commute times and availability of mass transit and air transportation.

8. *Leisure:* Leisure is calculated by the available forms of entertainment and recreation.

9. *Arts and culture:* Symphony orchestras, museums, ballets, and libraries weigh in here.

The best cities by category are given in Tables 10.1 through 10.3. (Note that these rankings were published based on a 2003 report.) Most of the categories will be similar from year to year, but the economic figures could change drastically. Here are some excerpts from the book:

Table 10.1 Best and Worst Cities by Cost of Living

Rank	Best	Rank	Worst
1	Texarkana, TX	373	San Francisco, CA
2	Anderson, IN	372	San Jose, CA
3	Danville, VA	371	Salinas, CA
4	Altoona, PA	370	Santa Ana, CA
5	Decatur, IL	369	New York, NY
6	Longview, TX	368	Honolulu, HI
7	Youngstown, OH	367	Santa Rosa, CA
8	Victoria, TX	366	Oxnard, CA
9	McAllen, TX	365	Santa Cruz, CA
10	Clarksville, TN	364	Oakland, CA

Table 10.2 Best and Worst by Climate

Rank	Best	Rank	Worst
1	Salinas, CA	375	Lewiston, ME
2	Oakland, CA	374	Portland, ME
3	Santa Cruz, CA	373	Bangor, ME
4	San Francisco, CA	372	Burlington, VT
5	Honolulu, HI	371	Hartford, CT
6	San Louis Obispo, CA	370	Norwich, CT
7	Santa Barbara, CA	369	Pocatello, ID
8	Los Angeles, CA	368	Springfield, MA
9	Riverside, CA	367	Albany, NY
10	San Diego, CA	366	Glens Falls, NY

Table 10.3   Best and Worst Cities by Leisure

Rank	Best	Rank	Worst
1	Los Angeles, CA	375	El Centro, CA
2	Chicago, IL	374	Jackson, TN
3	New York, NY	373	Cheyenne, WY
4	Seattle, WA	372	St. Joseph, MO
5	San Francisco, CA	371	Dothan, AL
6	Nassau, NJ	370	Victoria, TX
7	Boston, MA	369	Gadsden, AL
8	Santa Ana, CA	368	Jonesboro, AR
9	Riverside, CA	367	Midland, TX
10	Phoenix, AZ	366	Danville, IL

Decision Factors for Two Cities

The Chicago Skyline

SOURCE: © Stuart Berman/istockphoto.com

Every city has its merits and demerits. We will discuss the strengths and weaknesses of two quite different cities: Savannah, Georgia, and Chicago, Illinois.

Savannah, a quaint little city located on the Atlantic Ocean, just north of Florida and south of Hilton Head Island, South Carolina, has been known as a tourist destination in the South, famous as the setting for the book and movie *Midnight in the Garden of Good and Evil* (Berendt, 1994).

Savannah also is an important and growing port for shipping. Let's take a look at that aspect of Savannah.

Port Location: Savannah

There is not a lot a city can do to attract business to its ports. For starters, the infrastructure and capital required to attract shipping business to a city's ports is

City Hall in Savannah, Georgia

SOURCE: © Bill Manning/istockphoto.com

enormous. Plus, the city has to be at an advantageous geographical position. Here are the 10 busiest ports in the United States:

Port	Total Containers (in Millions)	Port	Total Containers (in Millions)
Los Angeles, CA	7.32	Hampton Roads, VA	1.81
Long Beach, CA	5.78	Tacoma, WA	1.80
New York/New Jersey	4.48	Seattle, WA	1.78
Oakland, CA	2.04	Vancouver, WA	1.66
Charleston, SC	1.86	Savannah, GA	1.66

The small city of Savannah, Georgia, has reached the 10th place by tripling its business from 1994 to 2006 (Machalaba, 2005). This business generates 120,000 jobs for South Georgia. The angle Savannah took to this path was to encourage retailers to build warehouses in lower-cost areas in the South. Savannah has benefited by the logjam in the California ports, so some Asian exporters have found Savannah a lower-hassle alternative. The presence of major distribution centers for Wal-Mart and Home Depot brought a number of retailers into the region.

Why Locate in Chicago?

Chicago, the third largest city in the United States, boasts strengths in transportation, hospitality, and commerce. Unlike other midwestern cities that depend heavily on manufacturing, Chicago offers a diversified economy, a balanced portfolio, which is helpful for cities to fend off the negative effects of economic down cycles.

The decision to locate a headquarters, plant, or warehouse is influenced by many factors: for instance, costs to ship, ease of getting there, local amenities, and cost of living. Chicago certainly cannot attract companies based on its winters, which are quite cold. But the falls are very nice, and the summers are very pleasant.

A quick examination of the top 20 companies headquartered in the Chicago area shows a very diverse collection of food, drugs, service and retail, and financial institutions (see Table 10.4).

Table 10.4   The 20 Largest Public Firms in Chicago

Rank	Firm	Industry	# Employees Worldwide
1	Boeing	Aerospace	153,000
2	Sears	Retail	355,000
3	Walgreen	Drug stores	155,200
4	Motorola	Communications	69,000
5	Caterpillar	Farm equipment	85,116
6	Archer Daniels	Agricultural	25,641
7	Allstate Corp.	Insurance	38,900
8	Kraft Foods	Food	94,000
9	Abbott Labs	Pharmaceuticals	59,735
10	Deere and Co.	Farm machinery	47,400
11	McDonald's	Fast food	447,000
12	Sara Lee	Food	137,000
13	UAL Corp.	Airline	57,000
14	Exelon Corp.	Electricity	17,200
15	Illinois Tool Work	Industrial	50,000
16	CAN Financial	Insurance	10,100
17	Baxter Intl	Health care	47,000
18	AON Corp.	Insurance	46,600
19	Office Max	Office supply	29,000
20	R.R. Donnelley	Printing	50,000

Chicago's location, on the banks of Lake Michigan, was the prime reason for its growth in the 19th century. After rebuilding from the destruction of the Chicago fire, the city was able to rise from the ashes with a more manageable city plan. Eventually, it phased out its claim to fame as the "slaughterhouse" of America, a reputation it gained from its position as the largest meat-processing city in the world. The city relies heavily on public transportation, with two rail systems (the El and the Metra) and a large fleet of buses. Major efforts have been made to beautify the city in the past decade, most notable being the building of Millennium Park, a beautiful park right by Michigan Avenue.

Chicago has two major airports, O'Hare and Midway, and is a hub for both United and American Airlines. Because it is so centrally located within the United States, it ranks with Atlanta as a major intersection for air travel.

Global Location Factors: China and India

In the 21st century, the growing economic powers are China and India. China has made its mark in manufacturing and India in technology and services (Bremner & Engardio, 2005).

China anticipates more than U.S.$1.5 trillion in merchandise exports by 2010, up from U.S.$0.3 trillion, a fivefold increase. Meanwhile, India expects to export more than U.S.$75 billion in IT and services, an increase from only U.S.$6 billion in 2002 (Engardio, 2005).

From 2000 to 2004, India's gross domestic product (GDP) per capita grew from only U.S.$410 to around U.S.$500. During the same time period, China's GDP grew from about U.S.$825 to U.S.$1,050.

The current population of India is about 1.1 billion and of China, 1.25 billion. By 2050, they are anticipated to rise to 1.6 billion and 1.4 billion, respectively. The population of the United States is 300 million and is predicted to be 400 million by 2050. With "a billion" customers with increasing purchasing power, it is no wonder that these markets are highly sought after.

A limiting factor in China is the actual scarcity of laborers. As job opportunities increased, the availability of workers diminished. There has been a rapid rise in wages as opportunities for employment increased. (For the 2005 figures in China, see Table 10.5.)

Table 10.5 Wages in Major Chinese Cities

City	Percentage of Annual Wage Increase, 2005	Average Annual Pay for Manual Labor (U.S. $)
Beijing	9	2,756
Chengdou	10	1,489
Nanjing	12	2,353
Shanghai	9	2,979
Chongqing	11	1,787
Wuhan	9	2,681
Suzhou	10	2,413
Guangzhou	8	3,349

Honda Motors opened an automobile plant in Guangzhou in 2005. Honda has found the efficiency there to be equal to that of its plants in Japan and the United States, opening the door for an industry expected to have a capacity of 8 million units by 2008.

India is also a player in the automobile industry, although its domestic autos are yet to be popularized abroad. The Tata-produced Indica costs a mere $6,600. However, it is in telecommunications that India has made the biggest impression. The move of the largest cellular company, Bharti, to outsource its cellular network to three equipment suppliers was innovative in the industry (Hamm, 2005).

Bangalore has been a popular location for call centers, mainly from U.S. companies. Bangalore can provide a well-educated workforce with good English language skills. Many U.S. workers voiced their displeasure at the outsourcing of call centers and IT functions to India. However, companies have increasingly found this to be the economic solution.

As Roberts (2006) stated in *Business Week*, "In the coming decades, China and India will disrupt workforces, industries, companies, and markets in ways that we can barely begin to imagine."

Made in Taiwan

Although challenged by its lack of diplomatic relations with many countries, Taiwan has grown into a major exporter of manufactured goods. In fact, by 2006, it was the third largest exporter in the world, behind China and Japan, with the value of its exported goods totaling U.S.$215 billion (Insight Guide, 2006). Much of this comes from the IT hardware industry, totaling U.S.$30 billion per year. Taiwan is the world's leading manufacturer of laptop computers and a leading exporter of computer chips, bicycles, and chemicals.

The GDP of Taiwan is half that of the United States but much higher than that of neighboring Thailand and China. The population's use of the English language has enhanced its ability to bargain with English-speaking businesspeople. It also has a heavy Japanese presence, as Asian and Western influences blend into a sophisticated economic system. Trade with China is common despite the absence of a diplomatic relationship.

Taipei, the largest city in Taiwan, is a very sophisticated city, with a mass rapid transit (MRT) system providing quick access around the city. Taipei boasts the world's largest skyscraper (at present), Taipei 101, and a shopping district comparable to the one in Hong Kong.

Importantly, Taiwanese are friendly to foreigners, making it a good country for a corporate presence.

Northern Ireland

Belfast, in Northern Ireland, has become a popular location for foreign companies, with Citigroup, Microsoft, Oracle, Liberty Mutual, and Allstate Insurance locating there. Belfast has two highly recognized universities, Queen's University,

Belfast (QUB) and University of Ulster (UU), and this has proven to be a magnet for IT, financial services, and biotechnology firms.

A major consideration of locating in Northern Ireland is the political climate, and the recent stability has been a positive factor in the economic climate. A major factor that attracts business is the well-educated and highly motivated workforce available at lower salaries than in the rest of Britain and Europe. Foreign direct investment is mostly from the knowledge-based sectors.

The Best European Cities for Business

A survey of 500 board directors giving their opinions of the best European cities in which to conduct business gave the following results:

1. London	6. Amsterdam
2. Paris	7. Madrid
3. Frankfurt	8. Berlin
4. Brussels	9. Munich
5. Barcelona	10. Zurich

The survey asked participants to rank the most important location factors, and easy access to markets was listed first, with communication and transportation and availability of staff ranked high. Quality of life was listed as the least important factor to these executives. Make of that what you will.

Going the Other Way: Closing Plants

On April 1, 2006, Delphi announced that it was closing 21 of its 29 plants. This cut 17,000 union jobs, which paid an average of $27 an hour.

Other than the economics of the situation, the *Chicago Tribune* reported the reason the eight plants that survived would remain open:

The eight key plants, which employ 16,000 union workers, are in Kokomo, Ind.; Warren and Vandalia, Ohio; Grand Rapids, Mich.; Lockport and Rochester, NY.; and Brookhaven and Clinton, Miss.

Logistics explain why Delphi will maintain these U.S. plants. Components built at these plants, such as electronic controls; safety, communications and entertainment systems; and engine management systems, are shipped to assembly plants hours before they are installed on a vehicle.

On the other hand, brake pads and door hardware are low-margin "commodity" parts that can be built anywhere and easily shipped from low wage countries and stored in boxes until needed. Plants that produce such parts, including those in Milwaukee; Dayton, Ohio; Anderson, Ind.; and the Michigan cities of Flint, Lansing, Saginaw and Coopersville; are rendered expendable. (Popely, 2006, p. 8)

Delphi also eliminated 8,500 salaried workers globally. In Mexico, Delphi's workers are paid an annual wage of $7,000. Delphi employs 70,000 in Mexico, and these reductions bring the U.S. total to 30,000.

The headline read, "Nokia's German Closure Sparks Political Anger" (Euronews.net, 2008). Nokia had been given financial incentives to locate a plant in Germany for 2,300 workers. The incentives expired in September 2006, and 15 months later, Nokia announced that it was moving to Romania and Hungary. This followed moves by Motorola and Ben Q to move their cell phone manufacturing out of Germany, at a cost of 6,000 jobs. The German politicos were indignant, but Nokia felt that it had met its obligations and moved in search of cheaper labor.

In 1999, the Philip Morris plant closing in Louisville, Kentucky, was done due to declining sales in the cigarette industry (Hayes, 1999). With a 1% to 2% annual decline in sales, the writing was on the wall, and the plant was running at under 50% capacity.

This reduction of 1,400 jobs was due to a combination of factors, according to Philip Morris: increased productivity at other facilities, technological advances, and marketplace changes. The closing cost $200 million in severance packages.

In 2005, General Motors cut 30,000 jobs in a bid to reduce costs, cutting 9% of its global workforce (MSNBC.com, 2005). The cuts were largely from the United States and Canada.

When companies consider which plant or plants to close, they sometimes consider manpower difficulties. Called the "Runaway shop," this means that the company selects plants to close where it has experienced labor difficulties. Some of the factors to be considered in a plant or office closing are as follows:

- Total cost
- Total productivity
- Reduced sales
- Plant condition
- Technology requirements
- Labor costs
- Labor relations
- More attractive sites
- Incentives from other locations
- Industry or product decline

These are the realities that many companies face. When business turns downward, they have to examine their existing plant structure (or hotel structure or restaurant structure) and decide how to go about reducing the locations in a way that makes economic sense.

Conclusion

The facility location decision is one of analyzing the appropriateness of present locations, considering future new locations, and considering possible closures. The plant or headquarters closing can be a traumatic event for employees, so it is wise to consider new locations with that in mind.

A variety of mathematical approaches are available for plant location decisions, including simple-to-use methods such as the center-of-gravity and the factor-ratings methods. GIS have attained wide popularity for their ability to track demographic data. Perhaps as often as not, a simple intuitive decision is made without much thought given to these tools. However, the more thorough the analysis, the better informed the decision maker will be.

Summary

- One of the most strategic aspects of operations management has to do with its location of plants and offices. Access to markets, customers, and raw materials is an important consideration in plant location decisions.

- Location decisions range from regional to local and site selection. The global decision includes a study of labor availability, skills, shipping costs, political and economic factors, competition, and labor unions.

- The factor-rating method is a technique in which important factors are compared and weighted.

- The center-of-gravity method is applied for situations of existing plants or stores needing a central warehouse.

- GIS are used for location decisions frequently and offer the ability to show where things are and give demographic data.

Key Terms

Center-of-gravity method

Factor rating method

Geographic information systems (GIS)

Review Questions

1. How do facility location decisions differ when they are being considered at a global level?

2. What are the major issues one would face if looking for a location for an automobile plant? Hotel? Hospital? Waffle House?

3. What method of location analysis would be best to select a site for a new mega mall?

4. If a company sought a location that would be less likely to unionize, how would they go about finding that information?

5. What would be the major factors to be considered when selecting plants to shut down in a multiplant network?

Problems

1.   Best Buy presently has 41 locations in Illinois. Table 10.6 gives population density and latitude (X) and longitude (Y). Using population density as a proxy for volume, apply the center-of-gravity method to determine a good location for a distribution warehouse.

Table 10.6   Location Coordinates in Illinois

City	Population Density (/Sq. Mile)	X	Y
Forsyth	1,157	39.9	88.9
Bloomington	2,880	40.4	88.9
Springfield	2,064	39.7	89.6
Champaign	3,975	40.1	88.2
Peoria	2,543	40.7	89.6
Joliet	2,791	41.5	88.1
Fairview Hgts	1,349	38.5	89.9
Moline	2,806	41.4	90.5
Matteson	1,811	41.5	87.7
Bolingbroke	2,747	41.6	88.0
Orland Pk	2,668	41.6	87.8
Aurora	3,712	41.7	88.2
Downers Grove	3,420	41.7	88.0
Geneva	2,321	41.8	88.3
DeKalb	3,094	41.9	88.7
Crestwood	3,682	41.6	87.7
Lansing	4,189	41.5	87.5
Countryside	2,227	41.7	87.8
Burbank	6,687	41.7	87.7
Bloomingdale	3,204	41.9	88.0
N. Riverside	4,331	41.8	87.8
Addison	3,808	41.9	88.0
Melrose Pk	5,466	41.8	87.8
W. Dundee	2,041	42.0	88.2
Norridge	8,014	41.9	87.8
Schaumberg	3,967	42.0	88.0
Chicago	12,750	41.5	87.6
Chicago	12,750	41.5	87.6
Chicago	12,750	41.5	87.6
Rockford	2,680	42.2	89.0

City	Population Density (/Sq. Mile)	X	Y
Skokie	6,309	42.0	87.7
Niles	5,118	42.0	87.8
Arlington Hts	4,633	42.0	87.9
Crystal Lk	2,340	42.2	88.3
Evanston	9,584	42.0	87.2

2. Given the following coordinates and loads, find the preferred location, using the center-of-gravity method:

Location	X	Y	Loads
St. Louis	0	0	1,000
Columbia	80	0	400
Kansas City	200	0	1,000
Denver	700	0	2,000

Projects

1. Find the location coordinates of the Wal-Mart stores in your state (walmart.com), and determine a good location for a central warehouse serving these locations. Assume all the stores will have the same shipments.

2. Go to Bestplaces.net and find your best place to live. How does it differ from where you are?

3. Plot the McDonald's restaurants in your city on a map. If you were to locate a new one, where would it go?

4. Do the same for Starbucks.

5. Discuss the movement of jobs in manufacturing and customer service to locations outside the United States. Is this good or bad for the national economy?

6. Review major plant location decisions in your region. Were there new plants opening? Old plants closing? What is the unemployment rate in your region, and is it attractive for a future plant?

7. Assume you are assigned to select five U.S. cities to establish regional headquarters for a growing company that presently has only a national headquarters in Philadelphia. The business is hospital patient billing software. What places would you go?

8. What advantages do the following countries offer to manufacturers? Mexico, Taiwan, and Ireland.

9. The United States has several mints that print money for the economy. Analyze the present locations and suggest a new one.

10. Analyze the air traffic out of northern California airports and suggest an office location for a company requiring its managers to travel extensively.

11. Julia won the lottery. She actually won $100 million! For years, she had spent $10 a week on the lottery and it paid off. She had fantasized about what she would do with the money for so long that she had a plan on how to spend the money—quickly. Her decision is to spend $10 million by purchasing four houses. She intends to do her entire search over the Internet by consulting with three sources.

- *Bestplaces.net:* This site will give her the basic information on many of the cities.

- *move.com/?poe=homestore:* This site will show her available houses for sale.

- *Zillow.com:* This site gives her an estimate of the value of the property.

Assignment: Find four locations for Julia. Explain why you chose each one.

12. Joe Faryar owns several 39-dollar hotels along the interstate in Nevada. He is looking to expand to Utah and Arizona. He has enough cash to open three more locations. What would his criteria be for selecting these locations?

Web Sites

www.bestplaces.net

www.businessfacilities.com

www.citymayors.com

www.gis.com

www.move.com/?poe=homestore

www.zillow.com

References

Berendt, J. (1994). *Midnight in the garden of good and evil.* New York: Random House. (The movie was released in 1997)

Bremner, B., & Engardio, P. (2005, August 22–29). China ramps up. *Business Week,* 118–119.

Engardio, P. (2005, August 22–29). A new world economy. *Business Week,* 52–58.

Euronews.net. (2008, January 17). *Nokia's German closure sparks political anger.*

Hamm, S. (2005, August 22–29). Scrambling up the development ladder. *Business Week,* 112–114.

Hayes, C. (1999, February 25). Philip Morris plant closing to cost 1400 jobs. *www.nytimes.com.*

Insight Guide. (2006). *Taiwan.* London: Author.

Machalaba, D. (2005, August 22). How Savannah brought new life to its aging port. *Wall Street Journal,* pp. A1, A4.

MSNBC.com. (2005, November 21). *GM slashing 30,000 jobs.*

Popely, R. (2006, April 1). Disappearing Delphi. *Chicago Tribune,* pp. 1, 8.

Roberts, D. (2006, March 27). How rising wages are changing the game in China. *Business Week,* pp. 32–35.

Sperling, B., & Sander, P. (2007). *Cities ranked and rated.* Hoboken, NJ: Wiley.

CHAPTER 11

Facility Layout and Waiting Lines

SOURCE: © Britta Kasholm-Tengve/istockphoto.com

Learning Objectives

In this chapter, we will

- Learn about the importance of waiting-line management
- Review the major types of layouts
- Investigate process layout planning
- Study product layouts and assembly line balancing
- Study service layout planning
- Review waiting-line management practices
- Analyze waiting-line psychology

(Continued)

(Continued)

- Read about waiting lines in Hawaii
- Review waiting-line statistics
- Perform a simulation of a waiting line
- Study a case illustrating how long individuals are willing to wait
- Review basic waiting-line theory

Process Design and Facility Layout

The type of process used to make a product will determine the arrangement of the facility. A lot of thought must go into layout, to ensure a smooth production and distribution process.

Types of processes include the following:

- *Continuous flow:* In this type of process, the product moves like a river to its final destination. Oil, chocolate, and beer are examples of products that flow through pipes and undergo several processing steps before being packaged and distributed to the consumer.

- *Assembly lines:* In this process, a product moves down the line and is assembled, with workers usually staying in the same workstation area. The product is built up from one station to the next. This is the traditional way of manufacturing an automobile or a consumer product such as a DVD player.

- *Batch flow:* In this process, the product is moved from one machine to another in batches. A **batch flow** process does not have the characteristic of a linear arrangement like the assembly line. Musical instruments such as violins and guitars are manufactured in this way.

- *Job shop:* This is a process design in which there are several processing stations for products. Some products may only require one machine; others move from job to job. The classic job shop example is the hospital, in which some patients must move among departments, while others require only one unit.

- *Project:* These processes are temporary and have a completion date. The installation of new software or new equipment and the creation of a new office or new building are examples.

The type of process design should be applied to products according to their characteristics. Hayes and Wheelwright (1979) wrote that products must match the process that fits.

Continuous flow: high volume; commodity products

Assembly line: high volume; variety among products

Batch flow: moderate volume; multiple products

Job shop: low volume; many products

Project: one-of-a-kind products

A manufacturer may choose to use a process that does not match the product characteristics if there is some strategic reason to do so.

Service-Process Design

Chase and Tansik (1983) introduced the concept of customer contact: the idea that the degree to which the customer is involved in a process has an impact on production efficiency. For example, Internet banking or ATM usage, by removing the customer from face-to-face interactions with employees, results in higher efficiency for the bank.

The introduction of self-check-in kiosks at airports dramatically changed the operations at the airline ticket counter. With the exception of the occasional technophobe who has no idea how to operate a kiosk, customers may now find their own reservations and do everything but put their bags on the conveyor belt. The old system, which involved long lines of customers who had to be individually dealt with by a ticket agent, required much more labor, and customers frequently missed flights.

Some airports are experimenting with different security clearance lines, classifying passengers as "experts" or "beginners," to streamline the process.

Facility Layout

The facility layout is important: The workplace should be pleasing to the eye and make efficient use of available space. The building should be set up so that work is effectively accomplished. This is something we typically take for granted until we find ourselves working in a place with a poor layout.

Notice the difference between the layouts of typical McDonald's and Wendy's restaurants. McDonald's usually offers a row of cashiers, and customers pick the shortest line to wait in. Behind the cashiers, the meals are prepared in assembly line fashion.

Wendy's has one line leading to one cashier. The cashier passes on the orders to the assembly line in the rear. In some Wendy's restaurants, a long line will trigger a wandering cashier to take the orders in advance. The type of line is a choice a manager must make in laying out a fast-food restaurant. (In different situations, either line would be faster. A hesitant customer is all it takes to bring a single waiting line to a halt.)

Layout planning involves four basic elements: (1) space planning units (SPUs), which are typically functional departments; (2) affinities, which are the SPUs that need to be close to each other; (3) space, which is simply the amount of allocated space; and (4) constraints, which are limitations on arrangements. These elements go into the jigsaw-puzzle-solving aspect of layout planning. We know how houses are arranged. If you have an attached garage, it typically does not connect directly to the living room. Instead, it has a side entrance, maybe to the kitchen. The thinking that an architect brings to home design is similar to planning a plant layout, with the added complexity of product movement or customer interaction.

Types of Layouts

There are a number of basic layout forms, and some businesses combine elements of several at the same time.

1. *Product layout:* A product layout is one in which the product is assembled and travels down an assembly line of workstations. Any auto assembly plant is an example of a product layout. McDonald's, Taco Bell, Subway, and most fast-food places employ the assembly line layout as workers "build" hamburgers and sandwiches.

2. *Process layout:* In this type of layout, the building is arranged so that different processes are performed in different locations. A hospital is a classic process layout, in which the emergency room, the radiology department, the intensive care unit, the operating room, the cardiology department, the pharmacy, the nursery, and so on are located in different areas. Thought must go into the relative distance between the critical areas and the emergency room and supply areas. The challenge in hospital design is to enable efficient movement of patients and supplies.

3. *Fixed position:* Here, the product is so large that it stays in one place and the workers go to it. Airplane and ship manufacturing facilities are good examples of fixed position layouts.

4. *Retail layout:* The classic layout in which customers can select what they want to buy and bring it to the cash register is called a retailing layout. Any retailer or supermarket would be an example. (There is always the matter of customer trust—ideally, customers will pay for what they pick up in the store.)

5. *Warehouse layout:* In a warehouse setting, products are arranged for storage. Some retailers such as Costco and Sam's Club have this warehouse element because the products are sold in bulk quantities that cannot fit on grocery store shelves. But most large retailers have distribution centers that store products for delivery to all their stores.

6. *Project layout:* A one-time layout, like the construction site of a building or dam. The workers are there for a while, and then they move on to the next project.

7. *Cellular layout:* In this layout, work is arranged so that machines with similar processing requirements are grouped together. The layout is also called "group technology."

8. *Office layout:* In "cubicle world," we have various configurations of cubicles and fixed offices. The cubicles can be rearranged. The office walls can be torn down to make the offices bigger or smaller. The arrangement simply needs to suit the way work passes from one person to another. Here, we have the dwellings of Dilbert and the characters in "The Office."

Examples

Home Depot combines retailing with warehousing. Since some of their biggest customers are contractors and builders, they often sell in bulk quantities.

An amusement park, Disney World for example, has many types of layouts. It could be said that the park itself is one big fixed position layout because the rides stay in the same place and all the workers and the customers have to go to the rides. There are many shops offering the retailing layout. Underneath the park is the warehouse layout for all the park's supplies. (You could make a philosophical argument that the areas of the parks are like different processes.) There is a land for small children (Fantasy Land) and a land for older children (Future Land). Finally, there are elements of the product layout in their restaurants.

Visits to movie theaters reveal a number of different layouts. A movie theater is a fixed position layout in that the screen stays in the same place and all the workers and customers go to the product. Some theaters with certain concessions also offer customers the chance to select their own snacks in a retail-like layout. In a sense, these theaters are process layouts housing the movie theater, concessions, and game areas. A movie theater in Evanston, Illinois, includes a bar and a coffee shop.

Department store layouts often reflect different philosophies. A few principles should be kept in mind: When large appliances are to be moved off the floor to a customer, they should be located so that they may be easily moved to the loading dock. Easily stolen articles should obviously be located in a high-visibility area.

Note that the children's department is nowhere near the fine china, silverware, or kitchen appliances, for good reason. One department store refused to include store directories, because they wanted customers to wander around lost, looking for the items they wanted to buy. Then, they loaded the aisles with items for impulse purchases. A guy wandering around looking for a pair of shoes may come home with a Championship White Sox leather jacket, his sixth Polar fleece jacket, a GPS watch, and some Maui Jim sunglasses, simply because he couldn't find the shoes.

Impulse-purchase items are typically placed by the cash register. Customers can't remember if they have enough AA batteries, so they buy some more. Then they buy their eighth flashlight, a deck of playing cards, their 17th set of nail clippers and toe clippers, and a new city map, updated to include the changes in the Interstate.

In her book *What to Eat* (2006), Marion Nestle outlined a number of supermarket layout principles:

- Place the highest-selling food departments in the parts of the store that get the greatest flow of traffic—the periphery. Perishables—meat, produce, dairy, and frozen foods—generate the most sales, so put them against the back and side walls.

- Use the aisle nearest the entrance for items that sell especially well on impulse or look or smell enticing—produce, flowers, or freshly baked bread, for example. These must be the first things customers see in front or immediately to the left or right (the direction, according to researchers, doesn't matter).

- Use displays at the ends of aisles for high-profit, heavily advertised items likely to be bought on impulse.

- Place high-profit, center-aisled food items 60 in. above the floor where adults, with or without eyeglasses, easily see them.

- Devote as much shelf space as possible to brands that generate frequent sales; the more shelf space they occupy, the better they sell.

- Place store brands immediately to the right of those high-traffic items (people read from left to right), so that the name brands attract shoppers to the store brands too.

- Avoid using islands. These make people bump into each other and want to move on. Keep the traffic moving, but slowly. (p. 19)

Process Layout Approaches

A process layout, like a hospital or a job shop, must be designed so that the cost of moving materials around is minimized. In a hospital, there are many things moving: Supplies and materials are distributed around the hospital, as are drugs, linen, laundry, and food. Finally, patients are often taken from one unit to another. Hospital design has to take into account all these movements.

One approach to process layout is to set up a matrix of costs-to-move. This matrix resembles the distance grid you see on many maps. The costs are the costs to move one unit. For example, one move between Departments 1 and 2 costs $6.00.

From/To	1	2	3	4	5
1	—	6	4	0	5
2	6	—	7	3	8
3	4	7	—	9	4
4	0	3	9	—	6
5	5	8	4	6	—

Assume that these 5 departments are arranged in a parallel sequence:

Department	1	2	3	4	5
Position	A	B	C	D	E

The goal is to reduce the distance between department pairs with the highest-cost moves.

The highest-cost move is between Departments 3 and 4 ($9). So we start by placing those departments together at A and B. Our next-highest-cost move is between Departments 2 and 5 ($8). Placing them next to each other leaves Department 1 in the E position. Now the departments are arranged as follows:

Department	3	4	2	5	1
Position	A	B	C	D	E

However, the matching process is much harder than that. A simple 5-department setup such as the one above still has 5! combinations (5 × 4 × 3 × 2 × 1 = 120). In a setup with 20 departments, we would have 20! combinations, which is more than what a typical human can accommodate without a computer:

A	B	C	D	E
F	G	H	I	J
K	L	M	N	O
P	Q	R	S	T

Product Layouts

The typical approach to the assembly line is to attempt to balance the workstations so that the number of workstations and the idle time at workstations are both minimized.

In an automobile assembly line, the auto starts on the line with the chassis assembly and progresses down the line acquiring the seating, the body, and the engine. Some assembly lines may operate with tandem lines operating in parallel for most processes and eventually joining at the end.

Cycle time is important to the assembly line. It is measured by the work time per day divided by the output per day. If a plant operates from 7 a.m. to 11 p.m., its work time is 960 min. If the output is 100 units per day, it makes the cycle time 9.6 min or 576 s.

The concept of a 576-s cycle time becomes important to each workstation. No workstation can be assigned tasks that exceed this cycle time. Otherwise, you would have an out-of-control situation where the line is moving faster than the workers can keep up.

To balance the assembly line, the manager must itemize all the tasks, the task times, and the precedence relationships, just as in project scheduling (see Chapter 15).

Task	Task Time (Seconds)	Precedence
A	200	—
B	240	—
C	180	A
D	250	B
E	420	C
F	510	C
G	390	D
H	400	D
I	150	G, H
J	60	E, F
K	40	I, J
Total task time	2,840	

This is an example of two tandem lines that join together at K. The objective is to group the work into as few stations as possible. In theory, it may be possible for workers to move from one line to another if the lines are in close proximity.

There are several grouping rules. The longest-operating-time rule groups tasks according to the available task with the **longest operating time**. By *available*, we mean that all preceding tasks have been completed. Another rule groups tasks according to the largest number of following tasks.

Using the longest-operating-time rule, in this case, we assign tasks as follows:

Workstation	Tasks	Total Task Time (Minutes)	Idle Time (Minutes)
1	B, D	490	86
2	A, C	380	196
3	F	510	66
4	E	420	156
5	H	400	176
6	G	390	186
7	I, J, K	250	326

In continuous time, the tasks would proceed as follows:

0–200	201–400	401–600	601–800	801–1000
A (200)	C (380)		E (800)	F (890) J (950)
B (240)		D (490)		G (880) H (890)
				I (1040) K (1080)

The theoretical number of workstations is given by total task time divided by the cycle time:

$$\frac{2840}{576} = 4.93$$

However, we are only able to assign to seven workstations because of the precedence relationships. It may be possible to leave out the last workstation by assigning tasks J and K to G, and I to H. That may be physically impractical, but the point of balancing is to try to minimize the idle time at each workstation. This scenario has a lot of idle time. The efficiency of the line is measured by T/(actual workstations × cycle time).

In this case,

$$\frac{2840}{7 \times 576} = 70.43\%$$

Service Assembly Lines

The assembly line production method is not limited to manufacturing. Any fast-food restaurant is designed to produce tacos, hamburgers, and sandwiches in an assembly line manner.

Quizno's, for example, has three workstations.

1. *Workstation 1*

   Tasks:

   Take order, determine type of bread, size of sandwich (small, regular, or large), and whether order is dine-in or take-out.

   Assemble sandwich.

   Feed into oven.

2. *Workstation 2*

   Task: Retrieve from oven and package.

3. *Workstation 3:* Cashier

At Quizno's, the oven presents a physical barrier between the first two workstations. If only two servers are present, usually the cashier will serve at Workstations 2 and 3.

Any trip to Quizno's, Subway, Taco Bell, or McDonald's illustrates the principles of **assembly line balancing**.

Western Versus Japanese Assembly Lines

A number alternative features exist in the Japanese assembly line of a just-in-time inventory plant.

- The shape is a U, rather than an L.
- Workers can stop or slow the line.
- Workers are trained to do many maintenance activities, rather than relying on a maintenance department.

Cellular Manufacturing

One layout that has found increased acceptance is the cellular layout, also called group technology. In this arrangement, groupings are made according to similar processing requirements. The U-shaped arrangement reduces movement of materials and increases ease of utilization.

The Environmental Protection Agency (EPA) of the United States has recommended that manufacturers explore shifting to this style of layout because it helps reduce overproduction. Overproduction increases the number of products that must be disposed of, the amount of raw materials used, and the amount of energy, emission, and wastes required to produce.

The EPA outlined the three steps necessary to move from traditional batch manufacturing to cellular manufacturing (U.S. EPA, n.d.).

- *Step 1:* Understand current conditions. Assess current work using flow diagrams. Measure cycle time.
- *Step 2:* Convert to a process-based layout. Rearrange the elements so that processing steps are adjacent.
- *Step 3:* Continuously improve the process. Fine-tune all the aspects of cellular manufacturing using TQM and Six Sigma tools.

The EPA listed several features of effective cellular design (U.S. EPA, n.d.):

SMED. Single-minute exchange of die (SMED) enables an organization to quickly convert a machine or process to produce a different product type. A single cell and set of tools can then produce a variety of products without the time-consuming equipment changeover and the setup time associated with large batch-and-queue processes, enabling the organization to quickly respond to changes in customer demand.

AUTONOMATION. Autonomation is the transfer of human intelligence to automated machinery so that machines are able to stop, start, load, and unload automatically. In many cases, machines can also be designed to detect the production of a defective part, stop themselves, and signal for help. This frees operators for other value-added work. This concept has also been known as "automation with a human touch" and *jidoka,* and it was pioneered by Sakichi Toyoda in the early 1900s when he invented automatic looms that stopped instantly when any thread broke. This enabled one operator to manage many machines without risk of producing vast amounts of defective cloth. This technique is closely linked to mistake-proofing, or *poka yoke.*

RIGHT-SIZED EQUIPMENT. Conversion to a cellular layout frequently entails the replacement of large equipment (sometimes referred to as monuments) with smaller equipment. Right-sized equipment is often mobile, so that it can quickly be reconfigured into a different cellular layout in a different location. In some cases, equipment vendors offer right-sized equipment alternatives, and in other cases companies develop such equipment in-house. A rule of thumb is that machines need not be more than three times larger than the part they are intended to produce.

Waiting Lines

The average human sleeps 8 hr/day. If you live to be 80 years of age, you have slept for more than 25 years. Undoubtedly, the average human has spent another 25 years waiting in line. That leaves only 30 years of life! The challenge, then, is to reduce the time we spend waiting in line.

Customers do not want to wait, but most stores cannot hire enough cashiers to prevent a line from developing. So the idea is to minimize waiting time while maintaining a high degree of customer satisfaction. If the lines get too long, customers will walk into the store, take a look at the line, and walk away. The length of time a customer is willing to wait is directly proportional to the value of the item to the customer.

Years ago, if you went to an amusement park, the lines were always straight lines to infinity. Somewhere around the 1970s, they came up with the idea of forming the line in the shape of a coiled snake. Meanwhile, they sprinkled objects to hold your attention as you approached, for example, signs that said, "Entry 45 minutes from this sign."

Banks used to have one line for every teller. Then it was the luck of the draw. If you got behind the guy cashing in his collection of coins, it could be a half an hour wait in line. They finally came up with the one-line idea, and the customer now goes to the first available teller.

The FASTPASS at the Disney Parks is a wonderful way to reduce the time one spends in line. Since they put a limit on the number of FASTPASSes you can hold at any one time, the efficient way to proceed is to enter the park and immediately get a FASTPASS for a high-demand ride with a long line, guaranteeing an easy entry later in the day. Then, you can get in one of those long lines and ride. Go to the FASTPASS counter. Get a second FASTPASS for another ride, get in a long line, and so on. The FASTPASSes have the effect of increasing the number of rides you can experience per day.

Waiting-Line Psychology

Maister (1985) outlined a number of principles active in the psychology of waiting lines.

1. *Unexplained waits seem longer than explained waits.* If you don't know the reason you are waiting, it can become frustrating. For example, if you are caught in a traffic jam with no idea why you are waiting, it can be exasperating. A simple electronic sign that tells you of an accident ahead lets you know what is going on and may give you a chance to exit.

2. *Preprocess waits seem longer than in-process waits.* If you are waiting for a table at a restaurant, there is uncertainty about when you will get a table, and anxiety can arise when you exceed the expected wait time. This waiting time seems worse than the time you spend waiting to be served at your table, because once you are at the table, you feel more relaxed.

3. *Anxiety-producing waits seem longer.* The longest waits can be to hear serious news. Perhaps the longest 60 s would be to await the results of a pregnancy test. Waiting in a hospital waiting room for news about either your own condition or a loved one's condition can seem to take forever.

4. *Unoccupied waits seem longer.* If you have nothing to entertain yourself with, the wait can seem endless. Think of sitting in a waiting room with no reading material, for example. The long line in an amusement park can be extremely boring, so ride producers try to keep you entertained by placing small TVs in line with some sort of lead-in to the ride.

5. *The more valuable the product or service, the more willing a customer is to wait.* If you are waiting in line for extremely valuable event tickets, perhaps to a concert by Radiohead or Arcade Fire, your patience with waiting is increased because you expect to wait a long time. Similarly, you will endure the wait for sporting-event tickets to events such as a World Series game or an ACC basketball game. The author of this book once willingly waited 12 hr to get a ticket to the LSU-Georgia basketball game in Athens, Georgia, to see Pete Maravich. The reward was probably the most amazing demonstration of basketball skills in history. In overtime, with LSU assured a victory, Maravich put on a dribbling exhibition during the final 2 min; as the last seconds ticked off, he dribbled to half court and launched a left-handed hook shot that stripped the nets. This concluded a 60-point performance.

6. *Unfair waits are the worst.* To have to wait in line for something for a while and see someone break in line in front of you wrecks your day.

Line Etiquette in Hawaii

An article in the Honolulu Advertiser (Hoover, 2000) noted that culture plays a part in line behavior. Hawaiians are used to waiting in line for scarce resources. The Hawaii "line of lines" forms at the state office buildings where citizens must get state IDs and driver's licenses. (For some reason, the driver's license bureau in all states seems to be the line that will go on to infinity and in which you may stand for 2 to 4 hr to reach the counter.)

Albert Robillard, a University of Hawaii sociology professor, sees Hawaii's lines as remarkable because the islands become a meeting place for line and nonline cultures. This merging of different cultures probably adds to the unique, more laid-back flavor of lines in Hawaii.

"You have Samoans, Hawaiians, Filipinos, and haoles mixed with Japanese tourists, and they each display great sensitivity to the local line formation," he said, referring to the checkout line at Costco in Salt Lake (Honolulu). "Some of these people don't come from line cultures, but they see what's going on and comply and become line members right on the spot."

Leon James, a UH social psychologist who teaches traffic psychology at the University of Hawaii, has studied what he calls "Line rage." He has concluded that line behavior is contagious, be it good, bad, or ugly. One single member of a line can make all the difference in the mood or personality of a line.

That could mean Hawaii enjoys something of a social advantage, he contends. Recently, after patiently waiting his turn at a health clinic, James turned to the woman behind him, who was toting a heavy bag in one arm and a fidgety kid in the other, and invited her to go ahead of him.

"She was so happy," recalled James. "And that made me feel so good that I didn't mind waiting the extra minute. It's important to think of being nice as a sort of cultural resource. You might call it the aloha spirit." (p. 2)

Hawaiians have been reluctant to order event tickets online, not trusting the process and preferring to wait in long lines for the tangibility of a hard ticket.

One woman waited 18 hr in line to buy a ticket to *The Lion King*. For once in her life, she wanted to be first in line. It may have been worth the wait. By the time the box office opened, more than 500 people had joined the line (Gordon, 2007).

Marion Nestle, in *What to Eat* (2006), notes several elements of supermarket layout psychology. She says that companies want customers to

- listen to the background music. The slower the beat, the longer you will tarry.
- search for the loss leaders (the items you always need, like meat, coffee, or bananas, that are offered at or below their actual cost). The longer you search, the more products you will see.
- go to the bakery, prepared foods, and deli sections; the sights and good smells will keep you lingering and encourage sales.
- taste the samples that companies are giving away. If you like what you taste, you are likely to buy it.
- put your kids in the play areas; the longer they play there, the more time you have to walk those tempting aisles. (p. 23)

Waiting-Line Statistics

The management of a waiting line only requires three pieces of information: the arrival rate of customers, the service time of workers, and the number of servers. To calculate the arrival rate, you must have a representative sample broken down for different times of the day. A visit to any fast-food restaurant will show that the arrival rate slows between 9:00 a.m. and 11:30 a.m. and then picks up dramatically until 1:30 p.m. Lunch and dinner crunches are the times when the arrival rates jump.

A typical arrival rate could look like this:

Time	Customers/Hour	Time	Customers/Hour	Time	Customers/Hour
6 a.m.	20	12 p.m.	100	6 p.m.	120
7	70	1	150	7	90
8	60	2	90	8	70
9	50	3	50	9	50
10	30	4	30	10	20
11	40	5	60	11	20

The service rate is calculated by the average time it takes to handle a customer. This time is determined when the customer arrives at the cash register. The time from the initial processing to the exit of the customer is the service time. The waiting time lasts from the time the customer gets into line to the time he or she arrives at the cash register. The combined times of waiting and service are called the system time.

Once we know the three pieces of information (arrivals, service rate, and number of servers), several waiting-line statistics become available.

A = Arrival rate

S = Service rate

$1/A$ = Average time between arrivals

$1/S$ = Average service time

$U = A/S$ = Server utilization rate

$W\# = A^2/S(S - A)$ = Average number of customers waiting

$WT = W\#/A$ = Average waiting time

$SYS\# = A/S - A$ = Average number of customers in system

$SYST = SYS\#/A$ = Average time in the system

To use a numerical example, assume 40 customers arrive per hour and that the server can handle 60 customers per hour.

A = Arrival rate = 40/hr

S = Service rate = 60/hr

$1/A$ = Average time between arrivals = 1/0.67 = 1.33 min

$1/S$ = Average service time = 1/1 = 1.0 min

$U = A/S =$ Server utilization rate $= 4/6 = 0.67$

$W\# = A^2/S(S - A) =$ Average number of customers waiting $= (40)^2/60(60 - 40)$
$= 1,600/1,200 = 1.33$

$WT = W\#/A =$ Average waiting time $= 1.33/40 = 0.033$ hr $= 1.8$ min

$SYS\# = A/(S - A) =$ Average number of customers in system $= 40/(60 - 40) = 2$

$SYST = SYS\#/A =$ Average time in the system $= 2/40 = 0.05/$hr $= 3$ min

This information reveals that customers will spend 3 min from the time they get in line until they exit the cashier line. That is the total time of the system. They will be waiting to be served for 1.8 of those minutes, and then the cashier will take 1 min to process them.

Line Structures

Customers queue into several types of line structures. The types vary according to the number of lines, servers, and processes.

- *One line, one server:* A single ATM is an example. A customer simply goes to the ATM, makes a transaction, and exits. The next in line follows.

- *One line, multiple servers:* At the post office, customers enter one line, and several servers process them.

- *Multiple lines, multiple servers:* At some fast-food restaurants, and at all supermarkets and retailers, we see lines everywhere and servers for each line.

- *One line, multiple servers, and multiple processes:* In this situation, the customer is not finished at the end of the first transaction and must enter a second line. For example, at the driver's license bureau, you must get in line to pay the fee, enter a second line to take a test, and go to a third line to get your photograph taken.

Basic Principles of Line Structure

FCFS: First come first served.

LIFS: The elevator rule (whoever is in last goes first).

Priority: In the emergency room, a gunshot wound takes precedence over carpal tunnel syndrome. The seriousness of the case determines the order. If a VIP enters a line to get into a disco, he or she immediately gets to the front.

FISH: First in, still here. The customer gets in line and watches with amazement as others are served as he or she is still waiting.

Simulation of Waiting Lines

Managers are constantly challenged to balance the number of servers with customer satisfaction. Customers don't enjoy waiting in line, unless the line moves so fast that they can't read the latest exploits of Tom Cruise, Lindsay Lohan, Jessica Simpson, and Paris Hilton in the tabloids.

One approach to determining the right number of servers is to use a computer simulation. This way, you can see the effect of each number of servers. You need to know how many customers will leave the system if there are too many in line. You need to get the average waiting time for those who stay, to make sure it is not unreasonable.

To do this simulation, data must be collected over a period of time so that the arrivals and service times can be modeled. This information can be arranged in a probability distribution table.

We will use Sam and Dave's barbershop as an example. Sam hired Dave a year ago, but he has seen business slack off and wonders if he really needs Dave. So for a week, he collects information on the arrival times of customers and the service times of the shop.

Sam will assign an equal number of random numbers to the probability and then simulate a shop with Dave and a shop without Dave.

Arrival times:

Time Period (Minutes)	Number	Probability	Random Numbers
5	36	22.5	1–22
10	40	25.0	23–47
15	42	26.3	48–73
20	30	18.8	74–92
25	12	7.5	93–0

Service times:

Time Period (Minutes)	Number	Probability	Random Numbers
10	20	12.5	1–12
15	25	15.6	13–28
20	30	18.8	29–46
25	40	25.0	47–71
30	30	18.8	72–90
35	15	9.4	91–0

Since 160 customers came in during the 6 days the shop was open, Sam chose to simulate a typical day with Dave and a typical day without Dave by generating random numbers from a random number table (Table 11.1).

Table 11.1   Table of Random Numbers

39634 62349 74088 65564 16379 19713 39153 69459 17986 24537
14595 35050 40469 27478 44526 67331 93365 54526 22356 93208
30734 71571 83722 79712 25775 65178 07763 82928 31131 30196
64628 89126 91254 24090 25752 03091 39411 73146 06089 15630
42831 95113 43511 42082 15140 34733 68076 18292 69486 80468
80583 70361 41047 26792 78466 03395 17635 09697 82447 31405
00209 90404 99457 72570 42194 49043 24330 14939 09865 45906
05409 20830 01911 60767 55248 79253 12317 84120 77772 50103
95836 22530 91785 80210 34361 52228 33869 94332 83868 61672
65358 70469 87149 89509 72176 18103 55169 79954 72002 20582
72249 04037 36192 40221 14918 53437 60571 40995 55006 10694
41692 40581 93050 48734 34652 41577 04631 49184 39295 81776
61885 50796 96822 82002 07973 52925 75467 86013 98072 91942
48917 48129 48624 48248 91465 54898 61220 18721 67387 66575
88378 84299 12193 03785 49314 39761 99132 28775 45276 91816
77800 25734 09801 92087 02955 12872 89848 48579 06028 13827
24028 03405 01178 06316 81916 40170 53665 87202 88638 47121
86558 84750 43994 01760 96205 27937 45416 71964 52261 30781
78545 49201 05329 14182 10971 90472 44682 39304 19819 55799
14969 64623 82780 35686 30941 14622 04126 25498 95452 63937
58697 31973 06303 94202 62287 56164 79157 98375 24558 99241
38449 46438 91579 01907 72146 05764 22400 94490 49833 09258
62134 87244 73348 80114 78490 64735 31010 66975 28652 36166
72749 13347 65030 26128 49067 27904 49953 74674 94617 13317
81638 36566 42709 33717 59943 12027 46547 61303 46699 76243
46574 79670 10342 89543 75030 23428 29541 32501 89422 87474
11873 57196 32209 67663 07990 12288 59245 83638 23642 61715
13862 72778 09949 23096 01791 19472 14634 31690 36602 62943
08312 27886 82321 28666 72998 22514 51054 22940 31842 54245
11071 44430 94664 91294 35163 05494 32882 23904 41340 61185
82509 11842 86963 50307 07510 32545 90717 46856 86079 13769
07426 67341 80314 58910 93948 85738 69444 09370 58194 28207
57696 25592 91221 95386 15857 84645 89659 80535 93233 82798
08074 89810 48521 90740 02687 83117 74920 25954 99629 78978
20128 53721 01518 40699 20849 04710 38989 91322 56057 58573

(Continued)

Table 11.1 (Continued)

00190 27157 83208 79446 92987 61357 38752 55424 94518 45205
23798 55425 32454 34611 39605 39981 74691 40836 30812 38563
85306 57995 68222 39055 43890 36956 84861 63624 04961 55439
99719 36036 74274 53901 34643 06157 89500 57514 93977 42403
95970 81452 48873 00784 58347 40269 11880 43395 28249 38743
56651 91460 92462 98566 72062 18556 55052 47614 80044 60015
71499 80220 35750 67337 47556 55272 55249 79100 34014 17037
66660 78443 47545 70736 65419 77489 70831 73237 14970 23129
35483 84563 79956 88618 54619 24853 59783 47537 88822 47227
09262 25041 57862 19203 86103 02800 23198 70639 43757 52064

SOURCE: www.mrs.umn.edu/sungurea/introstat

Assuming that the shop opens at 8 a.m. and closes at 6 p.m., we generate 37 random numbers for the arrivals and 36 random numbers for the service times to see if the customers have to wait. The random numbers are then compared with the probability tables and assigned times.

Simulation of Sam alone:

Random Number	Arrival	Random Number	Service Start	Service Finish	Waiting
39	8:10 a.m.	63	8:10 a.m.	8:35 a.m.	0
46	8:20 a.m.	23	8:35 a.m.	8:50 a.m.	15
23	8:30 a.m.	49	8:50 a.m.	9:15 a.m.	20
74	8:50 a.m.	08	9:15 a.m.	9:25 a.m.	25
86	9:10 a.m.	55	9:25 a.m.	9:50 a.m.	15
64	9:25 a.m.	16	9:50 a.m.	10:05 a.m.	25
37	9:35 a.m.	91	10:05 a.m.	10:40 a.m.	30
97	10:00 a.m.	13	10:40 a.m.	BALK	
39	10:10 a.m.	15	10:40 a.m.	10:55 a.m.	30
36	10:20 a.m.	94	10:55 a.m.	BALK	
59	10:35 a.m.	17	10:55 a.m.	11:10 a.m.	20
98	11:00 a.m.	62	11:10 a.m.	11:35 a.m.	10
45	11:10 a.m.	37	11:35 a.m.	11:55 a.m.	25
14	11:15 a.m.	59	11:55 a.m.	BALK	
53	11:30 a.m.	50	11:55 a.m.	12:20 p.m.	25
50	11:45 a.m.	40	12:20 p.m.	BALK	
46	11:55 a.m.	92	12:20 p.m.	12:55 p.m.	25
74	12:15 p.m.	78	12:55 p.m.	BALK	
44	12:25 p.m.	52	12:55 p.m.	1:20 p.m.	30

Sam goes on lunch break from 1:20 p.m. to 1:45 p.m., losing 3 customers.

Random Number	Arrival (p.m.)	Random Number	Service Start (p.m.)	Service Finish (p.m.)	Waiting
55	1:45	45	1:45	2:05	0
26	1:55	22	2:05	2:20	10
35	2:05	69	2:20	2:45	15
32	2:15	08	2:45	2:55	30
30	2:25	73	2:55	3:25	30
47	2:35	15	3:25	BALK	
71	2:50	83	3:25	BALK	
72	3:05	27	3:25	3:40	20
97	3:30	12	3:40	3:50	10
25	3:40	77	3:50	4:20	10
56	3:55	51	4:20	4:45	25
78	4:15	07	4:45	4:55	30
76	4:35	38	4:55	5:15	20
29	4:45	28	5:15	5:30	30
31	4:55	13	5:30	BALK	
13	5:00	01	5:30	5:40	30
96	5:25	64	5:40	6:05	15
62	5:40				

Two customers who come in between 5:40 p.m. and 6:00 p.m. are lost.

The shop closes.

Eight customers balk, and 5 are lost during lunch and prior to closing, for a total of 13 lost customers. Customers wait a total of 570 min. Sam serves 28 customers, so they average 20.4 min waiting.

Simulation of Sam with Dave:

Random Number	Arrival Time	Random Number	Service Start	Server	Service Finish	Waiting
39	8:10 a.m.	63	8:10 a.m.	Sam	8:35 a.m.	0
46	8:20 a.m.	23	8:20 a.m.	Dave	8:35 a.m.	0
23	8:30 a.m.	49	8:35 a.m.	Sam	9:00 a.m.	5
74	8:50 a.m.	08	8:50 a.m.	Dave	9:00 a.m.	0
86	9:10 a.m.	55	9:10 a.m.	Sam	9:35 a.m.	0
64	9:25 a.m.	16	9:25 a.m.	Dave	9:40 a.m.	0

(Continued)

(Continued)

Random Number	Arrival Time	Random Number	Service Start	Server	Service Finish	Waiting
37	9:35 a.m.	91	9:35 a.m.	Sam	10:10 a.m.	0
97	10:00 a.m.	13	10:00 a.m.	Dave	10:15 a.m.	0
39	10:10 a.m.	15	10:10 a.m.	Sam	10:25 a.m.	0
36	10:20 a.m.	94	10:20 a.m.	Dave	10:55 a.m.	0
59	10:35 a.m.	17	10:35 a.m.	Sam	10:50 a.m.	0
98	11:00 a.m.	62	11:00 a.m.	Dave	11:25 a.m.	0
45	11:10 a.m.	37	11:10 a.m.	Sam	11:30 a.m.	0
14	11:15 a.m.	59	11:25 a.m.	Dave	11:50 a.m.	10
53	11:30 a.m.	50	11:30 a.m.	Sam	11:55 a.m.	0
50	11:45 a.m.	40	11:50 a.m.	Dave	12:10 p.m.	5

Dave goes on lunch break and returns at 1:10 p.m.

Random Number	Arrival	Random Number	Service Start	Server	Service Finish	Waiting
46	11:55 a.m.	92	11:55 a.m.	Sam	12:25 p.m.	0
74	12:15 p.m.	78	12:25 p.m.	Sam	12:55 p.m.	10
44	12:25 p.m.	52	12:55 p.m.	Sam	1:20 p.m.	30
52	12:40 p.m.	66	1:10 p.m.	Dave	1:35 p.m.	30
73	12:55 p.m.	31	1:20 p.m.	Sam	1:40 p.m.	25
93	1:20 p.m.	36	1:35 p.m.	Dave	1:55 p.m.	15

Sam goes on lunch break from 1:40 p.m. to 2:40 p.m.

Random Number	Arrival (p.m.)	Random Number	Service Start (p.m.)	Server	Service Finish (p.m.)	Waiting
55	1:45	45	1:55	Dave	2:15	10
26	1:55	22	2:15	Dave	2:30	20
35	2:05	69	2:30	Dave	2:55	25
32	2:15	08	2:40	Sam	2:50	25
30	2:25	73	2:50	Sam	3:20	25
47	2:35	15	2:55	Dave	3:10	20
71	2:50	83	3:10	Dave	3:40	20
72	3:05	27	3:20	Sam	3:35	15

Random Number	Arrival	Random Number	Service Start	Server	Service Finish	Waiting
97	3:30	12	3:35	Sam	3:45	5
25	3:40	77	3:40	Dave	4:10	0
56	3:55	51	3:55	Sam	4:20	0
78	4:15	07	4:15	Dave	4:25	0
76	4:35	38	4:35	Sam	4:55	0
29	4:45	28	4:45	Dave	5:00	0
31	4:55	13	4:55	Sam	5:10	0
13	5:00	01	5:00	Dave	5:10	0
96	5:25	64	5:25	Sam	5:50	0
62	5:40	88	5:40	Dave	6:10	0
91	6:00	26	6:00	Sam	6:15	0

The shop closes.

With Dave, there is a total of 295 min of waiting for the 41 customers, an average of 7 min per customer. None balk at the system. Meanwhile, both Sam and Dave get a lunch.

The question for Sam is whether losing 13 customers (at about $20 per head) is worse than paying Dave. Let's assume Dave gets to keep $15 per haircut and Sam keeps $5. With Dave, Sam cuts a total of 21, with Dave cutting 20. Sam then gets $100 from Dave, plus his own $420, for a take per day of $520 for Sam and $300 for Dave.

Without Dave, Sam served 28 customers for a total of $560. Sam is up $40, but the question is, how long will the shop maintain its business if the wait continues at 20 plus minutes? Sam may find he is losing his customers as a result of the long wait. He has also lost a half hour of his lunch break, and will probably have trouble taking a vacation. In the end, Sam decides to keep Dave (which is a good thing, since Dave named his second son Sam).

This is the crux of the waiting line, after all. How long is a customer comfortable in waiting and what is the cost to reduce that wait?

Conclusion

A good facility layout is important for the smooth processing of work and products. As in the design of a house, a workplace should be arranged so that its occupants can get the assigned tasks done in an efficient manner. The type of layout will dictate many of the work arrangements that follow.

Customers spend a lot of time waiting, and the management of that time is a crucial aspect of good customer service. Long waits can make customers irritable and unruly, and management must make an effort to minimize this period.

Modeling customer arrival patterns and service patterns enables the manager to simulate the waiting-line system, which is a helpful way to analyze the needs of the system. Three pieces of information—the arrival rates of customers, the service times of servers, and the number of servers—are the keys to analyzing the waiting-line statistics.

Summary

- The basic types of processes are continuous flow, assembly line, batch flow, job shop, and project. These processes should be matched to fit the product characteristics.

- The degree of contact a customer has in a service system will affect the production efficiency of the system.

- The basic types of layouts are process, product, fixed position, cellular, project, warehouse, and office.

- The process layout is one in which different types of work are performed in different areas of the company.

- A product layout is one in which the product is assembled to its finished form.

- A fixed-position layout is one in which the product is too large to move and the workers move to the product.

- The method of minimizing the number of workstations in an assembly line is called assembly line balancing.

- Managing a waiting line requires knowledge of some psychology. For example, unexplained waits feel longer than explained waits, and preprocess waits feel longer than in-process waits.

- The number of servers and the number of lines together dictate the type of waiting-line structure.

Key Terms

Assembly line balancing	Office layout
Batch flow	Process layout
Cellular layout	Product layout
Continuous flow	Project layout
Cycle time	Retail layout
Fixed position	Warehouse layout
Longest operating time	

Review Questions

1. What type of layout would be found at a department store? A police station? A hospital? A driver's license bureau?

2. What types of businesses are best suited for the assembly line?

3. How would you determine the optimal layout for a process, using the process layout?

4. What factors would render a layout less than optimal in any process or product layout?

5. What are the different types of waiting-line psychology issues that managers should be concerned with?

6. What layout improvements could be made in your workplace?

7. It is possible to bypass the waiting line in the movie theater by buying the tickets online. Survey a local movie theater to determine its current use of online ticketing.

8. Compare offices with walls with offices with cubicles. Do employees prefer one to the other? What are the advantages and disadvantages of both?

9. List the basic types of layouts and discuss businesses that use each type.

10. Consider the times when you have willingly waited in line for something you felt valuable. Was it worth it?

11. Consider the times when you have been treated unfairly in a waiting line. What were the reasons why this happened? How could the experience have been avoided?

12. What is the most anxiety-producing wait you have experienced?

13. When applying for a driver's license or a license plate, are there ways in which the wait could be improved?

Problems

1. Given the following number of arrivals, determine the probabilities and assign two-digit random numbers to create a probability table.

Time (Minutes)	Number of Customers	Time (Minutes)	Number of Customers
0–5	61	16–20	67
6–10	74	21–25	32
11–15	125		

2. If the customers arrive at the rate of 80 per hour and the service rate is 120 per hour, calculate the average wait time, server utilization rate, average time in the system, and so on.

3. In the following assembly line, we have these tasks, precedence relationships, and times (in seconds). Balance the assembly line using the longest-operating-time rule:

Task	Task Time (Seconds)	Precedence
A	42	—
B	58	—
C	12	A
D	34	B
E	27	D
F	43	C
G	52	F
H	8	G
I	12	E
J	24	H, I

4. In the following assembly line, we have these tasks, precedence relationships, and times (in seconds). Balance the assembly line:

Task	Task Time (Minutes)	Precedence
A	1.3	—
B	2.1	A
C	2.7	A
D	1.2	B, C
E	4.0	D
F	3.2	D
G	2.5	D
H	3.2	E
I	5.6	F, G
J	1.0	H
K	2.3	I
L	3.5	J, K

5. Given the following task times, balance this assembly line. Assume a cycle time of 70 s. How many workstations can you group the tasks into? What is the efficiency of the line?

Task	Task Time (Seconds)	Precedence
A	60	—
B	55	A
C	25	A
D	50	A

Task	Task Time (Seconds)	Precedence
E	55	B, C
F	35	C, D
G	25	E, F
H	45	G

If the cycle time was 120 s, how many workstations would it require?

6. Balance this assembly line, assuming a cycle time of 100 s. How many workstations are needed? What is the best efficiency rate attainable?

Task	Task Time (Seconds)	Precedence
A	85	—
B	42	A
C	54	A
D	38	B
E	30	C
F	62	D
G	50	E
H	47	F, G
I	80	H

Projects

1. Visit four local bank branches and compare the layouts. Do a waiting-line analysis over several different hourly periods.

2. Compare the layout of a nonchain fast-food restaurant to the layout of a chain restaurant. Has the independent company incorporated many of the chain's methods?

3. Visit a local manufacturer and determine the type of layout.

4. Analyze the concession layout of your local movie theater.

CASE   Waiting for Radiohead

Radiohead will play for four nights at the United Center in Chicago. Attempting to purchase a ticket the day they go on sale would mean that the caller has to continuously redial for up to 2 hr for the opportunity to purchase a ticket. (These tickets go on sale on Saturday morning and are invariably sold out within 2 hr.)

To avoid the experience of redialing all morning, the customer can let someone else do the work and then pay a scalper's price for the tickets. The prices will start at $200 per ticket and range up to $2,000 per ticket, depending on how close the seats are to the stage. The question for the customer is, "How much is it worth to you?"

1. If you have seen Radiohead before, was the experience desirable enough for you to want to see them a second time? If it was a wonderful show, you can simply acknowledge that you saw them once in a great show and call that a lifetime's chance of seeing Radiohead. Or the show may have been so good that you want to see them again and again.

2. If you have not seen them live before, it is a totally different story. How close do you want to get? The closer you get, the more you pay, but, of course, the better the experience is. To see Radiohead from the upper regions of the stadium is like watching a mouse on your kitchen floor. It may sound a little better, though.

Chapter Note: Waiting-Line Theory

The probability distribution is important to waiting-line calculations. In general, we use the exponential distribution to model arrival distributions, that is, the interval between arrivals. We use this distribution when we assume random arrivals. If we have a continuous arrival pattern, as in a machine-controlled system, we will not use the exponential distribution.

The exponential probability function gives an expected value for an arrival rate of λ as $E(X) = (1/\lambda)$.

The number of arrivals in a period follows the Poisson probability distribution. This gives the number of arrivals in a certain period of time.

The formula for the Poisson distribution is

$$F(k, \lambda) = \frac{e(-\lambda) \, \lambda(k)}{k!}$$

where

e = the base of the natural log(2.71),

k = the number of occurrences of an event,

$k!$ = k factorial, and

λ (Lambda) = a positive number of occurrences that occur in a given interval.

If the distribution is not random, other distributions are applied. Also, the formulas in this chapter assume an infinite population. In cases with a finite population, when each customer is served, that customer leaves the population, and there is no replacement.

Web Sites

Cellular manufacturing: www.epa.gov/lean/thinking/cellular.htm

Plant layout: www.strategosinc.com/plant_layout_elements.htm

Wait line psychology: www.Davidmaister.com/articles

References

Chase, R. B., Jacobs, F. R., & Aquilano, N. J. (2004). *Operations management for competitive advantage* (10th ed.). New York: McGraw-Hill.

Chase, R. B., & Tansik, D. A. (1983). The customer contact model for organization design. *Management Science, 29*(9), 1037–1050.

Gordon, M. (2007, April 28). 19 Hours for "Lion King"? Hakuna matata! *Honolulu Advertiser,* pp. 1, 9.

Hayes, R. H., & Wheelwright, S. C. (1979). Line manufacturing process and product life cycles. *Harvard Business Review, 57*(1), 133–140.

Hoover, W. (2000, March 26). Hawaii has its own style of waiting in lines. *Honolulu Advertiser,* p. 2.

Maister, D. (1985). The psychology of waiting lines. In J. A. Czepiel, M. R. Solomon, & C. Suprenant (Eds.), *The service encounter* (pp. 113–123). Lanham, MD: Lexington Books.

Nestle, M. (2006). *What to eat.* New York: North Point Press.

U.S. Environmental Protection Agency. (n.d.). *Cellular manufacturing.* Retrieved August 31, 2007, from www.epa.gov/lean/thinking/cellular.htm

PART III

Inventory, Logistics, and Supply Chain Management

CHAPTER 12

Supply Chain Management

SOURCE: © Demonoid/istockphoto.com

Learning Objectives

In this chapter, we will

- Study the concept of supply chain management (SCM)
- Review the different stages of SCM
- Review the major transportation modes of SCM
- Study the bullwhip effect in SCM
- Analyze outsourcing and make versus buy decisions
- Review warehousing principles
- Discuss ethics in SCM
- Discuss customer relationships to SCM
- Study a case: Shiraishi Garments

Stages of the Supply Chain

Supply chain management (SCM) is the movement of materials from the distribution of raw materials to manufacture to the distribution of finished products to the customer. *SCM* is actually a term for what used to be called logistics and materials management. Logistics may be considered to involve getting the raw materials into a plant (inbound logistics) and then distributing the finished product to customers (outbound logistics). Materials management is the control and planning of all inventory items in stock. SCM combines these two areas into a complete management of all areas involving supplies.

Definitions

One definition of SCM proposed by the University of Tennessee's Supply Chain Research Group is as follows: "The systematic, strategic coordination of the traditional business functions within a particular company and across businesses within the supply chain, for the purposes of improving the long-term performance of the individual companies and the supply chain as a whole."

Logistics, the heart of SCM, is defined by Frazelle (2002) as "the flow of material, information, and money between consumers and suppliers" (p. 5).

A retailer such as Target will have the following supply chain for its clothing lines:

Stage 1: *Raw materials suppliers*—The raw materials, such as cotton, rayon, and buttons, are provided by the suppliers to the textile manufacturer.

Stage 2: At the textile mills, these materials are cut to the design for shirts, blouses, trousers, jackets, and so on.

Stage 3: In some cases, the clothing would go through a distributor to the retailer. In other cases, the retailer will deal directly with the manufacturer.

Stage 4: The retailer receives the supplies of clothing.

Stage 5: *Delivery to the customer*—Clothing is taken by the customer, so there is no home delivery in this case.

For Infiniti motors, the supply chain will go like this:

Stage 1: *Raw materials suppliers*—These are the producers of commodities such as steel, aluminum, glass, and plastics. Radio manufacturers are already in Stage 2 of their supply chain because they have assembled commodities such as steel, plastic, and microchips into a radio.

Stage 2: *Subassembly suppliers, fabricators, and so on*—Another manufacturer, such as Bose stereos, will assemble raw materials and deliver to Infiniti. One company alone takes glass and transforms it into windshields and delivers them to Infiniti.

Stage 3: *Infiniti*—Here, the automobile is manufactured.

Stage 4: *Infiniti dealerships*—The cars are shipped to the lots.

Stage 5: *Customer delivery*—After customer inspection, the car is either ordered from the manufacturer or, if available on the lot, prepared for delivery and final inspection.

Of the five stages mentioned above, the first two are concerned with inbound logistics and the last with outbound logistics.

SCM has evolved, so that an entire industry has blossomed. Integrated service providers (ISPs) provide all the logistical functions, from order entry to customer delivery. ISPs are also known as *third-party logistics* companies. Companies such as United Parcel Service (UPS) and Federal Express, which were formerly known only as courier companies, have the ability to perform as totally integrated ISPs for other companies. Similarly, some transportation companies, Ryder Truck, for example, have parlayed their transportation expertise into becoming leaders in the SCM industry.

UPS in the Supply Chain

UPS is emblematic of changes in the supply chain. UPS, which employs more than 400,000 employees, including 65,000 outside of the United States, has benefited from companies that seek to streamline their SCM. UPS now finds many of its employees employed full-time in the shipping areas of manufacturers. UPS workers are stationed permanently at Birkenstock, where they handle all the shipping of shoes directly to retailers. This eliminates the need for Birkenstock to hire a shipping department. UPS has similar arrangements with many companies, including Nike and Gateway.

Best Buy, the retailer for electronics, appliances, and music, sources televisions from manufacturers such as Sony, Pioneer, and LG. Pioneer would source from different component suppliers, and these, in turn, may also source from various raw material and commodity suppliers. The chain goes all the way from the makers of metals to the finished product in the consumer's hands.

SCM is the aggregation of the total supply activities. Best Buy is involved with inbound logistics when it brings the Pioneer screens to the store. The direction from the supplier to the retailer is called the upstream direction. Then, it is involved with outbound logistics when it ships to the customer. This is the downstream direction. The reverse supply chain is the upstream movement of returned or defective merchandise. This term especially fits because customers having to return defective products often feel like they are swimming upstream to return the product. "Do you have the receipt?" is the dreaded phrase of the returning customer who does not have one.

Transportation Methods

One of the important decisions in SCM is the method of transporting goods from one source to another. This is most important for outbound logistics. For inbound logistics, the buyers of a commodity care little *how* it gets to them, so long as it is on time.

Here are the major forms of transporting goods.

Rail: Many location decisions are dictated by access to the rail system. Shipping in bulk rail is a cost-effective method.

Truck: Shipping by truck increases speed and flexibility over rail but is very susceptible to rises in fuel costs.

Air: The fastest and the most expensive method to ship is by air.

Courier: For cross-town deliveries, nothing beats the courier.

Pipeline: Pipeline is ideal for transportation of fluid materials, that is, oil and gas.

Boat: Boat is the slowest and least costly method of transporting materials.

Transportation activity profiling (TAP) is a method for tracking the key performance aspects of transportation. A transportation manager would want to know information such as weight per shipment, time requirements, carrier availability and capacity, and shipping rates.

Frazelle (2002) gave two examples of TAP: one for the chemical industry and the other for health and beauty aids (see Tables 12.1 and 12.2).

Table 12.1 Multicommodity Transportation Activity Profile for the Chemical Industry

T&D Profile	Unit	Commodity Feedstock	Intermediate	Polymers	Total
Shipment/value	$ Per	64,726	55,247	44,911	52,256
Order value	$ Per	21,670	56,964	39,950	44,753
Shipments/order	Shipments	0.33	1.03	0.89	0.86
Freight/order	$	613	1,746	2,790	1,896
Freight/shipment	$	1,831	1,693	3,136	2,214
Weight/order	Tons/order	40	101	56	74
Weight/shipment	Tons/ship	118	96	62	87
Miles/shipment	Miles	1,118	352	725	538
Ton-miles/shipment	Ton-miles	333.43 million	700.831 million	569.911 million	16.56 million
Ton-miles/order	Ton-miles	111.63 million	722.61 million	506.97 million	1,418.42 million

Table 12.2   International Transportation Activity Profile in International Health and Beauty Aids

	Revenue (in $000s)	Freight (in $000s)	Weight (000 lb)	Cases	Shipments	Freight/Revenue (%)
Asia-Pacific	28,630	581	599	25,118	57	2.03
NAFTA	18,164	499	59	3,100	11	2.74
Overall	46,794	$1,080	658	28,218	68	2.32

SOURCE: Frazelle (2002).

Frazelle (2002) suggested a number of transportation performance metrics:

- Claims-free shipment percentage—how many shipments have no damage claims
- Damage-free shipment percentage—the actual percentage of damages
- Time between accidents—the days since the last accident
- On-time arrival percentage—like an airplane, goods have to get there on time
- On-time departure percentage—it helps to leave on time if you want to get there on time
- Perfect delivery percentage—for each delivery, what percentage is complete
- Perfect route percentage—breaks down the delivery percentage into routes
- In-transit time—time from boat to delivery
- In-transit variability—the standard deviation of in-transit times
- Vehicle load/unload time—an efficiency percentage
- Delayed in traffic time—not the fault of the driver, that is, *Stuck Inside of Mobile With the Memphis Blues Again!* (pp. 185–186)

Ultimately, the total transportation cost is the essential productivity measurement. The cost of shipping is negotiated between the buyer and the supplier.

Transportation modes have shifted significantly from 1980 to 2004. According to a report of the Council of Supply Chain Management Professionals (Wilson, 2005), the past 20 years have seen an increase in trucking as a means of moving freight around the United States, with a corresponding decrease in rail. Table 12.3 shows the shifts from railroad to trucking.

The Bullwhip Effect

Because a supply chain is made up of several stages, a problem that occurs in any one stage causes a ripple effect throughout the system, called *the bullwhip effect.* For example, a backorder from a raw material source will cause backorders throughout

Table 12.3   Shifts From Railroad to Trucking (1980–2004)

	1980	1990	2004
Truck	72.6%	76.9%	79.0%
Railroad	13.1	8.5	6.5
Water	7.1	5.7	4.1
Pipeline	3.5	2.3	1.3
Air	1.8	3.9	4.8
Other	1.6	2.1	4.0
Total (in $ billions)	213.7	350.8	644.0

SOURCE: Adapted from Wilson (2005).

the system. Similarly, an increase in customer demand will cause a short-term problem for manufacturers. This variability, compounded throughout the system, has to be accommodated or the buyer can risk serious shortages.

Fluctuations in ordering patterns anywhere in the supply chain can cause discrepancies in demand forecasting all the way through the chain, making it very important to have supply chain coordination. Chopra and Meindl (2001) suggest quantifying this effect by comparing the variability of customer orders with the variability of their orders with suppliers. If a manager can have an idea of the impact of the bullwhip effect, the cause can be traced and reduced.

In a typical situation, an increase in demand at the retailer will lead to increasing demand from the distributor, leading to increased production at the manufacturer. Similarly, a stockout at the manufacturer will cause disruptions throughout the system.

This illustrates the need for coordination in the system. Mentzer, Myers, and Stank (2007) listed the areas that require intercorporate coordination: marketing, sales, research and development, forecasting, production, purchasing, logistics, information systems, finance, and customer service.

Electronic Data Interchange

Electronic data interchange (EDI) is the electronic interface between buyers and suppliers throughout the supply chain. A buyer for a manufacturer, for example, may check the warehouses of several suppliers of materials to determine current price and availability. It is the industrial equivalent to shopping on the Internet. EDI can help combat the bullwhip effect with vigilant checking of important supplies.

Outsourcing

An important consideration within the supply chain is whether or not to outsource some activities within the supply chain. Students see examples of outsourcing all over the campus. Many universities have made financial arrangements with companies such as Barnes and Noble and Follett's to manage the bookstore.

In this way, the university completely removes the difficulties of managing the bookstore—handling returns, book buybacks, retailing, computer sales, hiring staff, and so on—and surrenders them to a specialist. Barnes and Noble will then agree on a financial arrangement with the university.

Similarly, many university cafeterias are outsourced to vendors who manage the employees' food and supplies. Customer service and satisfaction are obviously important to renewing the contract, so the company has more of an incentive to come up with good food and service than would a university, since universities have other things to worry about, such as students.

Formerly, manufacturers such as General Motors handled the manufacturing of most of the components of a car. Now, much of the car is outsourced and car manufacturers are becoming increasingly assembly operations.

The decision to outsource is basically a "make versus buy" decision. Each offers advantages and disadvantages:

Make

Advantages

- Creates in-house expertise
- Can be cost-effective when managed well
- Can give a vertical integration competitive advantage

Disadvantages

- A burden for management
- May not be a distinctive competence
- May not be cost-effective

Buy

Advantages

- Fewer headaches
- Can be cost-effective
- Can focus on other things the company does better

Disadvantages

- Can lose control of the accounting
- May not be cost-effective over the long run
- May lose production expertise and may not be able to return to make the product in the future

Postponement and Mass Customization

A method applied to the supply chain is postponement, which means that the product is finished with differentiating product features late in the supply chain. Dell

Computers, for example, will assemble a basic computer and then postpone complete assembly until the customer specifies which components he or she actually desires: for example, size of hard drive, memory, screen size, and so on.

Mass customization is when a basic design can be specified to each customer's tastes. Panasonic builds bicycles this way, configuring with different frame sizes and brake and gear shift components. Nike allows customized versions of its Nike Free 5.0 shoe on its Web site.

Warehousing

There are a number of types of inventories that must be warehoused:

- Raw materials inventories
- Work-in-process inventories
- Finished goods inventories
- Distribution center inventories

The inventory management within a warehouse involves much planning and organization. The flow of materials through the warehouse and the method of movement are important.

Warehouse activities include receiving, putting away, storing, order picking, packaging and pricing, sorting, and shipping. In a hospital warehouse, for example, materials management workers receive supplies from shippers. They check the packing slip for completeness and attach it to a copy of the purchase order. Then, they "put away" the product in a preassigned warehouse location for storage. The order picking takes place when a hospital unit requests the product. Then, packaging takes place, if necessary, and codes are placed on the product for pricing and inventory scanning. The products are sorted according to delivery destination within the hospital and then "shipped" to the unit.

A retailer would go through a similar process. Best Buy, for example, receives plasma television sets from Pioneer, matches the invoice to the purchase order, and places the sets in a warehouse location with an attached bar code for pricing and location. When a set is ready to be delivered to a customer, it is "picked" and shipped.

Automated guided vehicles (AGVs) for inventory require a major capital investment. Tracks are laid along the warehouse floor. If an inventory picker wants a box of nails, he or she specifies that box on a computer, and an AVG moves to the correct location and extends a crane to the location and retrieves the box of nails, tipping it into a bucket.

Automatic depletion from the computer inventory is an important planning consideration. If a stock picker for a paper company withdraws a case of toilet tissue to ship to a supermarket, it should automatically deduct the case from the computer inventory using the bar code.

Bar codes have been integrated into retailing and supermarket information systems, so that in a supermarket when the cashier scans an item it not only deducts it from the inventory but may actually trigger a reorder of the item.

Other mechanized materials-handling systems include forklifts, Ryder trucks, towlines that may be either in the floor or mounted overhead, tractor trailers, conveyors, and carousels.

RFID Technology

Radio frequency identification (RFID) systems have become an effective way to track inventories. An RFID tag is a device that communicates with a label that contains a computer chip or an antenna. According to Sophos (2004), an enterprise architect's blog,

> [The] RFID reader may be a fixed antenna or it may be portable, like a bar code scanner. The tag itself is an extension of the bar code labels you see everywhere today, but with more intelligence. The advantage of these more intelligent systems is that, unlike bar code tracking systems, an RFID system can read the information on a tag without requiring line of sight or a particular orientation. This means that RFID systems can be largely automated, reducing the need for manual scanning.

An example of an "active" RFID tag is the tollbooth that reads a device installed in your car. An example of a "passive" RFID is a bar code reader typically used in warehouses.

Numbers Only is a vendor that produces a handheld scanner using RFID that enables six functions:

1. *Cart count:* Perform inventory count operations at remote inventory locations or carts

2. *Cycle count:* Perform cycle count as well as physical count operations on the handheld

3. *Receive:* Receive inbound items from vendors at the receiving dock on a handheld and update the actual receipt of items

4. *Put away:* Put away the received materials into the inventory and confirm materials into the inventory and confirm the put away location on the handheld

5. *Pick:* Pick the requested items from the inventory and confirm the pick quantity and pick location on the handheld

6. *Deliver:* Perform delivery and distribution operations of inbound items to the requested departments and capture recipient's signature for confirmation

Handheld devices of the size of a Treo or Blackberry can now interface with the computer inventory system at the point of location.

Many rental car dealers use this technology. When you return your car, the agency scans the car, notes the mileage and fuel consumption, and voilá! You have a bill. They then service and park the car and can find it on the lot easily.

Pick-to-Light Systems

A pick-to-light system guides stock pickers to the correct amount of product to select by lighting the carousel with the correct amount.

Ethics in the Supply Chain

The supply chain is one area that is constantly faced with ethical situations. A company may be dealing with suppliers that have unfair labor practices, and they may have to deal with buyers who expect to be paid bribes.

Target is one company that has implemented a Standards of Vendor Engagement. Among the issues facing Target is the employment of persons under the age of 14. As a consequence, Target established a Corporate Compliance Organization, comprising auditors who check on subcontractors and vendors. Vendors are educated about the legal and ethical ramifications of the Fair Labor Standards Act of 1938 and require vendors to attend an "Approved for Purchase" program.

The ethical situations that often arise in the purchasing function are discussed in detail in Chapter 13.

Customer Relationship Management (CRM) and the Supply Chain

An important component of modern SCM software is the customer relationship management (CRM) module, which tracks customer statistics. Frazelle (2002) listed a number of aspects of this system:

- Order entry
- Order processing
- Contact management
- Customer activity profiling
- Order pattern recognition
- Customer transaction databases
- Open order databases
- Customer service policy maintenance
- Customer service performance measurement
- Call/customer transaction management systems
- Customer satisfaction monitoring
- Online order assignment to optimal shipment and pick waves (pp. 88–89)

CRM is more than just providing the statistics about the customer service. It is also a holistic approach to customer relations and involves the teamwork of marketing, sales, and customer service.

Conclusions

The heart of operations management is the inventory system, the logic of moving materials from the supplier to the customer. The importance of coordination through the supply chain has magnified the need for an integrated management approach. This chapter shows the role SCM plays within the organization and why it has become a critical entity for organizational success.

A critical aspect of successful SCM is coordination. A backorder in one element of the chain can cause what is called the "bullwhip effect," causing supply disruptions throughout the system.

Summary

- SCM is the coordination of functions within the supply chain, including logistics and materials management.

- SCM has several stages according to the industry. For a retailer, there may be five stages: (1) raw material suppliers, (2) textile mills, (3) distributor, (4) retailer, and (5) customer.

- The major modes of transportation for SCM are rail, truck, air, courier, pipeline, and boat.

- Any backorder in one of the stages of SCM causes a "bullwhip effect" in which supply disruptions can occur throughout the chain.

- The make versus buy decision is an important aspect of SCM as companies must decide whether to outsource or perform tasks in-house.

- Warehouse activities include receiving, putting away, storage, order picking, packaging and pricing, sorting, and shipping.

- The relationship between suppliers and customers calls for an ethical approach to these interactions.

- CRM is a holistic approach to customer relations and involves the teamwork of marketing, sales, and customer service.

Review Questions

1. Define SCM.

2. What are the stages of SCM?

3. How would the stages of SCM differ from a retail company to a manufacturer?

4. List the major forms of transportation for SCM.

5. Look at the furniture and equipment in the room you are presently in. What transportation method do you think got them there?

6. What is EDI, and what are its advantages?

7. Define postponement and mass customization. Give examples of each.

8. What are the major tasks involved in warehousing?

9. What are some methods of automation employed in warehousing?

10. Find examples of companies that use AGVs. What is the cost justification for these systems?

Projects

1. Trace SCM at your own company. Take one item in the inventory and try to discover its history: where it came from, what its lead time from the supplier was, and so on.

2. Discuss SCM with a supply chain professional. What does he or she list as the most important coordination issues?

3. Consult with one of the industry professional organizations, and attend one of their meetings. There is always an informative speaker at organizations such as the American Production and Inventory Control Society (APICS).

CASE   Shiraishi Garments Co.

Bin Jiang and Patrick Murphy

On February 9, 2005, Takashi Shiraishi, the president of Shiraishi Garments Co., stood in front of his office window where there was a view of the afternoon sun sparkling on the Tokyo Bay. Since last year, Shiraishi Garments had begun to outsource its businesses to China to improve its profit margins. Even though Takashi did see some benefits of outsourcing, he also found that buying low-cost goods at the expense of Chinese workers' health, safety, and welfare was morally bankrupt. Doing so was unsustainable, because such a supply chain model was increasingly showing cracks. Furthermore, as a consumer goods company, Shiraishi Garments was more exposed to labor scandals than capital goods companies, because its market success largely depended on its brand, which was vulnerable to reputation risks.

Since the Snow Brand Milk poisoning episode in 2000, which resulted in more than 13,000 people falling sick, Japanese companies had to wrestle with falling public trust. Simultaneously, exploiting cheaper overseas labor was blamed as the main reason for Japanese companies' moving operations out of Japan and as the main trigger of Japan's increasing unemployment. Under increasing public pressures, many companies that had outsourced business overseas were seriously boosting their demonstrable commitment to good corporate citizenship.

Shiraishi Garments worked very hard to improve labor conditions in its supply chain in China. For instance, Takashi found local suppliers to be reluctant to make the initial financial investment to provide first aid training in factories, so Shiraishi Garments footed the bill for the first sessions. Having seen the benefits of less time lost through worker injury, local suppliers were then more prepared to continue the investment. Two major suppliers had taken advantage of this scheme, and Shiraishi Garments had taken a similar approach with other initiatives, including the production of a handbook and posters about hazardous substances. From this experience, Takashi was wondering if working with local partners might be a sustainable way to improve labor conditions.

Shiraishi Garments Co.

Japan has one of the biggest and most sophisticated apparel industries in the world. To understand why the Japanese are so fastidious about their clothing, one should understand that throughout Japanese history, a woman's most prized possessions were not silver, gold, or precious stones but rather her kimonos. More than in other societies, clothes in Japan signify one's station in life and advertise one's tastes and sensibilities. The fact that most modern-day Japanese live in nondescript apartments reinforces their willingness to spend on clothes.

Takashi Shiraishi established his Shiraishi Garments Co. in 1978, after watching an interesting report on TV. In that year, the oil crisis was biting hard; the Japanese government announced an "energy suit" (a sort of short-sleeved safari suit) for its staff, which was designed to allow companies to save on air conditioning. The experiment was a failure; although a few ministers wore these suits for a week or two, no one felt they were "correct" clothes for the office. A TV reporter said,

> The businessman puts on the darkest suit he owns, a white shirt, and a sober tie, and that is what he wears in Japan, no matter what the temperature might be outside. . . . Many Japanese find such rigidity comforting because it eliminates the nerve-racking necessity of making choices.

As a recent art school graduate, Takashi believed that such a conservative dressing habit gave him an entrepreneurship opportunity—introducing customization into the drab business attire market. He believed that customer values should be reflected in different tastes, preferences, and lifestyles, even among those in the same age-group. There should be more diversified purchasing patterns. He opened his first men's clothing shop in a department store in Tokyo. In the small shop, even though Shiraishi products were still in the conservative colors (e.g., blue, gray, brown, and black), it was amazing to see so many varieties of drab suits and neckties. Based on each particular customer's skin color, hairstyle, and other personal characteristics, Takashi helped his customer select the best-matched color, accessories, suit style, and even shape of tie knot. He was the master of the art of making his customers feel special and important. This personal attention made all the difference. Those customers liked to believe that the deal with them was the most important thing Shiraishi Garments was engaged in at the moment.

Each finished design was transferred to Shiraishi sewing subcontractors, which were located in the suburbs of Tokyo. Shiraishi Garments usually asked for smaller quantities, but with more designs, while other apparel retailers wanted larger quantities and fewer designs. Even though it was much easier to provide services to other apparel retailers than to Shiraishi Garments, those subcontractors were still interested in Shiraishi orders. The problem with the other retailers was that they wanted low price but high quality and, to provide such a service, the subcontractors could only engage themselves in a price war. On the contrary, the relationship between Shiraishi Garments and its sewing subcontractors was very strong. Shiraishi Garments made a detailed report to its subcontractors on any defects and gave them advice on how to improve the quality and production of the components they produced. Furthermore, Shiraishi Garments shared its customers' comments and its prediction of fashion changes with them, so that these subcontractors and suppliers could keep pace with the changing market.

Within 2 weeks of placing the order, the customer would get his or her customized garments from Shiraishi Garments. The deliverer not only sent the clothes to the customer's home but also helped him dress up. The deliverer would visit the customer again in 10 days to see whether everything went well. Even after the monetary transaction, customers still felt Shiraishi Garments' sense of obligation. They were convinced that Shiraishi Garments would still be there to service the product later on.

The results of this customer-oriented customization strategy led to a strong relationship with suppliers. Shiraishi Garments' prices were only 15% higher than ready-made garments, but the consumer was able to choose from more than 10,000 variations in styles. Takashi made its company's name synonymous with quality and prestige. With the Japanese economy's boom in the 1980s, Shiraishi Garments expanded to a middle-size prestige brand. By 1991, the total annual sales of its 11 retail outlets in department stores amounted to more than 22 billion yen.

Since the 1990s, however, the globalization of the economy and a shrinking and aging population have dramatically changed the Japanese apparel market. Rather than purchasing complete designed garments, the younger generation tends to purchase items at several different shops and then mixed those items freely to match their sensitivities. Young shoppers now display a strong tendency to purchase products at select shops located at railway stations, commercial districts, and fashion-specific buildings rather than the conventional department stores where retail outlets and products were expected with greater sophistication and higher quality. There has been a trend toward more casual clothes among males. Perhaps some disillusion with life as "salary men" has contributed to a more laid-back attitude. Simultaneously, the Japanese economy entered the "lost 10 years" as soon as the real estate and stock market bubble burst in 1990. Japanese consumers trimmed spending on clothing by making fewer purchases and shifting to lower-priced items. From 1991 to 2004, clothing's share of total household expenditures decreased 13 years in a row.

Because the Japanese male clothing market was becoming both fashion and commodity oriented, Shiraishi Garments' customized/designed business attire could not meet this trend very well. Since the late 1990s, Takashi had been struggling with shrinking sales and profit margins (see Table 12.4). He believed that Shiraishi Garments had to cut costs to survive. In 2004, Takashi outsourced Shiraishi Garments' sewing tasks to Chinese companies.

Table 12.4   Shiraishi Garments Co. Financial Highlights

For the Years Ended March 31	2000	2001	2002	2003	2004
Sales	236,225	232,819	221,781	215,822	189,313
Operating income	17,661	14,032	15,275	12,910	12,872
Net income	7,266	6,026	5,049	4,567	4,347

NOTE: Figures are in millions of yen.

The Allure and Challenge of China

The eyes of the world were fixed on the Chinese economy. Some 1.3 billion potential consumers and low labor costs had lured numerous Western or Japanese companies to China. Around the globe, shelves were stacked with the low-cost goods, such as clothes, sports goods, toys, computers, and DVD players, churned out by "the world's workshop." Further liberalization following China's accession to the World Trade Organization (WTO) in 2001 had further increased the attractiveness of China as a manufacturing location. According to the World Bank, by 2010 China could account for half of the textiles manufactured in the world.

Actually, Takashi found that China was not necessarily the cheapest place to source (see Table 12. 5). For the apparel industry, however, Takashi believed that there was always a "best place" for manufacturing at a given time, and right now, it was China—because of low labor costs and also because of the tremendous investments made in textile and apparel factories. There were high-tech sewing facilities there that did not exist, to the same magnitude, anywhere else in the world. Takashi visited several Chinese "supply chain cities" and was impressed that he could find everything needed for manufacturing garments in a single location. Many Chinese vendors were located within supply chain cities, with factories located near textile mills and suppliers of various components. By aggregating decent factories, political stability, time, availability of fabric, talent pool, infrastructure, and speed to Japanese market, Takashi was sure that China had some favorable components compared with other Asian countries.

Takashi also noticed that the salary in the coastal regions of China was four times higher than in the Western areas. As a result, many laborers had left the inland countryside in droves preferring to take their chances in the new factories along the coast than live in rural poverty. At the advent of the Chinese New Year 2004, Takashi was in China and was surprised to learn that up to 120 million migrant laborers traveled by either road or rail to reunite with their families in the countryside. The large migration movement was putting pressure on wages for unskilled workers. On the one hand, migrant laborers had provided a cheap, mobile, and largely compliant workforce, which had attracted foreign direct investment and ensured the viability of millions of domestic businesses. On the other hand, Chinese prosperity had been achieved through the suffering of these ruthlessly exploited migrant laborers. In the Pearl River Delta, one local vendor in Shiraishi Garments' supply chain told Takashi, "There are plenty of girls with good eyes and strong hands. If we run out of workers who would like to accept our current wages, we just go deeper into the inland regions to recruit new workers." In this vendor's factory, some workers were earning a basic monthly wage of $37 and working up to 16 hr a day for 7 days a week.

Table 12.5 Wage Comparison (Hourly Rates for Sewer Workers in Asian Urban Regions)

Country	Rate ($/Hour)	Country	Rate ($/Hour)
Laos	0.04	Pakistan	0.23
China (inland areas)	0.12	India	0.25
Vietnam	0.12	Indonesia	0.42
Sri Lanka	0.14	China (coastal areas)	0.48
Bangladesh	0.19	Japan	13.5

SOURCE: Cal Safety Compliance Corporation.

Low wages and poor labor conditions in Chinese factories were a negative side of the attractive labor costs and were not generally addressed effectively by domestic policies in China. Takashi found that while workers in factories that were state owned were fairly well treated, the same was not true of those in the private sector, which employed a high proportion of young, migrant, female workers. At the root of the problem was the failure of local authorities to enforce the law. He believed, "The problem is that local authorities are flexible in interpreting the law and have scarce resources; their priority is to attract foreign investment. Labor law enforcement is a selling point when trying to attract foreign inward investment."

To operate in China, Takashi had to face the concerns of labor conditions. Clothing and sports goods companies had been in the focus of NGO (nongovernmental organization) campaigns criticizing low pay, overtime, safety problems, and child labor in supply chains. An NGO criticism could lead to significant damages to a company's reputation. Other risks associated with poor labor conditions included quality problems, low productivity, and high employee turnover rates. Takashi summarized the business risks associated with operating in China as reputation risks (poor labor conditions could create negative publicity and damage the value of brands) and operational risks (poor productivity and high employee turnover due to poor labor conditions).

Foreign companies having their own factories in China were less exposed to the two risks than companies that outsourced production to local companies, where control was limited. For those companies with their own factories in China, most of them had implemented occupational health and safety programs as part of their operating management. They paid basic wages above the legal minimum and their social security payments and working hours complied with the local legal regulations as a minimum requirement. Some companies even provided extra benefits for employees, such as housing subsidies and additional holidays. However, these factories required a consistent minimum volume of business and must continually reinvest in updating their technology capabilities. All these added up to overhead costs that an outsourced vendor would be spreading over 100 to 300 clients. Based on Takashi's experience, in 3 years a new factory could not get access to the best practices, platforms, and intellectual property that a third party could potentially provide. This was why Takashi decided to use Chinese suppliers rather than establish his own factory in China.

Shiraishi Garments' Chinese Suppliers

In China, Shiraishi Garments had two major suppliers: one producing accessory goods (Supplier 1) and another sewing garments (Supplier 2).

Located on the outskirts of Wenzhou, Zhejiang, Supplier 1 employed 1,500 workers producing accessory goods. Its overtime hours were a significant problem, with 78% of the workers working more than 132 hr of overtime in 1 month. Most workers arrived at this factory with low-level skills. Because they were often paid by the piece, without an overtime premium, the factory had no direct financial incentive to reduce long hours. Workers built their skills "on the job" so that the factory did not pay directly for training, but faced the hidden costs of low productivity, low quality, and factory overhead for long hours.

The factory ran a system of warnings and some fines and did not provide any productivity bonuses. It published a rulebook that instructed workers on every aspect of factory life. Harsh penalty systems included imposing fines (deductions from pay) for any violation of the rules (e.g., coming to work late, talking during work, leaving the workplace, spitting, and so on). Supervisors and middle managers had a tendency to speak rudely and shout at workers when production goals were not met.

Employees were unhappy about the long hours, compulsory overtime work, low pay, fines, and poor quality of food. Workers said that there were few ways to talk to managers and many did not want to. Relationships between workers and their supervisors were strained. Supervisors were suspected of not accurately recording the number of pieces made by each worker and of extending working hours further than the management had planned.

Although it seemed that health and safety management was generally good, with accidents recorded by the medical center and minor injuries dealt with in the first aid room in each production unit, Takashi had concerns over the poor ergonomic design of workplaces. Problems identified in this factory also included inappropriate storage and handling of chemicals, improper protection equipment for workers, and the lack of chemical safety training.

For Supplier 1, management of its own suppliers was difficult. Problems with the quality and late delivery of raw material inputs delayed the start of production and squeezed the window of time for production. Supplier 1 used multiple-source purchasing, which means having a list of potential suppliers and buying from several to avoid getting locked into a sole source.

Supplier 2 was a small factory in Dongguan, Guangdong, which employed around 400 workers sewing garments for Shiraishi Garments and a few other foreign retailers. The factory's managers described the relationship with these foreign purchasers as uncomfortable, particularly in terms of tight lead times, late sample approval, and last-minute alterations to product specification. All these problems put increased pressure on this factory to deliver orders and led to poor communication between merchandisers, factory management, and production.

Insufficient communication about changes to product specification could lead to increased levels of rework and thus overtime. High reworking levels were recorded up to an average of 7% during production and 10% following final inspection. On some lines with some styles, reworking could reach levels of more than 50%. Piece rate workers were not paid for reworking, that is, a significant proportion of working time was not only unproductive but also unpaid. While very few workers were aware of the amount of the legal minimum wage, they were aware that they were not properly compensated for overtime and believed their wages to be unfair. Two-way communication between workers and management was poor, so that changes in pay or hours were frequently not understood, and on occasion were resented, by workers. This created a situation where there were few effective channels for workers to raise their concerns with managers and managers often did not respond to workers' concerns or suggestions. The factory operated fines for 18 different offences, and workers did not receive any skills training for their jobs.

Poor performance was noted in a number of other areas. For example, there were inadequate escape routes and locked or blocked fire exits. Systems for tracking and improving productivity and quality were poor. No formal line quality control system existed, and no records were kept of reworking rates during the production process. Piece rate workers were set daily targets, and supervisors made daily estimates of how many pieces each worker made. However, these records were not kept for more than a few days. The factory estimated that 70% of fabric supplies were delivered at least 1 week late.

The annual turnover of workers in the factory was extremely high (140%). Many workers wanted to leave the factory because of the long overtime hours and because they felt that the management was too strict.

The Need for a New Approach

Audit was the dominant tool for tackling Chinese labor standards in supply chains. However, audits alone were not sufficient to drive positive change. It was impossible to socially audit a supplier.

Even health and safety audits were difficult. For instance, Takashi found that "The supplier has a fire alarm" was a box that was ticked or not ticked in an audit. "But does it work?" "Do workers know what it is?" "Do they have the right to use it?" "Do they know what to do in an emergency?" "Can everyone hear it?" The black-and-white audit approach could not answer these questions. Furthermore, if very short time frames were set for improvements to meet a coming audit, they often proved unrealistic for tackling the fundamental problems of labor conditions. As a result, the follow-up was poor and resulted in few sustained improvements being made on the ground.

Audits could even lead to dishonesty, a lack of openness, and fraud, when suppliers felt forced to provide the "right" answer or face serious business implications. Chinese factory managers were becoming increasingly professional at faking records and coaching workers to give acceptable responses during worker interviews. This trend toward concealment was a serious barrier to improving labor conditions, as it wasted time and money without making any change at all in the workplace.

Also, while workers did not want to work the excess hours, which were currently being demanded of them, they were willing to work more than the low limits set by Chinese national law to increase their pay packets. If a factory suddenly reduced working hours to legal limits as a result of audits, without any effort to increase productivity, workers' wages would dramatically decrease.

The sun was low and darkness was descending over the man-made islands of Tokyo Bay. Takashi walked away from the window and turned on the light on his desk. He believed that the current approach, which often depended heavily on compliance-focused audits, had made little progress in tackling poor labor conditions in China. Assessments therefore needed to become more focused on supporting continuous improvement and should be supplemented with capacity-building activities. So a new approach that could provide a sustainable solution was needed (Figure 12.1).

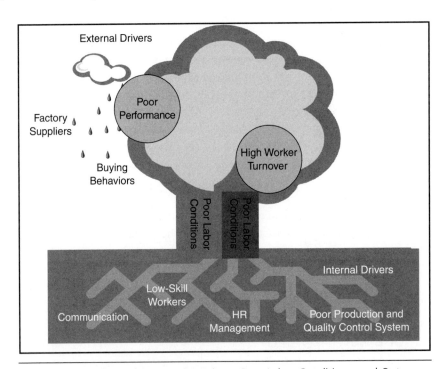

Figure 12.1 Relationship Between Drivers, Poor Labor Conditions, and Outcomes

SOURCE: Used with permission from the *Journal of Business Ethics Education*.

Web Site

www.supplychainittoolbox.com

References

Chopra, S., & Meindl, P. (2001). *Supply chain management.* Upper Saddle River, NJ: Prentice Hall.

Frazelle, E. H. (2002). *Supply chain strategy.* New York: McGraw-Hill.

Mentzer, J. T., Myers, M. B., & Stank, T. P. (Eds.). (2007). *Handbook of global supply chain management.* Thousand Oaks, CA: Sage.

Sophos. (2004). *RFID technology: An Introduction.* Posted September 30, 2004, at and retrieved September 15, 2006, from http://blogs.ittoolbox.com.

Wilson, R. (June, 2005). *16th Annual state of logistics report.* Oak Brook, IL: Council of Supply Chain Management Professionals.

CHAPTER 13

Inventory Management and Purchasing

SOURCE: © Anton Gvozdikov/istockphoto.com

Learning Objectives

In this chapter, we will

- Study the basic philosophies of purchasing
- Learn negotiation principles for buying
- Study negotiation tactics
- Learn "when" to order
- Review basic inventory costs
- Study the economic order quantity
- Review the ABC method of inventory control
- Learn the importance of accuracy and cycle counting
- Study the just-in-time and lean inventory systems

The Basics

The basic inventory policy decisions are as follows:

- When do we order supplies?
- How much do we buy?
- Who do we buy from?

These basic questions drive the materials management function, which is responsible for supply management within a firm. Materials management, a key component of the supply chain, involves the purchasing or sourcing of materials and the management of the inventory while still in the facility.

A buyer who has been trained to understand the products he or she is buying usually staffs the purchasing function. For example, a hospital purchasing agent has to know the difference between types of surgeon's gloves and the differences between brands of sutures. This person may be required to do extensive research prior to buying capital equipment, such as MRIs or digital echocardiography machines. Similarly, the purchasing agent for Apple Computers must know the differences between hard drive manufacturers before sourcing that essential part to computers.

A professional association, the Institute for Supply Management (ISM), guides the conduct and certification of purchasing professionals. Its principles and standards highlight the importance of ethical conduct within the profession (see Box 13.1). Since the purchasing agent spends as much or more of a company's budget than is spent on labor, the purchasing function has the potential of realizing significant cost savings if managed prudently.

The first policy decision is, basically, "Where do we get it?" The availability of a commodity varies from product to product. Some parts and supplies are commodity items that can be purchased from countless suppliers, while others are in scarce supply. Sometimes parts and supplies are protected by patent, and can only be sourced from one manufacturer until the patent expires.

BOX 13.1	**Principles and Standards of Ethical Supply Management Conduct**

LOYALTY TO YOUR ORGANIZATION
JUSTICE TO THOSE WITH WHOM YOU DEAL
FAITH IN YOUR PROFESSION

From these principles are derived the ISM standards of supply management conduct. (Global)

1. Avoid the intent and appearance of unethical or compromising practice in relationships, actions and communications.

2. Demonstrate loyalty to the employer by diligently following the lawful instructions of the employer, using reasonable care and granted authority.

3. Avoid any personal business or professional activity that would create a conflict between personal interests and the interests of the employer.

4. Avoid soliciting or accepting money, loans, credits or preferential discounts and the acceptance of gifts, entertainment, favors or services from present or potential suppliers that might influence, or appear to influence, supply management decisions.

5. Handle confidential or proprietary information with due care and proper consideration of ethical and legal ramifications and governmental regulations.

6. Promote positive supplier relationships through courtesy and impartiality.

7. Avoid improper reciprocal agreements.

8. Know and obey the letter and spirit of laws applicable to supply management.

9. Encourage support for socially diverse practices.

10. Conduct supply management activities in accordance with national and international laws, customs and practices, your organization's policies, and these ethical principles and standards of conduct.

11. Develop and maintain professional competence.

12. Enhance the stature of the supply management profession.

Approved January 2005

A key philosophical consideration is whether to single-source or multisource an item. Do you award a contract for nuts and bolts to one vendor, giving them an exclusive agreement for a period of time, or do you purchase as needed from whoever offers you the best price at the time?

Industrial purchasing is analogous to the consumer shopping experience. Consumers go to the supermarket and purchase what they need when their inventory has reached the **reorder point** at their homes. Some consumers clip coupons from the newspaper and purchase whatever they can get discounts on. Others only buy the highest quality of everything they purchase. Still others buy the cheapest items available. All these behaviors are also typical of professional purchasing agents.

The award of a contract to a **single source** has many advantages. It reduces the paperwork through the accounting system, cutting the numbers of receiving documents and accounts payable invoices. Dealing with only one vendor can help the supplier to forecast better. A contract can lock in a price for an extended period of time and protect against price increases. Some contracts are negotiated with a "cost-plus" clause to protect vendors against price changes in rapidly changing commodity markets.

A disadvantage of dealing with a single source can be that the purchasing agent locks in a deal that is ultimately more expensive than multiple sourcing, and the company is stuck with a contract. For example, a supplier can make a contract for 10 items, and 1 commodity alone is overpriced, but that is exactly the one on which you spend the most money. That is why there is a lot of talent required in smart purchasing. Not to watch prices is a fatal mistake for buyers.

Those who encourage a competitive atmosphere among their suppliers favor the multiple-sourcing option. It increases the paperwork and requires a lot more vigilance in watching prices, but it can result in cost savings. The buyer can run into trouble when a commodity becomes scarce; however, loyal buyers are always served first.

Just-in-time (JIT) sourcing relies on the single-sourcing method. In cases where assembly lines operate JIT, the dependence on the delivery of a reliable supplier is paramount, and any failure on the part of the supplier will result in a shutdown of the line. As a result, JIT companies' strong dependence on their suppliers changes their purchasing philosophy to one of guaranteed long-term contracts and much cozier relations with suppliers than you would typically find in a multiple-sourcing environment.

JIT suppliers are considered an extension of the manufacturer itself. The main point is that there is a total reliance on suppliers in JIT, so they had better perform.

The selection of a supplier should be based on the following criteria:

- Price
- Quality
- Service

Ultimately, quality/price is called value.

Price

The contract negotiations should not end with the negotiated price alone, however. Who pays for shipping? Buyers may find out that they were gouged on shipping costs after they have negotiated what they thought was a good contract. Shipping is a negotiable item, too. If Company A pays for shipping but Company B does not, it may mean that Company A is overall less expensive, although its prices are higher.

The terms of payment also can be negotiated. A "Net 30" contract means that the bill must be paid within 30 days of receipt or a penalty will be invoked; "10% 10 net 30" means that a 10% discount is available if the invoice is paid within 10 days, otherwise the price holds for 30 days. Buyers can realize a significant discount by taking advantage of payment discounts, yet these are sometimes not even mentioned in the negotiations of a contract. Therefore, buyers have a total cost of the item to consider: Actual price + Shipping price + Payment terms.

Negotiation Principles for Purchasing Agents

Negotiation is one of the required skills of the professional purchasing agent. It is their job to establish continuous sources of materials for the company. In a large manufacturing company, the buyers typically are divided into commodities, and they will specialize in that area, usually for several years, and sometimes shift to another area of the firm. A large automobile manufacturer would have dozens of buyers, some for items such as sheet metal, others for stereos. A large retailer would have a similar setup: clothes buyers, household goods buyers, computer and peripheral equipment buyers, and so on.

A starting point for buyers to approach negotiations is the *price range.* Buyers have to preestablish in their minds what their goal price to purchase would be. The goal price is usually positioned between the *optimal price* and *bottom price.* The optimal price is usually their first offer. It is not expected, but sometimes it is accepted on the spot with no further negotiations. The bottom price is the absolute most the buyer will pay before walking away from the deal. Usually, buyers are in the best possible negotiating position if they can walk away from the negotiating table and buy either the same product or a substitute product from somewhere else.

The price range is best illustrated in a house purchase. When house sellers list a house for sale, they rarely expect a buyer to walk in through the door and pay the list price, unless there are competing buyers making bids or it is a rapidly shifting upward market.

As an example, let us say that a seller lists a house at $515,000. The seller has priced the house about $50,000 above her goal price of $465,000. Since she is purchasing another house, she needs enough for a down payment for the next house, so she has established that she cannot sell at a price lower than $435,000, which becomes her *bottom price.* She originally paid $375,000 for the house 5 years earlier, and as of now has an outstanding loan balance of $320,000. She will be paying 6% commission to her sales agent, which means that if she sells at $500,000, her commissions would be $30,000, netting her $470,000 and a balance of $150,000 after paying off her existing house loan.

The house is listed, and 1 month later, there is a very interested buyer. The buyer must also set his own *price range*. This buyer has been preapproved for a loan of $475,000. Since that is the maximum the bank will loan, it becomes the buyer's *bottom price*. Now, when looking at the prospect of buying a house, there has to be some research as to how much houses have been selling for in the neighborhood and how far from the listing price they usually go for. Although the buyer cannot afford $515,000, he thinks it is about 10% higher than what the house will sell for (about $463,000). Therefore, the buyer does a sketchy estimate that the seller is looking for something in the range of $460,000 to $465,000. The *optimum price* for this buyer would be to walk away with a real deal, and researching that the seller purchased the property for $375,000 and knowing that the realtor will get 6%, the buyer estimates that the seller has a break-even price of about $397,000, the point at which the seller makes no money on the deal. The buyer now sets his lowball price above that, at $430,000. With the optimum price at $430,000 and the bottom price of $475,000, the goal price is about in the middle, at $452,000.

Seller's range:

Optimum Price	Goal Price	Bottom Price
515,000	465,000	435,000

Buyer's range:

Optimum Price	Goal Price	Bottom Price
430,000	452,000	475,000

In a case like this, that is, in the absence of any other potential buyers, there is a very real chance that there will be a deal. At this point, however, the art of negotiation takes over, and the psychology involved could result in no deal. In the case of both the buyer and the seller, they should expect at least two rounds of offers and counteroffers, and maybe as many as four.

In this case, it goes like this:

Round 1: Buyer offers $430,000. Seller counters at $498,000.

Round 2: Buyer offers $450,000. Seller comes down to $478,000.

Round 3: Buyer offers to split the difference at $464,000. Seller accepts the offer.

This negotiation has seen the seller do slightly better than the buyer in approaching the goal, but both are satisfied parties.

Negotiation Objectives

The primary objective in a negotiation is for both parties to feel that they have won, creating a **win-win** situation. This is particularly important in professional purchasing, where a continued business relationship will exist. The buyers have to feel that they have purchased at a fair, competitive price, and the sellers have to feel that they have made an adequate profit on the deal and that forging a relationship will help their company in the long run.

Negotiations over automobile prices have changed somewhat with the recognition on the part of automobile dealers that they are not only trying to sell *this* car to the buyer but also *all their future automobiles!* So negotiations take the form of giving a fair price right off the bat, one that is hard to match by a competitor. The days of "*take it or leave it*" have passed.

A **win-lose** situation exists when one party takes advantage of the situation and gets a much better deal than the other party. Examples of this would be the house buyer who knows that the seller is on the verge of foreclosing the mortgage and is desperate to sell, so he or she offers a rock-bottom price, or the unscrupulous car dealer who takes advantage of the poor credit of the buyer to jack up the price, knowing that the buyer is simply grateful to get a loan of any kind.

A *lose-lose* situation happens when both parties make bad deals and neither party even thinks that they have made a good deal. Take, for example, a baseball team so desperate to get rid of a good player because of his bad behavior that they accept a lesser player from the other team, which does not even need the player in the first place but just wants to keep him so that a good team does not get him.

Negotiation Tactics

Once a buyer has established his or her range of acceptable outcomes, the process of dealing with the next buyer begins. Many people are afraid to negotiate, as Herb Cohen (2004) pointed out in his book *You Can Negotiate Anything*. People who are afraid to negotiate pay the list price on automobiles or the list price on houses—and ultimately cost themselves a lot of money. The two biggest purchases for a consumer are the house and the automobile, and these present the most room for negotiation. In the arena of industrial purchasing or retail buying, trained professionals look to get their companies good deals.

1. *Approach the goal with care.* When a negotiator makes a first offer, it should be at or above his or her optimal price, not at the goal price. The logic is that if you offer your goal price, then there will be a counteroffer immediately, putting you below your optimal price. Therefore, you start higher, wait for the response, and then respond to the response. Be careful not to go to the goal immediately either. If things are handled well, initial offers that seem far apart can be reconciled as long as the parties remain respectful of each other's role as negotiator.

2. *Watch out for the Trojan horse!* Some negotiations are concluded only for one of the parties to then make a number of additional demands. "I want this, and that,

and this, and that. Or the deal is off." Try to include all their terms within the contract and avoid unnecessary haggling over added demands. This can happen after a home inspection, when the buyer makes a number of unrealistic demands not expected by the seller. At this point, the seller either holds firm or kills the deal.

3. *Do in-depth research.* Buyers cannot afford to be ignorant about what they are buying before entering into negotiations. They must study all available comparable products, pricing, and terms. The process of purchasing an automobile is analogous to typical professional purchasing. If a buyer wants a new SUV, the buyer learns that there are several tiers of SUVs: luxury SUVs (Cadillac Eldorado, Porsche Cayenne, Range Rover), near-luxury SUVs (Lexus 300, BMW X5, Acura MDX, Infiniti FX45), and economy SUVs (Honda CRV, Toyota RAV4, Ford Escape).

Once the buyer picks the tier of SUVs desired, he or she compares the prices, quality, service, and availability of all the models in that tier. For example, if you have to drive 50 more miles for service for one of the models, you may reconsider in favor of a couple of brands that can be serviced within a 20-min drive. The astute buyer will study consumer reports and www.edmunds.com plus read automobile reviews in magazines and online sites (*Car and Driver, Motortrend,* etc.), and then he or she is ready to set foot in a car dealer's.

Also, showing the seller that research has been done is an important tactic. "I'm comparing this model with the BMW X5; what is the difference? I can get this car for this price on an online site; can you beat that?"

One of the ways automobile dealers make profits is on the trade-in. You will not get as much on a trade-in as you will if you sell it yourself. The dealers are offering to take the car off your hands and relieve you of the hassle of selling it yourself, a hassle that can cost you thousands of dollars.

A professional buyer's research is much the same. A hotel buyer purchasing mattresses will know all the manufacturers and the prices and will most likely actually sleep on the mattresses, since they are a critical hotel purchase.

Notice the tires on your automobile. A lot of negotiations went into sourcing that particular tire to the automobile manufacturer.

The Team Approach

When buyers work in teams, they must prepare their negotiating strategy and remain consistent. One approach is the *good guy/bad guy* approach. One buyer finds all the flaws and problems in the product, while the other tries to find the good side of the product. Many auto buyers have learned about this tactic firsthand. They negotiate with the salesperson, who always plays the good guy. When he offers a price and you counter it, he will say, "Let's see what my manager says we can do." He leaves, and the invisible manager becomes the *bad guy.* When the salesperson returns with the news that the bad guy would only budge a few dollars off their already low offer just because it is Thursday and they are cleaning the lot on Friday, make sure you know that the salesperson is both the good and *the bad* guy.

Escalating Authority

The power to negotiate different prices increases as you move up the chain of command in the organization. A hotel desk clerk has the power to offer a certain rate, but he or she cannot go below that rate. The hotel manager, however, can make a lower offer than the desk clerk. This is because the clerk has been given *limited authority*. The process of moving up the organizational hierarchy to negotiate is called *escalating authority*. A copier salesman has the ability to offer a certain price, but the marketing manager can refine the offer even further.

The Street-Smart Negotiator

Harry Mills (2004), in his book *The Streetsmart Negotiator,* described negotiations as a seven-step process:

Step 1: *Ready yourself*—Do your research, set your range, and make your tactical plan.

Step 2: *Explore needs*—Know the other party's expectations. If you know that a fleet of new cars is arriving at the lot the next week, you know they will try harder to sell the cars on the lot today. If you know that someone is eager to sell because they have bought a new house, you know they are willing to negotiate more.

Step 3: *Signal for movement*—Someone has to get the ball rolling in negotiations with the first offer. In real estate, it is a signed offer. In business, it is usually a request for a quote.

Step 4: *Probe with proposals*—"Would you consider?" is the catch phrase. Negotiators do not expect to settle things in one phase.

Step 5: *Exchange concessions*—Moving from the optimal toward the goal happens here.

Step 6: *Close the deal*—"If I offer you this, do we have a deal?" Getting the signature on the line is actually quite an art.

Step 7: *Tie up the loose ends*—All of the contractual details, delivery, and fine points have to be sorted through and then you are on your way!

Probably the best investment any business student can make would be in books on how to negotiate. These are life skills well worth knowing, whether you get involved in professional buying or not.

When to Order

Once a source has been settled on for materials, the next issue is when to order. If you run a hardware store that sells an average of five Eveready flashlights per day and it takes 5 days on average to receive them, how many should you have in stock when you place an order for more?

If you answered "25," you are halfway right. The reorder point is a function of average demand and average lead time (the time it takes from the moment you place an order to the time it is received). If you sell 5 per day and it takes 5 days, you should place the order when you have 25 and be at 0 about the time you receive some additional flashlights.

The problem centers on the word *average*. Because we are dealing with averages, all it will take is an increase in demand or an increase in lead time, and the hardware store will run out of stock. An out-of-stock position often results in lost sales. Thus, we have the concept of safety stock to hedge against these fluctuations in demand or lead time.

There are several ways to determine the necessary safety stock. The customary way, which we will call "**Grandpa's Intuition**," is to simply have a time period buffer, which gives the buyer enough time to react to any changes in demand. If Grandpa's Intuition is that we need an extra 3 days to protect against a stockout, our reorder point becomes Grandpa's Intuition = Average lead time demand + Average day's demand.

In this case, Grandpa's Intuition reorder point = 25 + 15 = 40.

The higher the average inventory, the more dollars are invested in it.

Another way to calculate the reorder point is to use a statistical method based on the standard deviation of demand and the order quantity.

Step 1: Calculate the standard deviation of demand.

Week	Demand	Deviation	Deviation Squared
1	42	7	49
2	27	8	64
3	36	1	1
4	35	0	0
Average demand			35
Total			114

The standard deviation is the square root of the sum of the squared deviation values divided by N (4): $\sqrt{114/4} = 5.34$

Step 2: Determine the desired service level. For example, if you want to be 99% sure that you will not run out of stock, then 99% is the desired service level.

Step 3: Find the value for 99% on a Z table.

Common Z scores:

50%	0.67	90%		1.65
75%	1.15	95%		1.97
85%	1.44	99%		2.58

(*Note:* Since *Z* tables specify the area under the normal curve, to find the area for 95%, for example, you would look for the value on the table that is closest to *half* of that. The value of 0.475 is located at 1.96.)

Step 4: Multiply the *Z* score by the standard deviation: $(2.58 \times 5.34) = 13.78 = 14$ units.

Step 5: Add that safety stock to the lead time demand to find your reorder point: $25 + 14 = 39$ units.

In other words, if you set the reorder point at 39, you can be 99% confident that you will not run out of stock and are well protected against a spike in demand or lead time. Then, of course, there is that 1% to worry about!

The Costs of Inventory

It is expensive to keep inventory. An examination of your refrigerator and storage cabinets reveals that you have some money invested in food. In theory, you could have no food in the house, but all the money in the bank, and every day buy what you need. That would be a form of the JIT inventory management system. But, since you don't want to go to the store every day, you keep enough in the house to tide you over until the next visit to the supermarket. This system is similar to the industrial inventory system.

Holding Cost

The most expensive cost of inventory is the **holding cost.** This is also called the "carrying cost" of inventory. The holding cost is simply the cost of storing inventory. The most significant part of this is the opportunity cost of capital. Since you have the option of putting the money in the bank and drawing inventory *or* buying inventory, the opportunity cost is what you lose by not putting the money in the bank. Whatever the interest rate a bank offers for large accounts of deposit, is that rate lost? If the inventory were $1 million and the current holding cost is 8%, then the annual cost of capital for the inventory would be $80,000.

Holding cost is also made up of the following:

- Cost of insurance on the inventory.
- Obsolescence cost: If you store a number of units and a newer model comes up, you may be stuck with the old units, and you may have to unload them at a reduced price, thus experiencing a loss.
- Shrinkage cost: Customers and employees steal some inventory.
- Breakage cost: Some inventory is broken or damaged and can't be returned.
- Cost of utilities in the warehouse: You have to have a place to store inventory, and that requires air-conditioning, heating, cleaning, and perhaps even construction of a new facility.

If the holding costs are added, they may approach as high as 25% to 35% of the cost of inventory. For $1 million in inventory, the annual inventory cost would be in the range of $250,000 to $350,000.

The enormous cost of carrying inventory is the reason why materials managers try to keep their inventories as low as possible while still maintaining high service rates. Reducing an inventory in half from $4 million to $2 million could save a company $500,000 or more! That would more than pay the salary of the materials manager.

Purchasing Cost

A second cost of inventory is the **purchasing cost** or order cost. This is the labor cost of the purchasing and accounts payable staff. Typically, this is broken down into a "cost per purchase order." So if the purchasing payroll totaled $500,000 and they made 1,000 purchase orders per year, their cost per purchase order would be $500. This cost forces purchasing and accounts payable to be efficient in their operations, trying to consolidate orders and avoiding placing orders for just a few products at a time.

Back-Order Costs

If a company runs out of stock, it may lose an order to a competing company. This is called the **"back-order cost"** or "stockout cost." It is difficult to determine what the cost actually is unless someone keeps track of the lost customers. This does impress on the purchasing staff the importance of making sure that they keep items in stock when customers want them.

The Total Cost of Inventory

These inventory costs are combined in an equation to determine the annual cost of inventory:

$$TC = DC + (D/Q)PO + (Q/2)CH,$$

where

TC = Total cost,

D = Annual demand,

C = Purchase cost,

Q = Order quantity,

PO = Purchase order cost, and

H = Holding cost percentage.

We will get into how to determine Q next, but for purposes of illustrating this equation, if

$D = 1,000,$

$C = 4.00,$

$Q = 100,$

$PO = 20,$ and

$H = 25\%,$

then

$$TC = (1000 \times 4) + (1000/100)20 + (100/2)(4 \times 0.25)$$
$$= 4000 + 200 + 50 = 4,250.00.$$

What this equation tells us is that if we purchase the item in quantities of 100 at a time, at a cost of $4.00 per item, the annual cost of the item would be $4,250. If we were to double the *size* of our orders to 200, it would have an impact on both the holding cost and the purchase order cost:

$$TC = 4000 + (1000/200)20 + (200/2)1$$
$$= 4000 + 100 + 100 = 4,200.$$

Trading off the cost of the purchase order against the holding cost, we would see a decrease in total cost annually by $50. This happens because the cost of holding is less than the cost of the purchase order in this particular example. That will not always be the case, however.

The Economic Order Quantity

The order quantity is an important consideration. If the cost of holding is minimal, you may purchase in larger quantities, particularly if the warehouse is very large.

The optimal order quantity, derived from the total cost equation, is called the **economic order quantity (EOQ)**. It is given as

$$EOQ = \sqrt{[2D(PO)]/(CH)}.$$

From the previous example,

$$EOQ = \sqrt{[(2 \times 1000)(20)]/(4 \times 0.25)} = \sqrt{40000} = 200.$$

We would then purchase an EOQ of 200.

Although the EOQ is the least costly quantity to purchase, there are times when a purchasing agent would not buy in these quantities:

1. If the company uses the JIT inventory method, the EOQ is assumed to be 1.

2. The EOQ may call for quantities that exceed the warehouse space allocation for the products.

3. To decrease the inventory on hand, frequently purchased items may be purchased in smaller quantities rather than the EOQ.

To calculate the total annual cost when purchasing in EOQs, the EOQ is substituted by Q in the equation

$$TC = DC + (D/Q)PO + (Q/2)CH,$$

considering the EOQ against a quantity discount.

If quantity discounts are offered for a product, a process of evaluating the total annual cost at each price break must be undertaken.

In the following example, three price breaks are offered to a music chain for buying copies of the latest CD by Surfjan Stevens.

1,000+ copies	$6.00
999–500 copies	$6.50
Under 500 copies	$7.00

Anticipated demand for the CD is 600 copies for the year. The holding cost is 25% of the price. The purchase order price is $10. The steps involved in this evaluation are as follows (Chase, Jacobs, & Aquilano, 2007):

1. Calculate the EOQ at the lowest price discount.

2. If the EOQ is enough to take advantage of the price break (over 1,000), you will automatically purchase that amount.

3. If the EOQ is not over that amount, substitute the lowest number possible for that price (1,000), and determine the total annual cost for that price break.

4. Move on to the next price break, and recalculate the EOQ for that price.

5. If that EOQ falls within the range (999–500), substitute the EOQ for the Q in the equation, and determine the total annual cost.

6. If it does *not* fall within the price range, calculate the Q as the lowest quantity in the range (500). Calculate the total cost for that quantity.

7. Repeat Steps 4 to 6 for the next price break ($7.00).

Example:

1. $EOQ(6.00) = \sqrt{[2D(PO)]/(CH)}$

   That is, $EOQ = \sqrt{[(2 \times 600)5]/(6.00 \times 0.25)} = \sqrt{6000/1.50} = 63.2$

2. Since you cannot purchase 63 units and get the quantity discount for 1,000 units, calculate the total cost of purchasing 1,000 units: $TC = DC + (D/Q)PO + (Q/2)CH.$

3. That is, TC = (600)6.00 + (600/1000)5 + (1000/2)(6.00 × 0.25).

4. TC = 3600 + 3 + 750 = 4,353.00.

5. For the next price break ($6.50), recalculate the EOQ.

6. $\sqrt{6000/1.63}$ = 60.7. Again, this is not within range, so calculate the total annual cost of purchasing in increments of $500.

7. TC = (600)6.50 + (600/500)5 + (500/2)(6.50 × 0.25). Thus, TC = 3900 + 6 + 406.25 = 4,312.25.

8. Finally, compare the total cost if you do not take the price discounts and pay $7.00:

$$EOQ = \sqrt{6000/1.75} = 58.5$$

$$TC = (600)7 + (600/59)5 + (59/2)(7 \times 0.25)$$

Thus, TC = 4200 + 50.85 + 51.63 = 4,302.48.

Comparison: Buying 1,000 units at a time, total annual cost = $4,353.00. Buying 500 at a time, total annual cost = $4,312.25. Buying 59 at a time, total annual cost = $4,302.48.

In other words, there is no effective price advantage in the discount when considering all the costs involved.

Purchasing at Fixed Time Intervals

Some purchasing agents buy materials according to delivery schedules. For example, if one supplier delivers weekly and another delivers monthly, they do not buy the EOQ. Instead, they order according to this equation:

Q = (Average demand × Time period of review) + Lead time demand + Safety stock − On-hand inventory.

For example, if a truck delivers every 4 weeks with an average demand of 7 units per day, the buyer would check the on-hand inventory and place an order. Assume a lead time of 4 days, a safety stock of 21 units, and an on-hand balance of 80 units for this example:

$$Q = (7 \times 28) + 28 + 21 - 80 = 165.$$

If on Monday the inventory on hand is 80, and the demand during the lead time is 28, 52 units will be on hand when the truck delivers the 165, bringing the stock back up to 217.

Bin Systems

Probably the easiest types of inventory systems to manage are bin systems. This is exactly like the management of groceries in your house. There are two ways you can stock. In a two-bin system, you have a box of cereal you are presently eating from and a backup. When you eat the first box, you buy another one.

In a one-bin system, you only have one box of cereal and will reorder when the box gets to a certain level. This system works best when movement of inventory is particularly slow and the lead time is fairly quick. Obviously, if the grocery store is 2 min away, you can operate with a one-bin system at home.

The ABC Analysis

Most inventories follow the Pareto principle. If you analyze how the inventory dollars are spent, the majority of the money is spent on just a few of the items in stock. An analysis of a hardware store, a hospital, or the storage for a hotel would yield similar results; that is, around 70% of the annual expenditures are spent on about 20% of the products in stock. This phenomenon enables the materials manager to study the inventory and apply different policies according to how the money is spent.

An **ABC analysis** is conducted in the following manner:

1. Calculate the total *annual* dollars spent for each product in stock.

2. Decide on a classification scheme in which the high-dollar items are classified "A," the next level is "B," and the lowest level is "C." Popular stratifications are 70% for A, 20% for B, and 10% for C and 80-10-10.

3. Multiply the total expenditures for all products by the chosen percentages (70-20-10, etc.). The first 70% of the dollars will be classified as A, the next 20% as B, and the last 10% as C.

4. Assign each product according to dollar class.

5. Once the items have been classified, the strategy is to reduce inventory levels for A items and increase the inventory turns. B will turn more frequently than C. C items are usually purchased with the EOQ.

6. A close watch should be placed on A items to make sure that the inventory counts are accurate, since the levels are reduced.

Table 13.1 provides an example of ABC analysis. In the table, 38 items total $19,329 per year in expenses. Multiplying by 70%, we find that the first $13,530 should be the cutoff for A items, the next $3,866 for B items, and the rest allocated as C.

Table 13.1 ABC Analysis

Item	Annual Expenditure (Cost × Demand) ($)	Class
1001	2,543	A
1020	432	B
1027	16	C
1031	1,576	A
1040	49	C
1042	876	A
1050	1,098	A
1060	125	C
1064	390	B
1066	27	C
1070	41	C
1077	78	C
1080	230	C
1087	27	C
1090	198	C
1200	20	C
1204	76	C
1210	765	A
1212	430	B
1213	65	C
1215	42	C
1217	65	C
1219	100	C
1227	201	C
1230	756	B
1232	300	C
1235	98	C
1240	765	B
1245	66	C
1251	309	C
1255	786	A
1260	1,206	A
1270	3,009	A
1275	1,200	A
1280	654	B
1290	34	C

(Continued)

Table 13.1 (Continued)

Item	Annual Expenditure (Cost × Demand) ($)	Class
1300	9	C
1303	560	B
Total	19,329	A 13,530
		B 3,866
		C 1,933

The A items actually total $13,059 because the highest-dollar B item would cause the As to exceed the cutoff value of $13,530. Similarly, the B items cutoff becomes $17,046. Nine items have been classified as A, 7 items as B, and 23 items as C. In this small sample, 23% of the products take up 67% of the annual expenditures.

Now the materials manager will put a closer watch on these products, keeping the inventories low but adequate to cover demand. Also, since the materials manager now knows where the money is spent by the company, he or she should spend proportional amounts of time in negotiating good prices for the high-dollar items.

Accuracy and Cycle Counting

Inventory accuracy is critical in successful inventory control. If the inventory system states that there is a balance of 5 on hand, but there are really 2, and the reorder point is 4, this may result in a stockout.

Periodic inventories are taken at least once a year. If the inventory balances are only reconciled once a year, there is a strong possibility that the counts may be wrong. Systematic counts of a sample of the inventory, called a **cycle count,** could help adjust balances more frequently.

These counts are especially important for the A and the most critical items. The cycle count does not eliminate the reasons for the inventory imbalances. A variety of factors may play into this:

- *Unit-of-issue errors:* A case of 24 boxes is received into the stock. If the inventory system records this as 1 box rather than 24 boxes, immediately the system would be off by 23 units.

- *Theft and loss:* some items get lost or broken and are not properly recorded.

- *Scanning errors:* Missed scans can result in inventory inaccuracy.

- *Items simply not recorded:* In a supermarket, for example, a box may be damaged and removed from the shelf, but this may not be recorded.

Periodic cycle counts should reveal that counts are no more than 95% correct. If the counts reveal a lower number, corrective action should be taken.

JIT and Lean Inventory Methods

The JIT production system was popularized by Toyota and other Japanese manufacturers. Toyota's inventory system, called **Kanban,** uses a card system to manage inventory. It is a form of JIT, although not the only form.

In a Kanban system, a "withdrawal" kanban (card) from a container of parts is swapped for a production kanban when the container is used. The production kanban signals the need for another container. This is somewhat akin to a two-bin system, earlier described in this chapter.

The JIT system as practiced in major Japanese corporations requires suppliers to deliver parts as needed—sometimes daily, sometimes weekly. It enables the plant to exist without a massive inventory of safety stock.

This system has a number of other features:

- *Worker preventive maintenance:* This feature enables quick response.

- *Total quality management (TQM):* JIT plants are very quality conscious, and the elimination of waste, that is, lean manufacturing, is the predominant theme.

- *Judoka:* Quality at the source. Production is stopped, and problems are corrected at the source rather than pulling the defective items from the assembly line while it continues to roll.

- *Long-term supplier relationships.*

JIT production is often called *lean* production because of its emphasis on the elimination of waste.

JIT has a major impact on location decisions for suppliers since they must locate at a proximity enabling them to make the frequent deliveries required for the system to work. In Tokyo, JIT is so prevalent that it has caused traffic problems for deliveries, with so many suppliers clogging the roads.

JIT in Services

Imagine a hospital set up to receive supplies the same day they are needed. Perhaps it would be possible if every procedure in the hospital were scheduled weeks in advance, but imagine the day when an unanticipated procedure occurs or a delivery is late. It is one thing to delay an assembly line while waiting for a delivery. It is another thing to risk a life while awaiting supplies.

Service companies such as hospitals, banks, hotels, and restaurants need to keep their inventories low, but they also need to be careful that they have an adequate buffer. Restaurants must manage some items that have short shelf lives, for example, fish, in a JIT approach, but they certainly don't want to run out of their main types of meat. Perishable inventories are by necessity run as a JIT system since their freshness is dependent on time.

Lean and Inventory

There has been a lot of discussion about what is really meant by *lean*. Shah and Ward (2007) performed a research study to find out what factors actually defined lean production. They surveyed 280 managers with a questionnaire designed to find the major factors in **lean systems.**

They found 10 distinct dimensions to a lean system:

1. *Supplier feedback:* The buyer provides feedback to the supplier, although this should work both ways.

2. *JIT delivery by suppliers:* This may mean different things to different managers. A true JIT system is virtually without inventory. Some managers prefer to think of JIT as supplies arriving "before I need to ask for it."

3. *Supplier development:* The manufacturing firm develops ties with suppliers who have an involvement in the production process and are tuned in to the need for prompt delivery.

4. *Customer involvement:* This refers to the internal focus on a firm's customers.

5. *Pull oriented:* Lean implies a pull production system, triggered by customer orders, rather than a push system.

6. *Continuous flow:* There is a "continuous flow of products."

7. *Setup:* This refers to the reduced time to prepare for a product changeover.

8. *Total productive/preventative maintenance:* A focus on preventative maintenance reduces downtime.

9. *Statistical process control:* Lean includes important quality tools.

10. *Employee involvement:* Employees are included in problem solving.

This study has focused on manufacturing firms, since service firms are not involved in pull systems and machine setups. The components of lean systems cross a wide range of operations management principles. Lean can be discussed in process improvement, quality management, and inventory management because it is key to an efficient firm.

Of the 10 factors, several are important to the service firm:

- Supplier feedback and development
- Customer involvement
- Employee involvement
- Statistical process control

However, a department store will have a different take on supplier delivery. The priority is to have it available for the customer. If a customer orders a washing machine from ABT Electronics, ABT will check its warehouse. If the item is unavailable, it will have to place another order from the supplier. Then, the company sets a delivery date for the customer that is timed in groupings by zip code. It does not want to receive a steady stream of washing machines from the vendor unless customers are ordering them at a reliable rate.

Professional Organizations

Two professional organizations guide the activities of supply chain managers and operations managers. The Institute for Supply Chain Management (ISM, www.ism.ws) guides purchasing and supply chain professionals, offering certification, conferences, seminars, and publications for its members.

The Association for Operations Management (APICS, www.apics.org) offers similar benefits for the operations management professional. APICS is probably more on the inventory side than ISM, while ISM is more on the sourcing side. Both organizations have chapters in major cities and present an ideal networking opportunity.

Conclusion

Materials management is the art of managing inventory. It includes the purchasing function, which is the important sourcing activity for supplies and materials. Supplies and materials are as costly as labor for most firms, which means that the effective cost management of this activity can result in savings.

Effective negotiation can result in major cost savings to a firm, so it is important that purchasing agents become adept at it.

Summary

- The basic supply questions are "When to order?" and "How much?"

- Purchasing managers must decide whether to single-source or multisource their supplies.

- Purchasing managers must learn negotiation techniques to get the best prices for their companies. The negotiations begin with an idea of an acceptable range of prices.

- The seven steps of negotiations are to ready yourself, explore needs, signal for movement, probe with proposals, exchange concessions, close the deal, and tie up loose ends.

- The basic costs of inventory are the holding cost, the purchasing cost, and the back-order cost.

- An ABC analysis is the stratification of inventory according to money spent per year.

- EOQ is an equation for setting an order quantity based on overall costs.

- Lean systems involve both JIT and TQM and include supplier, customer, and employee involvement.

Key Terms

ABC analysis

Back-order cost

Cycle count

Economic order quantity (EOQ)

Grandpa's Intuition

Holding cost

Just-in-time (JIT)

Judoka

Kanban

Lean systems

Purchasing cost

Reorder point

Single source

Win-lose

Win-win

Review Questions

1. How would you set reorder points for materials at your place of work?

2. How would you plan your grocery list?

3. What is the relationship between TQM and JIT?

4. Describe the negotiation steps taken in your last automobile purchase. How well did you do as a negotiator?

5. List the dos and don'ts of negotiations.

6. What is the difference in vendor relationships for JIT purchasing?

7. What is the economic difference between the Grandpa's Intuition method for setting reorder points and a statistical approach?

Problems

1. With the given information, calculate the following (TC = total cost, D = annual demand, C = purchase cost, Q = order quantity, PO = purchase order cost, H = holding cost percentage):

   a. EOQ

   $C = \$27.00$

   $H = 33.3$

   $D = 500$

   $PO = \$7.00$

   $EOQ = \sqrt{(2D \times PO)/(C \times H)}$

b. EOQ

$C = \$41.00$

$H = 25$

$D = 1,390$

$PO = \$11.00$

c. The reorder point

Average demand = 6

Average lead time = 4 days

Safety stock = 2 days' supply

d. The reorder point

Average demand = 42

Average lead time = 3 days

Safety stock is set at 95% confidence with a standard deviation of 2

e. The total annual cost of inventory

$TC = DC + (D/Q)PO + (Q/2)C \times H$

$D = 4,000$

$C = \$30$

$Q = 40$

$PO = \$9$

$H = 0.30$

2. Change the Q to 400 and recalculate.

3. What would be the best Q if price breaks are offered in the above case as follows?

500+	$22.00
499–100	$27.00
Under 100	$30.00

4. Will it make a difference in the Q if the price breaks shift as follows?

1,000+	$22.00
999–500	$27.00
499–100	$29.00
Under 100	$31.00

5. In the Children's Hospital of Milledge County, the new manager would like to set some inventory levels, so she collects information from the computerized inventory system. Evaluate the inventory information given in the following table to make some policy decisions.

a. Classify the items with a 70-20-10 stratification: 70% for As, the next 20% for Bs, and the last 10% for Cs.
b. Calculate the reorder points. Estimate lead time for all items as 5 days, and build in a 3-day safety stock.
c. For C items, calculate the EOQ. For A items, calculate Q as equivalent to a 3-week demand. With B items, calculate Q as equivalent to a 6-week demand.

Item	Demand	Cost	Reorder Points	Order Quantity	Class
101	47	3.11			
102	58	6.98			
103	21	12.61			
104	90	38.00			
105	130	37.00			
106	21	1.98			
107	170	21.00			
108	250	15.99			
109	37	7.90			
110	560	11.75			
111	307	11.90			
112	2	17.00			
113	59	50.00			
114	78	29.99			
115	130	65.00			
116	65	6.98			
117	49	3.50			
118	708	3.80			
119	39	45.00			
120	60	56.00			
121	123	57.00			
122	17	19.00			
123	8	34.00			
124	80	3.00			
125	450	4.00			
126	54	4.00			
127	571	3.78			
128	54	45.00			
129	32	27.00			

Item	Demand	Cost	Reorder Points	Order Quantity	Class
130	76	45.10			
131	120	42.00			
132	89	32.00			
133	32	11.00			
134	55	9.00			
135	71	9.01			
136	56	8.76			
137	988	12.00			
138	765	54.55			
139	12	127.00			
140	45	1.00			
141	77	2.98			
142	79	34.00			
143	90	125.00			
144	12	18.00			
145	15	3.90			
146	1000	4.78			
147	90	19.10			
148	710	4.00			
149	14	14.00			
150	88	52.00			

Projects

1. Visit a local flea market. Keep a record of the savings you make through negotiations. Try to find a friend who will negotiate over similar items, and see who performs best.

2. Consult with a local company's purchasing agent and learn how they handle negotiations, sourcing, and inventory management.

Web Sites

Institute for Supply Management: www.ism.ws

Karrass negotiation seminars: www.karrass.com

References

Chase, R. B., Jacobs, F. R., & Aquilano, N. J. (2007). *Operations management for competitive advantage.* Boston: McGraw-Hill.

Cohen, H. (2004). *You can negotiate anything.* New York: Jaico.

Mills, H. (2005). *The streetsmart negotiator.* New York: AMACOM.

Shah, R., & Ward, P. T. (2007, June). Defining and developing measures of lean production. *Journal of Operations Management, 2*(4), 785–805.

CHAPTER 14

Resource Planning

SOURCE: © Paul Mckeown/istockphoto.com

Learning Objectives

In this chapter, we will

- Study dependent demand inventory systems, known as materials resource planning (MRP)
- Consider how capacity planning affects MRP
- Study the MRP files: Master Production Schedule, Bill of Materials, and the Inventory Master File
- Review how MRP interfaces with enterprise resource planning (ERP)

Dependent Demand

In this concluding chapter on inventory topics, we will examine a form of inventory management for dependent-demand items called **materials resource planning** (MRP), also referred to as "materials requirements planning." When inventory is controlled independently at a hospital or a retail store, the inventory is managed item by item. The inventory manager orders Band-Aids based solely on the reorder point and demand levels for that one product. In independent-demand situations, we are concerned with the average demand and lead times for that specific product.

However, assembled products have a demand relationship. For instance, if you examine the overhead projector in the classroom, you will find that it consists of a projector bulb, a glass top, some steel parts, nuts and bolts, and an electrical cord and power unit. If there are 16 screws in the projector and someone orders three projectors, that signals to the inventory manager that 48 screws will be required.

A computer is an assembled product. It has a screen, a screen casing, a hard drive, a CPU, circuit boards containing hundreds of parts, a power unit, assorted wires, a keyboard consisting of a bunch of keys, a mouse, perhaps an external drive, and other accessories. If someone orders a computer through Apple, it will trigger the need for the keyboard, of course. And the keyboard has to be assembled, too. Some of the keys are bigger than others. There is one space bar on the computer, one larger shift key, a larger tab key, and a lot of individual keys for all the letters, numbers, and functions.

When there are orders for computers, somewhere down the line, the keys have to be ordered and manufactured. This is a dependent relationship between the computer order and the keyboard order.

MRP is the inventory system designed to handle assembled products. MRP was introduced on mainframe computers, for it is far too complex to handle manually. The second generation of MRP software (MRPII) integrated MRP with the general accounting software of the firm. Today, leading software companies—SAP, Oracle, and PeopleSoft, for example—bundle MRP within **enterprise resource planning** (ERP) systems.

ERP systems include software for project management, human resource management (HRM), MRP, electronic data interchange (EDI), customer relationship management (CRM), and quality control, among many packages. The advantages presented by one all-encompassing package are in the familiarity with the menus and in the compatibility between packages. That being said, ERP is very expensive, and some packages never find practical application for users. However, when fully integrated, it provides users a wealth of information that facilitates inventory decision making. The finance department can verify with the warehouse online about the status of an order instead of making a phone call. Some companies tie in to the HRM module, to quickly alert the company that there is a need for added employees to meet the forecasted demand.

The Components of MRP

MRP consists of several computer programs: the **Master Production Schedule** (MPS), the **Bill of Materials** (BOM), and the **Inventory Master File.** Once the files are completely implemented, all that is necessary to drive the MRP is to schedule production through the MPS.

Master Production Scheduling

The MPS is set by reviewing orders for finished products. If the typical lead time for the product is 4 weeks, the scheduler will only take new orders four periods out or more. The MPS combines the scheduler's knowledge of the forecast with actual orders to determine production. It is customary to have a schedule that is for actual orders in the short term and a schedule for the forecast for the long term.

Item 1010:

Week	1	2	3	4	5	6	7	8	9
Orders	16	21	27	15	11	8	5	2	2
Forecast	24	24	26	26	20	20	16	16	16
MPS	16	21	27	15	20	20	16	16	16

In this schedule, the schedule is for production of actual orders in Periods 1 through 4. Although there is a forecast for 20 units in Week 5, only 11 units have been ordered. When the week rolls over, the scheduler will change production to reflect the actual orders.

If the scheduler were to produce to the forecast, there would be a surplus of 8 units for the end of Week 1. These are reflected as on-hand inventory for the next period and are available for sale. It is probably a good idea to have some finished products for unexpected last-minute orders.

The MPS is usually constructed by balancing the short term with the longer term. The short term may be defined as up to four periods and has to reflect the firm's policy of freezing the schedule so that interruptions to the scheduling system are minimized. So the scheduler could schedule actual orders for production and have a schedule that rolls (the "rolling horizon"), so that when Period 5 becomes Period 4, it shifts from the forecasted production to the actual orders placed.

Capacity Planning

Another consideration in production scheduling is the capacity of the plant. Adjustments have to be made according to this capacity consideration.

Item 1010:

Week	1	2	3	4	5	6	7	8	9
Orders	16	21	27	15	11	8	5	2	2
Forecast	24	24	26	26	20	20	16	16	16
Capacity	20	20	20	20	20	20	20	20	20
MPS	20	20	20	20	20	20	16	16	16
On-hand inventory	4	3	4	1					

Here we have a case in which the forecasted demand exceeds the capacity of the plant. If the scheduler calculates that there are 79 orders in the next 4 weeks, producing 20 per period will smooth the production schedule. In Week 3, there will be 4 expected back orders, which can be replenished in Week 5.

The MPS is considered "frozen" when it is too late to add an order into the mix. This is usually at the minimum period required to assemble a finished product.

Inventory Item File

This file contains the basic inventory information for the part:

- On-hand inventory balance

- *Safety stock:* Safety stock is a minimum stock level that balances should not go below. It is like keeping a minimum balance of $500 in your checking account. Going below that figure means that the bank will charge you. Going below the safety stock puts you in jeopardy of a stockout.

- *Lot size:* When the exact amount to meet the net requirements is met, we say that we are using lot-for-lot (LFL) sizing. The economic order quantity (EOQ) is a typical lot size. If there is a quantity discount available at a certain size, then that quantity may be the lot size. Or the part may come in certain increments. For example, if the reorder point is reached and the net requirements are 125, and the part must be ordered in increments of 100, then 200 must be ordered.

Bill of Materials File

This file details all the components of the finished product. A product structure tree is a diagram of the BOM file.

Orders for finished products interact with the BOM to "explode" the inventory needs of all the components, subcomponents, and parts involved in the product.

A BOM is composed of levels in the product structure tree:

Level 1: Finished product

Level 2: Major components

Level 3: Subcomponents of components

Level 4: Subcomponents of subcomponents

A product structure tree can look like the one shown in Figure 14.1. In this tree, we list the Level 1 Product A and its lead time, 92 weeks. A is composed of subcomponents B, C, and D, and each of the lead times are given. Additionally, D is composed of two Es.

This product structure tree will dictate the product "explosion" when orders are made.

Suppose that we have orders for 200 As in Period 8 and 100 in Period 10. We will work through an MRP sheet to see how the explosion works (Table 14.1).

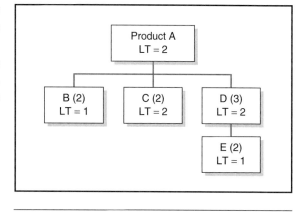

MRP Sheets

MRP sheets are spreadsheets with the following rows:

Figure 14.1   Product Structure Tree

- Gross requirements: from the MPS
- **Scheduled receipts:** any previously scheduled receipt of parts
- On-hand inventory: Gross requirements + Scheduled receipts − Ending inventory from prior period = On-hand inventory
- Net requirements: Gross requirements − On-hand inventory
- Planned receipts: net requirements in that week, affected by lot size
- Planned order release: offsetting the planned receipt by the assembly lead time

Following through the spreadsheet, the planned receipts row of a parent (A), signals the gross requirements of the components (B, C, and D).

Similarly, the planned receipts of Component D result in the gross requirements for Subcomponent E (see Table 14.1).

Adding Inventory Information

If we add information on scheduled receipts, inventory balances, and lot sizes, the planning sheet grows in complexity (see Table 14.2).

B: Scheduled receipt of 100 in Period 2: Starting inventory = 100.

C: Starting inventory = 20. Lot size = 20.

D: Starting inventory = 200.

E. Starting inventory = 400. Lot size = 400 (Table 14.2).

The planned receipt for E is 800 because of the lot size requirement of 400. Because the net requirements are 600, there will be a 200 balance for E at the end of that period.

Table 14.1   MRP Sheet 1

Period	1	2	3	4	5	6	7	8	9	10
A										
Gross requirements								200		100
Scheduled receipts										
Ending inventory										
Net requirements								200		100
Planned receipts								200		100
Planned order releases						200		100		
B										
Gross requirements						400		200		
Scheduled receipts										
Ending inventory										
Net requirements						400		200		
Planned receipts						400		200		
Planned order releases					400		200			
C										
Gross requirements						400		200		
Scheduled receipts										
Ending inventory										
Net requirements						400		200		
Planned receipts						400		200		
Planned order releases						200				
D										
Gross requirements						600		300		
Scheduled receipts										
Ending inventory										
Net requirements						600		300		
Planned receipts						600		300		
Planned order releases						300				
E										
Gross requirements						600				
Scheduled receipts										
Ending inventory										
Net requirements						600				
Planned receipts						600				
Planned order releases			1,200		600					

Table 14.2 MRP Sheet 2

Period	0	1	2	3	4	5	6	7	8	9	10
A											
Gross requirements									200		100
Scheduled receipts											
Ending inventory											
Net requirements									200		100
Planned receipts									200		100
Planned order releases							200		100		
B											
Gross requirements							400		200		
Scheduled receipts			100								
Ending inventory	100		200					0			
Net requirements							200		200		
Planned receipts							200		200		
Planned order releases						200		200			
C											
Gross requirements							400		200		
Scheduled receipts											
Ending inventory	20	20	20	20	20	20	0	0			
Net requirements							380		200		
Planned receipts							380		200		
Planned order releases					380		380				
D											
Gross requirements							600		300		
Scheduled receipts											
Ending inventory	200	200	200	200	200	200					
Net requirements							400		300		
Planned receipts							400		300		
Planned order releases					400		300				
E											
Gross requirements					800		600				
Scheduled receipts											
Ending inventory	400	400	400	400			200				
Net requirements					400		600				
Planned receipts					400		800				
Planned order releases				400		800					

The Integration With ERP

The advantage of connecting MRP into the ERP software modules is that information is available at the manager's fingertips. The old way was for departments to have independent software packages that did not interface. For example, the production manager might see a big spike in demand approaching that will require additional employees, so the manager can go directly into the HRM module to post openings, instead of completing a number of paper forms, sending them via interoffice mail, and awaiting a response that may take days.

MRP in Services

Some manufacturing-oriented writers have suggested various applications for MRP in service organizations such as hospitals and restaurants. That is rather like feeding dog food to a cat. In concept, one could propose that a particular type of surgery would require the same supplies and that surgeries could trigger a supply explosion. Unfortunately, hospitals may have 500 types of surgeries and procedures, and trying to set up an MRP system for them all would result in total futility.

MRP was meant, and is only suited, for assembled products.

Conclusion

ERP is an advanced system of software that incorporates most of the planning modules needed for business. MRP is the inventory module of the ERP system, when using assembled products. ERP systems do not always include MRP, but when they do and the packages are put into place, the inventory modules become the driving force.

The implementation of these systems requires great commitment. Once mastered, these packages provide useful information for planning and opportunities for substantial inventory savings. The success of the programs often depends on the installation, for it is difficult to turn the ship in turbulent waters.

MRP is the coordination of a number of software programs: the MPS, the inventory item file, and the BOM. The logic is that the production schedule causes the explosion of orders throughout the system, based on the BOM and the inventory item information.

Summary

• MRP is used to control inventory for assembled products that have a dependent-demand relationship.

• ERP is a larger system that incorporates a number of software packages, including MRP, Project Management, EDI, Quality Management, and HRM, into an integrated package.

- The inputs to the MRP are the BOM, the inventory item master, and the MPS.

- The MPS is a production schedule that combines the forecast and the actual customer orders into a plan.

- Capacity planning takes the MPS and considers the plant or machine capacity in scheduling.

Key Terms

Bill of materials	Master Production Schedule
Dependent demand	Materials resource planning
Enterprise resource planning	Safety stock
Inventory Master File	Scheduled receipts
Lot size	

Review Questions

1. How is MRP different from the management of independent demand inventories?

2. What is the difference between the terms *planned order receipt* and *planned order release*?

3. How would forecasting errors affect MRP?

4. Why would an MRP planner not produce exactly according to forecast?

5. What does "available to promise" mean?

6. How would MRP apply in a JIT system?

Problems

1. Given the product structure tree (Figure 14.2), complete planning sheets using this inventory information:

   A
   MPS: 6 in Period 5, 10 in Period 6, and 12 in Period 7
   B
   On-hand inventory: 5
   Lot size: 5
   C
   On-hand inventory: 12
   Lot size: 6

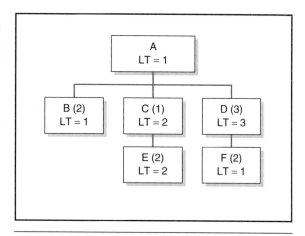

Figure 14.2 Parent Structure Tree (Bill of Materials)

D
   Scheduled receipt in Period 1: 15
   On-hand inventory: 21
E
   On-hand inventory: 0
F
   On-hand inventory: 10

2. Continuing with the same product structure tree, change the MPS of A to 25 units in Period 6 and 41 units in Period 8.

   Change D to a lot size of 9.

3. If the MPS for A calls for 40 in Period 5
   a. What would the gross requirements for B be and in what period?
   b. What would the gross requirements for D be and in what period?

4. If a planned order receipt for B was 50 in Period 6
   a. When would its planned order release be?
   b. What would the gross requirements be for D and when?

5. Given the following forecasts and actual orders, make an MPS:

Period	1	2	3	4	5	6	7	8
Forecast	20	20	18	18	18	27	27	27
Orders	15	19	27	23	11	16	10	6

6. Recalculate the MPS for a capacity of 20.

7. Consider the following indented product structure tree:

A	C (2)	H (1)
	D (1)	
	E (3)	F (2)
B	F (1)	
	G (2)	I (3)
		J (2)

A's components are C, D, and E. C's component is H. E's component is F. B's components are F and G. G consists of J and I.

Inventory on hand

C	40
E	26
G	11
I	18
J	20

Lot sizes

F	24
J	20

MPS

A	40 orders in Period 9, 50 orders in Period 12
B	20 orders in Period 7, 30 orders in Period 10

Devise a planning sheet for the above situation.

CASE   Whirlpool Corporation—Giving ERP a Spin

Helen LaVan

Whirlpool Corporation (NYSE:WHR) is the world's leading manufacturer and marketer of major home appliances. The company has principal manufacturing operations and marketing activities in North and South America, Europe, and Asia. Whirlpool's primary brand names—KitchenAid, Roper, Bauknecht, Ignis, Brastemp, Consul, and its global Whirlpool brand—are marketed in more than 170 countries worldwide. In North America, Whirlpool is the largest supplier of major appliances to Sears, Roebuck & Co. under the Kenmore brand. This accounts for nearly 20% of Whirlpool's sales. With brand names recognized by anyone, Whirlpool is the world's Number 2 producer of major home appliances, after Sweden's Electrolux, and is Number 1 in the United States. The company makes washers, dryers, dishwashers, dehumidifiers, microwave ovens, ranges, refrigerators, freezers, and air conditioners. Products are also marketed under brand names such as Whirlpool, KitchenAid, Roper, Inglis, and Speed Queen. Whirlpool, which manufactures its products in 13 countries and sells them in 170, makes about 25% of its sales in Europe and is concentrating on emerging markets in Asia and Latin America. At the time of this case example, it had 59,000 employees, a decrease of 3.3% over the previous year.

Regional Operations Summary

North America. Whirlpool operations in the United States, Canada, and Mexico together form the North American Region (NAR). The combined operations work with a unified strategy for manufacturing and marketing appliances in the three countries. This strategy focuses on delighting customers and giving them compelling reasons beyond price to choose Whirlpool-built appliances.

Latin America. Whirlpool defines the Latin American region as including Central and South America and the Caribbean. The Latin American Appliance Group (LAAG) of Whirlpool and its affiliates have the largest market share and one third of the manufacturing capacity of the region. The Latin American home appliance market is expected to expand more rapidly than either North America or Europe in the decade ahead.

Asia. Whirlpool has been exporting home appliances to Asia for more than 30 years. From 1993 to 1995, Whirlpool moved aggressively to increase its presence throughout the region by establishing marketing and manufacturing joint ventures. In Asia, Whirlpool focuses on four key products: clothes washers, refrigerators, air conditioners, and microwave ovens.

Europe. With a staff of approximately 11,000 and 11 factories in six countries, Whirlpool Europe ranks as the third largest producer and marketer in Western Europe. It commands the leading position in Central and Eastern Europe and is growing steadily in the Middle East and Africa. A strong focus on the needs of customers in each of Europe's various markets, combined with a coordinated, pan-European approach to many common operations and activities, provides Whirlpool Europe with a strong foundation to build for the future.

Company Vision and Values

The Whirlpool Vision

Every Home . . . Everywhere with Pride, Passion, Performance. We create the world's best home appliances that make life a little easier and more enjoyable for all people. Our goal is a Whirlpool product in every home, everywhere. We will achieve this by creating: Pride . . . in our work and each other; Passion . . . for creating unmatched customer loyalty for our brands and Performance . . . results that excite and reward global investors with superior returns (www.whirlpool.com).

Values

Five fundamental values: Respect, Integrity, Teamwork, Learning to Lead and Spirit of Winning, represent the essence of who we are as a company. They provide a framework of expectations for how we behave and relate with others. The power of these values and the behaviors that support them lies in how they help us achieve a consistently high level of performance, regardless of business or economic cycles (www.whirlpool.com).

ERP at Whirlpool

The following portions of the ERP at Whirlpool are provided for analysis: dispatcher assignment, centralized pricing, vendor interfaces, the Internet application decision, the Internet application problems, response time monitoring, and application integration.

Dispatcher Assignment

Sophisticated geographic routing software is helping Whirlpool Corp. consolidate 22 field service offices into a single hub operation, slashing millions of dollars in real estate costs in the process, but not without creating some thorny personnel issues.

The $200,000 Resources in Motion Management System (RIMMS) from Lightstone Group in Mineola, New York, is expected to help Whirlpool manage and coordinate its 440 appliance technicians across the United States from one service hub in Knoxville, Tennessee.

Whirlpool is replacing the colored pins and giant wall maps that have been used in its regional service centers for years.

Automation will mean that dispatchers may lose the intimate knowledge they had of local routes and traffic trouble spots. But with the manual system, it sometimes took dispatchers a full day to plot a daily service route for a single technician.

Using RIMMS, Whirlpool dispatchers can lay out each technician's route within an hour, but the consolidation has presented Whirlpool with some tricky personnel problems. Under the service overhaul, technicians are asked to cover new territories and squeeze in extra work in the same amount of time.

For example, RIMMS, with its street-level routing capabilities, has shortened technicians' daily mileage by 5% to 10% in preliminary tests, which in turn has reduced wear and tear on Whirlpool's trucks.

Whirlpool's technicians typically handle 10 customer calls per day. The hope is that by using the most efficient routes from one customer call to another, each service technician will be able to squeeze in an extra customer job each day.

A spokeswoman for Whirlpool said that RIMMS isn't expected to lengthen workdays for technicians, who are paid on an hourly basis.

Downsizing is another issue. Whirlpool's service center consolidation also means that it will probably need only 5 or 6 dispatchers, not the 24 it once used to support its field service centers.

Whirlpool's staffing situation is common, according to one geographic decision support consultant. "You're asking fewer dispatchers to do more work using technology, and there's more stress on them that's tricky to deal with," said Larry Daniel, president of Daniel Consulting Group LLC in Wimberley, Texas (Hoffman, 2000).

Centralized Pricing

When Frigidaire Co. drops freezer prices, a flurry of faxes and FedExes fly from Whirlpool Corp.'s offices in a fight to match those prices.

It's a chore for Whirlpool, which has been in this familiar fracas in the appliance business for 85 years with rivals such as Maytag Corp. and General Electric Corp.

But soon Whirlpool will be able to match competitors' pricing with a few key strokes, allowing the company to react quickly to market changes or launch a special promotion for a single product.

The $8.6 billion maker of stoves, dishwashers, and other appliances is implementing a centralized pricing configuration system from Trilogy Development Group, Inc., in Austin, Texas.

Scheduled to go live in July, the pricing software will allow Whirlpool to cut by more than half the 110 days it now takes to reprice its entire product line of more than 2,000 models each quarter.

Most important, the application will give the Benton Harbor, Michigan–based company a centralized pricing structure. Previously, the company used separate pricing models and order entry systems for each Whirlpool division, from small appliances to large goods to spare parts.

"The big driver for all of this is to make Whirlpool easier to do business with," said Bill Hester, a senior information systems project manager at Whirlpool.

According to Nick Heymann, an industry analyst at Prudential Securities, Inc., in New York, the appliance market is fiercely competitive, with Whirlpool leading the pack in front of General Electric in Louisville, Kentucky, and Maytag in North Newton, Iowa.

Combined, the three manufacturers own about 85% of the marketplace. Companies such as Electrolux Corp., the maker of Frigidaire, and Raytheon Co., which makes the Amana brand, take the rest of the market share.

Heymann said that Whirlpool's technology overhaul, which also includes implementing SAP AG's R/3 and a massive operational reorganization, is necessary to prime Whirlpool for the dishwasher wars in the years to come.

It is also necessary as competitors such as General Electric undergo their own operational and information technology overhaul, he added. Heymann estimated that the entire IT overhaul will cut $160 million from Whirlpool's operational budget over 5 years.

Although Whirlpool wouldn't release the exact budget of the project, Hester said that the company expects that the new pricing system will pay for itself within a few years "because the benefits are so great, like better managing our pricing and reducing customer claims."

Historically, Whirlpool's customer claims usually resulted from pricing discrepancies. Customers, ranging from mom-and-pop stores to mega-retailers such as Sears Brand Central, were quoted one price when they ordered a product and received an invoice with a different price when the product arrived. The earlier approach made finding information difficult, said Kathleen Descamps, business project manager for Whirlpool's new pricing system.

With one centralized pricing system, sales agents will be able to meet that goal. The same information will be replicated in sales agents' laptops for quick reference when making field calls to trading partners. "They will have the same sales history information that is used to make [production] forecasts," Descamps said, so they will have the same information to help meet the forecasts.

Bruce Richardson, an analyst at Advanced Manufacturing Research Inc. in Boston, said that Whirlpool is ahead of many manufacturers in aggressively attacking its outdated pricing system. The faster a company such as Whirlpool can react, the more likely it is to win customers in a rapidly changing market.

"People [in manufacturing] are starting to realize that pricing is everything," he said. "You want to do real-time pricing so you can align the street price of a product with the actual amount it costs you to make a product."

Whirlpool's current pricing system is highly dependent on spreadsheets, a laborious and time-consuming system.

Bill Hester, a project manager at the appliance giant, said that the quarterly job of revamping the pricing of every product takes 110 days and is prone to errors. Pricing has to be entered for every product under 11 different brand names.

"It took roughly 180,000 cells in the spreadsheet," Hester said. "Since pricing is formula driven, if someone changed a formula, you wouldn't know the effects somewhere else in the spreadsheet. It took a lot of work to get the pricing masters printed."

Creating the quarterly pricing masters requires calculating new prices, reviewing them, printing them, reviewing them again, and feeding them into the old mainframe system. After that, the new pricing must be mailed, faxed, and sent by overnight delivery to trading partners and regional sales representatives, Hester said.

"There were a lot of places where errors could occur. So in our new environment we have one pricing table for the company, and one person is the pricing administrator."

If a marketing manager needs to change the price of dishwashers to match General Electric's pricing, that person can now enter the information, do a profitability analysis on the change and then, if acceptable, enter the new price. Hester said,

> Then a message is automatically sent to the pricing administrator, who sets up any rules for the pricing, and as soon as they hit "enter," if the pricing is effective today, the next person that places an order gets that new price (Weston, 1998).

Vendor Interfaces

A warehouse automation system has propelled Whirlpool Corporation's Parts Distribution Center in LaPorte, Indiana, into a new era of customer satisfaction. The system, comprising an elaborate configuration of computers and automatic conveyors, reduces the order-processing cycle time for customers around the world. "It helps us better manage our inventories with the ultimate improvement being customer satisfaction," says Tom Harrow, a customer service supervisor.

Although installation was completed several months ago, refinements to the system are continuing to this day. According to Harrow, the technological fine-tuning will eventually lead to an even faster response time to customer orders.

Whirlpool Corp. hopes that a new e-commerce initiative will cut down supply-chain expenses and enhance efficiencies. Next month, the $10 billion appliance maker will launch Easy EDI.

Easy EDI's goal is twofold: to eliminate the paper process used by Whirlpool's 300 smaller suppliers and to save Whirlpool up to $600,000 a year in operational costs for the EDI network used by Whirlpool's 300 largest suppliers, according to David Tibbitts, Manager of Strategy and Planning in Global Procurement at Whirlpool, in Benton Harbor, Michigan.

Initially, Easy EDI will involve four small and midsize suppliers that rely on paper transactions to conduct business with Whirlpool's 14 North American manufacturing facilities. Four to six weeks later, the service will expand to about 30 suppliers; all small and midsize suppliers should be online by year's end.

Whirlpool then expects to gradually roll out Easy EDI to its largest suppliers, which use a public value-added network (VAN) for EDI transactions. The company hopes to phase out VAN-based EDI, Tibbitts says, along with the $40,000 to $50,000 a month it pays for the service. Tibbitts also expects that "the savings through improved efficiencies will be tremendous." He estimates that Whirlpool will get a return on investment from Easy EDI within a year of the pilot's launch.

Whirlpool is waiting to move its largest suppliers on to Easy EDI in the hope that Internet technologies will become more reliable over the next year. Reliability is crucial because many of Whirlpool's suppliers must ship parts to the company's factories within hours of receiving an order.

Easy EDI is an example of how the consumer goods manufacturing industry is moving in the same direction as the automotive industry, according to Susan Cournoyer, an analyst at Dataquest. "Agile, just-in-time manufacturing and its use of the Internet will cut costs and improve communications and responsiveness to customers," she says.

Whirlpool is working with the integrator Litton Enterprise Solutions, a division of the government contractor Litton Industries, to develop Easy EDI. The service uses GenTran Web Suite e-commerce software from Sterling Commerce, which interfaces with GenTran Server, the back-end supply chain transaction software.

Easy EDI is just one of several e-commerce initiatives at Whirlpool. Among other projects, Whirlpool lets retailers order appliances and other products over the Net (McGee, 1998).

Easy EDI at a Glance

Goal: To eliminate paperwork and EDI network expenses related to supply chain transactions by migrating to an Internet-based system

Project rollout: Four small Whirlpool suppliers online in January; 26 more small and midsize suppliers added by March, and 300 online by the end of 1999; 300 largest suppliers online starting in 2000

Systems Integrator: Litton Enterprise Solutions

Key software: Sterling Commerce's GenTran Web Suite and GenTran Server

Savings: Minimum of $40,000 per month (Stedman, 1999)

Internet Application Decision

Late this year, Whirlpool Corp. plans to turn on SAP R/3 and link it to the Internet so that retailers can place and track orders online.

But that doesn't mean the call center workers who take orders over the phone will go away. In fact, their jobs will become more important and more complex, said Senior Project Manager Bob Briggs.

At a conference held by Boston-based AMR Research Inc. last week, Briggs said that Whirlpool plans to use SAP AG's R/3 applications to give call center employees access to all the information they need to answer questions about pricing, promotions, and billing from retailers that sell its appliances.

Whirlpool isn't the only company that's changing but still depending on its call center while moving more routine business transactions to the Web.

Ovum Inc., a U.K.-based consulting firm, released a report last week predicting that call centers will remain central to business strategies because they have "a crucial advantage" over e-commerce Web sites.

But change won't be easy. At Benton Harbor, Michigan, for example, Whirlpool's call center workers will be fielding "bigger and more sophisticated questions" on matters such as credit and pricing promotions, Briggs said.

This will require them to learn both R/3 and a new set of business processes before the combination of SAP's software and Whirlpool's retailer extranet goes into use in the fourth quarter, Briggs added (Collett, 1999).

Internet Application Problems

Whirlpool Corp. made a risky and ultimately damaging business decision by going live with its SAP R/3 implementation over the Labor Day weekend knowing that "red flags" had been raised, according to SAP AG officials.

Fixing the problem would have delayed Whirlpool's go-live date by a week, SAP said. But pressure to take advantage of the long holiday weekend and to get off of its legacy system well before 2000 pushed Whirlpool ahead.

The decision resulted in a botched shipping system that, until it was fixed on November 1, 1999, left appliances sitting in warehouses. Some stores experienced 6- to 8-week delays before receiving their orders.

"We suspected there would be problems, but the customer made a decision to go live" despite warning signals, said Jeff Zimmerman, the senior vice president of customer support services at SAP.

Officials at the Benton Harbor, Michigan, unit wouldn't discuss details of the snafu. "We have had some delays, partially due to the new [SAP] implementation and also due to record levels of orders," said Christopher Wyse, a Whirlpool spokesman.

In a statement, Whirlpool Chairman and CEO David R. Whitwam said that shipping delays, "most of which are already behind us, are due as much to the strength of our North American business . . . as to issues we've already addressed with the new system." He added that the problems shouldn't force the company to miss its fourth-quarter earnings targets.

According to Zimmerman, 90 days before Whirlpool was scheduled to go live on September 7, 1999, SAP assigned a postimplementation consultant to check for any functionality problems that might affect the launch. The testing raised two red flags.

Two batch-processing transactions were taking a long time to feed into the decision support database and into the customer service system.

"We made recommendations on what to fix," which included stripping out some instructions and making the transaction smaller, said Zimmerman. But Whirlpool and its implementation partners, Deloitte Consulting in New York and SAP, decided to hold off on the fix. "A lot of customers go live [with red flags] without any problems," he said.

Things seemed to be running smoothly days after the launch, when 1,000 system users processed appliance orders. But by September 18, 1999, with 4,000 users placing orders, performance started to disintegrate, Zimmerman said.

That's when stores that sell Whirlpool appliances started feeling the pinch. Foremost Appliance in Chantilly, Virginia, which gets one third of its revenue from Whirlpool sales, had shipments from Whirlpool's Carlisle, Pennsylvania, distribution center delayed by 6 to 8 weeks.

"Some people are ordering four or five appliances, and we get one this week, none for them the next week. Then one more the week after. It's been a dilemma," said Bill Brennan, the store manager. Brennan said that he's been steering customers who don't want the long wait to other brands.

Whirlpool's is the latest in a recent spate of ERP implementations in which user companies have grossly underestimated the complexity.

"These implementations are like doing open-heart surgery. There was an expectation on the part of the companies that was completely unreasonable," said Chris Selland, an analyst at The Yankee Group in Boston. Selland said that SAP has recorded more implementation successes than failures and that it's common to find "a hundred little problems and 10 that are major" when going live—not just two like Whirlpool had. "You also have to blame SAP because, for companies like Whirlpool, you have to set the expectations," said Dave Boulanger, an analyst at AMR Research Inc. in Boston. SAP has been under pressure to change its image from that of a company whose software requires multiyear, multimillion-dollar implementations to one that offers shorter, easier projects, Boulanger said. SAP's plan to bring overseers into the project 90 days before going live is relatively new, he said, but users would be better served if SAP were present at the project from the beginning to the end.

Regardless of who's fueling the impression that companies can launch an ERP application quickly, "companies have to realize that the onus is on you and the consulting firm to make it work," Selland said.

Officials at Whirlpool said that the company suffered delays in shipping products in the United States after it installed new ERP software from SAP.

Officials at the Benton Harbor, Michigan, unit—which supplies washing machines, refrigerators, and other products to retailers in more than 100 countries—said in a statement that the company ran into difficulties in meeting some of its orders after the company installed SAP's R/3 business software in the beginning of September 1999.

A Whirlpool representative would not say what problems the company had encountered, but he did say that the R/3 problems have since been addressed. He also declined to say whether Whirlpool intends to take any legal action against SAP.

The United States is the sixth country in which Whirlpool installed the SAP software, and in each country the company had similar problems following installation, said a Whirlpool representative, who asked not to be identified.

Record sales of Whirlpool's product in North America contributed to its inability to meet all its orders, Whirlpool officials said.

Whirlpool isn't the first customer to have run into problems with the German software maker's products. In March, the Australian Wine Society (AWS) said that it suffered delivery delays, billing errors, and other problems after its installation of SAP R/3. One AWS source at the time told the IDGNS sister publication *Computerworld Today Australia* that the software "runs like a dog," and complained that the ERP company had "oversold" its product.

Whirlpool issued its statement in response to a report in *The Wall Street Journal* about its problems with SAP's software.

Observers noted that the ERP software, which is designed to enable companies to run their operations by bringing together financial, manufacturing, and human resources applications, is by its nature complex and difficult to install.

It would be "facile" to blame a company's installation problems entirely on the software vendor. Consultants, integration partners, and even the customer could be equally responsible, says Joshua Greenbaum, a principal analyst with Enterprise Applications Consulting in Berkeley, California.

"The crux of the issue more often than not hinges on how well the implementation team and the customer understand the requirements of the system, and how well they can bring those requirements to bear," Greenbaum says. "You don't have to have a single weak link."

Nevertheless, Greenbaum cautions that software vendors must be careful not to "oversell" their products by exaggerating their capabilities (Niccolai, 1999).

Response Time Monitoring

The premise behind enterprise management frameworks has always been easy to understand: Monitor every resource across the enterprise, and the company can ensure end-to-end delivery of critical IT services. But what happens when the company no longer owns the infrastructure that delivers those services? Do enterprise frameworks still make sense in the world of e-business? How can network managers deal with the reality that service levels now depend not only on their own network infrastructures but also on those of multiple ISPs, business partners, and customers?

Extranet computing is forcing IT managers to look beyond element-level monitoring and focus on the actual response times that end-user business partners and customers experience. "Business success isn't determined by the seek time on a disk or a processor utilization level," says Richard Ptak, the vice president of systems and applications management at the consultancy Hurwitz Group Inc. "It's based on the end-user experience."

This idea of monitoring end-to-end application response times never caught on for internal users but has become critically important now that IT is servicing paying customers. "A company's real customers used to be insulated from IT problems," explains Ptak. "But if something goes haywire now, you get written up on the front page of *The Wall Street Journal*."

There's more at stake than just bad publicity. Network managers simply can't afford to depend on help desk calls to find out about performance outages when those problems affect a paying customer.

"Internally, we have a lot of feedback mechanisms," says Walt Zilahy, the vice president of distributed computing at Travelers Property Casualty Corp., now part of the $49.8 billion Citigroup Inc.

Users are very vocal, and when things start to go south, they're right on top of us. External customers, on the other hand, may just end up going to another vendor. They're not a captive audience, so it's more important to be proactive with them.

These new pressures have IT managers scrambling to find solutions that will let them effectively monitor response times to external users. And they want these response-time-monitoring tools to work with their existing management architectures—which are often based on one of the leading enterprise frameworks.

Take Jim Haney, the director of architecture and planning at the $10.3 billion Whirlpool Corp. and a Tivoli user. His company chose Tivoli Systems Inc.'s management system to support a worldwide SAP R/3 rollout. "Tivoli lets us do everything we need to do to manage our SAP infrastructure—problem management, job scheduling, network management, OS management—across the board," he says.

Like many framework users, Haney uses element-specific tools that plug into his centralized management console. "We use CiscoWorks to manage our routers, but we can see whether they're up or down from the Tivoli console."

Because he is accustomed to using third-party tools in conjunction with Tivoli, Haney has been reviewing new third-party products that promise to track performance issues in outward-facing network services. But he hasn't yet found what he's looking for.

One problem he sees is that many of the vendors selling such tools aim too high. "All I really need them to do is to tell me when the experience for the end user is exceeding an acceptable business threshold," he says.

But a lot of these vendors are trying to sell me something that also goes out and gathers information about each network hop, so that you can see exactly where the problem is. I already have tools that will let me drop down and do that if I get a notification that there's a problem.

Haney also says that few vendors are prepared to deal with his ATM backbone. "They just haven't engineered ATM monitoring into their software yet," he says.

So, for the moment, he is pinning his hopes on Cross-Site, a solution from Tivoli itself. Announced in April 1998, Cross-Site is a suite of tools that lets IT shops manage applications across internal and external networks—what Tivoli calls "collaborative management." The tools include an agent that can reside on a customer's PC and track service levels at that point.

Zilahy is another Tivoli user who sees the potential benefits of using a monitoring solution that comes from his framework vendor. "The assumption is that it will integrate better, and that it will do a better job of capturing alerts and sending them to the central console," he says. "The integration should also help us generate the kind of reports we need, so we don't have to do that work ourselves" (Liebmann, 1998).

Application Integration

Connecting disparate elements together in the enterprise takes planning and time.

Enterprise application integration (EAI), which facilitates business process integration across multiple applications, is becoming a critical factor in today's IT world.

But like most complex IT solutions, a concise implementation strategy must be in place and effectively communicated up and down the executive ladder before embracing the process.

"You have to understand how the systems interconnect and work with each other," said Klaus Schulz, the vice president of Internet strategies and IT at 3Com Corp., Santa Clara, California.

IT departments aiming to make applications work together see the disparate elements that must be drawn together, but the link between business and IT personnel is often missing, Schulz said. "You need to build the teams and have a vision, and you also need the tools."

A team of IT implementers with the necessary tools have to go the extra step to interact with company executives to get the most out of this process, other IT professionals said.

"You have to make integration pay off," said Bob Briggs, the senior vice president and manager of applications engineers for Whirlpool Corp., Benton Harbor, Michigan. "The business bottom line is the reason to make any change, and you have to tie IT and business together."

This point was hammered home recently at the AMR Research Enabling Technologies Strategies conference held in San Francisco.

"Application integration is about getting data from one point to another," said Kimberly Knickle, the senior analyst of enabling technologies strategies for AMR Research, Boston. "But enterprises have to remember that integration is ultimately about sharing information with customers and channel partners," Knickle said.

IT professionals involved with EAI have the responsibility to identify business processes and create a planning and design team to prioritize them, Knickle said. "Sometimes it's hard to get everyone—IT and businesspeople—to buy into this, but you need to identify an overarching goal for a business."

Whirlpool is just one company that made integration pay off. Whirlpool, one of the world's largest manufacturers of household appliances, had a large number of systems doing the same functions.

"We had over 11 different general ledger programs and 6 general databases," said Briggs. "We needed an ERP integration system with interfaces to lower costs," he said.

Whirlpool embarked on an EAI process to integrate applications and processes such as its best-of-breed pricing and promotion system from Trilogy Software Inc., Austin, Texas, with its SAP R/3 ERP platform, Briggs said. "We wanted to keep SAP our center focus, but it had to interface with our legacy systems to be of any value," he said.

The company first had to decide the most effective way to create and maintain these interfaces and decided on the EAI approach over building custom code, Briggs said.

Whirlpool chose CrossWorlds Software Inc., Burlingame, California, to create the SAP-Trilogy interface, and it quickly saw results, with Trilogy pricing information sent back to SAP in less than 5 s, said Briggs. "Before, we had to do this overnight using batch processing."

Clearly, this rethinking has a lot to do with monitoring e-business services across multiple corporate and service provider networks. Whirlpool's Haney says,

As we start to integrate the entire supply chain—from raw material through delivery to the customer—across the Internet, it's going to become increasingly important to be able to monitor what's going on outside the traditional corporate IT infrastructure, where you own everything. That's going to make things very interesting.

And that's why it's time to look beyond the enterprise (Tiazkun, 1999).

Discussion Questions

1. What went wrong with the Whirlpool implementation of ERP?

2. What are the benefits of each software component implemented by Whirlpool?

The SAP R/3 System Overview: Thinking and Acting in Business Processes[1]

Companies' Dynamic Strategies to Meet the Challenges of Today's Fast-Paced Business World

The ability to respond nimbly to new customer needs and seize market opportunities as they arise is crucial. A powerful, open IT infrastructure that will optimally support business activities and permit flexible adjustment to change and progress is the answer: SAP's R/3 System, the world's most used standard business software for client-server computing.

Flexible. R/3 enables the company to respond quickly by making the company more flexible—so that changes can be leveraged to the company's advantage. Everyday business will surge, letting the company concentrate on strategically expanding to address new products and markets.

Comprehensive. SAP's R/3 System is ideal for companies of all sizes and from all industries. It gives them both a forward-looking information management system and the means to optimize their business processes.

At SAP R/3's core are powerful programs for accounting and controlling, production and materials management, quality management and plant maintenance, sales and distribution, HRM, and project management. Information and early warning systems are also available. And the Business Information Warehouse conveniently edits external and internal data to support decision making at all corporate levels.

Open. The SAP R/3 System is an unbeatable combination of functionality and technology. Although designed as an integrated system, SAP R/3's modules can also be used individually. The company can expand it in stages to meet the specific requirements of the company's business. SAP R/3 runs on the hardware platforms of leading international vendors and will mesh smoothly with in-house applications. Open to allow interoperability with third-party solutions and services, it is quick and efficient to install. The SAP R/3 System enjoys full, 24-hr support from SAP's global service network. Companies in more than 90 countries are already benefiting from this system.

Integrated. SAP R/3 overcomes the limitations of traditional hierarchical and function-oriented structures like no other software. Sales and materials planning, production planning, warehouse management, financial accounting, and HRM are all integrated into a work flow of business events and processes across departments and functional areas. Employees receive the right information and documents at the right time on their desktops. SAP R/3 knows no organizational or geographical boundaries. Corporate headquarters, manufacturing plants, sales offices, and subsidiaries all merge for integrated handling of business processes.

Beyond the company. SAP R/3 does more than open up completely new IT solutions within the company. Its applications also link the company's business processes with those of customers and suppliers to create complete logistical chains covering the entire route from supply to delivery. SAP R/3 lets you integrate banks and other business partners into intercompany communications, both nationally and internationally.

Best business practices. SAP R/3 software lets you integrate all the company's business operations in an overall system for planning, controlling, and monitoring. You can choose from 800+ ready-made business processes—and their number continues to grow. They include best business practices that reflect the experiences, suggestions, and requirements of leading companies in a host of industries. SAP R/3 lets you profit directly from this wealth of business and organizational know-how.

New technologies. SAP R/3 continues to evolve in close dialogue with its users. Cutting-edge technologies such as object orientation are incorporated into development work and translated into practical user benefits. Innovative applications are also harnessed to extend the ways in which you can use SAP R/3. Take the Internet, for example. More and more companies are using the Internet not just for marketing and communications but also for procurement, customer service, and order processing. SAP R/3 is directly linked to the Internet and ready for electronic commerce.

SAP R/3: Dynamic Information Management for Enterprises of All Sizes From Diverse Industries

Today, companies compete fiercely for market share and work hard to operate profitably. SAP R/3 is a major strategic tool for achieving these aims. SAP R/3 gives enterprises of all sizes and from all types of industries a flexible software base for their business infrastructure.

Moreover, they profit from the quality and powerful functionality of SAP R/3's applications, which meet the information management needs of both medium-sized and large multinational companies. This flexibility as regards enterprise size is demonstrated by the fact that more than 50% of SAP R/3 installations are in small and medium-size companies.

SAP R/3 solutions are hard at work in some vertically structured industries. Automobile manufacturers use SAP R/3 to build flow factories, in which just-in-time materials and assemblies flow from the supplier into production and then flow as finished products to the customer. Retail companies use SAP R/3 to boost consumer response. The pharmaceutical and chemical industries use SAP R/3 to integrate commercial and technical applications.

Banking and insurance businesses use SAP R/3 to coordinate revenue and risk management and to optimally manage their financial assets. Manufacturing companies use it because SAP R/3 simultaneously supports several types of production. Special enhancements to the SAP R/3 System enable government agencies to make their services more efficient and cost-effective. In wholesale businesses, SAP R/3 speeds up all processes from suppliers to final customers and permits simultaneous optimization of wholesale and consumer prices. Publishers and media take advantage of SAP R/3's flexibility to respond to short-term changes in the markets. Utilities use SAP R/3 to reorganize their business processes and improve the quality of their services. These examples illustrate the versatility that has persuaded companies in more than 90 countries around the globe to adopt SAP R/3.

With its integrated processes for complete handling of enterprise processes, SAP R/3 holds considerable potential for reengineering conventional structures and organizational methods. SAP R/3 enhances performance by redesigning your core business processes to revitalize and optimize them. This overcomes the divisions of labor that restrict productivity. For multienterprise business processes, SAP R/3 covers companies, their vendors, customers, and banks (www.sap.com/solutions/r3/index.htm).

Overview of the Supply Chain: The SAP Advanced Planner and Optimizer (SAP APO)[2]

The SAP APO consists of a number of integrated modules using a constraint-based planning and optimization philosophy.

Collaborative Planning. The goal of SAP APO Collaborative Planning, as the name suggests, is to help enterprises carry out collaborative supply chain planning activities with their business partners.

Supply Chain Cockpit provides users with a bird's-eye view of all activities and applications and models, monitors, and manages the supply chain with a specially designed graphical user interface.

Demand Planning. Demand Planning identifies and analyzes patterns and fluctuations in demand and creates accurate, dynamic demand forecasts. Supply Network Planning matches purchasing, production, and transportation processes to demand and balances and optimizes the entire supply network.

Production Planning and Detailed Scheduling. This optimizes the use of resources and creates accurate plant-by-plant production schedules to shorten production life cycles and respond rapidly to changes in market demand forecasts.

Global Available-to-Promise. This matches supply to demand on a truly worldwide scale and gives the customers reliable delivery commitments by means of both real-time checks and sophisticated simulation methods.

SAP Business Information Warehouse (SAP BW). This is a preconfigured data warehouse ideal for SAP environments and provides access to both internal and external information from multiple sources, as well as providing sophisticated reporting and analysis tools.

The SAP Logistics Execution System (SAP LES). This system offers advanced warehouse management and transportation management functionality. It enables companies to improve customer service and to gain a more coherent view of their logistics operations.

Notes

1.   The source of this document is the Web pages of SAP and is primarily intended for sales purposes. The reader should take this into account when reading this overview
2.   The source of this document is the Web pages of SAP.

Web Sites

www.hoovers.com

www.oracle.com

www.sap.com

www.whirlpool.com

References

Collett, S. (1999, November 8). SAP gets stuck in the spin cycle. *Computerworld, 33*(45), 1, 16.

Hoffman, T. (2000, January 10). IT plan has Whirlpool spinning. *Computerworld, 8*(1).

Liebmann, L. (1997, July 19). Look beyond the enterprise. *InformationWeek, 34*(1).

McGee, M. K. (1998, June 1). Whirlpool jumps on the Net: E-commerce project will cut paperwork, save on EDI costs. *Computerworld, 32*(22).

Niccolai, J. (1999, November 8). Whirlpool lays delays at SAP's door. *Network World.* Retrieved from www.network world.com/news/1999/1104whirlpool.html

Stedman, C. (1999, April 26). Whirlpool plans to spin R/3 for call center. *Computerworld, 33*(17), 10.

Tiazkun, S. (1999, May 10). EAI is fast becoming critical solution for enterprise accounts. *Computer Reseller News*, pp. 1, 6.

Weston, R. (1998, March 23). Appliance firm gives pricing system a whirl. *Computerworld, 32*(12), 1.

CHAPTER 15

Project Management

SOURCE: © Rick Hyman/istockphoto.com

Learning Objectives

In this chapter, we will

- Study how to make a work breakdown structure (WBS)
- Learn about the critical path method
- Study PERT's equation for time estimates
- Discuss earned-value analysis
- Review the critical success factors of projects

E very organization is faced with a number of projects that have to be carried out while the daily work gets done. When a hospital builds a new wing, it can't shut the facility down while the construction is going on. Highway construction continues while the traffic flows. Universities may decide to switch from the semester system to the quarter system or vice versa, and when they plan the change, classes have to continue. A company might change its computerized accounting systems, but it must continue to use one while implementing the other.

At some time in every manager's career, he or she is asked to participate on a project team while he or she continues with the rest of his or her work. Sometimes, multiple projects are carried out simultaneously. Projects can be very time-consuming, expensive, and stressful.

Projects are being implemented everywhere you look. Outside, you can see construction projects: houses, buildings, shopping centers, retail establishments. At your workplace, there are probably a number of projects that are ongoing: a new product introduction, a marketing promotion, a special banquet or event, a software introduction, and so on.

Projects take careful planning. A successful project is one that is done on time and within budget. Often, that is not the case. In this concluding chapter, we will study methods of project scheduling that are in use today.

Gantt Charts

For many years, the major method of project scheduling was the **Gantt chart**, which was devised by Henry Gantt in the 1920s. The Gantt chart is a graphical chart that shows the tasks of a project in relation to the dates that they are to be accomplished. A simple illustration is to plan for a Thanksgiving Day (T-day) dinner.

Task	11/1		11/8	11/15	11/22 (T-day)
Invite guests		--------------]			
Confirm guests				--------------]	
Purchase turkey			--------------------------]		
Purchase groceries				--------------]	
Clean house				--------------]	

On Thanksgiving Day, the cooking project is undertaken.

Task	8		9	10	11	12	1	2	3	4
Prepare turkey		----]								
Cook turkey				--------------------]						
Cook veggies				------]						

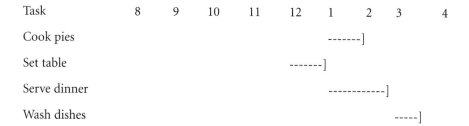

Task	8	9	10	11	12	1	2	3	4
Cook pies						-------]			
Set table					-------]				
Serve dinner						-----------]			
Wash dishes							-----]		

The line shows when the task is being performed, and the bracket indicates the end of the task. Some of the tasks overlap, as work is going on simultaneously. Intuitively, the planning for a large dinner is done, usually with a handwritten list. A Gantt chart is one step further in project planning than a simple list of tasks, because it gives a visual depiction of when things are done.

Project Planning

When a project is undertaken, all these questions must be clearly addressed:

- What is the goal of the project?
- What is the scope of the project?
- What are the tasks involved?
- What is the goal completion time?
- How long will each task take?
- Who is responsible for each task?
- What is the reporting relationship for the project?
- How is the project progress communicated to the top management?
- What is the method of interproject communication?
- What is the budget for the project?
- How is the budget allocated during the project?
- What constitutes project success?

The standard definition of a successful project is that it is finished on time, within budget, and with a high degree of quality.

The need for precision in project planning of the Olympic Games can be illustrated with the case of the two American sprinters in 1972, who were not told about a change in the time of their heats. As a result, they missed the Games. What are their names? We don't know, and that is the point. They missed their opportunity for fame, probably after training for many years, due to poor communication within the project system.

The Work Breakdown Structure

A starting point for planning is to create a **work breakdown structure** (WBS), a diagram of the project that resembles an organizational chart. Instead of the CEO at the top of the chart, we have the program. At this point, the team brainstorms to try to think of every task they will encounter in the project. After they set out the

SOURCE: © Mike Clarke/istockphoto.com

tasks, and the expected task times, they allocate responsibility to certain individuals. There are six levels to the structure:

Level 1: The program—the global project

Level 2: The project—the major project

Level 3: The task—a task inside the project

Level 4: The subtask—a secondary task

Level 5: The work package—where the work is performed

Level 6: The activity—a segment of the work package

Horine (2005) had a list of guidelines for developing a WBS.

All the work of the project is included in the WBS.

- The WBS should be "deliverable focused."

- The WBS should be developed "with the team."

- The WBS is refined as the project progresses.

- The WBS is a top-down decomposition and is logical—the summary tasks go with lower level tasks.

- The WBS should be organized in a manner that emphasizes the most important aspects of the project and that best communicates the entire scope of the project to your stakeholders.

- The lowest level of the WBS, the work package or activity level, is used for schedule and cost development. This is the level where effort and cost can be reliably estimated.

- Unique identifiers are assigned to each item in the WBS to allow for better management reporting of costs and resources.

- WBS elements should be consistent with organizational and accounting structures.

- The coding scheme should clearly represent a hierarchical structure.

- Review and refine the WBS until all key project stakeholders are satisfied.

- Each WBS element represents a single deliverable and should be an aggregation of lower level WBS elements.

- Each WBS element has only one parent.

- Upper levels of the WBS represent major deliverables or project phases.

- The WBS should include project management tasks and activities. (p. 74)

The following are the six levels for the Chicago Marathon:

Level 1: The program—annual Chicago Marathon

Level 2: The project—the 2008 Marathon

Level 3: The task—registration

Level 4: The subtask—online registration

Level 5: The work package—registration confirmation

Level 6: The activity—mailing confirmations

A marathon that is held annually usually begins its preparation as soon as the results are printed and a review is made of any glitches that happened in the most recent marathon.

Several marathons have more than 20,000 runners: Chicago, New York City, Honolulu, Los Angeles, and Boston, and the coordination necessary to move that many people safely for 26 miles and 385 yards requires a lot of police. In 2004, at the Summer Olympic Games, an insane spectator ran onto the course and knocked down the lead runner in the race. The marathoner, from Brazil, pulled himself away and managed to finish third, but this moron undeniably altered the final result. No amount of security can prevent such an odd occurrence, but that is one of the issues of good project planning—to anticipate the unanticipated.

In 2007, the Chicago marathon was held on a day of intense heat, and when the number of runners in heat distress became unmanageable, the event was cancelled 3 hr into the event.

Marathon organizers want a seamless event. That means there is no cheating, and security is enforced along the course.

A line-indented WBS is simply an outline form rather than the org chart form.

Chicago Marathon

1. Registration

    1.1. Online begins January 1

    1.2. Reminder messages

    1.3. Mail-in registration begins February 1

    1.4. Close at 40,000 entrants

    1.5. Registration processing

        1.5a. Seeding processing

        1.5b. Team processing

2. Elite runners

    2.1. Elite recruiting

    2.2. Elite announcements

    2.3. Elite housing

    2.4. Elite transportation

    2.5. Elite logistics to race

    2.6. Elite staging area at start

3. Security

    3.1. Route security

    3.2. Starting line security

4. Media

    4.1. Press passes issuance

    4.2. Press releases

    4.3. Press conferences

    4.4. Results coordination

5. Starting line

    5.1. Seeding corrals

    5.2. Corral volunteers

    5.3. Supplies

5.4. Timing

5.5. Chip mats

5.6. Clean-up

6. Volunteers

6.1. Registration processing

6.2. Expo

6.3. Start line

6.4. Course

6.5. Water, gels, and Vaseline

6.6. Finish line

7. Expo

7.1. Registration area

7.2. Vendor area

7.3. Receiving area

7.4. Hotel shuttles

8. Finish line

8.1. Timing

8.2. Security

8.3. Medal volunteers

8.4. Chip removal

8.5. Refreshments and blankets

8.6. First aid

9. Web page

9.1. Updating

9.2. Results posting

10. Publications

10.1. Race program

10.2. Newspaper results

10.3. Results postcards

10.4. Finisher certificates

10.5. Results book

The vast amount of planning that goes into this singular event makes one wonder why anyone would want to organize the event in the first place. Race organizers cannot control everything. A very hot day can mean a big increase in visits to the medical tent, so the experienced race director will watch the weather forecasts and try to increase ambulance support if the weather looks forbiddingly hot. Bad weather one year often means a drop-off in entrants in the following year. By comparing race entrants at similar periods from one year to another, the race director gets some idea of how much advertising of the race they may need to do.

The WBS aspect of project planning serves the purpose of forcing the project manager to consider all tasks. The WBS does not arrange tasks in their sequential order. It does help catalogue everything that has to be done.

Every quarter or semester, a student is faced with numerous projects. A student taking four courses learns in the first week of class all the assignments and test dates. At that time, time is allocated for all the test preparations and projects to be accomplished.

Operations Management:

Midterm examination	Monday, October 15
Paper assignment	Monday, October 29
Final examination	Monday, November 12

Marketing:

Midterm examination	Tuesday, October 16
Project assignment	Tuesday, November 6
Final examination	Tuesday, November 13

Negotiations:

Midterm examination	Tuesday, October 23
Project assignment	Tuesday, November 13

Finance:

Exam 1	Wednesday, October 10
Exam 2	Wednesday, October 24
Exam 3	Wednesday, November 14

October:

Sunday	Monday	Tuesday	Wednesday	Thursday	Friday	Saturday
	1	2	3	4	5	6
7	8	9	10 Fin. #1	11	12	13
14	15 Ops. #1	16 Mkt. #1	17	18	19	20
21	22	23 Negot. #1	24 Fin. #2	25	26	27
28	29 Ops. paper	30	31			

November:

Sunday	Monday	Tuesday	Wednesday	Thursday	Friday	Saturday
				1	2	3
4	5	6 Mkt. project	7	8	9	10
11	12 Ops. final	13 Mkt. final, Negot. project	14 Fin. final	15	16	17
18	19	20	21	22	23	24
25	26	27	28	29	30	

A calendar gives the student a visual sense of when things have to be done. Breaking them down into calendar order, things happen this way:

October 10	Finance exam
October 15	Operations exam
October 16	Marketing exam
October 23	Negotiations exam
October 24	Finance exam #2
October 29	Operations paper
November 6	Marketing project
November 12	Operations final
November 13	Marketing final, Negotiations project
November 14	Finance final

Perhaps the student allows 20 hr each week for study and working on projects. Smart students are not going to wait until the day before the finance test to crack the book. They have been allocating their time each week, with more time spent toward the finance class in the beginning because its test comes first. As soon as the dust clears from the first finance test, the emphasis switches to the other two courses, and after operations and marketing tests are over, the emphasis switches to negotiations and finance.

A WBS for the quarter is as follows:

Fall term

1. Finance

    1.1. Exam #1

    1.2. Exam #2

    1.3. Exam #3

2. Operations

    2.1. Exam #1

    2.2. Paper

        2.2a. Research

        2.2b. Write

    2.3. Exam #2

3. Marketing research

    3.1. Exam #1

    3.2. Project

    3.3. Exam #2

4. Negotiations

    4.1. Exam #1

    4.2. Project

        4.2a. Research

        4.2b. Write

        4.2c. Present

In a real sense, every term is a project for a student. It requires a lot of planning and work allocation to get everything done on time, prepare for examinations, and complete projects. If students used project management techniques, it might help them stay organized. The nice thing about projects is that they end. The exams are done, the grades are placed, and you move on to the next one. Semester after semester, quarter after quarter, the students plod on through graduation. Meanwhile, your friendly professor has projects of his or her own. Is it any wonder that students get sick during examinations?

The project process of penetrating a college term is analogous to projects in the workplace. College students have personal lives and jobs they have to juggle in the remaining hours. They go to sporting events, parties, social events, and informational events, while getting an education. To study 20+ hr a week and do all the things college students must do is a formidable task. That being said, life does not get any better for the college student. Whether an undergraduate or a graduate student, these are some of the greatest years. You may as well make the most of them by planning your activities!

The Critical Path Method

The basic aim of any project should be to attain the project's goals on time and within the budget. A project's planning phase begins once it has been studied as financially viable for the organization and one that meets the company's goals. Since the schedule must then be mapped out to match budget and time, a scheduling method that incorporates both variables must be used. Clearly, the Gantt chart is inadequate to map a complex project. For this reason, a network diagramming technique gained acceptance. The critical path method (CPM) is a method that identifies the "**critical path**" of a project and attempts to reduce the project length by attacking the critical path. We put resources into reducing the critical path, the "bottleneck" for projects.

The method begins with the identification of all the tasks involved in the project and an estimate of how long they will take to complete. This is taken directly from the WBS. Then, we need to know in what order things have to be done. The precedence relationship is depicted as a network flow diagram (Figure 15.1).

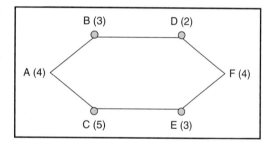

Figure 15.1   Precedence Relationship

Task	Task Time (Days)	Precedence
A	4	—
B	3	A
C	5	A
D	2	B
E	3	C
F	4	D

The method of drawing the network precedence diagram is called *Activity on Nodes (AON)*. Some books depict the project with Activity on Arrows or Activity on Arcs (AOA). However, the AON method is the most frequently used, so we will stick with that method. This project has two identifiable paths through the network, ABDF and ACEF.

The first step in identifying the critical path is to calculate the early and late times for each task. This is done as follows:

1. The initial task(s) starts at Time 0.

2. The initial task(s) finish time is found by adding the task time to 0. A's early finish time is 4.

3. The early start times for a task are equal to the early finish time of the preceding task.

4. The early finish times are the early start times + task times.

A (4)	B (3)	C (5)	D (2)	E (3)	F (4)
ES = 0	ES = 4	ES = 4	ES = 7	ES = 9	ES = 12
EF = 4	EF = 7	EF = 9	EF = 9	EF = 12	EF = 16

NOTE: ES = early start; EF = early finish.

When multiple tasks precede a task, as illustrated by D and E preceding F, the start time of the following task is determined by the latest time of the preceding tasks. Since D finishes at Day 9 and E finishes at Day 12, F cannot begin until Day 12. Imagine that the task is a car waiting for two passengers. You cannot drive until they both get in the car.

Also, note that when the early finish time of a task is 9, the early start time for the succeeding task also should be 9. Some people make the mistake of assuming lag time and start the next task at Day 10. Project planning assumes no lag between tasks.

The late starting and finish times are found by tracing backward from the end node (F). The end node has the same late and early times because it is the conclusion of all the preceding tasks.

Again, if you are working through a project manually, you must be careful when multiple tasks precede a task. B has a late start of Day 7. C has a late start of Day 4. Thus, A must have a late finish of the earlier of the two following tasks and that is at Day 4.

A (4)	B (3)	C (5)	D (2)	E (3)	F (4)
LS = 0	LS = 7	LS = 4	LS = 10	LS = 9	LS = 12
LF = 4	LF = 10	LF = 9	LF = 12	LF = 12	LF = 16

NOTE: LS = late start; LF = late finish.

When there is a difference between the early and late times in the project, it is identified as *slack time*. This indicates that the task is not on the critical path. The critical path is the one that takes the longest to complete and has the least slack of all the paths.

In path ABDF, we see slack at Tasks B and D. There is no slack in ACEF. Therefore, our critical path is ACEF. This path takes 16 days to complete. By adding the task times of ACEF, we find a project path of 16 days. The total task time in ABDF is 13 days.

The value in knowing the critical path is that if we are to reduce the total project time, *it must be* from the critical path. Putting resources into reducing B from 3 days to 2 would result in a net project reduction of 0 days, since the critical path will still take 16 days. If we want to reduce the path from 16, it has to be by attacking the critical path.

Crashing the Critical Path

After estimating the task times, drawing a precedence diagram, and determining the critical path, the manager must look over the project to see where reductions in the project can be made. The method for reducing the project length is called *crashing*. Here are the rules for crashing:

1. Only *crash* from the critical path.

2. Crash tasks that are the least costly to crash first.

3. When there are critical paths of equal length, crash all paths in the same increments.

4. Do not crash if there is no net reduction in the project length.

5. Changes in the critical path can cause new critical paths, so monitor all the paths for changes.

Crashing requires knowledge of the cost and time to get things done faster. Let's look at one project with 10 tasks:

Task	Precedence	Normal Time (Days)	Crash Time (Days)	Cost/Day (Dollars)
A	—	4	3	125
B	—	7	5	105
C	A, B	9	6	180
D	C	4	3	65
E	C	6	4	100
F	D	9	7	110
G	E	12	8	80
H	G	8	8	—
I	G	7	5	120
J	H, I	10	7	150

There are six distinct paths in the project. The first step is to identify these paths and check the length of each one:

Paths	Days	Paths	Days
ACDFJ	36	BCDFJ	39
ACEGHJ	49	BCEGHJ	52
ACEGIJ	49	BCEGIJ	52

In this case, we have two critical paths: BCEGHJ and BCEGIJ. In crashing, a project manager will have two objectives, either to reduce time by a number of days or to reduce time given a certain budget.

If the project manager were told that the project must be finished in 45 days, we would proceed in the following manner:

1. Although the cheapest task to crash is D ($65), it is not on the critical path. The lowest cost task on the critical path is G ($80). We cut the task by 4 days at a total cost of $320.

2. The next task to cut on the critical path is E ($100). We cut the task by 2 days at a total cost of $200.

3. Finally, B is cut by only 1 day to get to 45 days. This adds $105. Our total cost is $625 to get the project from 52 days to 45 days.

Perhaps the project manager is given $1,000 and told to cut the project until out of money. We would continue as follows:

1. B is cut by another day. We have now spent $730 and the project stands at 44 days.

2. Reducing J by 1 day adds $150, making the budget at $880 and the project at 43 days. Another day reduced at J would take us over budget to $1,030.

Let's take another project:

Task	Precedence	Normal Time (Days)	Crash Time (Days)	Cost/Day (Dollars)
A	—	16	12	400
B	A	11	7	350
C	B	14	10	600
D	B	9	7	250
E	D	12	8	550
F	D	10	10	—
G	E, F	30	21	100

Task	Precedence	Normal Time (Days)	Crash Time (Days)	Cost/Day (Dollars)
H	G	19	14	300
I	G	11	9	500
J	H, I	7	4	150
K	C	40	30	125
L	K	9	8	75
M	J, L	14	7	700

The five identifiable paths are as follows:

Paths	Days	Paths	Days
ABCKLM	104	ABDFGHJM	116
ABDEGHJM	118	ABDFGIJM	108
ABDEGIJM	110		

The critical path is ABDEGHJM. If we were to cut the project by 27 days, we would approach it something like this:

	Days	Dollars
1. G	9	900
2. J	3	450
3. D	2	500

At this point, we have reduced path ABDEGHJM to 104 days, equaling the path of ABCKLM. Now, we have to address both paths equally.

Since our objective is to get the project from 118 to 91 days, we need 13 more days from both paths. Reducing both A and B by 4 days each reduces the project by 8 days, since these tasks are common to both paths. A cut of H by 5 days, L by 1 day, and K by 4 days will complete the process.

The purpose of the CPM is to determine how to allocate resources so that the project can be accomplished in the minimal amount of time.

Program Evaluation and Review Technique

Program evaluation and review technique (PERT) is a method of project scheduling that calculates estimates for each task time. PERT asks for three time estimates: an optimistic estimate, a pessimistic estimate, and the most likely estimate. These three estimates are plugged into a formula:

$$\text{Time} = \frac{a + 4m + b}{6}$$

where a is the optimistic time, b the pessimistic time, and m the most likely time.

This formula was derived from a statistician on the original PERT team who believed that project tasks followed the statistical beta distribution. Subsequent studies have found that not to be true. However, the formula still exists.

If our project manager looked at a task and plugged in these values: $a = 4$, $b = 10$, and $m = 7$, then we would get a time estimate of 7.

If the project manager plugged in these values for the same task: $a = 3$, $b = 12$, and $m = 7$, then we would have an estimate of 7.17.

If the manager were not using PERT, he or she would use the most likely time for the value (7). The argument in favor of using PERT is that the process of making three time estimates forces the manager to consider all possible events for each task, and it gives one a realistic assessment of the time for each project. The argument against using PERT is that it is simply an educated guess in the first place and a waste of time. Whatever the rationale for using PERT, it is frequently included in popular software packages, using the same beta distribution formula.

However, the basic premise of PERT is to carefully study the expected time. The scheduler must anticipate that some things may go wrong, that weather might interfere, or some other interruption might delay the project. Realistic time estimates are important in planning any project.

Earned-Value Analysis

One method of measuring project progress is **earned-value analysis** (EVA). In EVA, three variables measure deviations from progress (Lewis, 1995):

BCWS (budgeted cost of work scheduled)—the starting point for the cost of the project.

BCWP (budgeted cost of work performed)—also called earned value. It looks at the budget for the tasks already accomplished.

ACWP (actual cost of work performed)—gives the value for the tasks completed.

Cost variance = BCWP – ACWP. This measure shows how far away from budgeted cost the project may be.

Schedule variance = BCWP – BCWS. This measure shows how much behind schedule the project may be.

Example:
Take the following project. Tasks A through G have been completed.

Task	Precision	Normal Time (Days)	Actual (Days)	Budgeted Cost (BC)	Actual Cost (AC)
A	—	16	14	12,000	12,800
B	A	11	13	6,000	7,800
C	B	14	10	9,000	11,400
D	B	9	9	15,000	17,500
E	D	12	8	17,000	23,000
F	D	10	10	11,000	12,000
G	E, F	30	37	9,000	14,000
H	G	19	13,000		
I	G	11	21,000		
J	H, I	7	12,000		
K	C	40	19,000		
L	K	9	9,000		
M	J, L	14	10,000		

The five identifiable paths are as follows:

ABCKLM   ABDEGHJM, ABDEGIJM   ABDFGHJM   ABDFGIJM

The critical path through the rest of the project is ABDFGHJM. Since G is completed, we have completed at least 83 days of the project.
    Table 15.1 shows the budgeted versus actual costs of the completed tasks.

Table 15.1   Budgeted Versus Actual Costs of the Completed Tasks

Task	Budgeted	Actual
A	12,000	12,800
B	6,000	7,800
C	9,000	11,400
D	15,000	17,500
E	17,000	23,000
F	11,000	12,000
G	9,000	14,000
Total	79,000	98,500

The project at present is as follows:

$$\text{Cost variance} = \text{BCWP} - \text{ACWP} = 79{,}000 - 98{,}500 = -19{,}500$$

$$\text{Schedule variance} = \text{BCWP} - \text{BCWS} = 98{,}500 - 163{,}000 = -64{,}500$$

This measure shows the dollars remaining. We still have $64,500. Unfortunately, our $19,500 overspending will cause the budget to rise to $182,500 if we spend the expected amounts for the remaining tasks.

Project Success Factors

A project manager armed with a project schedule using the CPM has a good tool, but it certainly does not guarantee that the project will get done on time. Slevin and Pinto (1987) studied a number of projects and listed the most important factors in achieving project success:

1. *Mission:* Each project team should have a clear understanding of what their project is supposed to do and where it fits in with the organization's overall mission. If the project team is given no sense of an overall mission, they can tend to be nonchalant about how the project comes off. The more specific the mission, the better it is. "We are building the tallest living space in the world" gives more direction than "We are building a skyscraper." The team needs to know the importance and function of the project they are working on.

2. *Top management support:* Projects that spin employees away from their daily tasks should have some acknowledgment from the executive offices that they are aware of their special project, they know it is getting done, and they support the efforts. If a project team feels that no one cares about what they are doing or even knows what they are up to, their chances of success are limited.

3. *The skills of the project team:* The composition of the team is important. Specific skills may be required, and the absence of individuals equipped with those talents can limit the team. Perhaps the team requires a spreadsheet expert, an industrial engineer, or someone who knows something about animation. The absence of individuals with the required skills can kill a project.

4. *A schedule:* No matter how the project is scheduled, via Gantt charts, CPM, or Microsoft Outlook, a project team needs a visual schedule with milestones so that they can stay on top of the schedule.

5. *Troubleshooting:* The ability to get a project back on track when it runs into an impasse or delay is critical. Perhaps, it means bringing in a consultant who can find out the problems, fix them, and move them back in the right direction.

6. *Client approval:* Clients involved in the process should be consulted and their approval of the schedule obtained, if it involves them.

7. *Monitoring, feedback, and communication:* Project managers have to keep abreast of progress and let people know the current status. It is important that there be communication among project team members and externally from the project to top management and concerned clients.

A study of software projects (Gray & Larson, 2000) found the following factors important:

1. *User involvement:* In software, the ultimate client is the potential user, who therefore must give a realistic assessment of his or her wants and needs.

2. *Top management supports:* It is this communication that helps the project team have a feeling of the importance of the project's success (also mentioned in the above list).

3. *Clear statement of requirements:* Vague or fuzzy requirements often result in vague and fuzzy projects. The team needs to know exactly what it wants to accomplish.

4. *Proper planning:* A project must begin with a planning stage where all the steps are laid out. Think of a poorly planned vacation. You forget to bring things, and you may have trouble catching planes and with other transportation and lodging.

5. *Realistic expectations:* It helps to have previous experience with similar projects to be able to estimate project duration. Many projects are considered failures when they don't deliver on time, although they delivered in the fastest time possible.

6. *Smaller project milestones:* Milestones along the project path are important signs of project progress. Missing the milestones may cause a reevaluation of the project's chances of success.

7. *Competent staff:* A solid team with all the skills and tools necessary to complete the tasks is an absolute necessity.

8. *Project team ownership:* The project team needs to feel empowered to deliver the project and should feel secure about the fact that outside interests aren't going to come in and claim credit for its work.

9. *Clear vision and objectives:* Similar to having clear expectations, it is important to have a thorough understanding of the project's intent.

10. *Hardworking, focused staff:* Once the project is in motion, a project manager can ill afford to be loaded with lazy and irresponsible individuals. Projects require time and labor.

Student teams formed in business school give a taste of what real-world projects are like. Students are often matched with classmates who they hardly know and are given a task. They may have great chemistry and the project is completed with nary a hitch. Or the students discover that they don't like each other at all and totally disagree with each other every step of the way. Either way, it is an introduction to what can happen in actual business projects.

Project Management Software

Most projects of any complexity will take advantage of one of the many project management software packages. Features that should be offered in the package include the following:

- The ability to automatically create a Gantt chart and network flow diagram by completing the WBS
- The ability to draw the network flow diagram using the AON method
- The ability to easily copy the previous tasks into current projects

The best-selling software package is Microsoft's MS Project. Primavera is probably the leader of the upper end of software packages. There are many others, such as CA Superproject, Harvard Total Project Manager, and Timeline, to list a few.

Conclusion

Projects are temporary assignments that have a beginning and an end point. To complete them successfully, a manager needs a schedule and then a plan to accomplish the tasks in the project. Project management is often assisted by software tools, which can visually track the project with Gantt charts, work breakdown structures, and critical paths.

The emphasis in project management is advance planning. Projects often take unlikely twists and turns, and obstacles confront the project manager. Planning to overcome the unexpected helps the project manager accomplish tasks.

Summary

- A project is a temporary assignment given to an organization that contributes to the overall mission of the firm.

- A Gantt chart is a visual illustration of tasks, dates, and milestones. It shows the planner where the team is and where they should be.

- The work breakdown structure is the organizational chart of a project, breaking it down into program, project, task, subtask, work package, and activity.

- The CPM is an approach to projects that uses a network flow diagram to detect the critical path in the project and effectively determines ways to get the project accomplished in a cost-effective manner.

- PERT is a formula, which incorporates three time estimates: most likely time, optimistic time, and pessimistic time.

- EVA looks at the budgeted costs of a project and compares them with the actual costs.

- There are a number of critical project success factors, any one of which can cause a project to fail if it is missing. However, an understanding and communication of mission is the foremost critical success factor.

Key Terms

Critical path

Earned-value analysis

Gantt chart

Program evaluation and review technique (PERT)

Work breakdown structure

Review Questions

1. Describe the major steps in the CPM.

2. When would you crash tasks that are not on the critical path?

3. What are the major success factors in projects?

4. How does earned value analysis help a project manager control the project?

Problems

1. Take the following tasks. Draw the network flow diagram and discover the critical path.

Task	Precedence	Normal Time (Days)
A	—	8
B	—	12
C	A, B	11
D	C	9
E	D	2
F	D	4
G	E, F	7

2. Take the following tasks. Draw the network flow diagram and discover the critical path.

Task	Precedence	Normal Time (Days)
A	—	3
B	A	3
C	A	2
D	B, C	6
E	B	6
F	C	5
G	D, E	4
H	F, G	4

3. For the given tasks, do the following:
   a. Draw the precedence diagram.
   b. Find the critical path.
   c. Reduce the path by 10 days.
   d. Reduce the path until you have spent $1,500.

Task	Precedence	Normal Time (Days)	Crash Time (Days)	Cost/Day (Dollars)
A	—	6	4	147
B	A	5	4	211
C	—	8	5	420
D	B, C	7	4	300
E	A	7	5	375
F	B, E	10	—	—
G	D, F	9	7	200
H	F, G	2	1	190

4. For the given tasks, do the following:
   a. Draw the precedence diagram.
   b. Find the critical path.
   c. Reduce the path by 20 days.
   d. Reduce the path until you have spent $10,000.

Task	Precedence	Normal Time (Days)	Crash Time	Cost/Day (Dollars)
A	—	20	17	600
B	—	14	11	500

Task	Precedence	Normal Time (Days)	Crash Time	Cost/Day (Dollars)
C	A	21	15	800
D	B	17	15	700
E	C, D	11	9	1,300
F	E	13	12	300
G	E	19	13	400
H	F, G	14	10	900

5. For the given tasks, do the following:
   a. Draw the precedence diagram.
   b. Find the critical path.
   c. Reduce the path by 10 days.
   d. Reduce the path until you have spent $1,500.

Task	Precedence	Normal Time (Days)	Crash Time (Days)	Cost/Day (Dollars)
A	—	7	4	300
B	A	4	3	250
C	B	3	2	175
D	A	6	3	240
E	D	9	8	275
F	C	8	6	325
G	E, F	11	5	140

6. Using the PERT formula, determine time estimates for the following tasks:

Task	Optimistic (Days)	Likely (Days)	Pessimistic (Days)
A	6	7	9
B	3	4	6
C	3	3	5
D	5	6	9
E	7	9	12
F	7	8	10

Using PERT, what is the estimated number of days to complete this project? Without PERT, how would it differ?

7. Using the PERT formula, determine time estimates for the following tasks:

Task	Precedence	Optimistic (Days)	Likely (Days)	Pessimistic (Days)
A	—	18	20	27
B	A	11	14	17
C	B	15	21	25
D	B	15	17	19
E	C, D	9	11	14
F	E	12	13	18
G	E	13	19	23
H	F, G	10	14	20

Using the precedence relationships from #4, what is the expected time if all optimistic times are met? Most likely times? Pessimistic times?

8. Revisiting this project:

Task	Precedence	Normal Time (Days)	Crash Time (Days)	Cost/Day (Dollars)
A	—	20	17	600
B	—	14	11	500
C	A	21	15	800
D	B	17	15	700
E	C, D	11	9	1,300
F	E	13	12	300
G	E	19	13	400
H	F, G	14	10	900

Here is the budget for the project tasks if they are accomplished in normal time:

Task	Expected Time (Days)	Actual Time (Days)	Budget (Dollars)	Actual (Dollars)
A	20	17	20,000	22,000
B	14	14	15,000	19,000
C	21	20	17,000	18,000
D	17	18	11,000	13,000
E	11	—	26,000	
F	13	—	10,000	
G	19	—	27,000	
H	14	—	34,000	

At this point, Tasks A through D have been completed. What is the expected cost of the project if all tasks are accomplished in the expected time? If asked to reduce the project by 5 days, what would the total budget be?

Projects

1. Create a Gantt chart and a network flow diagram for your school term projects.

2. Discuss a project in actual use with a manager involved in the project. Does he or she use any project management techniques? Software?

3. Outline the tasks that would be required to put on a concert at a stadium.

4. Create a work breakdown structure for the annual ESPN NBA draft show.

5. On your commute, note all the activities that involve projects, that is, construction projects, road repairs, and so on.

6. Study the release of a motion picture and its marketing campaign. Dissect the campaign into a project. Note the length of stay at theaters before the film dies out.

7. Study the steps involved in making an audio recording, and translate them into a work breakdown structure.

8. Dissect a new product introduction into a work breakdown structure.

9. Approach your income tax return as a project. What are the tasks and how long does each one take? What do you consider a successful tax return?

CASE 1   Software Installation in a Hospital

Community Hospital has signed a contract to change their general accounting and patient billing software to that provided by a firm that specializes in health care software. The plan is to install the software over a 16-week period while the existing software is still in use. John Ho, the project director for HSS, Hospital Systems Supreme, leads a team of four installers, who spend 5 days per week working on the installation.

HSS is based in Sacramento, and since Community is in Los Angeles, the HSS team must stay in hotels and work on expenses. The team comprises Dan Root, who has installed two systems of patient billing; Mary Hagan, who has helped Dan on both projects; Matt Dillon, a former actor, who quit the profession to become a software installer; and little Stevie Clark, who was just hired out of the Cal State Sacramento business school.

The group meets in the first week at a restaurant on Los Feliz Boulevard in Los Angeles.

"John," Dan opens, "I've never seen a project of this magnitude get done in 16 weeks. That's 80 working days for us. The last one took 20 weeks with 6 people. You've got us with 16 weeks and only 5 people."

"Let's try to be productive. You've done two billing systems."

"Yeah, but I had experienced people there, too. Here, we got a new guy on top of not having enough time."

"We'll work weekends if we have to."

"Let's try adding 4 people to the team if you want it in 16 weeks."

"Jenkins won't give me more than 4. He said that they did a job in Philadelphia in that time."

"Probably on the old system."

"Just try, and that is what we will shoot for."

The project took longer than expected. By the eighth week, Dan reported to Ho.

"I'd say we have 16 weeks more to go. No one told us we had to transfer detailed billing at the time of transition. That puts an extra few weeks on top of where we are automatically. You're going to have to tell the hospital."

Ho chewed on the sleeve of his shirt, a nervous tic that drove Root crazy. "I'll tell Jenkins we need all the people we can get to get it done in 8 weeks."

"It's not possible."

"Never say never."

"What are you? In Fantasyland?"

Meanwhile, the team was showing strains of constant travel. At least they were getting to know each other. Everyone ate dinner together, except for Ho, who always ate two pizzas alone in his room.

"How come you gave up acting?" Mary Hagan asked of Matt Dillon.

"Well, I would probably have had to change my name. There already was one Matt Dillon actor, and then of course there was a cowboy named Matt Dillon in Gunsmoke. I don't think there is any danger of a Matt Dillon software installer."

"How about you, Clark? Why'd you get into this business out of business school?"

"I figured health care was a good field to get into and software installation had less stress than actually working in a hospital."

"Well, if you were in Ho's shoes, you'd feel stress," Dan Smith replied. "He promised a 28-week job in 16 weeks, and we're at Week 8 where we would be in Week 6 normally. It's not going to be good for him."

"What do they do if you lead a project that doesn't come in on time?"

"They don't ask you to lead projects again. Which pretty much means that you stay at entry level in this firm. He'll spend the rest of his career doing what you are doing now."

"At least he gets to ride first class all the time," Mary said.

"Yeah, but that is only because he is so fat, he can't fit in economy seats."

Hagan suddenly made a confession. "I don't know how much longer I can continue on the road like this. My marriage is in jeopardy."

"How so?"

"My husband goes out every night I am out of town. When I come home I can smell the buffalo wings on his clothes."

"Maybe he just likes the food."

"Get real. I know why he goes out and it ain't for the buffalo wings!"

In Week 16, Jenkins added four brand-new employees to the team, all hired fresh out of their initial training. However, when they arrived at the site in Los Angeles, they found that the training had not taught them everything, and they needed help. Mary Hagan quit the team and took a job at a restaurant known for its buffalo wings, so she could spend more time with her husband.

In Week 24, when Ho told the hospital that they needed 8 more weeks for installation, the hospital cancelled the contract due to a loophole in the contract. HSS had spent 24 weeks meeting the expenses of five to nine people and it was all lost. The reason the hospital cancelled the contract was "loss of confidence in HSS." They expected the program to be running in 16 weeks. Now, when they said that it would be at least 32, they felt they were better off staying with their existing contract.

Ho never led a project again.

Discussion Questions

1. Why did this project fail?

2. How could the project have been done on time?

CASE 2 Trump International Hotel and Towers

On July 17, 2001, Donald Trump announced that the Trump Organization would build a 92-story skyscraper in Chicago that would include a hotel and condominiums. The residences would break the world record for the highest homes off ground level. The building would be built on the site of the Chicago Sun-Times Building, overlooking the Chicago River. The announcement in 2001 claimed that the building would be the world's tallest. However, after the events of September 11, 2001, the height of the structure was reduced.

Milestones of the project followed:

1. Original announcement	July 17, 2001
2. Narrowed to three design firms	July 18, 2001
3. Skidmore, Owings, and Merrill (SOM) chosen to design Trump Tower	August 6, 2001
4. SOM's design scheme revealed	December 14, 2001
5. Trump Tower submitted for building approvals	June 24, 2002
6. Tower approved by city	July 19, 2002
7. Trump kicks off condo sales	September 3, 2003
8. Sun-Times evacuates site	October 16, 2004
9. Trump closes on $640 million construction loan	February 19, 2005
10. Construction groundbreaking	March 17, 2005
11. Completion expected	June 1, 2008

a. What will be the major phases of construction for Trump Tower from groundbreaking to completion?

b. Is it realistic to expect a 92-story building to be constructed in 3 years? Substantiate your answer.

c. List the tasks accomplished prior to groundbreaking. What tasks were critical?

CASE 3   Finding the Photographer

An understanding of mission goes a long way to success in any project. On New Year's Eve 2007, Erika Gunderson got into a taxi in New York City and found a digital camera. The driver had no idea where the camera came from. The next day, Erika made it her New Year's resolution to find the photographer and return the camera.

She studied the photographs in the camera for clues. Her fiancé, Brian Ascher, consulted the taxi service to see if anyone had reported a lost camera. He placed ads in the lost and found section on Craig's List, but got only incorrect responses.

There were 350 pictures in the camera, mostly of New York City sightseeing locations. There was a picture next to the Beachcomber Restaurant in Clearwater, Florida. In another picture, the group in the photo wore name badges with the names Alan, Eileen, Noel, Noelle, and Ciarnan. Beneath their names was written "IRE."

Ascher called the restaurant to see if they had an Irish group on the date stamped on the camera, but no luck. Then, Ascher's mother became curious and studied the photos. By zooming in on a door-man outside a hotel in New York City, she found his uniform had the logo of the Radisson Hotel. Nancy Ascher had the hotel search its records for anyone from Ireland registered on that day and found a Noel had been registered. They provided Noel's e-mail address, but when contacted, he had not lost a camera.

So Nancy Ascher moved on to another photograph. She found a couple posing under a sign that read "Standings"—a bar in New York City. A Standings bartender did recall an Irish group and remembered one of them had told him she worked at the Playwrights Bar in New York.

The bartender from Standings contacted the Playwrights to see who had visited his bar, and he forwarded to Ascher a response from Sarah Casey, whose sister was the bartender at Playwrights. The Caseys had hosted a group from Ireland who had vacationed in Florida prior to New York City. They had stayed at the Radisson, but the hotel employee who had looked for Irish names missed their names.

The owner of the camera actually lived in Australia. Alan Murphy, a former Irishman, had met up with his friends in the United States and left his camera behind in the taxi. So with dogged determination, the project's mission was completed: find the owner of the digital camera. Such devotion to completing a project and accomplishing the mission is necessary in any business project if one wants to succeed (Bergstein, 2008).

CASE 4   The Weight Loss Project

Amy Munndein, having read the chapter on project management, decides that she will apply these methods to her own project: to lose 40 lb in 1 year. Amy entered her freshman year of college at a svelte 5 ft 4 in. and 125 lb. Away from home for the first time in her life, she made best friends with the vending machine around the corner from her dorm room. Being overstressed by exams and papers, she put on 40 lb in her first year. Although her parents were somewhat concerned about the weight gain, they appreciated the 3.8 grade point average Amy had delivered.

Amy did not dwell much on her weight gain until that summer, when her boyfriend from high school unceremoniously dumped her. She tried to watch what she ate in her sophomore year and weighed herself every morning. At the end of the year, she could celebrate the fact that she had not gained any weight.

In the fall of her junior year, an operations management class assignment was to find a personal way to use an operations technique, and she opted to use the project management for weight loss. She had 5 weeks, so she set a goal of losing the first 8 lb of the 40 in that time, but decided to continue for a year until she weighed what she did as a freshman. Her reward was to replenish her closet with Size 6 clothes, down from her present Size 14.

She listed her tasks as follows:

Task	Time (Weeks)	Task	Time (Weeks)
Read diet books	2	Increase exercise	5
Read exercise books	2	Weigh-in milestones	Every week; 1 lb
Reduce caloric intake	5		

This was an unusual project in that all the tasks started simultaneously. She decided that a Gantt chart made more sense than a project flow network.

TASK	10/1	10/8	10/15	10/22	10/29
Read books	——				—|
Weigh in	X	X	X	X	X
Reduce calories	——				—|
Increase exercise	——				—|

Amy was very motivated by grades, still holding a 3.8 entering her junior year. She wanted to make an A on the project, so she intended to put as much into the project as she did into her studies. The irony was that much of her project involved "Not" doing things, that is, not putting the wrong food into her mouth.

She read about the Atkins diet, the South Beach diet, the Sonoma diet, and the Biggest Loser diet. The low-carb diets did not appeal to her at all because she loved bread and pancakes so much. She settled on a form of the "Biggest Loser" diet. She would have an allocation of four fruits and vegetables, three proteins, and two grains every day. Then, she could splurge with a 200-calorie treat.

Her diet on a typical day is as follows:

Breakfast

A whole grapefruit—two fruits

Lunch

Turkey

Slice of bread

A little mayo

Lettuce—one vegetable

One grain

Two proteins

Dinner

Lean cuisine meal—one protein

One grain

One vegetable

Banana

Dessert

Sugar-free Jell-O

This was less than half of the calories she consumed on a normal day. Her previous diet would show a day like this:

Breakfast

Cereal and milk

Toast with jam and butter

Snack

Muffin

Lunch

Chicken Panini

Brownie

Snack

Candy

Dinner

Pizza or other fast food (two hamburgers was common)

Dessert

Ice cream sundae

On the very first day, Amy found her stomach growling in midmorning and it took everything she had to avoid the urge to raid the vending machine. She kept thinking, "4.0 this semester!"

Not eating was very hard but not as hard as starting to exercise. Amy learned from the exercise books that running and cross-country skiing were the biggest calorie burners, and it being September in Georgia rather limited her skiing. Amy had played on the high school softball team and that had been the only athletic endeavor in her life. However, she could really run the bases and cover the outfield, so she thought she could work into a running program.

She wrote out an ambitious schedule for the 5 weeks:

Week 1

　Walk/run 1 mile four times

Week 2

　Walk/run 1 mile 2 times, 2 miles 2 times

Week 3

　Run 2 miles 2 times, walk/run 3 miles 2 times

Week 4

　Run 3 miles 3 times, walk/run 4 miles 2 times

Week 5

　Run 3 miles 2 times, run 4 miles 2 times, walk/run 5 miles once

Amy stuck to the schedule. In her first attempt at running, she went to a track and made it halfway around the track before having to walk. In her fourth try, however, she made it four times around without stopping. It took her 12 min, but she was pleased.

In the second week, she did a 2-mile run in only 19 min. This gave her the confidence to sign up for a local 5-km race in Week 4. She did the 3.1-mile race in 28 min, and she was hooked.

Amy weighed 165 lb when she began her project. Here are her weekly weigh-ins:

Week	Pounds	Week	Pounds
1	161	4	154
2	159	5	150
3	156		

By the time Amy entered her senior year, she had settled in at 117 lb. She looked great and had already received three job offers for postgraduation. Amy became a motivational speaker and was asked to appear on the Oprah show. In one interview, she said,

It all started in my operations management class. That class opened my eyes to project management, which saved my life. Without project management, I would be like Herbie in "The Goal." But with it, I am in charge of my own critical path.

Amy formed the Critical Path Society and was nominated for the Nobel Prize for her contributions to the field of project management.

Discussion Questions

1. How could you have improved on Amy's project?

2. Is there a personal project of your own that could benefit from project management?

CASE 5   The Las Vegas Wedding

Joey B. and Cecilia have decided to tie the knot. On Labor Day 2007, Joey proposed to Cecilia, a young lady he had dated for 16 months, 12 days, 6 hr, and 30 s prior to the proposal.

"My darling, Cecilia, will you grant me paradise and be my wife?" he asked, as they rode in a horse-drawn carriage through Central Park in New York City.

"Oh, you can't be kidding me. You're not kidding me, are you?"

"No, I mean it." He opened a box containing a diamond engagement ring.

The carriage driver glanced back and smiled.

"Of course, I'll marry you!" She kissed him passionately, forgiving him for forgetting her birthday the day before.

"There is one catch," Joey B. said, gasping for air.

"I knew it. You're already married!" Cecilia frowned.

"No, that's not it. I want us to get married in Vegas in one of those Elvis impersonator weddings. And the date should be Mother's Day next year, since my mother is an Elvis fan."

"I would marry you in Peoria, Des Moines, Kansas, Provo, Sacramento, anywhere in the world. This is going to be the greatest day in my life! *Our* lives! Now, I will get to work and use my project management skills I learned in business school to plan."

"I knew you could do that. That is why I bought you *this* birthday present!" He opened a bag containing Microsoft Project.

"Oh, you are such a sweetie! Isn't he a doll?" she asked the horse carriage driver.

"He's a sweetie, all right!" the carriage driver smirked.

The project was on. Mother's Day, 2010. Joey B. and Cecilia, who live in Naperville, Illinois, began their planning. The first thing Cecilia needed was her laptop. Then, what next?

Discussion Questions

1. Take Cecilia's job and plan a Vegas wedding at Caesar's Palace.
2. Uh, oh. Cecilia discovers that it would really be a good idea to move up the wedding date to 1 month from now. Crash the project so it can be done in 4 weeks.

Web Sites

Dave Farthing's software project management links page: www.comp.glam.ac.uk/pages/staff/dwfarthi/projman.htm

Project Management Institute: www.pmi.org

References

Bergstein, B. (2008, February 5). Camera found; mystery begins. *Chicago Tribune*, pp. 5.1–5.9.

Gray, C. E., & Larson, E. W. (2000). *Project management.* Boston: McGraw-Hill.

Horine, G. M. (2005). *Absolute beginner's guide to project management.* Indianapolis, IN: Que.

Lewis, J. P. (1995). *Project manager's desk reference.* Chicago: Irwin.

Slevin, D. P., & Pinto, J. K. (1987, Fall). Balancing strategy and tactics in project implementation. *Sloan Management Review, 28,* 33–41.

Appendix

If the Shoe Fits: Wenzhou Aike Shoes Company, Ltd.

Bin Jiang

Patrick J. Murphy

This case study addresses critical aspects of the strategic management decision to be made by Wenzhou Aike Shoes Company, Ltd., a Chinese multinational shoe manufacturer. The specific focus is on Aike's operations in Elche, Spain. Over a period of several years, upheaval stemming from a multitude of Chinese new entrants to Elche's revered shoemaking industry reached a flashpoint. The Chinese new entrants run operations significantly differently than the local Elche businesses in terms of daily practices, production, imitation, price competition, and supply chain management. All of these aspects derive from deep cultural differences and are highlighted in the case. Several strategic options, such as foreign partnership, brand acquisition, and exiting Elche are presented for discussion.

Ma Juncheng was President of Wenzhou Aike Footwear Company. On September 16, 2004 he was anxiously waiting to hear from his Regional Manager in Elche, Spain. Ma was going to have to make big decisions fast about how to handle rising hostility toward his Elche operations. A large and growing number of Elche citizens were beginning to despise Chinese shoemakers. Business people resented the political deals with local officials and perceived dumping practices. The animosity and tension was about to reach a boiling point, as last week a sign was posted on the wall of one of Wenzhou Aike's manufacturing plants.

Citizens of Elche
DEMONSTRATE ON SEPTEMBER 16
Keep our families fed!
Burn all Chinese shoe shipments!
Shoemaking is our livelihood.
Neither the Mayor nor anyone else will help.
Stop complaining about the situation and ACT!
Defend our jobs and keep our city.

SOURCE: Jiang, B., & Murphy, P. J. (2007). If the shoe fits: Wenzhou Aike Shoes Company, Ltd. *Journal of International Business Education, 3.*

As Ma waited nervously to hear from his Regional Manager, he thought about the situation in Elche. The city is located 420 kilometers Southeast of Madrid. It is the capital of Spain's footwear industry. Elche is historically renowned in European and international shoe markets for the high quality and fine styles of the footwear produced by its artisans and sold in its shops. Because of this fame, growing numbers of shoemakers from China had moved to Elche and the surrounding areas during the past several years to run shoe businesses. Most of these immigrants came from Wenzhou, China's largest shoe manufacturing center. Wenzhou has at least 4,000 factories that produce massive quantities of low-priced shoes using cheap labor amidst poor working conditions. Once payoffs from Chinese shoemakers to the Elche government had led to a tidal wave of shoes from Wenzhou, the local politicians were hesitant to intervene, but the shoe industry was undergoing a sharp recession. In fact, 60% of its shoe stores and factories had gone out of business by 2002.

One response to these disturbing trends was a growing insurgency among Elche's populace. Ma had feared for a long time that it would reach a flash point. The reaction of the citizens was premised on a perception that competition with the Chinese was not just about low-priced products. The Chinese companies were smuggling large quantities of shoes into Wenzhou. Most of the Chinese shoe inventory was untaxed or the product of illegal markets, which made it impossible for law-abiding Spanish businesses to compete. As well, local entrepreneurs blamed the Chinese for not respecting Spanish business customs and allegedly forging political relationships with local government officials. The Chinese shoe stores in Elche were open for at least three hours longer than the locally owned ones. As well, Chinese businesses received shipments on Sundays while the Spanish ones were closed.

Fire!

Ma's Regional Manager finally came through on the telephone with a frantic update. The tension in Elche had reached a flashpoint on September 16. Over 7,000 citizens marched through the streets protesting the demise of their shoe industry. Angered by the loss of local jobs and businesses since the massive influx of shoes from China, infuriated protesters shouted loudly and carried large billboards, declaring "Chinese out!" Several hundred protesters entered Elche's Karus industrial area by force and hurled stones at Chinese wholesalers and footwear stores. Once they reached Aike's location, it was not long before a whole warehouse and large trailer were ablaze in flames. More than €1.2 million worth of Aike's shoe inventory—all manufactured in China and transported to Spain—was up in smoke. Several arrests were made. The Chinese implored local Spanish authorities to protect them and their property and the Chinese government asked about compensation to the businesses.

Ma was relieved nobody was hurt but very distressed about the predicament. He saw the destruction of his inventory as symptomatic of a longstanding deeper problem. Now the complexities of that problem were compounded, intensified, and more apparent than ever before. It was almost as though the fire that had just destroyed so much of his inventory was a metaphor for the "fire" of competition and other external forces that were spreading around his business. He needed to make some hard strategic decisions fast about how to stop the flames, but it was unclear to him how he could do so while keeping his company intact.

Background

Chinese Shoemakers

In China, shoemakers are widely known as "shoe locusts" because of their extraordinary reproductive capacity. As business organizations, they move fast in dynamic swarms and high-density droves. Their growth rates are very high, and they can destroy or transform any market system they enter if given free reign. Chinese shoemakers produced no less than six billion pairs of shoes in 2004. That level of production equated to at least one pair of shoes for every single person on earth.

Wenzhou is the source of this production activity. Though the shoes manufactured in Wenzhou dominate a global industry, virtually none of the millions of workers there speak Western languages. In fact, these workers tend to be so uneducated they cannot even speak standard Mandarin Chinese well. As such, they do not share or develop specialized knowledge about product quality. Instead, they only emphasize simple information about productivity and quantity. Most of them have only a primary school education that is supplemented by years of experience emphasizing volume and conducting fast business in flea markets. Thus, the only real business principle they understand is that lower prices mean higher sales. With this rudimentary orientation, they will dare entry into any new market. If there is an opportunity for profit, they rush in; if there is no opportunity, they hurry away. If a first mover generates profit, then a large swarm will follow quickly.

Sometimes the hoarding activity of Chinese shoemaking companies damages the natural environment. The effects include pollution, poisoning of natural waterways, and destruction of natural habitats. An intense production emphasis also tends to exploit physical labor in China. Organizational characteristics and norms deriving from these practices sometimes cause foreign markets to be unreceptive to Chinese shoemakers.

Wenzhou Aike

China suffered from many shortages of manufactured goods in the 1980s. Shoes, for example, were difficult to buy in the centralized economic system. Ma founded his company based on an opportunity he discovered to respond to this inefficiency. In 1992, with the help of a successful Hong Kong businessperson, Ma began to produce leather for a Belgian company. He invested his entire family fortune (about $100,000) in the operation and named the business "Aike" because of its phonetic similarity with the famous "Nike" brand. The Belgian company exported shoes made with Ma's leather to Russia, which was another centralized economy struggling with similar shortages. Aike's total sales in 1993 were about $1.3 million.

True to form, it was not long before many imitators cropped up in Wenzhou to chase the same kind of success. The hotness of the competition made Ma uncomfortable, and intermediaries such as the Belgian company had begun to capitalize on Chinese competition. This process drove Aike's prices down. As a result, Aike separated from its distributors in 1997 and opted to conduct its international business independently.

The first country Aike entered was Russia. The original installation was a large booth in a Moscow bargain market. When Aike arrived there were already two other Wenzhou shoemakers in the market. Soon there were more. Aike occupied the booth in 1999 at a rental rate of €10,000 per year. By 2000, there were more than 100 Wenzhou shoemakers in the market, which drove rent up to €25,000 per year. By 2002, there were more than 300 Wenzhou shoemakers in the market. Rising rent and a fierce price war with other Chinese shoemakers narrowed Aike's profit margins considerably and Ma decided to leave Russia.

Aike next moved into Hungary, Poland, and the Czech Republic. Ma decided on these locations for a couple of reasons. First, not many Chinese competitors had reached these markets yet. Second, Ma had acquired some business skills and cultural understanding during his Russian experience that enabled him to do business in these formerly centralized economies. Third, as most Eastern European countries had recently become members of the European Union (EU), Aike could eventually use them as pivot points to enter larger markets in Western European countries.

Aike Enters Elche

Aike finally entered the Western European market in 2000 with the purchase of a small shoe-manufacturing workshop in Elche. When Aike first began conducting business, the main shopping street in Elche was packed full of local shoe stores. Each one had a retail area near the front and a manufacturing facility in back. There were only two Chinese manufacturers in the entire city. Elche originally welcomed the Chinese, and local business people had very positive relations with them. By this point, Ma had learned a lot about the political aspects of establishing a business in a foreign environment, but would still marvel about the fact that smooth relations with local government officials were arguably more critical than economic concerns. Sometimes those relations involved political payments. At that point, there were no economic or political issues related to Chinese trade or immigration. For example, though there was a limiting quota on imports, some local shops even agreed to help absorb excesses by storing inventory for the Chinese stores. Ma visited several of the local stores and noticed their operations were very small. There were many such stores, but most had very few employees. Ma recognized that competition with these stores based on economies of scale would be easy. The strategic approach allowed Aike to thrive and grow in Elche for the next several years. During this time, relations with competitors began to cool, and political support from government officials became increasingly important.

By 2004, Elche's main shopping street had changed dramatically. Most of the shoe stores were now run by Chinese shoemakers who manufactured and sold inexpensive shoes. The average price for a pair of Chinese shoes was €9.00. The Spanish stores, by contrast, were selling shoes for €15.00–20.00. The strategy of the Chinese was to compete on price. Later, as Chinese shoemakers began to compete intensely with each other, the prices for shoes were driven very low. Before long, shoes in Elche could be bought from Chinese stores for €2.00–3.00. In the meantime, many Spanish shoe stores closed.

Chinese Operations and Competition in Elche

Chinese shoe businesses had distinct operational characteristics in Elche. Whereas the local stores were closed for a respite every afternoon from 2:00–4:00, the Chinese ones were always open during this time. Spanish stores were also closed every Saturday and Sunday, but the Chinese ones were still open. The Chinese stores almost never had local citizens working in them. Rather, they hired Chinese employees. The stores were linked with a supply chain that stretched from manufacturing to retail and populated only by Chinese people.

The dynamics of Chinese competition were intense. Unlike the Spanish shoemakers, Chinese manufacturers copied each other based on material, style, production technique, and any other notable practice. Once a popular style was identified, it was certain that exact imitations of it down to the last detail would be for sale on the main street in a couple of days. Soon enough, imitation amongst players in the shoe market and its effect on prices became a strategic enabler. For example, in 2000 a pair of popular shoes would be available for sale at 1–2 locations and generate €3 in profit. In 2004, a pair of popular shoes, or exact imitations, would be available at 20 locations and the same margin was down to €0.20. The dynamics of competition began to hinge on price and efficiency, at the expense of brand and quality.

Environmental Forces

The practices of Chinese shoemakers in Europe eventually met with objections from not only local but also international authorities. In 2003, Chinese shoes totaling €2 million were destroyed in Rome because of counterfeiting and smuggling. In June 2005, the EU began to investigate the Chinese shoe industry for dumping practices in Europe and began to inaugurate anti-dumping tariffs for all shoes made in China. A gradual increase in those taxes from 4% to 19% over a five-year period was planned by the EU.

In 2006, in the context of this environment, Aike faced two forces from a strategic management perspective. The first one, which was immediate, derived from Chinese competition in fierce price wars. The second one was more daunting and related to the general political and legal environment. It derived ultimately from the EU, which had already threatened tariffs and anti-dumping legislation. It was also germane to local towns and municipalities that did not appreciate so many Chinese shoemakers entering their markets. How could Aike deal with both challenges at once?

Next Steps for Aike

For Ma, how to engage the first challenge was straightforward but would be difficult. He knew that over the long run, the cost advantage of Aike and the other Chinese shoemakers was not sustainable. In Malaysia and Vietnam, for example, shoes could now be made even cheaper than in China. Noting as many of the parameters as he could identify, Ma pondered several potential strategic approaches for Aike as next steps.

First, he considered manufacturing in Africa, where labor was very cheap. It was true that Nigeria's government saw Chinese imports as destroying local industries and had just forced Chinese retailers out in 2004. Nigeria also announced that they would stop importing 31 different products from China, including shoes. One Chinese shoemaker saw an opportunity, however, and sought to invest in Nigeria by establishing a shoe factory that hired many local employees (over 2,000), trained local sellers, and shared technology. The shoemaker eventually gained access and also paid taxes to local governments, helped solve unemployment problems, and became the largest shoemaker in West Africa. By 2005, that shoemaker's production capacity exceeded one million pairs and sold for an average of €10. The highest quality shoes made in Africa could even be exported to the USA and Europe; because they were made in Africa, there were no anti-dumping regulations and they were not overtaxed. Could Aike move operations to Africa?

The second option involved establishing a brand. In the Chinese market, luxury shoes cost more than €120 and were only made by foreign brands outside China. Ma knew the reason was not only based on quality, but also because Chinese shoemakers did not understand how to establish brand recognition and loyalty. Foreign shoemakers used a brand advantage to attract Chinese customers. Therefore, some Chinese shoemakers had purchased foreign companies just for their brands. In 2002, for example, a Wenzhou shoemaker met the founder of Wilson, an Italian company with a revered 50-year history. Wilson was an original equipment manufacturer for Polo and Armani. The daughter of the founder had no interest in running the family business. Therefore, the Wenzhou company was able to buy Wilson's operations for €1.5 million. The acquisition afforded many strategic enablers. For one, imitation was not an issue because original designers were utilized to make the product. As well, Chinese competitors were not supposed to copy the design due to strict Italian intellectual property guidelines. In addition, there were no anti-dumping regulations because it was an Italian company. Aike had just enough resources to make such an acquisition, but it would be a massive change for the company. Was buying a foreign company an option?

The last option was to cooperate with foreign companies. Ma knew of a few examples of such cooperation. In 2004, a Wenzhou company allied with Geox, the largest shoemaker in Italy. The CEO of Geox, Diego Bolzonello, granted the Chinese company sole status as its Asian manufacturing base. The alliance involved completely sharing Geox's distribution network for products. Geox provided technology and international channels to market for the Wenzhou company. The cooperation helped the Wenzhou company establish an image. It was then able to produce highly desirable products and keep pace with the European market. If this option was viable, how could it be done?

IVEY

Richard Ivey School of Business
The University of Western Ontario

Rosenbluth: Supply Chain Management in Services

Professor John Kamauff

In October 1993, Mike McCormick, Director of Industry Relations for Rosenbluth International, an international travel services company based in Philadelphia, Pennsylvania, was preparing a series of negotiations with one of Rosenbluth's "preferred" airline suppliers. Ever since a new manager had taken over travel agency relations one year ago at this airline, the relationship with this supplier had deteriorated. As a result, Rosenbluth had been directing fewer of its corporate clients to the airline. McCormick wondered what he should do about the relationship. Should Rosenbluth continue to consider the airline a preferred supplier, or should it focus on other suppliers with whom the relationship was stronger and more cooperative? His primary obligation was, after all, to the needs of Rosenbluth's clients. Mike had to determine the best way to manage Rosenbluth's suppliers to satisfy those needs.

Rosenbluth International

Rosenbluth International was a worldwide travel management company with annual revenues of $1.5 billion. Started in 1892 by Marcus Rosenbluth as a steamship ticket office, the Rosenbluth family continued to own and manage it throughout its 100-year history. President and CEO Hal Rosenbluth started his career with Rosenbluth in 1974. In 1992, Rosenbluth had 550 locations in 335 cities and had established international alliances with 34 affiliates around the globe. Since 1992, annual revenues had grown from $40 million to $1.5 billion. Rosenbluth operated in three lines of business: leisure travel, meeting and motivation management, and corporate travel (which represented 90 per cent of the company's revenues).

According to industry observers, Rosenbluth's ability to exploit the opportunities offered by the deregulation of the airline industry in 1978 had fuelled its growth. The advent of deregulation meant that airlines could change fares and schedules any time they wished. This resulted in a massive increase in the number of available routes and fares, and the information became very volatile, as changes were made constantly. The printed medium was no longer an efficient way to conduct business for travel agencies, and a different approach was needed to keep up with tariffs and schedules. Computerized Reservation Systems (CRSs), provided by the large airlines, became a permanent fixture in the airline/travel agency distribution system. The CRS gave immediate access in a real-time environment to air tariff information, the availability of specific seats, and a sense of what discount opportunities were available. Changes in schedules, etc. were immediately reflected in the CRS system.

Deregulation had a profound impact on the travel industry and some experts predicted the demise of the travel agency as a factor in the industry. Hal Rosenbluth and his colleagues reacted differently.

> What did deregulation mean? We weren't sure we knew. But if all the bets were off, the company that could gather information faster and turn it into knowledge would win.

Rosenbluth was able to recognize early the impact that this information explosion would have on corporate travel expenses, and positioned itself to become an expert in managing corporate travel information. The corporate market wanted excellent service, coupled with a need for quick access to information that would allow any feasible cost savings to be realized. Information technology was the only mechanism for cost effectively managing the complexity that emerged in the industry following deregulation. Therefore, Rosenbluth set out to create an information systems infrastructure that would allow it to gather, track and report information on all of its clients' travel activity (Exhibit 1). It began by downloading information from the CRS and modifying the data locally to produce customized reports for corporate clients. In 1983, Rosenbluth introduced READOUT, a product that turned the flight selection process around, listing flights by fare instead of by time of departure. The CRS would display available flights by time of departure only; thus in order to find out the cost of a flight, the agent would have to switch back and forth between fare screen and the list of flights. In contrast, READOUT would display the flights for a particular city-pair in order of increasing fare, so that the cost implications of a particular flight selection were immediately apparent at the point of sale.

In 1985, Rosenbluth took another important step toward becoming a technology leader by developing systems that would allow it to operate in the back office independently from the CRS. The CRS was essential in performing the travel agency functions, and the CRS providers had leveraged this into control over virtually all aspects of the business. All hardware and software were closed systems with fixed functionality, including the "back-end" processing for accounting and travel management reporting, and the system was subsidized by the CRS provider, usually an airline. For Hal Rosenbluth, the primary issue was control over back-end processing. Overall, the CRSs were not sufficiently responsive to corporate clients' needs for reporting and control. The CRS subsidy further impinged on the agency's independence. As Hal Rosenbluth said:

> Knowledge is in the back office. If you are dependent on a CRS provider for your back office, you can't fully utilize the knowledge. How can you ask United Airlines' APOLLO to help you shift a client's business to American?

Rosenbluth developed its own back office system, VISION, in 1986, thus liberating itself from the control of the airlines who owned or operated the CRSs. The CRSs were still used for booking a reservation, but a record of the transaction always went into VISION also. The resulting VISION database provided complete and accurate information and gave considerable flexibility in reporting and analysis. Not only did VISION allow Rosenbluth to provide extensive reporting for corporate clients, it also allowed the agency to track its market share and volumes with the service providers. Rosenbluth was now able to identify opportunities for negotiating price and rebates with the airlines, based on historical fact. Exhibit 2 shows the categories included in a sample VISION report.

Travel Industry—Supplier Relations

The use of negotiated fares and rates was an important trend to appear in the travel industry in the 1980s. As early as 1982, about one-half of firms surveyed with in-house travel departments were negotiating rates directly with hotels and car rental agencies. These special prices were primarily corporate-wide discounts and special group prices for specific meetings and events. In the mid-1980s, a new frontier in price negotiation opened. By having access to detailed data on their corporate travel down to the city-pair, firms were able to identify their high-volume routes and negotiate with suppliers for preferential fares on a route-by-route basis.

Maximizing the opportunities for negotiated prices required consolidating travel information over an entire organization to lever purchasing power fully. The organization had to be able to demonstrate to the air supplier that the increase in the volume from a fare program would more than offset the lower fares. Using a single agency facilitated this consolidation of information. Moreover, the purchasing power of the travel agency itself could be an important factor in negotiations, creating a benefit for consolidating travel through fewer agencies. The ability of an agency to move market share dictated negotiated prices which required being able to demonstrate the effects of the program and to monitor compliance. Travel agencies were in a good position to encourage compliance with the firm's negotiated agreement at the time the reservation was made.

Rosenbluth was a pioneer in the industry in the use of negotiated route-by-route fares, thereby taking advantage of the trend towards consolidating travel accounts through a single agency. The VISION system was truly innovative in the industry at the time and allowed Rosenbluth to provide the detailed analysis required to its clients and to negotiate with travel suppliers on their behalf. Negotiated route-by-route programs led to a significant change in the way that Rosenbluth approached the corporate travel market. Corporate travel was sold almost exclusively by agency commission sharing. Travel agents would typically rebate to clients 15 per cent of their commissions. Rosenbluth adopted a more cooperative approach based on service and partnership. Instead of rebates, Rosenbluth offered guaranteed savings through lower airfares. Rosenbluth maintained that it could reduce overall travel costs for the client while still earning its standard 10 per cent commission. This claim could be backed up by reports from the VISION system, comparing prices paid to the lowest available fare.

Hal Rosenbluth described the Rosenbluth approach as follows:

> Rebating doesn't help anyone involved. When a service company gives away its commissions, it doesn't leave much to pay its people and to invest in the future. In the end it hurts the company and its clients. We try to hold firm to a position that makes everyone win. We might guarantee a client with a $20 million budget a $1 million reduction in travel costs through consolidated purchasing, specially negotiated fares and the manipulation of travel patterns toward less expensive alternatives. In effect we are saying, "Why assume you have to keep spending that $20 million?"

Rosenbluth formed an Industry Relations department to manage supplier negotiations on behalf of clients. This allowed all negotiations to be undertaken centrally, sending a consistent message to clients. Industry Relations personnel developed close ties with the relationship managers at the supplier companies. In 1991, Mike McCormick was appointed Director of Industry Relations. Mike joined the department in 1986 as a data analyst and in 1988 had been promoted to Manager of Industry Relations. As manager, he had been responsible for expanding the department to include a supplier relations management team. This team worked to improve and enhance Rosenbluth's preferred supplier relationships, by creating business and marketing plans, guiding Rosenbluth's business units in their supplier relationships, and ensuring that valuable supplier products and services were available for clients. Mike described the process the department undertakes as follows:

> We have positioned our department as a yield management group. As a travel company our clients are expecting us to manage their travel budgets. Once you have done that to satisfy the client's need to the lowest cost, you need to

take a macro bundling of all of our accounts to maximize our margins and to achieve overrides above the standard 10 per cent . . . Contracts are usually a year, but that's only a formality. With our primary suppliers, we start by setting joint objectives and then we back into how we are going to measure that to ensure that we jointly meet our goals. The negotiations are clearly different from a yearly sit down to hammer out costs. It is more like an on-going set of negotiations as we continually iron out details. The weekly and monthly management reports are used to help us manage our activities. We share all of our info with the airlines.

To provide the motivation for successful negotiations, Rosenbluth employed techniques such as taking inventory positions to secure the most economical routes for clients. Rosenbluth studied travel patterns, and suppliers were guaranteed a certain level of business based on historical data. The company shared information both with clients and suppliers. Rosenbluth's systems allowed the company to demonstrate exactly how much it cost a client to travel between two points on any given time of day, day of the week or week of the year. This information could then be used by the client to shift travel patterns to those times during which travel was more economical. Rosenbluth would then show clients how to shift business to the carrier that offered the best rates and services. Exhibit 3 shows a sample of an airfare activity report that would typically be used in negotiations. Exhibit 4 similarly depicts a typical travel pattern analysis that would be used to describe travel patterns, airline market shares and the impact of negotiated airfare programs. As Hal Rosenbluth described it, "The suppliers who participate get more business; our clients get significant savings, and we share in those savings."

Partnering with airlines allowed Rosenbluth to define clearly its role in the travel process. Negotiated agreements with clients and travel agencies assured the airlines of brand loyalty. According to David Miller, Director of MIS at Rosenbluth:

Developing brand loyalty is a real problem for airlines. For them, we are creating a mechanism that takes care of those facets of travel that they cannot handle. The ideal situation for airlines would be to have travel agency dealerships. We use this to our advantage by partnering with appropriate airlines to reinforce the relationship with the customer at a lower cost than the airlines can.

Hal Rosenbluth believed strongly in the benefits of forming close partnerships with both clients and suppliers. He said:

Companies can't overlook the importance of supplier relationships in helping to meet their client's needs. In our case, we rely on airline, hotel and car rental suppliers to provide the end product—the travel itself. We need to make sure that our suppliers are performing for our clients. We need to work in concert with our clients and suppliers in strategic partnerships. The way we see it, all three parties need to know exactly what to expect.

Rosenbluth's strategy was to appeal simultaneously to the airlines for lower costs and better services and to the customer for preferences.

Hal felt that more could be accomplished when clients and suppliers worked together like true partners in a venture than in a typical adversarial relationship. Supplier selection was predicated to a great extent on trust. Hal described the process of forming preferred supplier relationships as follows:

> Regarding the airlines, we went in with those executives who we thought would be respectful of a partnership. It had a three-way win. Any one of the three parties could destroy it. Trust and respect, the viability of the supplier, and geographical overlaps and linkages were key. We focused on the thought processes of their senior executives. One of the major issues was that we did not try to build long-term relationships with potentially competing companies, which was the game that most travel agencies tried to play.

According to Mike McCormick:

> We don't have these relationships with all airlines. We had to make decisions about aligning with preferred suppliers. Our ability to direct business is the lifeblood of our industry. The number of preferred suppliers has narrowed over the years and will continue to narrow. You can only give your true support to so many, both statistically and in terms of developing and sustaining ethical relationships. We have taken the high road here by making tough decisions often resulting in short-term sacrifices, but over the long term we have engendered open and trusting relationships . . . which is not necessarily indicative of our industry.

Rosenbluth was committed to maintaining open, trusting relationships. The company strived to be known as the ethical player in the industry. According to Mike Melvagh, Manager of Rosenbluth's Canadian operations:

> We will tell a client that we can't do something if it jeopardizes our relationship with a supplier. Our Industry Relations department has worked very hard to build Rosenbluth's reputation and image. Why would we want to risk damaging it?

Added Hal:

> One of the things we have always done, and we've made it very clear to our existing and prospective clients, is that we're going to be very straight with our suppliers in negotiating with them. We won't promise to deliver something that we don't know we can deliver.

This policy of openness and trust was entrenched throughout the company, as well as with its clients and suppliers. Hal Rosenbluth had endeavored to shape a culture based on team work and employee empowerment at Rosenbluth. His success was recognized when Rosenbluth was ranked among the top 10 in the book *The 100 Best Companies to Work for in America* (Exhibit 5).

Hal's philosophy was that there was no reason to hide anything from clients:

The more you try to hide something the more curious people become. We found that openness is reciprocal. The more candid we are with our clients and suppliers, the more candid they are with us. The level of trust we build is reciprocal.

Hal also insisted that Rosenbluth use its clients' products whenever feasible. Hal gave this example of the importance of this policy:

Because the James River Corporation is our client, we use only their paper products. Each time we visit the rest room, we're reminded of how important our clients' products are.

Hal's vision of partnership extended past the traditional client-supplier relationship.

The definite level in partnership is the idea of a "corporate marriage." This would be a form of interchange that takes place in an environment of complete trust. An exchange of people.

Hal felt that this level of partnership provided insight into the needs of clients that could not be attained any other way. As Hal put it:

The benefits are reciprocal. Our clients who participate in this degree of partnership come to understand the objectives we must achieve as a business and the challenges we face. A walk in each other's shoes builds the platform for true teamwork.

Achieving "corporate marriages" with key clients would truly entrench Rosenbluth's relationships. According to Hal:

The only thing that puts the relationships at risk is new management in the partners. If they differ in their beliefs, it can lead to catastrophic break-ups. It would take us less than a night to adapt to a change but only with the participation and understanding of our clients.

The Current Situation

A change in management at Global Airways was what had precipitated Mike McCormick's current troubles. Rosenbluth had first developed a preferred supplier relationship with Global five years earlier. Together with several of its largest national accounts, Rosenbluth had successfully negotiated route-by-route overrides with Global for many important domestic city-pairs, which represented very high volume routes for Rosenbluth.

Global was one of the three largest airlines in the United States and had established itself as a leader in the industry in providing quality in-flight services for corporate travelers. The U.S. airline industry, including Global, had faced serious financial difficulties during the period 1990 to 1992. (See Exhibits 6 and 7 for airline industry aggregate data for the years 1982 to 1992.) However, Global appeared to be recovering better than most U.S. airlines, following a restructuring and a significant cost-cutting effort in early 1992.

As part of the restructuring, many top managers were let go, including the management of the Corporate Relations department. Rosenbluth had enjoyed a very strong relationship with the former Vice-President of Corporate Relations, Rick Chadwick. Chadwick had supported Rosenbluth's approach to building corporate loyalty and moving share through negotiated fares. He recognized the importance of partnering with travel agencies to provide the travel management function that the airlines could not cost effectively perform for large corporate clients.

The restructuring had resulted in a significant downsizing of the Corporate Relations department at Global. The remaining staff now reported to the Vice President of Operations, Bill Whitherspoon. Whitherspoon had been hired in 1992, and had previously worked at one of the largest telecommunications companies in the United States. He had no previous experience in the travel or transportation industries. Whitherspoon's background was as a comptroller, and he had a reputation as a "real bean-counter."

Mike had scheduled a meeting with Whitherspoon immediately following his appointment. The meeting had been a disappointment. Whitherspoon announced that negotiated airfares on high volume routes were going to be seriously curtailed with all corporate clients. This would translate into a large increase in travel costs for Rosenbluth's clients that flew these routes, much to their dissatisfaction. Rosenbluth and its clients were starting to look around for possible discounts at other airlines. Mike felt that the options were fairly limited. The two other large carriers that flew these routes were both struggling with large operating losses and very high debt loads. Their future viability was not assured. The service levels on these airlines had also deteriorated with the decline in profitability, as they attempted to control costs. In addition, one of the airlines owned a minority interest in one of Rosenbluth's largest competitors. However, both airlines were showing willingness to negotiate on price, especially if the travel agency could demonstrate the ability to move market share away from the airlines' competitors.

Alternatively, Mike could try to salvage the relationship with Global. Although the clients in question were unhappy about fare increases, they all had very strong relationships with Rosenbluth and were extensive users of Rosenbluth's travel management products. Their combined travel accounts amounted to over $150 million. Perhaps working together to lobby Global for better service could sway Whitherspoon.

Whatever the solution was, Mike would have to be creative. Whitherspoon, although unyielding, appeared to be fair and possess integrity. Rosenbluth had been successful in demonstrating the benefits of the relationship to Global in the past. Now Mike had to determine how to demonstrate what benefits there might be in future co-operation, if he wanted to preserve the relationship.

EXHIBIT 1   Rosenbluth Travel: Domestic Technology Infrastructure

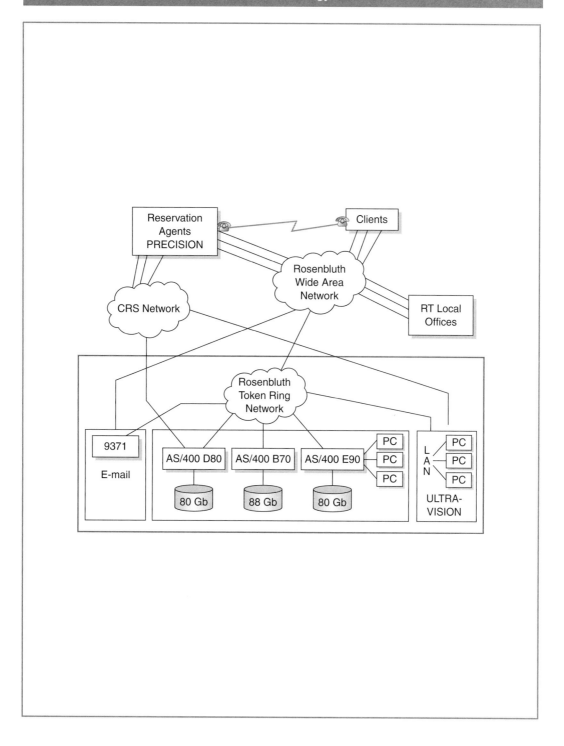

EXHIBIT 2   Airfare Cost per Mile—Detail by Time of Day

This report provides useful cost per air mile information by city-pair and carrier flown. By analyzing this report, a travel manager can either direct travellers towards a particular carrier or flight or be better equipped when negotiating with airlines. A report is also available by day or week, which determines the company's most popular travel day and time. Either non-directional or directional travel can be analysed.

1. DATE RANGE: Time period analysed on report based upon date of travel.

2. CITY-PAIR: Point-to-point arrival and destination cities for each segment flown.

3. CARRIER: Airline flown for corresponding city-pair.

4. NO. OF TRIPS: Number of segments flown within the corresponding city-pair.

5. FLIGHT NUMBER: Airline assigned flight number.

6. DEPARTURE TIMES: Time slots analyzed. Shown in military time.

7. CLASS OF TRAVEL: Categories applicable to class of service flown.

8. TOTAL FARE PAID: Total value of all segments within corresponding city-pair.

9. AVERAGE FARE PAID: Calculated by dividing *total no. of segments* into *total fare paid*.

10. CITY-PAIR MILEAGE: Air miles involved within corresponding city-pair. A consistent source is used to generate these figures.

11. AVERAGE COST PER MILE: Calculated by multiplying the *total no. of segments* and the *city-pair mileage* and dividing that figure into the *total fare paid*.

12. SUBTOTAL: Totals for each report field for each carrier flown or the selected sort field.

EXHIBIT 3   Airfare Activity Analysis

This section presents your company's total airline volume compared to both high and low fare benchmarks.[1] **The amount paid on airfares for this quarter, as noted in Figure 1, was $9,427,600.** This amount represents gross costs (before refunds) and includes all applicable taxes. **Refunds for this quarter totaled $625,672, thus yielding a net airfare expenditure of $8,801,928.**

We estimate that with your current travel policy and destinations, your airfare costs could have been reduced by approximately 2.7% had reservations been made seven days sooner and an additional 3.9% had reservations been made fourteen days sooner. On average, reservations were made ten days in advance this past quarter, which is the same as the previous quarter.

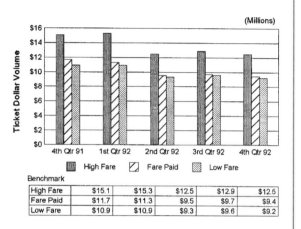

Benchmark					
High Fare	$15.1	$15.3	$12.5	$12.9	$12.5
Fare Paid	$11.7	$11.3	$9.5	$9.7	$9.4
Low Fare	$10.9	$10.9	$9.3	$9.6	$9.2

Figure 1

Air Expenditure by Division

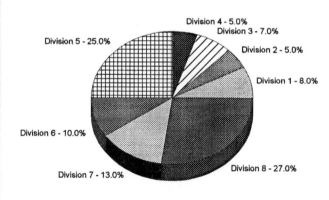

Figure 2

Spending/Savings Analysis

Airfare volume for this quarter was down 2.9% compared to last quarter; compared to this same quarter last year it was down 19.4% (Figure 1). Figure 2 further defines spending through a divisional breakdown.

Additional savings opportunities totaling $216,045, or 2.3%, were offered this quarter but not accepted by your travelers. Figure 3 illustrates why additional savings opportunities were not realized. Your company's ability to capitalize on all savings opportunities decreased 0.7% compared to last quarter, and increased 4.3% compared to this same quarter last year.

---

[1] *The high fare benchmark represents (define high fare benchmark as it applies to specific accounts), whereas the low fare benchmark represents the lowest possible airfare as defined by your corporate travel policy.*

(Continued)

EXHIBIT 3 (Continued)

Additional Airfare Savings Analysis

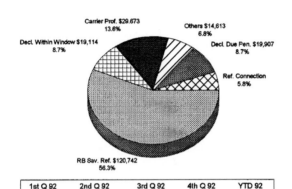

Carrier Prof. $29,673
13.6%

Others $14,613
6.8%

Decl. Within Window $19,114
8.7%

Decl. Due Pen. $19,907
8.7%

Ref. Connection
5.8%

RB Sav. Ref. $120,742
56.3%

1st Q 92	2nd Q 92	3rd Q 92	4th Q 92	YTD 92
$437,069	$184,043	$150,863	$216,045	$987,820

Figure 3

Carrier Analysis

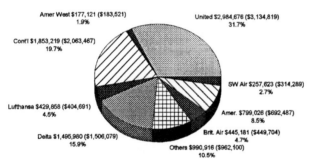

Amer West $177,121 ($183,521)
1.9%

United $2,984,676 ($3,134,819)
31.7%

Cont'l $1,853,219 ($2,063,467)
19.7%

SW Air $257,623 ($314,289)
2.7%

Lufthansa $429,858 ($404,691)
4.5%

Amer. $799,026 ($692,487)
8.5%

Delta $1,495,980 ($1,506,079)
15.9%

Brit. Air $445,181 ($449,704)
4.7%

Others $990,916 ($962,100)
10.5%

Figure 4

Total savings for this quarter were **$3,057,514, or 24.5%, compared to non-discount airfare equivalents; $385,900, or 12.6%, of savings for this quarter was generated by negotiated airfare programs.** Compared to last quarter, total savings are down 0.15; compared to this same quarter last year they are up 2.1%. Negotiated airfare program savings are up 7.8% compared to last quarter; compared to this quarter last year they are up 10.9%.

Figure 4 reflects your company's overall airline market share for this quarter. Noted in parentheses beneath your current market share is last quarter's market share with each airline.

Average Ticket Price Analysis

Domestic travel for this quarter totaled $5,322,798 and represented 56% of your company's total travel. A total of 11,361 tickets were issued in this area thus yielding an average ticket price of $469; this represents and increase of $43 (10.1%) compared to the last quarter and a decrease of $82 (14.9%) compared to this quarter a year ago. We suggest that this upward trend is largely due to _____, and exceeds what is reported on average from other industry sources by 3.8%.

International travel for this quarter totaled $4,104,802, representing 43.5% of your travel expenditures for this period. A total of 1,645 tickets were issued in this area with the resulting average ticket price of $2,495; this represents a decrease of $209 (7.7%) compared to last quarter and a decrease of $352 (12.4%) compared to this same quarter a year ago. We suggest that this downward trend is largely due to _____, and exceeds what is reported on average from other industry sources by 4.1%.

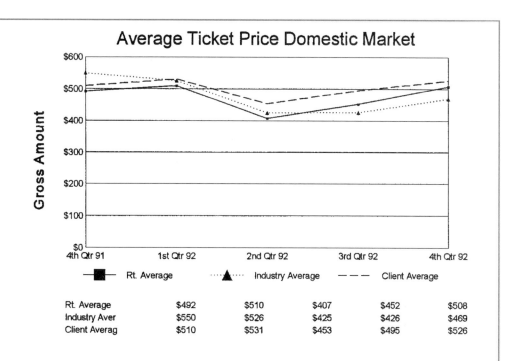

Average Ticket Price Domestic Market

	4th Qtr 91	1st Qtr 92	2nd Qtr 92	3rd Qtr 92	4th Qtr 92
Rt. Average	$492	$510	$407	$452	$508
Industry Aver	$550	$526	$425	$426	$469
Client Averag	$510	$531	$453	$495	$526

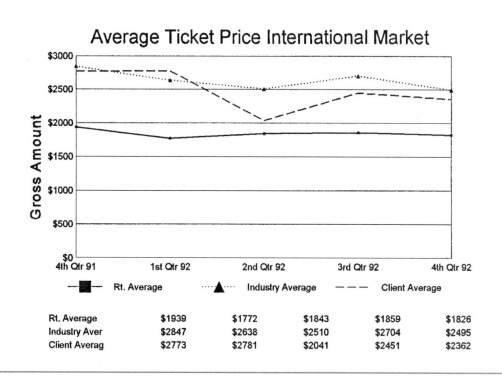

Average Ticket Price International Market

	4th Qtr 91	1st Qtr 92	2nd Qtr 92	3rd Qtr 92	4th Qtr 92
Rt. Average	$1939	$1772	$1843	$1859	$1826
Industry Aver	$2847	$2638	$2510	$2704	$2495
Client Averag	$2773	$2781	$2041	$2451	$2362

EXHIBIT 4   Travel Pattern Analysis

This section discusses travel patterns, airline market shares, and the impact of negotiated airfare programs. Comparative average ticket prices in your company's most frequently travelled markets and in total are also provided.

Impact Analysis of Negotiated Airfare Programs

The table below depicts your company's top 10 most frequently travelled markets, the actual number of one-way segments flown in each market, the actual share in each market, and a comparative airfare spending analysis. The spending analysis is projected from selected fare categories, representing the highest and lowest non-premium fares that were available to your travellers. The airfares employed in this analysis were compiled over the past quarter and do not take into consideration seat availability nor what was actually confirmed on behalf of your travellers.

| Negotiated Airfare Analysis Top 10 City Pairs | | | | | Market Value[1] | | | |
City Pairs	Segments	Coach[2]	LUF[3]	NEG[4]/LUF	Coach	LUF	NEG/LUF	Airline Share
IAH SFO	2,579	$700	$420	$319	$1,805,300	$1,083,180	$822,701	CO 87.1% UA 8.5%
LAX OAK	813	69	69	69	56,097	56,097	56,097	UA 61.5% WN 38.5%
IAH OAK	772	700	239	239	540,400	184,508	184,508	UA 44.2% HP 40.3%
IAH MSY	754	360	139	139	271,440	104,806	104,806	CO 100%
HOU MSY	629	89	89	89	55,981	55,981	55,981	WN 100%
LAX SFO	462	337	124	124	155,694	57,288	57,288	UA 69.2% US 18.5%
OAK ONT	393	69	69	69	27,117	27,117	27,117	WN 100%
SFO MSY	380	750	450	342	285,000	171,000	129,960	CO 48.8% UA 33.9%
SFO IAD	290	920	500	380	266,800	145,000	110,200	UA 96.9% CO 2.1%
OAK PHX	288	99	99	99	28,512	28,512	28,512	HP 69.8% WN 29.5%
					$ 3,492,341	$ 1,913,489	$ 1,577,170	
				Potential Savings (%)		45.21%	54.84%	
				Potential Savings ($)		$ 1,578,852	$ 1,915,171	

This analysis is designed to assess travel patterns from quarter to quarter and to demonstrate the potential savings impact of negotiated programs. It is also useful for identifying new opportunities for negotiated airfare programs.

[1] Market values shown are derived by multiplying the actual number of segments flown in each market by the airfares noted in each category.

[2] Coach represents the full coach fare.

[3] L.U.F. represents the published "Lowest Usable Fare" as defined by your corporate travel policy.

[4] NEG represents non-published airfares that were specifically negotiated for your company.

EXHIBIT 5

ROSENBLUTH INTERNATIONAL RECOGNIZED AS ONE OF THE TEN BEST COMPANIES TO WORK FOR IN AMERICA

Rosenbluth International, a worldwide travel management firm with unique and widely-acclaimed management and training strategies, recently was distinguished as one of the top ten companies to work for in the USA.

Since 1989, Robert Levering and Milton Moskowitz, co-authors of *The 100 Best Companies to Work for in America*, have been examining Rosenbluth's success through the eyes of Rosenbluth associates. Levering and Moskowitz's research included unsolicited visits to many offices, impromptu conversations with associates at every level, and a thorough examination of company policies, procedures, and philosophies. Their selection was based on the following criteria: Pay/Benefits, Opportunities, Pride In Work/Company, Openness/Fairness, and Camaraderie/Friendship. Rosenbluth International was also recognized as having one of the ten best training programs in America.

Learning opportunities covering a broad scope of disciplines focusing on personal and professional development abounds at Rosenbluth International. Committed to the concept of lifelong learning, Rosenbluth employs training strategies that foster a high level of intellectual stimulation throughout the company. Knowledgeable and innovative associates who adapt and control new market situations with an incredible amount of efficiency are the direct result of Rosenbluth's learning philosophies.

For years, Rosenbluth International has measured associate happiness and provided many opportunities for growth and training. At Rosenbluth, providing the service that exceeds client expectations is achieved because of enjoyable and creative workplace conditions. In 1991, Rosenbluth created Learning Frontiers, a training and development company that provides Rosenbluth's proven training programs to other companies. These programs focus on areas such as corporate culture, leadership development and award winning service.

The 10 Best Companies

Rosenbluth International
Beth Israel Hospital
Delta Airlines
Donnelly
Federal Express
Fel-Pro
Hallmark Cards
Publix Super Markets
Southwest Airlines
USAA

10 Best Training Programs

Rosenbluth International
Federal Express
General Mills
Haworth
IBM
J.P. Morgan
Motorola
J.C. Penney
Procter & Gamble
Quad/Graphics

EXHIBIT 6   U.S. Airline Industry Operating Profit and Net Income

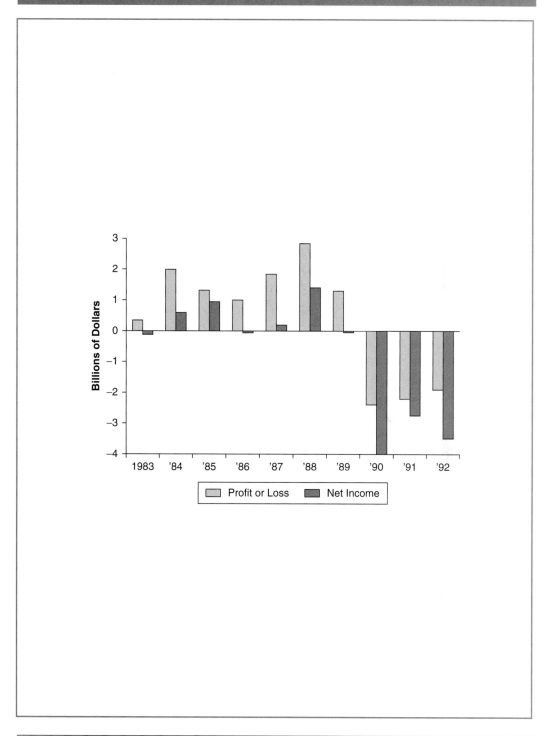

SOURCE: DOT Form 41 data.

EXHIBIT 7   U.S. Carriers' Operating Profit/Loss for International Passenger Operations

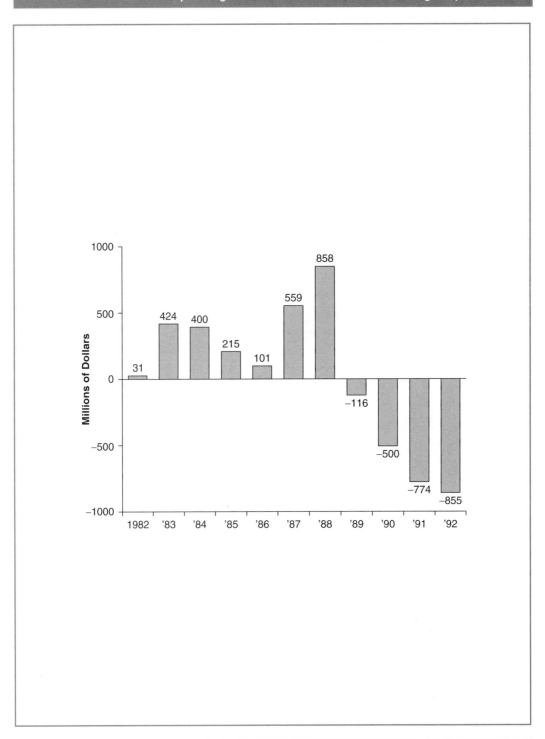

SOURCE: DOT RSPA Form 41 Data.

Richard Ivey School of Business
The University of Western Ontario

Wilkins, a Zurn Company: Material Requirements Planning

Professor Carol Prahinski

O n the morning of Monday, August 29, 2005, Jim Gerpheide, the materials manager at the Wilkins plant located in Paso Robles, California, was still stunned that the auditors had insisted that the plant undergo a second annual physical inventory count, after an inventory count had been completed two weekends earlier. In addition, Chris Connors, the general manager at the plant and Gerpheide's direct supervisor, had repeatedly expressed his concern about the high inventory level. Gerpheide knew that changes were needed, and he wondered what alternatives he should consider.

Background

In 1971, Zurn Industries acquired Wilkins Regulator Company, which commenced operations in 1906, and in 1998, it merged with U.S. Industries Bath & Plumbing

Products Co. (later known as Jacuzzi Brands, Inc.). Wilkins manufactured products for four markets: general plumbing, agricultural irrigation, commercial building and municipal water works. Wilkins used more than 14,000 different components for its production and stored them at the plant. The finished products were stored at the plant and 52 other stocking locations.

Gerpheide started employment at Wilkins in 1989. Prior to working at Wilkins, he had earned an undergraduate degree in chemistry and a Masters in Business Administration from California Polytechnic State University. At an entry-level position for a small electronics company, he commenced his career in materials management in 1978, and implemented its material requirement planning (MRP) system in 1982. Four years later, a syndicated store that sold lighting fixtures hired him to manage inventory and its MRP system. When Wilkins hired Gerpheide, he became involved with his third MRP system installation. Gerpheide's position at Wilkins had changed over the years from negotiating freight contracts, shipping product, organizing the warehouse and budgeting, to currently managing 400 projects in Asia, where 70 per cent of his time was spent sourcing materials.

The Materials Department

The materials department consisted of four employees. Gerpheide, as the materials manager, supervised three employees and was responsible for the purchase of all parts for the manufacturing plant. The purchasing manager, Cyd Lane, reported directly to Gerpheide and had been at Wilkins for 11 years. Lane directly supervised two purchasing agents, Tammi Keyes and Vivian Matthews, and was responsible for the purchase of castings and screw machine products. Keyes, who had been at Wilkins for nine years, purchased gate valves, plastic parts and springs. Matthews, who had worked at Wilkins for eight years, was responsible for the purchase of fasteners (such as bolts, nuts and screws), packaging, fittings, machine shop supplies and tooling. See Exhibit 1 for the Wilkins' plant organization chart.

The Material Requirement Planning (MRP) System

In 1990, Wilkins selected Manfact as the software for its financial system. Gerpheide commented:

> We actually did not buy the Manfact system for the MRP system; we bought it for the financial system and it happened to offer an MRP package as part of that system. We purchased the system with no consideration for the MRP package.
>
> After purchasing Manfact, we noticed several major system problems with the MRP software, which I mentioned to the company who created Manfact. Amazingly, the programmers were unaware of how the MRP system was supposed to work. When I questioned them further, the company said that only

two customers were attempting to use the MRP program, one of which was us. I helped the programmers rewrite part of the software to correct several errors so that we could use the MRP system. As of this time, we are not experiencing any problems with the MRP system. We are actually not utilizing it to the extent that we could be using it right now—we are using it at a basic level.

The materials department was the only group at Wilkins that used the MRP system. Their purpose in using the MRP system was to determine the timing and quantity to purchase components needed to produce the finished goods according to the schedule.

The MRP system was usually regenerated, or exploded, daily or weekly depending on the number of changes entered into the system. During the annual physical inventory count, the MRP system might not be regenerated for up to three weeks. The system changes were usually related to the receipt of raw materials, the production and sale of finished goods, or an update in the monthly sales forecast. Occasionally, changes were also made if new information became available, such as inventory corrections, product design changes that required modifications to the bill of materials, revised raw material lead-times, lot size requirements from the supplier and changes in managerial policy regarding the safety stock requirements. The system required only about two to five minutes to regenerate.

At the start of each quarter, the inventory manager, Bernie Barge, created the forecast master by determining the anticipated weekly sales by product family for the upcoming six to eight quarters. From the forecast master, Connors would generate the required production volumes for the major product families. After receipt of this email, Gerpheide would update the production volumes in the MRP system, which would then generate a materials plan report. At the same time, the production department would also use Connors' information to create a production plan for each production cell.

To update the production volumes in the MRP system, Gerpheide first had to convert the average weekly production volumes by multiplying the number of fiscal weeks in each month to determine the monthly production volumes for the product family. The plant used a four/four/five system representing that the first and second month of the quarter contained four weeks whereas the third month contained five weeks. Gerpheide then entered the anticipated monthly production volumes into the MRP system.

Connors updated the production volumes quarterly but sometimes sooner if there were any significant changes, such as unexpected demand. Besides updating the MRP system, Gerpheide compared the actual production rates to the anticipated production plan from Connors' email to determine whether the materials department had enough material. Gerpheide explained:

In most cases, the actual monthly volumes produced by the production department are the same as Connors' production volumes and so the materials plan is on track with the production plan. In some cases, it is not. We plan that we will have enough inventory to meet Connors' production volumes, and if there isn't enough inventory, something is wrong. So, I'll investigate the situation. If my department made a mistake, we'll try to expedite to get the materials into the plant in time for production, or if that can't be done, we'll ask the production department to delay the production schedule for that product. The production department does not have the same constraints as the materials department. Sometimes they will produce as much as they can as fast as possible with no consideration as to the amount of material that is available.

If the production department is overproducing and we have a low level of raw materials, I notify Connors of the discrepancy and request a clarification on the true production plan. If Connors revises the production volumes, I would update the production plan in the MRP system and try to get those materials quickly. If Connors had not officially revised the production volumes, I would not make any MRP system changes even though materials inventory is running precariously low. Connors then follows up with the production department to make necessary corrections in its schedule.

Prior to this process of updating the MRP system, we had some costly delays and lots of confusion within the materials and production departments. Frequently, I faced dilemmas, such as when the materials department planned to produce 10,000 units of a particular product for a specific month, while the production department planned to make 12,000. When the production department ran out of materials, I had to figure out how to get enough components to meet the production department's requirements, or how to convince them to modify their production schedule based on the amount of materials available.

Inventory System

Wilkins used a periodic review system for inventory control. All finished good shipments, materials receipts and production quantities were periodically updated in the inventory records.

Wilkins used backflushing to update the inventory records. Backflushing was described as the update of the component inventory balances when the finished goods are received into stock.[1] At Wilkins, the backflush method relied on data from the production activity report of the previous day's production to determine the quantities of raw materials used. Gerpheide commented about this approach:

It [the backflush method] works fine if everyone remembers to report his or her production activity. People are motivated to report their output because we use piece-rate bonus incentives. However, sometimes the production isn't reported or there were component changes that were not adequately communicated on the production reports. We relieve inventory based on what we say we've built, not on what we actually produced. That can cause us problems.

---

[1] T. E. Vollmann, William L. Berry, D. Clay Whybark, and F. Robert Jacobs, *Manufacturing, Planning and Control Systems,* 5th ed., Irwin/McGraw-Hill, 2005, p. 304.

We have also been experiencing some problems since the bill of materials is not always correct or the production department has mistakenly used the wrong part number, which may happen since some of our parts can be interchanged. It is a never-ending battle because we continue to have new products that are designed and customers who request some customization. Eventually it always gets fixed because we wonder why the materials run out. After we look at the bill of material, we realize the mistake—we have used the wrong part number or the bill of material is incorrect.

The current inventory system is not completely accurate and it needs to be 100 per cent accurate in order for the MRP system to work correctly.

The Generally Accepted Accounting Principles

The Generally Accepted Accounting Principles (GAAP) required Wilkins to have established inventory controls. The GAAP and the Security Exchange Commission (SEC) required that each facility conduct a physical inventory once per year in the last quarter of the fiscal year. At Wilkins, since the fiscal year ends on September 30, the physical inventory process began on July 28 when Wilkins' in-house auditors counted the inventory. External auditors visited the plant during the year to ensure that Wilkins was following the proper accounting principles. During the past year, Wilkins had six different groups of auditors, both internal and external, visit the plant.

The Sarbanes-Oxley Act (SOX), which was passed by the U.S. legislature in July 2002, was generally considered the most significant piece of legislation to change financial disclosure, corporate governance and public accounting practice since the early 1930s when U.S. securities laws were passed.[2] As a result of this Act, Wilkins and other American public companies (including wholly owned subsidiaries), private companies that were preparing their initial public offering and non-American companies that performed business in the United States were required to reveal their internal financial auditing controls to the Securities and Exchange Commission (SEC) annually.[3]

Gerpheide remarked on the physical inventory count:

Ten years ago, we had about half of the current level of inventory. It would take us five days of counting with 30 to 40 people involved. Now, with about twice the inventory, we can complete the counts in about one-and-a-half to two days.

To help make the physical count go more smoothly, we pre-count the materials to speed up the process. These items are stored in a box and we will put a "do not move, do not touch" tag on the box. We use the same system at our other stocking locations.

---

[2]http://www.pwc.com/Extweb/NewCoAtWork.nsf/docid/D0D7F79003C6D64485256CF30074D66C, accessed October 2005.

[3]http://www.sarbanes-oxley-101.com/sarbanes-oxley-faq.htm, accessed October 2005.

The Inventory Manager

Although Wilkins followed the accounting principles and standards, the plant continued to experience problems with the accuracy of inventory records. Gerpheide commented:

> I spend most of my time putting out fires. Eighty per cent of the parts have good inventory accuracy while the remaining 20 per cent are problematic. Inventory inaccuracy causes so many problems that ripple through the plant and it seems like every single error ends up coming back to haunt our sales/marketing manager, Rick Fields or me.
>
> Three and a half years ago, Rick and I decided that we needed to hire someone to focus on the inventory issues. We proposed to Chris that we get an inventory manager for several reasons.
>
> We had the finished good inventory available in the U.S., but it wasn't in the right place. For example, there were finished goods located at a stocking location that had never previously sold that product before. The sales force had an incentive to hold onto any finished good inventory that they could get because they were commissioned based on sales and they were not penalized for holding extra inventory. We needed an inventory manager to determine where the finished goods inventory should be stored. The inventory manager should decide how to stratify the country so that we can have inventory in the right location or very nearby so that if an order comes in we can meet a short lead-time.
>
> A second major concern was that our inventory inaccuracy caused a rippling effect throughout the plant, our customers and our suppliers. We were, and still are, spending too much time correcting errors or trying to expedite materials because of the errors.
>
> After about three-and-a-half years of asking for an inventory manager, Chris promoted Bernie to the position. In most plants, the inventory manager would report to the materials manager, along with the purchasing, logistics, transportation and other functions. However, at our plant, Bernie reports directly to Chris.
>
> This job hasn't been here before and there is no real job description. Bernie needs to respond like water—addressing all of the issues that don't have enough inventory and flooding the holes by giving it attention.
>
> Rick and I hadn't realized this at the time, but another reason for creating the inventory manager position was to have a front-person to handle all of the complaints. It is really nice not to be involved as heavily in fighting the fires.

Barge provided some details about the inventory inaccuracy:

> There are dozens of reasons for the discrepancies and we've gone over them again and again in our meetings. One reason for the discrepancies is the timing of transactions; we don't enter the data into the computer until that night or the

next morning. Another reason is a modification on the products; the product was redesigned but the bill of materials system wasn't updated or the customer requested a customized product and we didn't notice it when we entered the production. In addition, we might use the wrong components. I've seen the production guys use the wrong components simply because they couldn't find the right ones to use. Sometimes we don't input the transactions for the right components, such as with data entry errors. Finally, we have some part commonality, using the same part in multiple finished goods; part commonality creates some confusion in the real quantity of parts needed by production.

Because of our inaccuracy, we had to have a second inventory count. We've been doing the inventory count the same way forever. Perhaps SOX has caused the auditors to be pickier. With the second physical inventory audit, the external auditors randomly selected items to test-count. We did four test-counts for each item. There were many teams because the inventory process had to be completed as quickly as possible. As it was, it still took two full days to count everything in the plant. The procedure used in the inventory process had teams conducting the initial count. Then, an in-house auditor verified the teams' counts.

The 720 Product

The 720, a backflow preventer in the pressure vacuum breaker (PVB) valve family, was one of many standard products at Wilkins. The PVB was installed in potable water lines to protect the quality of water. The device would stop the flow of substances or the reverse flow of water into the potable water distribution system. Gerpheide considered it a popular and reliable product in a very competitive market, and that Wilkins had produced and sold it for more than 25 years. The 720 was available in six different models based on the dimensions of the in-feed pipes, ranging from the ½- to 2-inch diameter. A diagram of the 720, its dimensions and weights are shown in Exhibit 2. The installation diagram of the PVB is shown in Exhibit 3.

The 34-720 was a PVB valve with a ¾-inch diameter in-feed pipe. The assembly process of the 34-720 was as follows: three bolts were placed into the canopy, which was then connected to the bonnet, plastic washer and o-ring. Once these parts were connected, the subassembly was then joined to the poppet assembly (load nut, load washer, upper disc and poppet) and spring. The next step consisted of attaching these parts to the spider assembly, which consisted of a screw, lower disc, guide spider and nut. This subassembly was then connected to the body. Previously, the body had undergone machining and was attached to two test cocks and two ball valves. These components are listed and diagramed in Exhibit 4.

Wilkins sold a 720 repair kit directly to customers. Due to extreme weather conditions, the PVB occasionally failed to function properly. Some contractors preferred to service the 720 product instead of replacing the PVB. The components of the 720 repair kit are listed in Exhibit 5. Gerpheide planned to sell 400 to 500 720 repair kits per month and kept a safety stock of 400 units on hand. He could make the product within five business days. The sales forecast for the 34-720 and the 720 repair kit are shown in Exhibit 6.

MRP System Inputs

The primary purpose of the MRP system was to develop a detailed time-phased plan for when to place purchasing orders for raw materials and to determine how much material to order. To operate effectively, the system required information on the purchasing and materials inventory policies associated with each component, the bill of materials and the demand requirements for finished goods and components. The following are some MRP inputs, specifically focused on the 34-720.

Bill of Materials

The bill of materials (BOM) lists each of the components required to make the finished good, the required quantity of each component and the sequence dependence associated with the parent-component relationships, where level 0 represents the finished good. Wilkins' BOM for the 34-720 PVB is shown in Exhibit 4.

Production Schedule

The MRP system required the production schedule for all products. For the products that were sold directly to customers, Gerpheide's calculation of the scheduled monthly production volumes was input into the system as the gross requirements. The forecasted demand in Exhibit 6 was used for the production schedule in the MRP planning inquiry.

According to Gerpheide, the calculation of the gross requirements could become rather complex. Some components were used in a variety of products, which was called part commonality. Other raw material components might also be sold independently as replacement parts, such as the 34-850, a ¾-inch ball valve. The calculation of the gross requirements needed to ensure that the requirements for all demand were included. Exhibit 7 shows the gross requirements for several selected 34-720 components. (Note that the gross requirements in Exhibit 7 excluded the 34-720 and RK1-720 demand.)

Scheduled Receipt

Scheduled receipts represented orders that had been placed with the supplier or production that had been scheduled but the product had not yet been received or completed. The materials department had placed several orders with its suppliers, and these scheduled orders were called scheduled receipts in the MRP system. The scheduled receipts for the ½-inch plastic washer, 721A-12, was 55,000 units in September. The scheduled receipts for the instruction sheet, IS720, were 49,500 units for September; 49,500 units for October; 54,900 units for November; 9,000 units for December and 12,600 units for January.

On-Hand Inventory

The on-hand inventory for 34-720 components was higher than normal because the PVB sales to the agricultural irrigation market were hampered due to the long and wet winter of 2004. The inventory for several 34-720 components on September 5, 2005 is shown in Exhibit 8.

Planning Lead Times

The expected lead time for each of the 34-720 components is shown in Exhibit 4. For items produced at the Wilkins plant, the expected lead times were the manufacturing lead times, which included processing time, setup time, transit time and wait time. For the purchased items, the lead times varied predominantly due to the distance that the material had to travel to reach the Paso Robles plant. Some components were domestically sourced from California, Illinois, Wisconsin and Massachusetts. Other components were internationally sourced from Taiwan and China. Gerpheide explained:

> If we were to order valves from our supplier, for instance, we could expect that the supplier would have some backlog or materials lead time and may not be able to schedule our product immediately in its plant. Once the supplier has processed our order, it would take them approximately four weeks to schedule the production and then another four weeks to produce the product. For domestic components, we would receive the components in about eight weeks from the time we placed the order, but for international components, it could take up to five months because of the shipping lag time. I'm in the process of ordering materials that I don't even need until next February.

Purchasing Lot Sizes

The purchasing lot sizes varied for each component due to differences in suppliers. Some suppliers had established ordering policies, such as a fixed lot size. Other suppliers allowed some flexibility and the materials department found that they preferred using a periodic order quantity. In addition, some suppliers gave Wilkins purchasing discounts dependent on a sizable order quantity. The typical lot sizes for each component are listed in Exhibit 4.

Safety Stock

At Wilkins, the safety stock, as shown in Exhibit 4, was determined based on the product seasonality. Gerpheide illustrated:

> Our MRP system doesn't have a data field to handle a safety stock value. So, to obtain a planned safety stock, we fool the MRP system. I adjust the demand values that Chris gives me so that I add in a safety stock value. If

demand is doubling during the upcoming months, I know that I will need to have a two-fold increase in the amount of safety stock. Therefore, I make a system adjustment by adding the needed safety stock to the demand values. The initial amount of the safety stock is determined with a ballpark estimate. If we find that there isn't enough safety stock, we will boost up the safety stock inventory to a point where we are comfortable.

We keep a safety stock for a majority of the 34-720 components. The ball valve, 34-850, which has part commonality and is sold directly to customers, is one exception. It does not require safety stock due to low demand. Wilkins sells very little of this component, with an average demand of approximately 50 pieces per month, give or take 10 units. For the first time in seven years, we recently experienced a stock-out of the ball valve during our ordering cycle. I guess you could say that Wilkins has a 99 per cent chance of not being out of stock of the 34-850 during an ordering cycle.

Inventory Discrepancy

The external auditors concluded that the annual physical inventory count conducted in July was flawed and the results were inaccurate. The auditors re-examined the process and procedures and insisted that Wilkins have a second physical inventory count. Within a month, the Wilkins plant had undergone its second physical inventory count. As a result, the plant was shut down for an additional three days, two of which had been scheduled for overtime work. During the shutdown, Wilkins was not able to ship products to customers or receive materials from their suppliers. Gerpheide stated:

I have never heard of any plant having to take a second physical inventory count. When I was involved with the physical inventory, I noticed that mistakes occurred frequently, such as the counter miswrote the part number or the quantity within the box. In the past, we have always done the count, entered the data, examined any large variances (such as by recounting or verifying the data entry), corrected the database, and then sent the file to auditors. Usually, there were some discrepancies, but the auditors never raised it as an issue. Now the auditors claimed the process and procedures need revisiting. We just lost $100,000 to $200,000 because of the plant shutdown, and it was right at the end of our fiscal year during our largest selling period of the year. It certainly isn't because of anything we've done or not done on our part. The process hasn't changed. We've always used the same process.

On top of all of this, we continue to have inventory discrepancies within the MRP system. Now, I'm going to have to search to find why this particular inaccuracy has occurred and attempt to rectify it. Every little mistake can cause me to have big headaches with the MRP system.

We have to solve the inventory inaccuracy problem as well as the high level of components and finished goods inventory at the plant. In addition, I need to address the annual physical inventory recount situation so that we don't face this again. I wonder what alternatives are available to us.

EXHIBIT 1 Wilkins Organization Chart

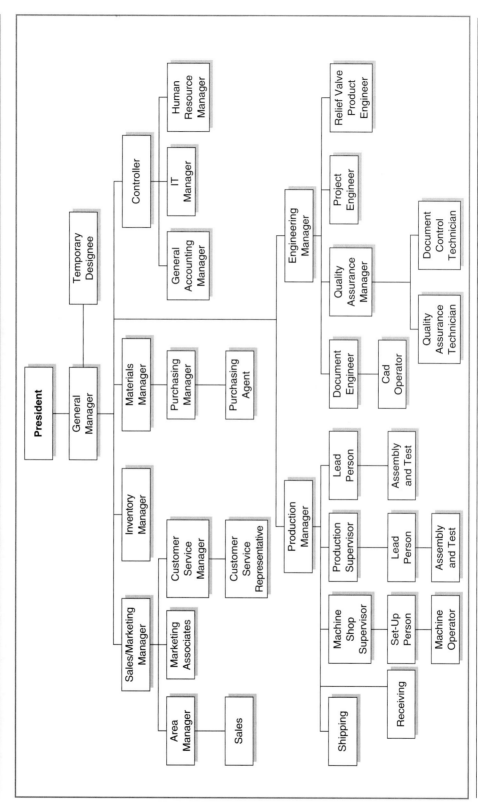

SOURCE: Wilkins plant data.

EXHIBIT 2 Dimensions and Weights of Model 720 PVB Product

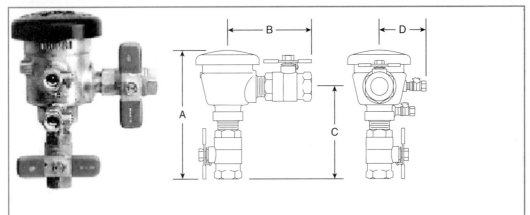

DIMENSIONS & WEIGHTS

| MODEL SIZE | | DIMENSIONS (approximate) | | | | | | | | WEIGHT | | | |
| | | A | | B | | C | | D | | LESS BV | | WITH BV | |
in.	mm	in.	mm	in.	mm	in.	mm	in.	mm	lbs.	Kg	lbs.	Kg
1/2	15	6 7/8	175	3 13/16	97	4	102	3 1/2	89	4	1.8	6	2.7
3/4	20	7	178	4 1/8	105	4 1/8	105	3 1/2	89	4	1.8	6	2.7
1	25	7 5/8	194	4 1/2	114	4 5/8	118	3 1/2	89	4	1.8	8	3.6
1 1/4	32	10 13/16	275	7 1/4	184	7 1/4	184	4 1/2	114	14	6.4	20	9
1 1/2	40	10 3/8	264	6 7/8	175	6 7/8	175	4 1/2	114	14	6.4	20	9
2	50	11	279	7 1/2	191	7 5/8	194	4 1/2	114	14	6.4	26	10.4

SOURCE: Wilkins sales data.

EXHIBIT 3 Installation Diagram of Model 720 PVB Product

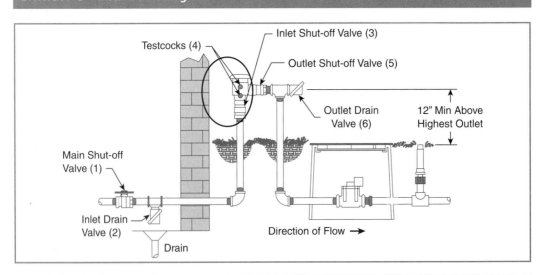

SOURCE: Wilkins sales data.

EXHIBIT 4   **Bill of Materials, Lead Time, Safety Stock and Lot Sizes for the 34-720 PVB and Its Components**

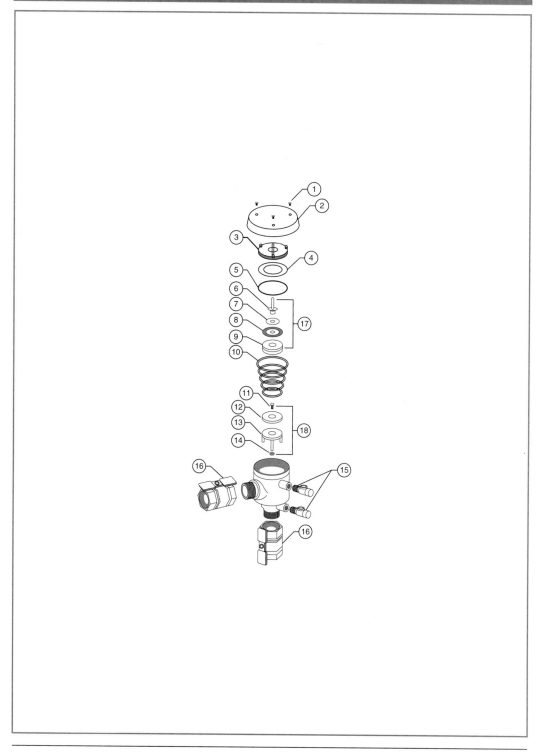

(Continued)

EXHIBIT 4 (Continued)

ITEM NO.	PART NO.	DESCRIPTION	COUNTRY OR STATE	QTY	LEVEL	LEAD TIME*	SAFETY STOCK	LOT SIZES
1	721-11	Bolt, 8-32 × 3/8 Fil. SS	Wisconsin	3	1	135	22,500	648,000
2	721-3	Canopy, ½" - 1" 720	California	1	1	36	9,000	90,000
3	721-20	Bonnet, ½" - 1" 720	China	1	1	59	0	31,500
4	721A-12	Plastic Washer, ½" - 1" 720	California	1	1	36	9,000	55,000
5	138N	O-Ring, FDA	California	1	1	9	1,800	126,000
6	721-90	Load Nut, ¼" - 2" Brass	California	1	2	45	900	292,500
7	721-80	Load Washer, ½" - 1" 720	California	1	2	19	3,600	216,000
8	721A-34	Upper Disc, ½" - 1" 720	California	1	2	54	9,000	99,000
9	721-30	Poppet, ½" - 1" 720	California	1	2	27	9,000	63,000
10	721-33	Spring, ½" - 1" 720	California	1	1	41	9,000	148,500
11	721-11A	Bolt, 8-32 × .620 Pan HD SS	Wisconsin	1	2	76	18,000	216,000
12	721B-34	Lower Disc, ½" - 1" 720	California	1	2	54	9,000	90,000
13	721-31	Spider, ½" - 1" 720	California	1	2	36	9,000	126,000
14	721-9A	Nut, 8-32 × 1/8 SS	California	1	2	4	18,000	216,000
15	18-860	Test Cock, 1/8" × ¼"	China	2	1	63	72,000	7,200
16	34-850	Ball Valve, ¾"	Taiwan	2	1	54	0	11,444
17	721-300	Poppet Assembly	California	1	1	0	5,000	—
18	721-310	Spider Assembly	California	1	1	0	5,000	—
N/A	722-1	Body, ¾" 720 Finished	California	1	1	0	—	55,800
N/A	34-720	¾" 720 w/BV	California	1	0	0	—	—
N/A	721-16	Guide Rod, ½" - ¾" 720	California	1	1	45	900	283,500
N/A	IS720	Instruction Sheet, ½" - 2" 720	California	1	1	9	27	54,000
N/A	PB5X7	5 ½ × 7 Plastic Bag	Illinois	1	1	9	900	18,900
N/A	PK361	Card, RK1-720	Massachusetts	1	1	18	90	4,500
N/A	722-1-000	Body, ¾" - 1" 720 Raw	California	1	2	14	—	56,413
N/A	PK002	Box, 8.75 × 7.625 × 7	California	1	1	14	0	20,187

*Lead time is in working days.

SOURCE: Wilkins plant data.

EXHIBIT 5   Components of the RK1-720 Repair Kit for ½-, ¾- and 1-Inch Model 720 PVB

PART NO.	QTY.	DESCRIPTION
721A-12	1	Plastic Washer
138N	1	O-Ring
721-33	1	Spring
721-300	1	Poppet Assembly
721-310	1	Spider Assembly
RK1-720	1	Card
IS720	1	Instruction Sheet, ½" – 2" 720
9B5X7	1	5 ½ × 7 Plastic Bag

SOURCE: Wilkins plant data.

EXHIBIT 6   Forecasted Demand for Model 34-720 PVB and 1-720 Repair Kit

Month	34-720 PVB	RK1-720 Repair Kit
September	5,000	517
October	5,000	662
November	5,000	578
December	4,000	650
January	4,000	858

SOURCE: Wilkins plant data.

EXHIBIT 7   Gross Requirements for 34-720 Components With Part Commonality or Independent Demand (Excludes Demand for 34-720 and RK1-720)

Month	722-1-000	721A-12	34-850	IS720
September	0	11,129	50	12,800
October	0	10,090	50	12,040
November	4,021	8,220	50	8,500
December	5,409	6,138	40	6,530
January	4,928	5,506	40	6,500

SOURCE: Wilkins plant data.

EXHIBIT 8 Material Requirements Planning Record for Selected 720 Components

ITEM: 34-720
¾" 720 w/BV

	08/29/2005	10/03/2005	10/31/2005	11/28/2005	01/02/2006
Level: 0					
Gross Requirements					
Scheduled Receipts					
Projected On-Hand	9,600				
Net Requirements					
Planned Order					

ITEM: RK1-720
Repair Kit, ½" - 1" 720

	08/29/2005	10/03/2005	10/31/2005	11/28/2005	01/02/2006
Level: 0					
Gross Requirements					
Scheduled Receipts					
Projected On-Hand	482				
Net Requirements					
Planned Order					

ITEM: 722-1
Body, ¾" 720 Finished

	08/29/2005	10/03/2005	10/31/2005	11/28/2005	01/02/2006
Level: 1					
Gross Requirements					
Scheduled Receipts					
Projected On-Hand	16,650				
Net Requirements					
Planned Order					

ITEM: 721A-12
Plastic Washer, ½"

	08/29/2005	10/03/2005	10/31/2005	11/28/2005	01/02/2006
Level: 1					
Gross Requirements					
Scheduled Receipts					

WILKINS MATERIAL REQUIREMENTS PLAN

				08/29/2005
Projected On-Hand	18,533			
Net Requirements				
Planned Order				

ITEM: 34-850
Ball Valve, ¾"

	08/29/2005	10/03/2005	10/31/2005	11/28/2005	01/02/2006
Level: 1					
Gross Requirements					
Scheduled Receipts					
Projected On-Hand	10,430				
Net Requirements					
Planned Order					

ITEM: IS720
Instruction Sheet, 720

	08/29/2005	10/03/2005	10/31/2005	11/28/2005	01/02/2006
Level: 1					
Gross Requirements					
Scheduled Receipts					
Projected On-Hand	64,372				
Net Requirements					
Planned Order					

ITEM: 722-1-000
Body, ¾" – 1" 720 Raw

	08/29/2005	10/03/2005	10/31/2005	11/28/2005	01/02/2006
Level: 2					
Gross Requirements					
Scheduled Receipts					
Projected On-Hand	612				
Net Requirements					
Planned Order					

SOURCE: Wilkins plant data.

Index

About the Author

Scott T. Young is Chairman of the Department of Management and Professor of Management at DePaul University. He has authored articles in management journals such as *Journal of Operations Management, Production and Operations Management, Interfaces, International Journal of Production Research, Business Horizons, Health Care Management Review*, and *Journal of World Business*. He is also the coauthor of *Managing Global Operations* (1996), with Winter Nie. Prior to joining DePaul University, Scott was at the University of Utah, where he served as Chairman of the Department of Management and Associate Dean for Academic Programs. The companies he has consulted for include American Express, Hill Air Force Base, Eimco, Baker Hughes, Eastman Christensen, PSC Development, and U.S. West (Qwest). He received his PhD in management from Georgia State University, his MBA from Georgia College, and his BA from the University of Georgia.

Scott is married to Luciana Young, a pediatric cardiologist who is on the medical school faculty at Northwestern University. They have two Jack Russell Terriers, a daughter, "GiGi," and live in Wilmette, Illinois. Scott's main hobby is distance running. He has logged over 56,000 miles of running and completed 33 marathons, six of them in under three hours.